THE CRUSADERS IN THE HOLY LAND

THE CRUSADERS
IN THE HOLY LAND

MERON BENVENISTI

THE MACMILLAN COMPANY, NEW YORK, NEW YORK

The Macmillan Company
866 Third Avenue, New York, N.Y. 10022
Collier-Macmillan Canada Ltd., Toronto, Ontario

First Published in Israel by
Israel Universities Press in 1970, Jerusalem.

First American Edition 1972.

Library of Congress Catalog Card Number: 70-1800293

Printed and bound by Keter Press, Jerusalem, Israel

Grateful acknowledgement is made to the following:

Jonathan Cape Ltd., London, for use of material from THE TRAVELS OF IBN JUBAYR, translated by R.J.C. Broadhurst, 1952;

Luzac and Company, Ltd., London, for use of material from THE DAMASCUS CHRONICLE OF THE CRUSADES, edited by H.A.R. Gibbs, 1932;

Columbia University Press, New York, for use of material from William of Tyre's DEEDS DONE BEYOND THE SEA, translated by E.A. Babcock and A.C. Krey, 1943;

Israel National Park Authority, for use of material from THE SURVEY OF ACRE, 1962;

Israel Department of Antiquities, for use of material and plans from the archives;

Dr. Richard Cleave, for many of the photographs.

PREFACE

This work tells the story of the Holy Land during the time of the Crusaders, and something of the history of the Crusaders themselves. My approach has been mainly through relics of the period that have been preserved to this day; the reader will thus find no description or analysis of the origins of the Crusaders, nor even a political and social history of the Kingdom of Jerusalem.

As I have limited myself to the description of the land and its inhabitants as seen in remains, I have not described the history of important cities such as Jaffa, Tiberias and Haifa for the simple reason that no Crusader sites are preserved in them. On the other hand, I have described all places, large or small, known or forgotten, in which Crusader remnants are to be found.

If this work is to be assigned to any particular discipline, it is that of historical geography. This is an inter-disciplinary subject that extends into the domains of history, geography, archaeology and architecture; and whereas I am not certain whether scholars dealing with particular fields will be pleased with my findings in their own fields, I do hope that they will find interest in the work as a whole.

The book is intended more for the interested general reader than for the professional and, thus, it does not contain a full scholarly apparatus of bibliography and notes. The opinions and conclusions are based on my own research and on the published literature, but I have not quoted all the sources, nor have I engaged in debate with divergent views.

The major part of the book consists of monographic descriptions of the sites; each section is preceded by a short introduction to the topic. This mode of presentation has given rise to an unusual picture of both the Holy Land and the Crusaders' way of life.

When the Crusaders arrived the Holy Land had apparently been in a period of progressive economic decline, but still something remained of the glorious ages that the land had enjoyed.

The Holy Land has been presented as in a state of decline, destruction, and decay since the Middle Ages. This picture is erroneous, at least as regards the time between the first part of the Crusader period and the end of the 12th century. The process of decay accelerated in the middle of the 13th century, and by the end of the 13th century the land reached a level of neglect from which it did not recover till the end of the 19th century.

The way of life of the Crusaders, or, to be more specific, of the Franks (this term refers to all inhabitants of the Holy Land, of European origin, and is not limited to those who took the Cross and became Crusaders), as illuminated by relics of the period, is here shown to be quite different from the picture generally represented.

In general, the Crusaders have been described in the heroic and romantic style, and as a result only their churches and castles have been depicted. Although it is true that castles and churches were the most outstanding expressions of the period, and are most impressive from the point of view of architecture, it should not be forgotten that there are many less magnificent but equally interesting relics, such as dwelling places, flourmills, water-works, ports, stables, and sugar refineries. Reconstruction of these structures enables us to derive some knowledge of everyday life of the period. Such a picture is a necessary complement to that given by the remains of churches and castles.

This work was commenced during one of those periods of relative calm that are so rare in the Holy Land. At that time I decided to limit the work to those places that I could reach and examine myself. After the war of June 1967, scenes and places that I had visited during my childhood were again accessible, so that the scope of my work was enlarged and many pages were added. The book now covers all the boundaries of the Crusader Kingdom of Jerusalem at the height of its expansion, excluding the mount of Edom and south-western Lebanon.

I would like to thank all those who have assisted me, directly or indirectly, to bring this project to fruition. First and foremost, I owe thanks to my teacher, Professor Joshua Prawer, who guided me through the intricacies of the period, and thanks to whom I started the study of the historical geography of the Crusaders. I sincerely hope that he will find in this book some echoes of what he taught me, despite the years that have elapsed. My good friend, Dr. Jonathan Riley-Smith, who accompanied me in this work in many of its phases and who also read the manuscript, was most helpful. In spite of the geographical distance between us I was able to enjoy his aid and to benefit from his profound knowledge of the subject. The map of Crusader Acre is the outcome of many long discussions that we held, although I am not sure if he will agree with the version published here. Special thanks are due to Mrs. Shifra Kolat, a colleague in the study of the historical geography of the period.

A part of the English version of this book was edited with great skill and understanding by the late Mrs. Hanita Shomron.

All the good photographs were taken by my friend Dr. Richard Cleave, who complied with all my wishes while collecting photographic material for another purpose. I also thank the workers of the Israel Universities Press for their devoted care in preparing the book: to Asher Weill, formerly Director of I.U.P.; to Derek Orlans, the Chief Editor; to S. Barlev, the graphic editor; and special gratitude is due to S. Yehudayan, who drew the maps and the plans, and prepared the photographs for printing. And, lastly, my thanks and my love to my son Eyal, my devoted companion in most of my tours, who was of great help.

JERUSALEM
SUMMER, 1970   M.B.

TABLE OF CONTENTS

x

LIST OF MAPS AND PLANS

Part I INTRODUCTORY REMARKS

HISTORICAL SURVEY

The Crusader host reached Palestine in the spring of the year 1099, and thus began a period of Frankish rule in the area which was to last for almost two hundred years. At the turn of the eleventh century the country was under the domination of the two rival Moslem powers, the Seljuk Turks and the Fatimids of Egypt. The Seljuks had migrated initially from the Central Asiatic steppes at the beginning of the 11th century, and had conquered Baghdad, the capital of the 'Abbasid caliphate, in the 1050's. In the 1070's they had arrived in Palestine, then held by the Fatimid caliphs of Egypt who were Shi'ites. The Seljuks expelled the Egyptians from the interior of the country and seized Jerusalem, but had not been able to take the coastal towns from them. In 1098, a year before the arrival of the Crusaders, the Egyptians had recovered Jerusalem.

conditions before
the First Crusade

The Crusaders passed swiftly over the maritime plain; in their haste to capture Jerusalem they did not stop to take the towns along the coast and only Jaffa, which they found abandoned, was secured. They laid siege to Jerusalem for five weeks, and after its capture small groups of knights seized control of the interior regions of the country, where no force remained to stand against them. Nablus and the mountains of Samaria were quickly overrun and Tancred, one of the Crusader leaders, took Beit Shean and Tiberias at the head of eighty knights, founding the "Principality of Galilee" in the north of the country. After Jerusalem had been taken, one of the leaders of the expedition, Godfrey de Bouillon, was proclaimed "Advocate of the Holy Sepulchre", but for various reasons he refused to take the title of king.

conquest of
Palestine

The Egyptians meanwhile gathered their forces for a counter attack, and a battle took place near Ascalon in 1099. The decisive victory of the Crusaders in this battle broke the power of the Egyptian army and secured their dominion over the country, despite the unavailing endeavours of the Egyptians to return to the attack against the Crusader kingdom on numerous occasions.

After the battle of Ascalon the greater part of the Crusader chivalry left the country, including most of the leaders of the expedition and the more important knights; having sworn to redeem the Holy Sepulchre, they felt under no obligation to remain and returned home when their pledge had been fulfilled. Only a small number of knights, electing to link their fate with the Holy Land, remained to settle, and it was on this minority that the burden of responsibility for the conquered country was imposed. They were faced with three urgent tasks, on whose fulfilment their continued hold on the country depended: the consolidation of power in the interior; the capture of the coastal towns and the opening of their harbours to European shipping; and the securing of defensible natural frontiers.

situation after
the conquest

The first of these tasks, the strengthening of their hold on the interior, presented few difficulties. No organized opposition remained and the Moslem pop-

3

ulation offered no resistance to the conquerors. The capture of the coastal towns, on the other hand, was more difficult, and success was vital to the Crusaders because ports were urgently needed to bring reinforcements, arms and supplies from Europe. Trading stations were also required at the ends of the long and busy trade routes through which oriental wares flowed to the shores of the Mediterranean.

conquest of coastal towns

To take the maritime towns the Crusaders, who had no naval forces, needed help from the fleets of the Italian mercantile cities, the most important of which were Genoa, Pisa and Venice. At first they were unwilling to cooperate with the Crusader land forces and, when they at last consented to do so, it was not without exacting concessions in return. Before agreeing to take part in the capture of a city, the merchants demanded privileges therein, including the ceding of quarters for their use, judicial autonomy and trade concessions, including exemption from customs and certain commercial monopolies. As a result of their subsequent cooperation all the coastal towns except Tyre, the largest and strongest, and Ascalon, close to Egypt and defended by the strong Egyptian fleet, were captured in the first decade of the kingdom's existence. Tyre was taken, after a prolonged siege, in 1124, and Ascalon continued to harass the Crusaders until its capture in 1153.

The third and fundamental aim of Frankish strategy was twofold: the establishment of secure frontiers on the desert borders, thereby preventing the danger of a Moslem force concentrating near their area, and the severance of land com-

establishment of secure borders

munication between the two power-centres of the hostile force. The centres of Moslem power, which threatened the kingdom for years, were the Emirate of Damascus in the northeast, and the Caliphate of Egypt in the southwest. Although hatred and religious envy prevailed between the Sunnite Seljuks in the north and the Shi'ite Fatimids in the south, nevertheless the danger was ever present that they would sink their religious differences in face of the common enemy.

Baldwin I, the second Crusader ruler, and the first to be crowned King of Jerusalem, directed his efforts to obtaining a hold in Transjordan and to conquering the heights of Golan and Gilead. In this area, indeed, he won important victories and was able to force the Damascenes to agree to the joint Frankish-Moslem control of Golan and Bashan, but he was unable to extend his dominion to the border of the Syrian-Arabian Desert. He thus failed to achieve the first aim of Crusader strategy, though he attained his second objective, the cutting of the land route between Damascus and Cairo. Baldwin I succeeded by brilliant campaigns in capturing the mountains of Moab and Edom and also the port of Eilat, thus gaining control of the "King's Highway" from Syria to Egypt, and of the "Pilgrims' Way" from Damascus and Cairo to Mecca and Medina. Indeed, during the eighteen years of his reign he brought the kingdom close to the peak of its expansion.

Baldwin I also attempted to invade Egypt, but met his end while leading his host in this campaign (1118). With the death of the conqueror-king the frontiers of the Kingdom of Jerusalem were finally crystallized; they remained in this form, with the addition of small areas in the vicinity of Ascalon in the south and of Banias in the north, until the first kingdom was lost in 1187.

The tasks facing the first generation of the conquest, therefore, were in greater part achieved; Jerusalem was in Crusader hands, a feudal kingdom on the European model had been established in the country, trade grew and prospered and the frontiers had been stabilized. But these many achievements had been made possible only because of the divisions and internal strife amongst the hostile Moslem forces.

The backbone of the Crusader frontier-defence was the geological rift of the Valley of Lebanon, the Jordan Valley and the 'Arava, and it was on the west and east sides of this boundary that the Crusaders built their castles. The natural geological boundary was indeed convenient for defence, but the failure of the Franks to reach the desert frontier left them powerless to prevent the dangerous concentration of Moslem forces near their borders. Luckily there were no such forces to assail them in the first period of the kingdom's existence.

New winds soon began to blow in the Moslem camp, heralding the end of the period of Christian offensive action and the beginning of the Moslem reconquest. The great Seljuk empire, which at the end of the 11th century had embraced all the lands of the Near East, progressively disintegrated. The aspiration to independence and to separatism took shape among the Seljuk rulers of the Syrian cities, influenced by the internal divisions prevailing among the local Arab population. This striving for independence grew stronger than the loyalty to the effete rulers of the empire. Though the Syrian city rulers paid lip service to the idea of Moslem unity and to the summons to a "Jihad", or Holy War, against the Christians, they refused to agree to a unity which would bring with it subjection and loss of local independence. The idea of the union of the Moslem world for war against the infidel, awakened in response to the humiliating defeats suffered by the Moslems at the hands of the Franks, had therefore to be realized by force.

political changes in the Moslem camp

This process of enforced unification began in the 1130's. Zengi, the ruler of the Iraqi city of Mosul at that time, seized control of the cities of Iraq and northern Syria. His pressure was felt both on the frontiers of the Christian principalities of the north and on the borders of the Moslem emirates in south Syria, but chiefly upon the Emirate of Damascus. The rulers of Damascus, the "Bride of Syria", who valued their independence highly, appealed to the Crusaders, their former foes, to join with them and present a united front against the common enemy. The alliance concluded between Damascus and Jerusalem, although unwritten, held good for twenty years and brought about a stabilization of the balance of power in the area. A buffer state was created between the forces of Islam, now in process of organizing themselves, and the Crusader kingdom. Damascus was the only point at which the Moslems could concentrate their army for an attack on the Frankish kingdom; so long as this base was denied to them, the frontiers of the kingdom were safe.

alliance with Damascus

5

The period of stability ended in 1144, when Zengi conquered the Crusader principality of Edessa. The fall of Edessa prompted a new wave of expeditions led by the kings of France and Germany, known as the Second Crusade. Of the multitudes of knights who set out from Europe only remnants reached the Orient. Once arrived, instead of directing their campaign to the liberation of Edessa, the knights, paying heed to the irresponsible advice of some of the knights of the Kingdom of Jerusalem, decided to attack and conquer their Moslem ally, Damascus. The failure of the siege of Damascus (1148) had disastrous results for the Kingdom of Jerusalem. The Franko-Damascene alliance, the cornerstone of the delicately contrived balance of power, was irreparably dislodged, and the legend of the "unbeaten Frankish host" was shown to be false. Within a few years Damascus, whose strategic position was of primary importance, had fallen to Nur a-Din, Zengi's heir.

beginning of the Moslem counterattack

With the fall of Damascus, the Moslems had acquired a decisive strategic advantage. The next phase in the unification of the Moslem lands and the encirclement of the Christians was the domination of Egypt, which possessed huge economic and human resources. In the 1150's Egypt was in a state of chaos; the ruling Fatimid dynasty was decaying, the military commanders were competing for power among themselves and constant squabbles were creating a political vacuum—circumstances which the Crusaders sought to exploit on the one hand, and Nur a-Din on the other. The struggle lasted for nine years (1159–68). King Amalric of Jerusalem invaded Egypt five times, and the Franks were able to establish a certain ascendency over the country, but, owing to their slender resources in manpower, they were incapable of seizing real control of the huge and populous state.

Egypt

Public opinion in Cairo, though Shi'ite, supported an alliance with Nur a-Din against the Christians. Anti-Frankish feeling was further aroused by the breaking of the Franco-Egyptian treaty by the Franks when they invaded Egypt in 1168. In that year the Crusader forces clashed with the Syrian army, led by the Kurdish general Shirkuh, which had invaded Egypt. Although the Franks won several engagements, they ultimately lost the struggle and were forced to retire to their territory. Shirkuh's kinsman, a young Kurd called Saladin, took part in these battles.

When Shirkuh died in 1171, Saladin became in effect ruler of Egypt, though complete unity between Syria and Egypt had not yet been achieved. While still refraining from opposing the rule of Nur a-Din openly, he converted Egypt into a state virtually independent of Syria. The existence of the Crusader kingdom suited his interests initially, since it acted as a buffer state between himself and Nur a-Din.

After the death of Nur a-Din, in 1174, Saladin attacked the Kingdom of Jerusalem, but was heavily defeated at the battle of Gezer (Montgisart—1177). This failure proved to the Moslem commander that the strength of the Franks was still something to be reckoned with, and that to destroy them he must unite the Moslems about him. For a time he gave up his attempt to obtain a decision

Saladin's first offensive

and devoted his entire energy to gaining control of Syria and Iraq. He had to overcome the opposition of the heirs of Nur a-Din and the separatist aspirations of the Syrian cities, which revived after the death of the old Sultan.

The Kingdom of Jerusalem thus enjoyed a long interval of repose, from 1177–87, punctuated by short outbreaks of fighting, but the lull was not exploited by the Crusaders for the reorganization or strengthening of their forces. The despairing appeals to the Christians of Europe for aid went unanswered, and the kingdom was on the brink of civil war. The leper king Baldwin IV was at the point of death, and power fell into the hands of a gang of corrupt and inept courtiers, so that almost nothing was done to forestall the approaching catastrophe.

When Saladin had completed the unification of his own kingdom, he turned his attention to that of the infidels. In July, 1187, he invaded Christian territory *fall of Jerusalem* and at the battle of Hattin, west of Tiberias, a decisive engagement took place which ended with the utter defeat of the Franks. No real strength remained anywhere in the kingdom capable of withstanding the triumphant Moslems. Jerusalem fell in October, 1187, and within four months most of the realm had been seized. At the end of 1188 only the city of Tyre remained in Christian hands.

The fall of Jerusalem caused profound shock among the nations of Europe. *Third Crusade* Thousands of knights and simple people took up the cross and wended their way eastward, headed by the great kings of Europe—Richard Coeur de Lion, king of England, Philip II Augustus of France and the German emperor Frederick I. Only shreds of the huge host reached the Holy Land, for the German emperor was drowned on the journey and his army dispersed; Philip II and Richard Coeur de Lion conquered the island of Cyprus on the way and arrived on the shores of the Holy Land in 1191, after numerous delays. The Crusader forces assembled before the walls of Acre, which had been besieged for over a year by the remnants of the local Crusader knights from Tyre. Although it was under siege, Saladin had enclosed the besiegers' camp with a siege-line of his own. This double investment dragged on indecisively for many months before the strength of its defenders gave out and Acre fell in July 1191.

After the capture of Acre the French king returned home and Richard Coeur de Lion became the sole leader of the expedition. Turning south, he inflicted a heavy defeat on Saladin near Arsuf (Tel Arshaf), following which the Crusaders overran the coastal belt from Tyre to Ascalon, though they were not strong enough to advance upon Jerusalem. By 1192 both sides were exhausted. A treaty *re-establishment* was signed at Ramla whereby the Kingdom of Jerusalem was re-established, to *of the kingdom* include in its mutilated form only the coastal plain from Tyre to Jaffa, but without its sacred capital, the centre of government being transferred to Acre: its territory was a narrow strip without defensive depth or economic hinterland.

Upon Saladin's death opportunity came for the Kingdom of Jerusalem. Saladin's realm disintegrated and his heirs fought one another. But this favourable moment too was wasted; the armies of the Fourth Crusade, organized in Europe, did not reach the country at all, having been diverted to Constantinople under the influence of the commercial interests of Venice. Constantinople was captured in 1204 and became the capital of a Frankish state for some sixty years.

Fifth Crusade Knightly contingents subsequently reached the Holy Land on several occasions, and with their aid several coastal towns were captured and raids conducted into Galilee, but no attempt was made to recapture Jerusalem. In 1218 Europe gathered itself for a renewed attempt, the contemporary strategic conception prevailing that there was no need to fight for Jerusalem to liberate it, but that Egypt must first be won, and that this would automatically bring about the capture of the Holy City. The forces of the Fifth Crusade were accordingly directed to Egypt. After an initial Frankish victory, the Sultan of Egypt agreed to cede to them the entire territory of western Palestine, including Jerusalem. The European Crusaders rejected the offer, although the knights of the Kingdom of Jerusalem demanded its acceptance, and continued their march to Cairo. The decisive battle took place near Mansura; the Crusaders were defeated and forced to evacuate Egypt. The episode of the Fifth Crusade proved that the strategic thinking of the Crusaders had been correct, but that through their fanaticism they had wasted their great opportunity

Frederick II Hohenstaufen The next attempt to recover Jerusalem was made at the end of the 1220's by the Emperor Frederick II Hohenstaufen, who claimed the crown of Jerusalem by virtue of being the husband of Yolanda, daughter of John de Brienne, King of Jerusalem. The emperor arrived in the country in 1228 and, by means of diplomatic negotiation and without bloodshed, reached an agreement with the Egyptian Sultan al Kamil, whereby Jerusalem (except the Temple Mount), Lower Galilee, Nazareth and the corridor between Jerusalem and Jaffa were annexed to the Crusader Kingdom. Although Jerusalem was restored to Christian possession, and remained in their hands for a period of sixteen years, only a limited number of Christians returned to the city.

During the emperor's sojourn the borders of the kingdom were indeed expanded, but its internal disputes were also intensified. The emperor attempted to impose a centralized regime upon the country, and the nobles, used to a weak feudal system, refused to pay allegiance to the emperor and were prepared to defend their ancient rights with force; violent disorders, and even battles, between them and the imperial army, were daily occurrences. The military orders, whose strength was constantly increasing, became independent factors to such an extent that they began to conduct their own foreign policy. The Italian communes, jealous of one another, came to blows over their commercial disputes. Battles were waged and blood spilt in Acre between the Pisan, Genoese and Venetian colonies. Henceforth the country was without firm central rule.

In the 1230's and 1240's the Franks secured some notable territorial achievements by exploiting the deep-rooted hostility prevailing between the rulers of Damascus and those of Egypt, both descendants of Saladin. Each Moslem ruler strove to attract the Franks to his side, and between them they restored almost the entire area of Palestine to the Franks; but the weakening of the kingdom through its internal discords continued.

8

At the beginning of the 1240's the country came under the influence of important events in the Far East. The migration of the Mongols headed by Jenghiz Khan led to the flight of numerous tribes who, in the course of their wanderings, reached the Middle East. Amongst these tribes were the Ḥwarizmians. The Egyptian sultan took them into his pay to fight his mortal enemy, the Sultan of Damascus. At this time an alliance existed between the Crusaders and the latter, so that they came under attack by the Ḥwarizmians, who took Jerusalem in 1244. A combined Damascene-Frankish host fighting the tribe and their Egyptian allies was defeated in the battle of Hirbiya (near Gaza), and the Egyptians occupied the entire south of Judea. The Kingdom of Jerusalem was thus reduced to the area of the northern coastal plain.

The second fall of Jerusalem caused renewed shock in Europe. The pious King Louis IX of France, later canonized, rose to save the Holy Sepulchre. He set out on a Crusade at the head of his French knights in 1249. As in 1218, and for the same strategic considerations, the Crusade was directed against Egypt. At first it was successful and the landing was accomplished. The sudden death of the sultan created chaos in the state and the Crusader host advanced towards Cairo; but, the flooding of the Nile having cut its supply lines, it was entirely surrounded and the Crusaders taken prisoner, with their king. Louis IX and the remnants of his army were only freed in exchange for the cession of all Crusader conquests in Egypt and on payment of a huge sum of money. The pious king reached Palestine and there spent four years trying to find a compromise between the rival parties. Failing, he returned frustrated to his own country, after strengthening the walls of the towns and castles, among them Caesarea, Acre and 'Atlit. *second fall of Jerusalem*

In the meanwhile a court revolution had occurred in Egypt, elevating to power a clique of Mamluk (slave) soldiers. Waves of Mongol tribes were approaching Syria and the hosts of Hulagu, the Mongol ruler of Persia, had captured Damascus and were preparing to advance on Egypt, but left the Crusader possessions unmolested. The inevitable collision between the Mamluks and the Mongols was looming, but the Crusaders, busy with their own quarrels, took no initiative whatever in this conflict. It was clear that the Mamluks were their mortal enemy, and there were signs that an understanding might have been reached with the Mongols. Nevertheless the Crusaders allowed the Mamluks to pass unhindered through their territory on their way to the decisive battle with the Mongols. *Mamluks*

In 1260 the armies met at 'Ein Ḥarod ('Ein Jalut): the Mamluks secured a great victory and in consequence their armies captured Damascus and southern Syria. The reunion of Egypt and Syria was a catastrophe for the Crusader kingdom, as it had been in the days of Saladin. But the approaching peril brought no change in the internal situation. Bloody disputes persisted and no real attempt was made to organize the kingdom for defence.

Sultan Baybars, having seized control of the Mamluk kingdom, began his campaigns of conquest in 1265. That year Arsuf and Caesarea were taken; a year later Safed was captured, and Jaffa fell in 1268. Baybars' successors, Kalaun *Baybars' conquests* and al-Ashraf Khalil, continued and completed the chapter of conquests. At the end of May, 1291, Acre was seized, and 'Atlit, the last Christian foothold in the Holy Land, was abandoned in August, 1291.

Jacob's Well church, near Nablus

BORDERS AND ADMINISTRATIVE DIVISIONS

The frontiers of the Kingdom of Jerusalem underwent many changes during the two centuries of its existence. The Franks gained control of the country within its natural frontiers in an astonishingly short time, and in a still shorter time lost that control. The borders established by King Baldwin I (1100–1118) remained in force, with minor modifications, until the decisive defeat of the battle of Hattin (1187), as a result of which the Franks lost their entire kingdom. At the end of the Third Crusade (1192) only a narrow strip of the coastal plain remained in their hands, extending from Tyre in the north to Jaffa in the south. This was retained, with slight modifications to its frontier, until 1229, when the Emperor Frederick II was able to annex to the kingdom Jerusalem (except for the Temple Mount), western Galilee, the north of Upper Galilee and the narrow corridors leading to Jerusalem and Nazareth. In 1241 the whole of Upper Galilee, the southern maritime plain and the Judean foot-hills as far as Beit Govrin were encompassed within the kingdom. But from 1244 the tables were turned. The realm began to dwindle as the Ḥwarizmians and the Mamluks bit off piece after piece, so that by the end of the 1270's only a restricted territory, from 'Atlit to Beirut, was left in Frankish hands.

border changes throughout the the period

The kingdom was at the height of its expansion in about the year 1160. At that time Ascalon had been captured and the Franks still held distant areas such as Banias and Eilat. Its northern frontier stood at the River Mu'amiltain north of Beirut, and continued eastward to the vicinity of the townlet of Zaḥala, the area between the latter and Beirut being divided between the Franks and the Moslem inhabitants of the mountain region. Near Zaḥala it turned southward along the valley of the River Litany, and thence east of Qal'at Shaqif (Beaufort) eastward, to include Marj 'Ayun and Banias, so forming a deep salient eastward encompassing the southern slopes of Mt. Hermon. South of Qal'at Subeibe the frontier crossed the Golan heights on a line more or less identical with the cease-fire line in the Arab-Israel war of 1967, impinging in part on the Ruqqad Valley. East of the Ruqqad estuary it crossed the Yarmuk and passed along the south bank to the vicinity of the Yarmuk confluence with the Jordan. It continued along the Jordan in the sector between the Yarmuk confluence and that of the Jaboq (Zerqa) river, where it turned east to take in the Plateau of Ammon, Moab and Edom as far as Eilat. The region of the central Negev was in fact a no-man's-land controlled by Bedouin tribes, and the only clear demarcation of the frontier was at Deir al-Balaḥ in the south. The area of the kingdom within the above frontiers amounted to 24,000 square kilometres.

border line at height of expansion

11

ADMINISTRATIVE DIVISIONS

fiefs and seigneuries
In any attempt to describe the administrative divisions of the Kingdom of Jerusalem, it must be remembered that we are dealing with a feudal state which contained no districts, or provinces, controlled by the officials of a central authority. The kingdom's administrative division was based on the laws of the feudal system, according to which the king, as suzerain and lord of the kingdom, granted tracts of land to nobles as fiefs, while a considerable part remained in the king's hands and was administered by him directly as his domain. The fiefs given to the nobles were of two types, the first being without judicial or administrative authority, and consisting of lands granted predominantly for economic exploitation. The second type consisted of "seigneuries", that is broad fiefs within which the lord received also judicial and administrative powers, which made him a ruler virtually independent of the central authority.

The Crusader kingdom was therefore divided into administrative units of two kinds: the royal domain, and the seigneuries, sometimes called counties. The fiefs without judicial powers were very numerous, both within the territory of the royal domain and in that of the seigneuries. Some of them were very small, down to half a village, while others were very extensive, covering vast areas. These however were not independent judicial units and do not interest us here.

administrative bodies
The sign that a fief was an administrative unit was the existence within it of a seigneurial court, the body through which the administrative and judicial affairs of the seigneurie were settled. This was composed of all the nobles holding fiefs from the seigneur within the territory of the domain. Its seat indicated the location of the chief administrative centre of the seigneurie. Only members of the nobility were tried by the seigneurial court; the European inhabitants of non-noble origin—the "bourgeois" (burgesses)—were tried in the burgesses' court, also subject to the seigneur. The head of the burgesses' court was known as the *Vicecomes* (Viscount). The seat of the burgesses' court or of the Viscount indicated the existence of a secondary administrative centre within the seigneurie. There was no dependence or connection between the seigneurial high court and the burgesses' courts, except the fact that both operated under the same feudal lord. Besides his judicial powers, the seigneur possessed a number of administrative prerogatives, such as the right to execute royal instructions. To these were added economic rights such as the monopolies of flour-mills and bakeries and tenurial dues; similar economic rights were also wielded by feudatories who were not independent seigneurs.

administrative functionaries
The seigneur was assisted in the administration of his domain by a number of officials. The viscount was responsible for the collection of rents and fines, and the maintenance of public order; the "dragoman" was in charge of relations with the native population and the "scribe" was the chief clerk. Besides these there were military and feudal officers such as the seneshal, constable, marshal, chancellor and chamberlain.

The royal domain was administered much like a seigneurie, there being no distinction between the general functions of the kingdom and the special administrative functions of the domain areas. The king's court of justice was simultaneously the supreme court of the kingdom *(Haute Cour)* and the domain court, so that the great nobles, the lords of the seigneuries and the knightly holders of fiefs within the domain, were all partners to it. The senior royal functionaries were engaged at one and the same time in the affairs of the whole realm and in the management of the royal domain.

The creation of the seigneuries, and the granting of independent judicial and administrative rights within them, was not a single non-recurring act but a relatively prolonged historical process. Godfrey, the first ruler of the kingdom, created no independent seigneuries. His successor Baldwin I began to grant fiefs, both in the areas won from the Moslems and in the areas which belonged initially to the royal domain. Some of these fiefs remained no more than landed estates and some developed into independent seigneuries. But as the seigneurial class grew stronger the king lost his influence and the seigneuries became petty states.

historical development of administrative units

The administrative-judicial borders, and the positions of the primary and secondary *chefs-lieux,* had been fixed when the seigneuries were set up, and they remained in force throughout the epoch, unaltered by the constant process of accumulation by the seigneurs, the annulment of the seigneuries, or the granting of fiefs within them. The perpetuation of the administrative borders was secured by virtue of the feudal law that no existing seigneurial court could be abolished, even if it had passed to another seigneur in consequence of legacy or sale.

The map of the administrative-judicial units of the kingdom took final shape in the 1150's, after the capture of Ascalon. Subsequently many changes occurred in the ownership of the seigneuries; some were united under one seigneur, others were created and split up, but these changes did not affect the administrative boundaries, as fixed when the original seigneuries were established. Several examples can be cited to make the matter clearer. The seigneuries of Mirabel, Ramla and Yavne were united in the middle of the 12th century under the Ibelins, but the old administrative units and centres continued to exist with separate administrative feudal institutions. Similarly, in spite of appearances to the contrary, Hebron was an administrative unit within the royal domain until 1161, when it was separated from it and made over to the lords of Oultrejourdain. Its administrative independence was not affected by this change of lords, and Hebron remained a separate unit under the lords of Crac-Montreal. Likewise, when the seigneurie of Joscelin de Courtenay was created in Upper Galilee and the Plain of Acre, it included areas belonging to the royal domain and areas belonging to the Seigneurie of Toron (the region of Maron), but despite the creation of this new seigneurial unit, the old administrative units remained unimpared and no change took place in the location of their centres. The creation of the seigneurie of Nablus in 1176 is a further instance. Detached from the terri-

permanence of administrative units

tory of the royal domain, the boundaries of this seigneurie continued to coincide with those of the administrative unit previously existing within the domain and administered by the Viscount of Nablus.

The grant deeds always specified the "territory" *(in territorio),* which indicated the administrative unit in which the property thus granted was situated. The boundaries of the "territories" remained unchanged even when the area had in the meantime become an independent seigneurie or part of a larger one. Thus villages within the Nablus region are defined in documents as situated *in territorio Neapolitano,* both before it had become an independent seigneurie and subsequently, and villages and districts are described as situated in the "territory" of Acre even after they had been transferred to the seigneurie of Joscelin.

This permanence of administrative regions continued in the 13th century. Even after the loss by conquest of most of the kingdom, the Moslem royal grants continued to indicate the location of villages given to emirs according to the former Frankish administrative divisions. In this way Baybars granted villages in "the land of Caesarea" and in "the land of Arsuf". We are thus able to sketch a map of administrative units that will be valid for most of the Crusader period. If, on the other hand, we wish to draw a seigneurial map, we shall need a series of maps describing the numerous changes that took place in their boundaries and areas in the course of the period.

administrative
borders coincide
with those of
earlier periods
The splitting up of the kingdom into administrative units was, as stated, a relatively prolonged and unplanned process. Nevertheless it is interesting to note that the lines of division created during the Crusader period generally coincided with those of the administrative division of the country as it had existed in the Byzantine period, and which had also been preserved by the Arab conquerors who succeeded them. The boundaries of the Principality of Galilee, within the territory of western Palestine, for example, are more or less the same as those of the Province of Palaestina Secunda, and the lordship of Caesarea covers the same area as the city territory of Caesarea at the end of the Byzantine period, after the addition of Dor. This is also the case with the boundaries between Sebaste and Neapolis, Neapolis and Jerusalem, and the town territories of Yavne, Ascalon and other cities.

The settlements which served as administrative centres in the Arab period were used as such by the Franks. Some of those which had been administrative centres in the Byzantine period, and ceased to fulfil these functions in the Arab epoch, recovered their ancient rank in the Crusader period; such were Yavne, Migdal Afeq (in place of Antipatris), Dor, Sebaste and Lydda. Only a few of the administrative centres were created in the Crusader period; amongst these were Safed, Mi'ilya, Tibnin, Yoqne'am, Hebron and Nazareth.

This continuity of administrative division and location of the centres of authority provides additional evidence of the manner in which the Franks adapted themselves to the prevailing conditions of the country, and of the great influence exercised by existing institutions and arrangements upon Crusader administration.

14

The number of administrative units was twenty-seven, the largest being the Principality of Galilee, whose area exceeded 3,000 square kilometres, and the smallest Yoqne'am (Caymont), 50 square kilometres in area. In the attached table all appear, the chief administrative centres being indicated and alongside these the secondary centres. The chief centres, apart from Sebaste and Migdal Afeq, are seats of seigneurial courts. In the two exceptional cases there were only burgesses' courts or even only a viscount, but we have information which enables us to state that these were separate administrative areas. The secondary centres are generally the seats of burgesses' courts, except for a few (Qaqun, Qalansuwa, Maron, Lajjun, Jenin, Wadi Musa, Tafila) in which these are not referred to in the sources, and only the existence of a viscount is mentioned.

Name	Area in Sq. Km.	Chef-lieu	Secondary Centres
Beirut	300	Beirut	–
Saiete (Sidon)	1,800	Sidon	Qal'at Shaqif
Tyre	340	Tyre	–
Toron (Tibnin)	570	Tibnin	Hunin, Marun ar-Ras
Belinas (Banias)	80	Banias	Subeibe ?
Galilee	3,250	Tiberias	Safed, Jenin, Nazareth, Lajjun
Scandalion (Iskandaruna)	60	Iskandaruna	–
Acre	970	Acre	Mi'ilya
Haifa	170	Haifa	–
Caymont (Yoqne'am)	50	Yoqne'am	–
Caesarea	1,900	Caesarea	Dor, Qalansuwa, Qaqun, 'Atlit
Bethsan (Beit Shean)	230	Beit Shean	–
Sebaste (Sabastiya)	500	Sabastiya	–
Naples (Nablus)	1,500	Nablus	–
Arsuf	210	Arsuf	–
Mirabel (Migdal Afeq)	150	Migdal Afeq	–
Ramla-Lydda	550	Ramla-Lydda	–
Jaffa	240	Jaffa	–
Ibelin (Yavne)	150	Yavne	–
Blanchegarde (Tel Tsafit)	100	Tel Tsafit	–
Ascalon	610	Ascalon	–
Bethgibelin (Beit Govrin)	210	Beit Govrin	–
Gaza	?	Gaza	–
Darom (Deir al-Balaḥ)	?	Deir al-Balaḥ	–
Jerusalem	2,000	Jerusalem	Bethlehem, Jericho
Hebron	2,900	Hebron	–
Transjordan	5,000	Karak-Shaubak	Wadi Musa, Tafila

POPULATION

The population which suddenly found itself under Frankish rule was varied in composition and extremely heterogeneous. It comprised a medley of peoples, religions and races that had settled in the Holy Land in the wake of waves of conquerors, migration and religious movements.

THE INDIGENOUS POPULATION

The largest and most important component of the vanquished population was of course the Moslems. This element was in no sense homogeneous, but fell into various groups according to its religious sectarian adherence, its origin, way of *Moslems* life and habitat. Most of the Moslems belonged to the Sunni sect, but a considerable Shi'ite population was to be found in the north of the country, chiefly in the vicinity of Nablus, Tiberias, Galilee and Tyre. Esoteric sects which had grown up among the Shi'ites also found a place in the country. In the mountainous regions of Upper Galilee, Mt. Hermon and south Lebanon, were small communities of Isma'ilites, Nusairis (Assassins) and Druzes.

The overwhelming majority of the Moslem population were village-dwellers. These *fellaḥin* were the descendants of ancient indigenous remnants that had been swallowed by the waves of Arab conquerors and had accepted their religion. They retained ancient traditions of local "saints", of sacred trees and customs, unaltered since biblical days. The number of city-dwelling Moslems was small, since most of them had been butchered or expelled by the Crusaders at the time of the conquest. In addition to the villagers and townspeople there were in the country numerous Bedouin tribes, located chiefly in the desert areas of Judea, the Negev and Sinai, but also in the heart of the inhabited area, as in the region of Nablus. The Turkmen tribes which had wandered from the deserts of Central Asia constituted an additional nomadic element; in the Crusader period we find them in the Banias area. Baybars also brought in Turkmen tribes.

The Christian communities within the population were likewise heterogeneous *Christians* in content. The two main communities were the Syrian-Jacobites and the Greek Orthodox. The Jacobites, whose liturgical language was Syriac, were chiefly village-dwellers. Besides these two groups there were Armenians, Georgians, Copts, Nubians, Ethiopians and others, but they were largely nuns and priests and they had no local adherents. A special place was held by the Maronites, who lived in the Lebanon and had united with the Catholic Church in 1182, though continuing to retain a certain independence. The Christian communities lived both in the towns and in the countryside, the regions of Bethlehem, Nazareth and Lower Galilee being populated by Christian peasants.

17

Jews
The Jewish population of the Holy Land had dwindled considerably in the generations preceding the Crusader conquest. Nevertheless there were large urban communities in Jerusalem, Ramla, Ascalon, Jaffa, Banias, Haifa, Tiberias and Tyre, and also in rural settlements in Central and Upper Galilee, where Jewish settlement had been continuous since the Second Temple period. The Crusaders, whose hands were already stained with the blood of the Jews of the Rhineland towns, annihilated the Jewish communities in the cities of Palestine which they had captured by force of arms. Other congregations left their homes and migrated. During the period of the Crusader kingdom Jews were prohibited from residing in Jerusalem, but as the situation grew more stable some Jews returned to the towns under Frankish rule. Benjamin of Tudela refers to Jewish communities in a number of Frankish towns and townlets.

Besides the Jewish community there was a large Samaritan element, its centres being at Nablus, Caesarea and Ascalon, and also a small number of Karaites.

The conquest of the country by Saladin began a new chapter in the history of the Jewish population; the sultan abolished the prohibition of Jewish residence in Jerusalem, and even encouraged Jews to settle there, but owing to the deterioration in the economic situation the centres of Jewish population remained in the maritime towns which continued under Frankish rule. The influx from the lands of Islam, which grew with Saladin's conquest, was swelled by immigration from Europe at the beginning of the 13th century. On the capture by the Mamluks of the Frankish cities along the coast, the centres of Jewish life moved inland once more, to Jerusalem and Safed.

The total number of indigenous inhabitants, in their various groups, amounted to half a million. We do not know how they were divided according to communities, but it may be conjectured that the proportion of Moslems among the local population reached 75–80 per cent.

THE FRANKISH POPULATION

The Frankish population living in the Holy Land was varied in geographical and social origin. We find among the local Franks people from all the countries in Europe, and deriving from all strata of European society. The variety became
origin
the more perceptible with the process of migration, which continued throughout the epoch, and the mixed marriages between Franks and local Christians, and even between Franks and Moslems. Despite this the Frankish group retained a homogeneous character. Owing to the numerical majority and social standing of the Franks of French origin, the Crusader kingdom assumed the semblance of a French colony in language, institutions and customs.

settlements
The Frankish population was overwhelmingly urban; of its total of 140,000, only ten to twenty thousand lived outside the large population centres. But,

18

despite this urban demographic concentration, there were many Frankish settlements throughout the land, and these were of several types. They included castles manned by permanent Frankish garrisons; isolated monasteries and churches with their communities of priests and monks; townlets inhabited by a considerable Frankish population; Frankish villages and native settlements in which a limited number of Franks lived temporarily or permanently.

The following is a classified list of the Frankish settlements in the Holy Land:

Cities	Townships	Villages	Administrative Centres	Fortresses
Jerusalem	Gaza	Akhziv	Qula	Habonim
Acre	Qaqun	Dabburiya	Tsuba	Belvoir
Tyre	Qalansuwa	al-Bira	'Imwas	M. 'Ateret
Tiberias	Yavne	Qubeiba	Tour Rouge	Montfort
Haifa	Beit Govrin	Sinjil	H. Manot	Subeibe
Ascalon	Tel Tsafit	Beit Nuba	al-Mirr	Hunin
Caesarea	Deir al-Balah	Jezreel	Jericho	Yalu
Nablus	Safed	Beit Suriq		Ma'ale Adumim
Banias	'Atlit			al-Fula
Nazareth	Mi'ilya			Latrun
Arsuf	Tibnin			Qal'at Shaqif
Ramla-Lydda	Tsipori			Samu'
Bethlehem	Yoqne'am			Shaubak
Sidon	Dor			Tafila
Beirut	Migdal Afeq			Eilat
Karak	Jenin			Shefar'am
	Lajjun			
	Sebaste			
	Hebron			

Churches and Isolated Monasteries	Isolated Families or Temporary Settlements	
Mount Tabor	Jifna	Beit Horon
Abu Ghosh	H. Tannur	Tafuh
Quruntul	Bir Zeit	Zababida
Rantis	Beit 'Itab	Rantiya
Bethany	Beit Safafa	Lubban-Sharqiya
St Brocardus	Lifta	Raba
Nabi Samwil	Beit Hanina	Rama
Tayiba	Beit Iksa	Burj Bardawil
Cansie	al-Jib	Samariya
Deir al-Asad	Jab'a	Aqua Bella

This list gives us a total of some eighty settlements containing Frankish population. There are at least twenty-two additional settlements in which archaeological remains of Frankish occupation, permanent or temporary, have been found.

Given a total of seven hundred permanent settlements in the Holy Land, those with a permanent Frankish population amounted to fifteen percent of the total. Despite their relatively small number, the Frankish settlements, widely scattered in all parts of the country from the borders of Sinai to the foot of the Hermon range and from Jericho to the Litany valley, indicate a marked degree of settlement.

CONQUERORS AND CONQUERED

The Frankish kingdom was the state of a conquering minority, which maintained its rule by the economic exploitation of the local conquered population, preponderantly agricultural. The Crusader conquest did little to change the position of this population or the extent of its exploitation. Even before the conquest the land had been taken from its cultivators and belonged to religious foundations (*Waqf*), to the state, or to emirs and wealthy townspeople, who leased it to the peasants for a third or a half of their crops. It was but a slender difference that separated these tenurial relations from the feudal system inaugurated by the Franks. Hence the simple peasant scarcely felt any change in his daily way of life. The only difference, from his point of view, was that the place of the Moslem landlord had been taken by a Frankish one. The degree of exploitation and scale of taxes which he paid did not increase, nor was he driven from his land to make room for a Frankish peasant. Ibn Jubayr, comparing the plight of the Moslem peasants under the Franks to that under Moslem rule, came to the conclusion that the lot of those subject to the rule of the infidels was superior to that of those in the neighbouring Moslem countries:

> "The Moslem community bewails the injustice of a landlord of its own faith and applauds the conduct of its opponent and enemy, the Frankish overlord, and is accustomed to justice from him."[1]

judicial autonomy

The Franks allowed village communities to live their own lives and left in the hands of their headmen—*Rayises*—their traditional authority to judge cases and to conduct the daily affairs of their villages. These village headmen were also the intermediaries between the peasants and the feudal lords, and were responsible for the collection of taxes and crops. This judicial autonomy, as enjoyed by the various communities of the rural population (Christians, Moslems, Jews and Samaritans), existed to a certain degree also in the cities where indigenous groups were to be found. The local city population was judged in "the court of the market" (*Cour de la Fonde*) whose jurors were mostly Syrians sitting under Frankish presidents. This system of autonomous communal courts was in fact a product of feudal law, which required judgment by one's peers.

The mild occupational regime maintained by the Franks was based, not on any enlightened philosophy, but on force of circumstances: the state needed the labour of the peasants to conduct its economy. The Franks recognized that their numerical strength was insufficient to contend with an abandonment of the soil and a flight of the peasants across the frontiers of the kingdom as had resulted from the violent measures adopted during the first years after the Crusader conquest. They were therefore obliged to avoid the tension which would arise in conditions of severe oppression and exploitation, and which might endanger the peace and security of the realm. Moreover, any policy of suppression and imposed administration would have necessitated the employment of Frankish officials in large numbers, and these were not available.

The comparatively comfortable conditions of life enjoyed by the local inhabitants did not bring about close and loyal relations between them and their Frankish overlords, so that, although for most of the period the Franks enjoyed passive subjection on the part of the Moslems, outbreaks of violence did occur. Such revolts usually coincided with the invasion of a Moslem force. In 1113, when the Frankish army had been defeated in war, a rising broke out in the country. Of this Ibn al-Qalanisi related that on the defeat of the Franks, "there was not a Moslem left in the land of the Franks who did not send to the Atabek, begging that he should guarantee him security and confirm him in the possession of his property, and not a single cultivated estate was left between Acre and Jerusalem."[2] Other revolts took place in the years 1182–3 and also after the battle of Hattin, when peasant risings anticipated the overrunning of the country by the forces of Saladin. *passive subjection*

The relatively long period in which the Franks and the native population lived side by side did not lead to the forging of social ties between them, and, although Usamah tells of common hunting expeditions and reciprocal visiting, these were limited to the thin stratum of the Frankish nobility and the Moslem nobility of the neighbouring countries, and did not affect the local inhabitants. The Franks from Europe, and especially their sons and grandsons, born in the land, learned the manners, language and culture of the natives, understood them and appreciated them, and daily life in the same country created in the second generation of the Franks a tolerant attitude to their Moslem enemies, decidedly different from the hostile fanatical approach of their fathers and of the newly arrived Crusaders, but none of this could create a true feeling of kinship and common interest. To the end of the epoch the relationship between the Franks and the Moslems remained that of a conquering minority and a conquered and subject majority. Close relations were not established even with the local Christian communities. The latter, who might have been true allies of the Franks, could not forgive their haughtiness and pride, the treatment they had received as a subject class and above all the expulsion of their clergy and bishops from the churches, to be replaced by Latin prelates. Their hatred for the Franks was so violent that they saw in Saladin a saviour from their subjection. *no social ties between conquerors and subjects*

21

Part II CITIES AND TOWNS

INTRODUCTION

The cities encountered in the Holy Land by the armies of the First Crusade were numerous, large, wealthy and much more fully developed than those they were used to in their lands of origin. The advanced urban culture, which reached its height throughout the lands of the Roman Empire in the 3rd and 4th centuries A.D., had crumbled and declined in Europe.

Cities almost disappeared from the continental landscape during the Dark Ages, and only in the southern areas bordering on the Mediterranean did the urban tradition persist. The revival of the European cities began only at the end of the 10th century and at the beginning of the 11th century. In contrast to the impoverishment and decline of the European city, the oriental city retained its position and, despite the relative degeneration which had taken place since the brilliance of the Roman period, still acted as a political, administrative, economic and cultural centre.

cities in Europe

The Arab city of the 11th century was the administrative centre of a district *(kura)* whose borders coincided, with slight modifications, with the borders of the territories of the Byzantine towns (see p. 14). The military strength of the government was concentrated in the garrisons quartered in barracks within the cities, and hardly ever stationed outside their walls. The city was the focus of economic activity, both as a centre of consumption and of handicrafts, and as a local and international centre of commerce. The entire social élite—the military commanders, the high officialdom, the estate owners and merchants—resided in the city. Urban continuity expressed itself also in the actual physical structure of the cities. Their walls were Byzantine in most places, and the town plan was based on Roman models. In the majority the ancient systems of water supply and drainage still operated, and the dwellings and public buildings were in part hundreds of years old. Owing to the dominant position of the Arab city, the Crusader conquest of the country was expressed by the seizure of its urban centres. The capture of a city led in any case to the control of the whole surrounding area and to the seizure of the entire military, economic and governmental nerve-centres.

continuation of urban life in the east

In the first period of conquest, seizure of a city was accompanied by the brutal massacre of the whole population or, at best, by total expulsion. Numerous Franks took up immediate residence in such cities, which had thus become vacant but were not destroyed or damaged. The Crusaders, most of whom had not previously lived in towns, became city-dwellers, as their numerical inferiority impelled them to seek security in large concentrations of population, and the city walls ensured protection against the Moslem armies and robber bands. In the initial period the cities were half empty and the Franks' real control was limited to the walled areas. But the urban recovery was very swift; all the immigrants

the Crusaders become city-dwellers

from Europe, arriving in an endless stream, settled in the cities, and when the first period of fanaticism had passed some of the Moslem inhabitants who had been expelled were permitted to return. In the course of a generation the cities were restored to the size and status which they had possessed before the conquest, and in a short time their development outstripped the attainments of the Arab period.

functions of the
Frankish cities The Frankish city, indeed, was the successor of the Arab in respect not only of its walls and buildings, but also of the functions it discharged. Like its predecessor it was the centre of government, administration and the economy. The decisive importance of the Crusader city was all the greater because the majority of the Franks gathered there. Its dominant function was preserved despite the fact that, in contrast to the Arab period, the Crusaders established centres of military and administrative control outside it. These centres were vital for the protection of internal security and the management of the feudal estates, and they were set up in castles throughout the country. Frankish settlements grew near these centres and developed into new townships (see p. 173). But this decentralization was limited and the number of Frankish inhabitants living outside the cities did not exceed a few thousand. The estate-owners, great seigneurs and petty knights, dwelt in the cities which remained the nerve centre of the kingdom.

size and
population The demographic data concerning the towns of the Holy Land are slight and of doubtful reliability, as with all the statistical data recorded in the historical sources of the epoch. The only figures which can be relied upon to a certain extent are the numbers of the inhabitants of the principal cities, namely Jerusalem, Acre and Tyre, in each of which some thirty thousand people dwelt. The population of Crusader Jerusalem was more or less identical with its population at the end of the 19th century and not far from the number living within the walls today. As the area of the Crusader city (coinciding with the present "Old City") amounted to 860 dunams, the gross population density was 35 per dunam. If we subtract from the total the area of the Temple Mount, which was inhabited only by monks and members of the Order of Templars, the inhabited area, including churches, religious houses and institutions, amounted to 720 dunams, giving a density of 42 per dunam. If our reconstruction of ancient Acre is correct (see p. 88), its built-up area, including the quarter of Montmusard, covered 600 dunams. Acre's population density, therefore, was greater than that of Jerusalem, being 50 per dunam. The density at Tyre, the third chief town, resembled that of Acre.

The sources do not record the population of the other towns. In those whose built-up areas (or the course of whose walls) are known, we can estimate the population by assessing the density on the basis of the density data known from Jerusalem and Acre. The towns with known areas are Caesarea, Arsuf, Banias, 'Atlit, Sidon and Ascalon. (The walled area of Ascalon is known, but most of it was not built upon.) It is to be assumed that the population density of these towns was smaller than that of the principal cities, and it may also be supposed that it was greater in the coastal towns than in those of the interior. Proceeding from the calculations made concerning the towns of known area, we can arrive at the order of magnitude of the populations of the towns whose remains do not enable us to establish it otherwise. Thus, for example, it may be assumed that the population of Tiberias was somewhat larger than that of Banias, and that Jaffa resembled in size Caesarea and Sidon. The results of these calculations, which should not be regarded as other than approximate, are listed in the following table:

POPULATIONS OF THE TOWNS

Town	Area (dunams)	Total Population	Density per dunam	Serjeants	Jews and Samaritans
Jerusalem	720	30,000	42	500	—
Acre	600	30,000	50	500	200
Caesarea	120	4,800	40	50	400
Arsuf	90	3,600	40	50	—
Banias	75	2,625	35	—	—
'Atlit	90	3,600	40	—	—
Sidon	140	5,600	40	—	—
Tyre	—	30,000	—	100	400
Tiberias	130	4,500	35	200	50
Jaffa	—	5,000	—	100	—
Haifa	—	3,500	—	50	—
Ascalon	500	10,000	20	150	500
Ramla-Lydda	—	3,000	—	50	400

The table gives additional statistical data which may to a certain degree help to fix the order of magnitude of the population. In the view of scholars, the number of serjeants furnished by the various towns is not derived from the number of the Frankish population in the towns concerned but is rather a criterion of their economic strength. The number of Jewish and Samaritan inhabitants can only give a clue to the size of those towns possessing well-rooted Jewish and Samaritan populations unharmed by massacre or persecution. A reasonable estimate of Jewish and Samaritan population in the towns of Ascalon, Caesarea and Tiberias might vary between five and ten per cent of the whole. There is no point in drawing up a total from the above table, since the rise in population and prosperity of these towns did not take place at the same period. Acre's period of prosperity, for instance, came when Jerusalem lay deserted and in ruins. Nevertheless it can be estimated that at the peak of the Crusader kingdom's prosperity just before the battle of Hattin, the population of the cities amounted to not less than 120,000. To that we have to add several thousands who lived in townlets.

Several communities and classes lived together in the Frankish city, and differed from one another in social, legal and economic status.

communities in the cities

The Franks   The Franks were divided into two well-defined classes—the knights and the burgesses. As has been emphasized, all the nobles resided in the town, whether great seigneurs holding wide feudal domains, or poor knights living from money-rents. Though relatively small in numbers, this was the class that wielded a decisive influence in the kingdom. Below the knights was the class of burgesses, which included all the Latin Christians who were not knights, but were freemen. The burgess class shared the responsibility for urban government, although the cities never acquired any autonomy, such as was customary in Europe. No corporate bodies or corporations were developed in the cities of Palestine and none enjoyed a city charter or other sign of privilege. At the head of the administration stood the burgesses' court composed of twelve jurors, all rich and respected burgesses selected by the feudal lord of the city. They were headed by the viscount, who was also appointed by the lord. The burgesses' court was both the judicial and the executive authority. The supreme executive official was the viscount, whose function was to maintain public order in the city markets, to superintend the cleanliness of the streets, weights and measures, fair trade, the craftsmen, and everyday life as a whole. He was aided in the fulfilment of his duties by a police force. The constables were called *serjeants,* and served under a commander called a *Mathessep.* Besides fulfilling administrative duties, the burgesses' court was a judicial authority in all matters affecting the burgess class and also decided on certain cases concerning immovable property within the city. These courts existed in all the centres of Frankish population and the *chefs-lieux* of the seigneuries.

mercantile   A special place among the Frankish social groups was occupied by the "mer-
communes   cantile communes," the colonies of Italian, Provençal and Catalan commercial towns. These communes were autonomous units virtually exempt from local jurisdiction by royal or baronial privileges. Their quarters were extra-territorial units governed by the laws of their parent-cities in Europe, and they were administered by a special representative known as a consul or viscount, appointed by the authorities of the parent-cities. The members of the communes, whether permanent or short-term residents, enjoyed many commercial privileges which gave them preference over the local Frankish merchants.

indigenous   The stratum of indigenous subjects was a mosaic of numerous national, reli-
communities   gious and sectarian elements. Most of the native population of the cities was composed of local Christians, among them Syrians, Greeks, Armenians, Jacobites and others. This population engaged in all branches of trade and handicrafts and was allowed to own immovable property. It also enjoyed considerable judicial autonomy, but in certain matters the local inhabitants availed themselves of a special court known as the "Court of the Market" or *Cour de la Fonde.* This court was composed of Syrian and Frankish jurors. In some urban areas there were Moslem and Jewish minorities, and in such cases their individual members enjoyed liberty of cult and judicial autonomy, and did not suffer from commercial discrimination.

Having described the place of the city, its inhabitants and administration, in an introductory manner, we may pass to an account of its physical form.

TOWN PLAN, STREETS AND MARKETS.

The cities of the Crusader kingdom retained the Roman-Byzantine town plan. The city had four main gates facing the four cardinal points. From these led four main streets: the main north-south route, or *cardo,* began at the north gate and issued from the south gate, and the street crossing it from east to west, the *Decumanus,* began at the east gate and left at the west gate. This is the plan we find in *streets* Jerusalem, Ascalon, Caesarea, Arsuf and Acre. In the maritime cities the west gate opened on to the harbour and was known as the Sea Gate. Some cities possessed secondary gates from which streets led in all directions. In addition to the main streets, which were straight, there was a winding complex of lanes and alleys. The main streets had stone vaulting to provide shelter from summer sun and winter rain. A complete example of a covered street is the triple bazaar in Jerusalem and there are remains of vaulting also at Caesarea. Historical sources record the existence of covered streets in Jerusalem, Acre and Tyre. Describing the famous columned street of Sebaste, the traveller Burchard says:

"These columns used to support the vaults of the streets for the streets of this city were vaulted according to the custom of the Holy Land."[3]

Where stone vaults were not built, canvas was stretched across the streets. Since they did not exceed three metres in width, they were congested and passage through them was difficult. They were paved with flagstones, with an open channel in the centre. The sides of the streets were lined with shops (*stationes*), dark narrow niches with masonry verandahs projecting in front, on which the merchants set out their wares. The cities contained numerous markets, each of which concentrated on trade in a given type of goods. There were distinct markets for wholesale and retail trade, and in the central market or *funda* sat the court of justice concerned with its affairs.

The city was divided into quarters. In the maritime towns the mercantile communes had their own quarters fortified by walls; the Patriarch's quarter in Jeru- *quarters* salem was also defended. The various communities congregated in their own special streets and areas; there were streets for the English, Spanish, Germans, Provençals, Syrians and others. The craftsmen also kept to separate streets, special ones being erected for the butchers and tanners.

Although it is known that municipal cleaning services existed, the streets were filthy and the sewage systems primitive.

HOSPITALS AND INNS

The Crusader cities contained public buildings of various types. Besides the royal palaces, churches and monasteries, which we shall not deal with here, it would be well to mention the hospitals and inns. The hospitals belonged to the Orders or were maintained under the authority of the churches and monasteries. The

most important body maintaining such hospitals was the Order of St. John, known as the Order of Hospitallers, which maintained hospitals and infirmaries in Jerusalem, Acre and Nablus. Remains of hospitals of the Order have survived *hospitals* until our own day: in Jerusalem the hospital building occupied the west side of the Muristan square; the infirmary at Acre was situated in the vicinity of the Turkish bathhouse (now the Municipal Museum); ruins of a hospital are preserved at Nablus. The Teutonic Order maintained hospitals at Jerusalem and Acre. Remains of the Jerusalem building are preserved in the Jewish Quarter. There were also shelters for lepers at Jerusalem and Acre. The Eastern Christian communities also maintained hostels and infirmaries; one of the latter was situated near the church of St. Sabas in Jerusalem. The Greek Orthodox monastery of St. Theodosius maintained hospitals at Ascalon, Jaffa and in Cyprus. Medical care is described on page 381.

All the big cities contained large buildings resembling the oriental *khan* or *caravanserai,* that is, a square of rooms and halls built to second storey level, surrounding an inner court. These structures were called *funda* or *fundacum,* and served at one and the same time as markets, customs stations and hostels. The *funda* had two gates, at which the royal revenue officers were stationed to levy the taxes due from merchants. Having entered, the merchants unloaded their wares and stowed them in the storerooms in the lower storey, which also contained stables for the beasts of burden. The second storey contained rooms suitable for a night's lodging. The royal market *(funda regis)* of Acre is excellently described by the traveller Ibn Jubayr (see p. 111). In addition to the royal buildings there were also *khans* in each of the "communal" quarters. No archaeological remains of the Crusader *funda* survive, but the 19th century *khans* of Acre are built on their foundations and are identical in all details with those structures.

CEMETERIES

The Franks buried their dead in cemeteries situated outside the walls of their cities, but kings, nobles and prelates of the church were interred in crypts beneath the churches. Two Crusader burial grounds have been preserved in their entirety *Jerusalem* and many tombstones have also survived.

In one cemetery the laymen were buried with their heads to the west, but the priests lay with their heads to the eastward, perhaps so that at the resurrection the congregation should rise facing eastwards and the clergy with their faces to their congregation. Jerusalem had three burial grounds, one near the Church of St. Stephen, north of the Damascus Gate on the hill of Gordon's Calvary, the second on Mt. Zion not far from the Bishop Gobat School, and the third at Aceldama.

Remains of the graveyard near St. Stephen's Church survived till the end of the 19th century. A number of gravestones of the Crusader cemetery on Mt. Zion

31

Jerusalem, Triple Bazaar, vaults

which belonged to the Church of the Holy Sepulchre have been found. One tombstone is that of John de Valenciennes, a French knight, who lived in Jerusalem in the second half of the 12th century and whose signature appears on several royal documents between 1149 and 1174. The stone bears the words:

Hic requiescit Joh(anne)*s*
de Valencinis
(Here rests John de Valenciennes.)

The stone is an elongated trapezoid, but its lower portion is broken and has disappeared.

The third cemetery, at Aceldama, for pilgrims, was on the south of the Valley of Hinnom not far from the junction with the Kidron Valley. In 1143 the cemetery was given by the Patriarch to the Order of Hospitallers; the document making the grant mentions a church "in the field of Aceldamach, where the bodies of pilgrims are buried." The traveller Phocas describes this cemetery in the 1180's as that "in which they bury foreigners." A large excavation some 40 metres long is preserved here in the rock of the steep slope. The rock-face has in it the openings of ancient rock-cut tombs, and at the east end of the excavation is a pointed barrel vault 15 metres long and six metres wide, resting on two huge square piers made of drafted bossed masonry. The vault was the chapel of the cemetery. Two ancient rock-cut tomb chambers with galleries open from the south wall of the chapel, and steps lead to a third.

'Atlit   Another Crusader burial ground, completely preserved, is situated outside the wall of the lower town or faubourg of 'Atlit; this is on the shore at the north-eastern corner of the wall, and contains 1,700 graves, as well as dozens of tombstones. These bear engraved crosses but no inscriptions. The tombstone of a mason is of special interest; on it are carved, as was customary in the Middle Ages, the symbols of his craft—his builder's rule and hammer.

tombs   As well as in cemeteries, Crusader tombs were situated in the crypts of churches or in churchyards, the best-known being the tombs of the Crusader kings, which were on the south side of the Church of the Holy Sepulchre (today in the Chapel of Adam). These were destroyed in 1808 after the fire in the Church. Drawings of their tombstones, made before they were destroyed, give some notion of their form and inscriptions. Those of which drawings survive belonged to Godfrey de Bouillon, Baldwin I, Fulk, and the child-king Baldwin V.

At the foot of the column dividing the southern portals of the Church of the Holy Sepulchre, in the floor of the Parvis, was formerly the grave of Philip d'Aubigné, an English Crusader who lived in Palestine in the years 1222–1236 and was buried in Jerusalem. The tombstone bears the inscription: "Here is buried Philippus de Aubigné, may his soul rest in peace, amen," and also the engraved knightly shield of the family, with an escutcheon of four fusils.

Several tombstones have been found at Acre, including one which is possibly a gravestone, but may be a memorial stone, of one of the Grand Masters of

Jerusalem, Aceldama, chapel

'Atlit,
Frankish cemetery

the Order of Hospitallers, Peter de Vieille Bride, who died at Acre in 1242. This stone was found during the archaeological excavations made in the "Posta", and measures 1.80 by 0.50 metres. In addition to a lengthy inscription, which includes the date of his death and historical details, it is carved with a Maltese cross (the badge of the Hospitallers), and also the *fleur-de-lys*. The text of the stone differs from that customary on ordinary tombs; moreover it is known that the Grand Masters of the Order were interred in the 13th century in the Church of St Michael on the seashore.

JERUSALEM

The Crusaders caught their first glimpse of the walls and domes of Jerusalem on the morning of the seventh day of June, 1099, as they stood on the summit of the hill of Nabi Samwil. They had spent the night at Abu Ghosh (which they identified with Emmaus), and in the early morning hours had set out to traverse the last lap of their long and wearisome journey. It is easy to imagine their joy and emotion as they beheld the city upon which they had set themselves body and soul.

first glimpse of Jerusalem

Raymond d'Aguilers related how "the Christians could not prevent themselves, in the fervour of their devotions, from shedding tears; they fell on their faces to the ground, glorifying and adoring God, who, in His goodness, had heard the prayers of His people, and had granted them, according to their desires, to arrive at this most sacred place, the object of all their hopes."[4]

The city disclosed to their view was large, fortified, and "wondrously fair". The Persian traveller Nasir Husru describes Jerusalem in the year 1047, in the following words:

"The city is enclosed by strong walls of stone, mortared, and there are iron gates,--- Jerusalem is a very great city and at the time of my visit it contained twenty-thousand men. It has high, well built and clean bazaars. All the streets are paved with slabs of stones.—There are in the city numerous artificers, and each craft has a separate bazaar".[5]

The Moslem geographer al-Maqdisi, a native of the city, sang the praises of Jerusalem thus:

"The buildings of the holy city are of stone, and you will find nowhere finer or more solid construction.—In Jerusalem are all manner of learned men and doctors, and for this reason the heart of every man of intelligence yearns toward her.—As to the saying that Jerusalem is the most illustrious of cities—is she not the one that unites the advantages of this world and those of the next?—And as to Jerusalem being the most spacious of cities, why, since all created things are to assemble there, what place on earth can be more extensive than this?"[6]

A year before the arrival of the Crusaders, Jerusalem had passed back into the hands of the Egyptian Fatimid caliphate and was defended by a large and well-trained Egyptian army. As rumours reached them of the Frankish approach, equipment, supplies and arms were concentrated in the city. Units of the garrison destroyed crops, poisoned the wells and burnt all the timber in a wide radius around the city, in order to deny the Crusaders food, water and the materials required for a siege. The inhabitants of the villages and townships abandoned their homes and concentrated within the city walls. The population of Jerusalem, which in recent years had reached 20,000, was thus doubled. The walls were strengthened, fortifications being added mainly on the north side of the city, where a level area, favourable to a penetration, extended before the walls. Here a strong, lofty barbican was built. The entire Christian population

Moslem preparations for siege

35

was expelled just before the siege. The Jews gathered in their quarter on the north-east of the city.

The Crusader force approaching Jerusalem numbered some 40,000, among *Crusader deployment* them over 12,000 infantry and 1,500 mounted knights. On the 7th of June, at evening, the invading host encamped on the level ground north of the walls. The leaders of the campaign held a council of war, participated in by some of the Christian natives of Jerusalem who had been expelled, and settled the siege dispositions and the division of forces. It was clear to the Franks that the steep slopes of the Kidron Valley and the Valley of Hinnom made it impossible to break into the city from either of these directions and that the only prospect of a successful assault was from the north. They therefore divided the sectors of the wall between them: the Flemish force deployed in the sector facing St. Stephen's Gate (the present Damascus Gate); to the west of it the Norman force took up their post. Tancred took up his position opposite the north-west corner tower, called by the Moslems "the Tower of Goliath". The Provençal unit deployed before the north-western sector of the wall between the Tower of Goliath and the Tower of David, the citadel of the city. The commander of the Provençals, Raymond of St. Gilles, soon lost hope of breaching the wall alongside the huge citadel, and transferred most of his force to Mt. Zion.

After the disposition of the force had been settled, siege tactics were determined. From a military point of view there was no prospect of overcoming the city by prolonged siege, for it was known to be well-supplied and capable of resisting a long investment. Moreover, Egyptian forces had concentrated at *lack of provisions* Ascalon and were preparing to come to Jerusalem's assistance. The Crusaders' *and materials for* supply position was very grave, and they were suffering chiefly from lack of *siege* water, the only source at their disposal being the Spring of Gihon flowing in the ancient tunnel to the Pool of Siloam, whose foul water could not quench the thirst of tens of thousands of Crusaders in the oppressive summer heat. The besiegers were unable to build siege-engines as the Moslems destroyed all the trees around the city. But all these preoccupations were overshadowed by one irrational consideration: the Crusaders were psychologically unprepared for a long siege. They expected a miracle that would cause the city walls to fall before them and permit them to prostrate themselves upon the place where their Redeemer had been crucified.

After five days of preparations, during which time they were engaged in gath- *attempt to scale* ering supplies and in skirmishing with mobile Moslem forces, the Crusaders *walls repulsed* launched a frontal attack from the north. Approaching the wall with dauntless courage, the soldiers attempted to pull it down with mattocks and hammers. The Moslems poured boiling oil and hurled huge stones down on them. Despite heavy losses the Crusaders kept up their attacks and captured the barbican which had been built in front of the wall. "Had scaling ladders been prepared, we would have taken the wall," wrote an anonymous chronicler. But, since they had expected miracles, the Crusaders had not troubled to provide themselves with this vital piece of equipment. Tancred alone had a ladder, and he was the first to set foot upon it, but his knights prevented him by force from climbing to certain death. With evening the defeated combatants gave up their attempts and retired to their camp. No miracle had occurred and the walls of Jerusalem had not fallen before them as the walls of Jericho had fallen before Joshua.

The leaders met and decided to begin a planned and conventional siege. For this, timber was required to build siege-engines. Miraculously, a quantity was discovered, hidden by the Moslems in a cave. Natives led the Franks to a wood six miles away on the road to Nablus, where additional timber was cut and transported, but when it had been brought, it was found that there were no carpenters in camp who knew how to build the engines. In the meantime the problem of supplies and water had grown more grave. Most of the force was hungry, and the price of water was more than many of the Franks could afford. Some licked the dew from the grass, or sucked lumps of mud. Others sewed bottles from oxhides and filled them with stinking water which they brought at the risk of their lives from distant cisterns. Their suffering exceeded anything they had known on their long journey to the Holy Land. *preparations for prolonged siege*

On the 17th of June the news came that a small Genoese fleet had reached the port of Jaffa. The leaders determined to send a unit to Jaffa to enter into negotiations with its commanders and induce them to come to Jerusalem. A company of three hundred men set out westward, encountered an Egyptian force near Ramla, and suffered great losses. When they reached Jaffa they were able to convince the Genoese mariners of the need to break up their ships and all the equipment was brought to Jerusalem. Their carpenters immediately began to build siege engines; meanwhile a regular water supply was organized for the Crusader forces, and morale improved.

The Crusaders erected three moving siege-towers which were higher than the wall, and covered their exposed fronts and sides with iron plates or hides soaked in vinegar, to protect them from Greek Fire. The rear of each tower was of timber and on its top was set a drawbridge. When the towers had been erected the Crusaders began a fast of three days, at the conclusion of which they moved in procession around the city's walls, led by the clergy carrying sacred banners and pictures of saints, the entire host walking barefoot and bareheaded. The Moslems, who saw the procession from the walls, mocked the Christians and shot arrows at them; the Crusaders, having encircled the walls of the city like the Israelites at Jericho, expected them to fall, but they remained whole and menacing as before. *building of siege machines*

On the 10th of July the towers were set up in the places selected for the assault, one on Mt. Zion, one near the Tower of Goliath and one at the northeast corner of the wall. The assault was fixed for Thursday, the 14th of July, 1099. At dawn the towers approached the walls under cover of the fire of mangonels and archers. The fight went on all day without avail. By evening the siege-tower placed on Mt. Zion had been destroyed, and the towers under Tancred (at Goliath Tower) and Godfrey (at the north-east corner of the wall) had been seriously damaged. On the following day, Friday, the struggle was renewed. *assault*

37

In the early morning hours the Crusaders succeeded in breaching the wall, but the outcome was still in the balance. Suddenly, at nine o'clock, the hour of the passion of Christ, a Flemish knight called Lethold was able to leap onto the top of the wall opposite the drawbridge placed at the north-east corner of the rampart. Godfrey de Bouillon followed close behind him with several knights and, as a result of this penetration, the defenders collapsed in the northern sector and the Moslems retreated towards the Temple Mount. Tancred was also able to seize the Goliath Tower and burst into the city. Raymond of St. Gilles encountered numerous difficulties and was unable to penetrate the city until the evening. The Moslem garrison fortified itself on the Temple Mount and in the Tower of David, but the Mount was swiftly taken and the remnants of the garrison of the Tower of David surrendered to Raymond of St. Gilles and were permitted to depart for Ascalon. These were the only ones to escape from Jerusalem.

collapse of defence

The Crusaders, drunk with victory, conducted a massacre in the city such as has seldom been paralleled in the history of war; the troops ran amok through the streets, stabbing and slaying everyone they encountered. It is said that rivers of blood flowed through the narrow lanes, covering the horses' hocks. The Jewish community, gathered in the central synagogue, were shut in by the Crusaders and burnt alive. A few thousand people, remaining from a population which had numbered 40,000, were assembled near the gates and sold as slaves. The massacre aroused horror among the Crusaders themselves, and William of Tyre wrote:

massacre and plunder

"It was impossible to look upon the vast numbers of slain without horror; everywhere lay fragments of human bodies, and the very ground was covered with the blood of the slain. It was not alone the spectacle of the headless bodies and mutilated limbs strewn in all directions that roused horror in all who looked upon them. Still more dreadful it was to gaze upon the victors themselves, dripping with blood from head to foot, an ominous sight which brought terror to all who met them."[7]

The news of the catastrophe swiftly reached Damascus and Baghdad, and multitudes gathered in the mosques, stunned at the fate of the Holy City.

When no one remained alive, and the stench of the corpses could no longer be borne, the Crusaders compelled their prisoners to remove the bodies and to bury or burn them outside the city gates. The houses were divided among the conquerors. A shield or weapon placed over a gate or upon the roof was a sign of ownership. The city was full of foodstuffs and the choicest of merchandise. The heroes of the First Crusade could at last enjoy repose. When the orgy of slaughter and looting was at an end, they gathered at the Church of the Holy Sepulchre to give thanks. The leaders met to choose a ruler for the Holy City and, after prolonged debate, Godfrey de Bouillon was elected and given the modest title of "Advocate of the Holy Sepulchre" (*Advocatus Sancti Sepulchri*).

election of Godfrey

But the Crusaders were not permitted to enjoy the fruits of their victory for long. The Moslem host which had left Egypt to aid Jerusalem and whose march had been dilatory reached Ascalon on the 4th of August, 1099. When news came of the approaching danger, the Franks were forced to break off their rest, their prayers and their pilgrimages to the holy places, and to go out to meet the enemy. On the 9th of August, they left Jerusalem for a battle which was to decide whether the city would remain in their hands. On the 12th the armies clashed between Yavne and Ascalon: the Franks won a brilliant victory and returned to Jerusalem laden with plunder.

victory over Egyptian counter-attack

After they had awakened from the intoxication of their great victory the Crusaders became aware of the weakness and the dangers of their true position. Only a few thousand native Christians remained in the city, whose normal population prior to its capture had numbered 20,000. The Franks who remained after the departure of the leaders with most of the participants in the Crusade did not exceed three hundred knights and some thousands of footmen and civilians. The devastation of the countryside around the city prevented revictualling and as storehouses became empty there was a famine in the city. Bands of Bedouins and runaways roved freely in the vicinity, attacking anyone who left its walls. The main road to the coastal plain was controlled by highwaymen. The Egyptian garrison at Ascalon conducted frequent *razzias* against the isolated Frankish centres of settlement on the coastal plain, and on the roads to the capital, and sometimes reaching its very walls. The problems facing the new rulers of Jerusalem, therefore, concerned security, settlement and supplies. They took a series of steps to solve them, and these gradually brought about the strengthening of the position of the kingdom's capital. Their constant and stubborn efforts bore fruit and, at the end of fifty years of Frankish rule, the Holy City was larger, stronger and wealthier than in the period preceding the Crusader conquest.

situation in occupied Jerusalem

problems of security, settlement and supplies

A chain of fortresses was erected along the principal highways. In 1118 the Order of Templars received the task of protecting the roads from the maritime plain to Jerusalem. In the 1130's the south-western chain of border fortresses was set up in order to check the attacks of the Egyptian garrison at Ascalon. The improvement in security conditions along the main arteries of communication influenced the city's economic situation; the price of foodstuffs fell and supplies began to flow into the city. In 1124, in order to encourage trade, Baldwin II relieved the inhabitants and traders of the city of taxes and duties on the importation of goods to Jerusalem. By this privilege every inhabitant and merchant, whether a resident of Jerusalem or a stranger, whether Latin, Syrian, Greek, Armenian or Moslem, could buy and sell his wares in the city without tax or duty. As a result of this step supplies became more abundant, prices fell, and the flow of settlers into the city increased.

The number of pilgrims grew, and the city's economic situation improved in consequence, since a considerable part of its sources of livelihood was based on the provision of services to pilgrims. The kings of Jerusalem endeavoured to attract the great maritime communes to the city, granting them numerous privileges, the first being given to Genoa in 1104, and others to Marseilles in 1117, to Venice in 1123 and also to Pisa. However, this endeavour of the rulers failed,

improvement of economic situation

as the communes were guided by purely mercantile considerations and their preoccupation was with the great international trade, in which Jerusalem had no part. Throughout the existence of the Kingdom of Jerusalem the communes did not settle there or contribute to its economy, but it is interesting to note that despite their failure to exercise their privileges the communes insisted on the periodical reaffirmation of their rights. The Commune of Genoa, for instance, insisted that its charter be engraved on a panel in letters of gold, and that the panel be kept in the Church of the Holy Sepulchre. Its removal gave rise to a dispute which reached the Holy See of Rome.

The improved conditions of security led to the return of the village population to the vicinity of Jerusalem, whence it had fled just before the conquest. Ecclesiastical and secular elements, chief amongst these being the Church of the Holy Sepulchre and the Order of Hospitallers, took active steps to repopulate the areas around the city, steps which were so successful that in the 1150's, according to sources, no single plot remained uncultivated.

growing population The Frankish kings took equally energetic measures to enlarge the city's population; William of Tyre tells of the action taken by Baldwin I to this end in 1115:

> "The king felt that the responsibility for relieving the desolation of the city rested upon him. Accordingly, he made careful investigations in regard to some source whence he might obtain citizens. Finally, he learned that beyond the Jordan, in Arabia, there were many Christians living in villages under hard conditions of servitude and forced tribute. He sent for these people and promised them improved conditions. Within a short time he had the satisfaction of receiving them with their wives and children, flocks and herds, and all their households."[8]

Pilgrims settled in growing numbers in the city and with the passage of time the Frankish element grew stronger. To promote their settlement a special law was enacted, whereby a householder lost his rights if he did not levy rent from his lodgers for a year and a day. This law was directed against absentee householders who left the town for a prolonged period, and for the benefit of new inhabitants who settled there, and who thus could acquire empty houses.

Residence in Jerusalem was prohibited absolutely to Jews and Moslems. But this prohibition seems to have been enforced only during the first years of the occupation of the city; as early as the late 1120's Moslems are mentioned among its inhabitants. The privileges referred to above, which granted exemption from taxes to inhabitants and merchants, alluded explicitly to "Saracen" traders. The Jewish community, which had been completely wiped out in the massacre which followed the capture of the city, was not renewed, but Benjamin of Tudela found three Jews in Jerusalem who were engaged in dyeing linen.

cosmopolitan character The character of the city was cosmopolitan. In its streets the pilgrim from Norway could be seen side-by-side with the trader from Central Asia, Copts and Scots, Persians, Jews and Moslems from Spain. John of Würzburg says: "For there are Greeks, Bulgarians, Latins, Germans, Hungarians, Scots, Navarrese,

40

Bretons, English, Franks, Ruthenians, Bohemians, Georgians, Armenians, Jacobites, Syrians, Nestorians, Indians, Capheturici, Maronites, and very many others, whom it would take long to tell."[9]

Inter-community relations passed through many changes. The first meeting between the Crusaders and the local Christians was warm and affectionate, but when the Franks became rulers of the country the local Christians were still regarded as inferior subjects, precisely as they had been in the Moslem period. The Latin clergy dominated the local churches. This control reached its peak when the local clergy were expelled from the Church of the Holy Sepulchre (1101) and replaced by Latin clergy. The chroniclers relate that because of this act of expulsion the "Holy Fire" did not come down to light the candles in the Church, as it had done every year on Easter eve. (The ceremony of the Holy Fire is customary to this day among the oriental communities in the Church of the Holy Sepulchre.) It is to be supposed that the secret of the Holy Fire was known to the local clergy alone and that the miracle therefore did not occur after their banishment. The Latins, much alarmed by this sign of ill omen, permitted the local clergy to use the church, although the upper hierarchy remained Frankish.

The Franks seem at first also to have gained control of the Armenian, Greek and Syrian churches, but after some time restored them to their owners. In the course of the years toleration and cooperation prevailed, but the local communities remained humiliated and under-privileged. The result of this attitude was that the local Christians neither linked their fate with that of the Frankish regime, nor fought its wars, and some of them openly preferred Moslem rule. During the period changes also took place in the Frankish attitude to the Moslems; after a period of extreme fanaticism the Frankish rulers began to treat the Moslems decently, without discrimination between them and the other conquered groups. This tolerance expressed itself not only in the legal status and material rights accorded to them, but also extended to the religious sphere. The Franks permitted the Moslems to visit as pilgrims and to pray unmolested at their sacred shrines in Jerusalem, which in the meantime had been converted into churches.

Despite the fact that Jerusalem was a city of many nations and religions, no extra-territorial quarters were created there as in Acre. The only quarter which enjoyed judicial autonomy was that of the Patriarch, whose limits coincided with those of the present Christian quarter. This was the last remaining relic of the Church's demand, made at the time of the conquest, that the whole city be placed under the authority of the Patriarch.

Jerusalem's status as the capital and centre of the royal domain created certain differences between its administration and that existing in other towns. Here met the High Court which was at once the court of the domain, of the nobles resident in Jerusalem and of the whole realm. The burgesses' court was responsible for the city administration, but some of the municipal functions were discharged by the central authority of the realm.

The clear distinction between the status of the nobles resident in the city and that of the burgesses was to some extent obscured in Jerusalem, and the Franks of both classes made common cause in certain legal proceedings. In grants of property within the city the signatures of nobles and burgesses appear together. under the term of "men of Jerusalem" (*"de Viris Hierosolimitanis"*). The Jerusalem burgesses held special rights, as, for example, the right to act as host at the royal coronation banquet held in the ceremonial hall of the Order of Templars. As in every Frankish city, the viscount was the president of the court of burgesses and responsible for the local administration and for the collection of taxes and rents.

prosperity Frankish rule brought the city growth, prosperity and relative tranquility. The travellers who visited it in the 1170's emphasize the beauty of its buildings, the cleanliness of its streets, its thriving population and the multitudes of pilgrims from all parts of the world who visited it. The number of inhabitants in these years is estimated at thirty thousand. As a result of this relative quiet, the city's rulers saw no need to keep its walls in good repair. In 1177 part of the city wall collapsed from age, and only in the face of Saladin's invasion was it decided to allot an annual sum for essential repairs. It was in fact nine years later that Saladin stood before the walls of the Holy City.

Franks reject *offer of safe-* *conduct* Jerusalem's turn to be captured came after all the towns in the country, except Tyre, had been taken. The day Ascalon fell (4th September, 1187), a delegation of the inhabitants of Jerusalem came to Saladin's camp to ask for peace terms for the Holy City. A full eclipse of the sun occurred on the same day, an ill omen. Saladin proposed surprising terms: the Franks could remain masters of the city and might fortify it. An area of land of a radius of five leagues around it was also to remain in their hands, and the sultan would supply them with food and money. This settlement was to remain in force until the following Pentecost, and if by that time it became clear that the Frankish armies could come to Jerusalem's aid, the city would be theirs, but should it turn out that there was no prospect of saving it, they would surrender peacefully and depart for Christian lands.

The citizens of Jerusalem refused to accept this generous offer. "Under God's will they would never give up the city in which the Saviour died for them." The delegation returned to Jerusalem and the Sultan swore to take it with the sword. The citizens had nothing to rely on but a divine miracle, as the city was without knights or men-at-arms to defend it: all had perished by the sword or been taken prisoner at Hattin.

organization of *defence* The organization of the defence fell upon Balian of Ibelin, Lord of Nablus, who had reached the city from Tyre, having escaped thither from Hattin; he had asked the sultan's permission to come to Jerusalem to fetch his wife, Maria Comnena, and their children, who had fled there from their estates at Nablus. The sultan consented to Balian's request, but on condition that he remain in Jerusalem no more than a night, and swear never to bear arms against him again. But when he reached Jerusalem all the leaders, led by the Patriarch Heraclius, implored him to remain as its commander; when Balian refused on account of

42

his oath, the Patriarch absolved him from it with the words: "Know that it will be a greater sin if you keep your oath, than if you break it; it will be a great shame upon you and your heirs if you desert the city in the hour of its peril, and you will be unable to recover your honour no matter whither you turn." Balian, however, not content with the Patriarch's absolution, wrote a letter to the sultan in which he begged him to release him from his oath, and the sultan complied. When his wife and children had left the city, and gone to Tyre, Balian devoted himself to organizing its defence. He required of its leaders not only recognition as military commander but also a feudal oath of loyalty which made him Lord of Jerusalem.

The new commander, finding in Jerusalem only two knights, knighted all the sons of nobles over the age of sixteen and also promoted to the knightly class thirty burgesses. He sent units to the surrounding areas daily, to bring food and *preparations* supplies. By his order the gold and silver encrustations were stripped from the *for siege* Church of the Holy Sepulchre, and the royal mint made from them coins with which to pay the men-at-arms. In the middle of September the Moslem advance guard reached the outskirts of Jerusalem. The Frankish villages and townships were evacuated and their inhabitants fled to the city. The population of Jerusalem now numbered over 60,000, double the number in peacetime. The churches and monasteries around the city were captured and destroyed, and on the 20th of September the ordeal began.

Saladin, arriving from the west, placed his camp opposite the city's western

Jerusalem, Tomb of
the Virgin (St. Mary
Jehosaphat)

wall, between Tancred's (Goliath) Tower and the Tower of David. The besieged
made a sortie, which was easily repulsed, but the Moslems were surprised by the
courage of the Frankish inhabitants. After five days' hard fighting on the west
of the city Saladin decided to transfer his main effort to the north-east corner of
the wall between St. Stephen's Gate (the modern Damascus Gate) and the Valley
of Kidron. This move of the Moslems caused immense joy in the town, as the
Christians interpreted it as an intention to raise the siege, but they soon realized
their mistake. The Moslems set up siege engines which began to bombard the
city with "Greek Fire" and arrows. Ten thousand horsemen concentrated opposite St. Stephen's Gate to prevent sorties by the garrison. Sappers approached
the wall under cover of the rain of arrows and began to dig a sap beneath the

sapping barbican; within two days this attained a length of 30 metres, and when it was
completed its shorings were set alight and its collapse created a breach in the
barbican wall. The breach was precisely on the spot of the Crusader penetration
of 1099, and the great Cross which had been set up to mark it fell also. The attempts of the besieged to interrupt the work of the sappers failed, and the troops

barbican breached who manned the main wall fled from their positions, refusing to return even
when a reward of a hundred bezants had been promised to each of them.

Facing this crisis, the commanders met in council and after prolonged debate
decided to negotiate for the surrender of the city. While all this was going on the

negotiations for clergy passed in procession through the streets intoning psalms. Balian, going
capitulation out from the walls, opened conversations with Saladin, in the course of which
the fighting continued and the Moslems were able to gain a hold upon the main
wall. Seeing their standards upon the wall, the sultan broke off the negotiations
saying: "Why are you offering to surrender the city when it is already in our
hands?" At that moment the Christians delivered a counter attack and drove
the Moslems from the section of the wall which they had captured. Saladin,
abashed, stopped the negotiations and requested Balian to return the following
day.

For the city that was a night of prayer and lamentation. The women brought

a night of prayer tubs of water to the Church of the Holy Sepulchre, and stripping their daughters,
put them in the water and cut off their hair. Priests and monks made the circuit
of the walls bearing the *Corpus Domini* and the Syrian "true cross," which had
been kept in the city after the "true cross" of the Latins had fallen into enemy
hands at the battle of Hattin. In the morning Balian presented himself before
Saladin, who reminded him that he had sworn to take the city by force and to
avenge the massacre of 1099. Balian replied that, if acceptable terms of surrender
were not granted, the Franks would fight to the last drop of blood and would
themselves blot out the city and its inhabitants.

Balian's speech "O Sultan, know that we soldiers in this city are in the midst of God knows how many
people, who are slackening the fight in the hope of thy grace, believing that thou wilt
grant it them as thou hast granted it to the other cities—for they abhor death and desire
life. But for ourselves, when we see that death must needs be, by God we will slaughter
our sons and our women, we will burn our wealth and our possessions, and leave you

neither sequin nor stiver to loot, nor a man or a woman to enslave; and when we have finished that, we will demolish the Rock and the Mosque al-Aqsa, and the other holy places, we will slay the Moslem slaves who are in our hands—there are 5000 such,—and slaughter every beast and mount we have; and then we will sally out in a body to you, and will fight you for our lives: not a man of us will fall before he has slain his likes; thus shall we die gloriously or conquer like gentlemen."[10]

The Moslems knew that Balian's threat was no empty one, so the sultan stated that voluntary capitulation did not run counter to his oath. After prolonged bargaining the terms were settled: the ransoms to be paid by the city's inhabitants were fixed: a man was to pay ten dinars, a woman five and a child one. Seven thousand poor people were to be freed in return for a ransom of thirty thousand bezants. The Christians were granted forty days to deliver the ransom money and to liquidate their affairs in the city. Anyone found there after the appointed day was to be enslaved. The Christians were permitted to take from the city all the moveable property that they could carry. All the gates, except the Jaffa Gate, were closed and the keys were handed over to Saladin on the 2nd of October; he stationed officers in the streets to keep order. The Moslems were permitted to enter the town to purchase the property of Christians who needed ready money to pay their ransoms. Balian obtained from the Hospitallers the sum required to free the seven thousand poor and, having paid it over to Saladin, imposed upon two men in each street the preparation of the lists of the lucky ones who were to be set free. People of means paid their ransom at the Jaffa Gate or deposited it on trust with Moslem officers stationed in the city. They were given receipts on payment, and presentation of these was a certificate of departure.

terms of capitulation

Despite the explicit instruction that the sums collected were to be transferred to the royal chest, some officers of lesser rank put the ransoms in their pockets. When it emerged that thousands of Christians still remained in the city, Saladin freed many of them without ransom. It is also related that he provided food for the widows and orphans of the battle of Hattin and gave them valuable presents. The Patriarch Heraclius left the town taking with him his treasures, not deeming it fit to apportion part of them for the redemption of prisoners. The Moslem emirs proposed to the sultan to confiscate the Patriarch's money, but he refused, saying he did not wish to break his pledge that the Christians should take their property with them. Many of the wealthy also displayed astounding selfishness, refusing to aid the liberation of the indigent. When the time allowed for their departure expired, fifteen thousand remained in the city; they were assembled and taken in convoys to the slave-markets of Damascus. The ransomed were gathered in three groups: the Templars were placed in charge of the first, the Hospitallers of the second and Balian of the third. The sultan allotted fifty Moslem officers to each group to guard it until it reached Christian territory. A Christian chronicler relates that the Moslem officers could not endure the sufferings of the refugees and ordered their squires to dismount and to set aged Christians upon their steeds. Some of them carried Christian children in their arms.

Franks evacuate Jerusalem

The Frankish refugees from Jerusalem dispersed in all directions; some reached Alexandria and thence were taken to Europe. Others sought refuge in Tripoli, but its lord, Raymond, refused to allow them into the city, and they were forced to wander on to Antioch and to Armenia.

Moslems purify
the Temple MountThere remained in Jerusalem several thousand Syrian and Armenian Christians who were permitted to return to their churches and to pray there as they wished. The Church of the Holy Sepulchre was unscathed and only remained closed for three days. Liberated Moslem prisoners settled in the empty Frankish houses. The sultan began energetically to remove all symbols of the Christian religion and to purify the Moslem sacred places. The golden cross was taken down from the Dome of the Rock, dragged through the city streets and melted down in the Tower of David. The altar which had been set up on the rock was removed and the wall which the Templars had built in front of the praying-niche in the al-Aqsa Mosque was dismantled. The Temple Mount was purified with rose water and on the Friday following the conquest and purification of the city, the first public prayer was held in the Ḥaram, after 88 years of Christian rule. Multitudes gathered on the Temple Mount and not a single vacant space remained in all the huge area. In the presence of the sultan the Qadi of Aleppo, Muḥi a-Din, preached the sermon from the beautiful pulpit (minbar) which had been prepared in 1168 by Nur a-Din to be set up at al-Aqsa. This sermon opened with the following sentences:

"O men! Rejoice at good tidings! God is well pleased with what you have done and this is the summit of men's desires; he hath holpen you to bring back the strayed camel from misguided hands and to restore it to the fold of Islam, after the infidels had mishandled it for nearly a hundred years."[11]

Jews return to
JerusalemMoslem inhabitants began to return to the city and the Jewish community was also reconstituted after Saladin had rescinded the Christian prohibition of Jewish residence. The first members of the renewed congregation came from Ascalon, which had been destroyed, and after them came Jews from north Africa; in 1209–11 three hundred Jews came to the city from France and England.

Third CrusadeWhen the news of the taking of Jerusalem reached Constantinople the Byzantine emperor requested Saladin to restore the Church of the Holy Sepulchre to to Greek Orthodox Christians. The sultan conceded the request, but for four years no Frank entered the Holy City. Richard Coeur de Lion beheld its towers in the winter of 1191 as he stood on the height of the Hill of Nabi Samwil, but did not reach it. The English king refused to gaze upon the city he could not take, and covered his eyes with his shield.

In September 1192 the knights of the Third Crusade reached Jerusalem not as conquerors but as pilgrims. After the signing of the peace treaty between Richard and Saladin, the Franks were permitted to pray at the Church of the Holy Sepulchre. The knights went up to Jerusalem unarmed and were accorded a friendly reception by the Moslems. Hubert Walter, Bishop of Salisbury,

46

was received in audience by Saladin and obtained his agreement that two Latin priests be installed in the Church of the Holy Sepulchre.

The city, surviving unscathed the war of 1187, was destroyed by Saladin's nephew in 1219. Al-Mu'azzam demolished it during the invasion of Egypt by the Fifth Crusade, fearing lest it be restored to the Franks if they were victorious. The order for its demolition was not carried out at first as the Moslem commanders did not trust its authenticity. Only on the arrival of the sultan did the work of destruction begin, to be completed at the end of July. The city walls, towers and buildings were pulled down, except for the Tower of David, and also some of the houses in the city. Only the Temple Mount, with its mosques, and the Church of the Holy Sepulchre, remained unscathed. The Moslem and Jewish population evacuated the city, leaving behind them a few thousand local Christians.

al-Mu'azzam destroys Jerusalem

Ten years after this destruction, in 1229, the city returned to the Franks under the peace treaty between Emperor Frederick II Hohenstaufen and the Sultan al-Kamil—a diplomatic success achieved without bloodshed.

Under the "Jaffa Agreement" the Christians received the city, with the exception of the Temple Mount, together with Bethlehem, and a narrow corridor from Ramla to Jerusalem which included the two main roads. Thus the excommunicated emperor obtained the Holy City forty years after it had been lost. Moslem public opinion reacted with rage and mourning. The Christians, of course, rejoiced but, as the agreement was the work of the excommunicated emperor, the ecclesiastical leadership and the military orders tended to underrate the achievement and to represent its weaker aspects. The restoration of Jerusalem without a hinterland, they argued, would prevent the Franks from retaining a real hold on the city.

city ceded to Frederick II Hohenstaufen

The Sultan al-Kamil, desiring to justify his agreement to cede the city, said: "I have given to the Franks no more than ruined churches and demolished houses. The Ḥaram remains in Moslem hands and the Moslem rite will be celebrated there as always. The city's surroundings and countryside will also remain in Moslem hands." The near future was to prove that the achievement of the Franks was more spectacular than real.

At the beginning of March 1229 the emperor announced his intention of going up to Jerusalem. The sultan ordered the Egyptian garrison to evacuate the city, and the civil authority was also removed and transferred to al-Bira. The few Moslem inhabitants who remained after the destruction by Mu'azzam assembled in the Temple Mount area.

On the 17th of March the emperor entered Jerusalem. At the Jaffa Gate the city's keys were handed over to him and he took up his abode at the "Hospital" opposite the Church of the Holy Sepulchre. Great tension reigned in the city; the Christians were angry because the Moslems continued their rites on the Temple Mount and the local Christians who remained were afraid that the restored Frankish authority would expel them from their churches. Due to the interdict in force against the emperor, the Franks were forbidden all contact

Frederick in Jerusalem

and intercourse with him and only his troops and the members of the Teutonic Order ignored the ban.

On Sunday, the 18th of March, the emperor went to the Church of the Holy Sepulchre for an imperial crown-wearing. After this ceremony he returned to the Hospital and began consultations on the organization of the city's defence and the rehabilitation of its fortifications. The decision was taken to fortify the Tower of David and the area of St. Stephen's (Damascus) Gate. The Teutonic Order fortified itself in the old royal palace to the south of the Tower of David. Frederick II also found time to visit the Dome of the Rock and the Mosque of al-Aqsa, accompanied on his tour by the Moslem Qadi.

On the following day the Archbishop of Caesarea appeared, and imposed an interdict upon Jerusalem. Henceforth prayer in the churches was forbidden and all sacred rites ceased in the Holy City. The masters of the Orders of the Hospitallers and Templars hesitated to cooperate in the work of fortification and the embittered emperor had to announce his immediate departure from the city, before anything could be done to fortify it. A small number of pilgrims and a few Franks who were left in Jerusalem hastened to seize the empty houses. A few months after the emperor Frederick's departure the little Frankish settlement was in danger of annihilation; peasants from Hebron and Nablus broke into the city, still unwalled; the Franks fled to the Tower of David, and besought aid from Acre. Help was at once sent and the Moslem mob was expelled.

no renewal of Frankish population
The renewal of Frankish sovereignty over Jerusalem did not bring about its revival. No one of the institutions of the central government was transferred to Jerusalem; the Patriarch, the heads of the great monasteries of Jerusalem and of the military orders remained at Acre. No efforts at colonization worthy of the name were made, and even the city walls remained in disrepair except at two or three points. The neglect of the Holy City witnesses, perhaps better than anything else, to the political and religious bankruptcy of the Second Kingdom, which continued to bear the name of Jerusalem.

attack of 1239
The city dragged out a wretched existence, while a few pilgrims visited its holy places. In November 1239 it was attacked by al-Nasir Daud, ruler of Karak; the inhabitants fled to the Tower of David and the open city was left to be plundered. The Moslems besieged the citadel, and the Franks surrendered after twenty-seven days. The Moslems razed the fortifications of the Tower of David to their foundations, but in 1241 the city returned to Frankish hands under the treaty of Richard of Cornwall. In 1243 Christian control was extended to the area of the Temple Mount, and the Templars, as initiators of the new accord with Damascus, returned to their abode in the Mosque of al-Aqsa. But these political achievements were no better consolidated than those of the emperor Frederick. The city was not fortified and the number of its inhabitants did not exceed five thousand.

end of Frankish Jerusalem
In 1244 came the end of Frankish Jerusalem. Troops of Ḥwarizmians attacked the city and destroyed the Armenian Church of St. James. A counter-attacking Frankish force was repulsed and the Franks evacuated Jerusalem on the media-

tion of the ruler of Karak. The Hwarizmians massacred all who dared to remain; the clergy who refused to leave the Church of the Holy Sepulchre were butchered, the Church was looted and damaged, the tombs of the Kings of Jerusalem were opened and their bones scattered. The churches near the city were also destroyed, including the Church of the Last Supper on Mt. Zion and that of the Tomb of Mary in the Kidron Valley.

The city became a ruin and only recovered much later, with the establishment of Mamluk rule.

THE FRANKISH CITY

Crusader Jerusalem is so well-known to us that it can be visualized and mapped in its entirety; the churches, streets, markets and public buildings can be identified and named. The writings of pilgrims and archaeological and topographical researches have left hardly a corner unaccounted for and we can do no more here than repeat the descriptions so often given.

The area of the city coincided with the Old City of today, which has preserved not only the lines of the Crusader walls, but also the course of the streets and the outlines of the buildings. Those who rebuilt the city from its ruins, again and again from the 12th century onwards, found it easier to erect the buildings and city walls on their old foundations. The Turkish engineers utilized the remains of the Crusader ramparts when they came to build the 16th century walls that adorn the city still. Most of the churches of the Franks and of the local Christian communities are preserved to this day; others have been converted into mosques. Owing to the quantity of ancient debris that covers the area of the city, the result of thousands of years of settlement, the builders of the houses have preferred to erect them on the ancient foundations, since not to do so would have necessitated digging deeply into layers of residual rubble. As a result the street-lines have been preserved.

The Frankish city is the continuation of the Moslem town, which coincided in area and general plan with the Roman city of *Aelia Capitolina*. This urban continuity of a Crusader city occurred not only in the case of Jerusalem, but also in other places such as Ascalon and Acre.

WALLS AND GATES

The Fatimid walls were captured by the Crusaders almost undamaged and were used throughout the 12th century to defend the city. The historical sources record that they were restored and strengthened twice, firstly in 1116 and again in 1177. The line of the Crusader city wall diverges from the present one only in a few sectors.

Moslem walls undamaged

49

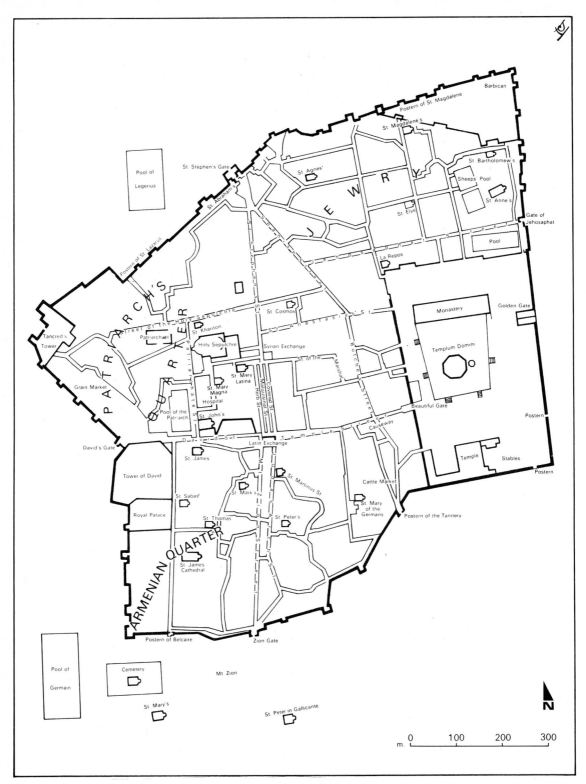

Jerusalem (Town Plan)

"Now", says Theodorich "the longest part of the city reaches from north to south, and the width of it is from west to east, and it is most strongly fortified by walls and bastions on the top of the mountains above the aforesaid valleys [Josephat]. There is also a barrier, or fosse, placed outside the wall, and furnished with battlements and loopholes, which they call the Barbican. The city has seven gates whereof they firmly lock six every night until after sunrise; the seventh [Golden Gate] is closed by a wall and is only opened on Palm Sunday and on the day of the Exaltation of the Cross. Now, the city, being of an oblong form, has five angles, one of which is transverse."[12]

The north rampart was built several metres north of the present line and its *city walls* north-western tower (Tancred's Tower or the Tower of Goliath) was built several metres further in than the present structure. At the north-east corner the present line coincides with the barbican which was breached in the sieges of 1099 and 1187, but the main rampart was nearly 100 metres farther in than the present course. On the eastern and western sides the Turkish line follows that of the Crusader walls. On the southern side, the line of the Crusader wall coincides with the present wall until a point west of the Dung Gate. From there it goes in a north-easterly direction to the south-western corner of the Temple Mount wall. Thus, the position of the postern of the Tannery (see below) is north of the present Dung Gate, and the area south of the al-Aqsa Mosque was outside the walled city. A rock-cut moat surrounded the ramparts on the north-west and south-west . Owing to the natural defences afforded by the slopes of the Kidron Valley, and the steep scarps of Mt. Zion and the City of David, there was no need to dig a moat on the east and south-east sides.

After the capture of the city in 1187 the walls were strengthened by Saladin, *Saladin's repairs* who is said to have utilized stones taken from Crusader monasteries outside the wall (St. Lazarus and St. Stephen's) to build the ramparts. He also brought fifty stonemasons from Mosul for this purpose. The northern moat was deepened and as recently as the late 19th century traces of rock-cutting, and Arab inscriptions such as "Allah", were visible in the counterscarp near the Damascus Gate. The walls were dismantled by al-Mu'azzam in 1219. We do not know the degree of destruction, but it may be supposed from our knowledge of similar acts of destruction in other places (such as Mt. Tabor) that it was not total, but confined rather to the burning of gates, the pulling down of towers and the breaching of curtain walls. The emperor Frederick II Hohenstaufen planned an extensive work of fortification, but in view of the attitude of the military orders and the interdict which had been laid upon the city, he abandoned the project before the work had been put in hand. It is related that between 1229–30 the *strengthening of* Tower of David was strengthened and the towers of St. Stephen's (Damascus) *gates 1229–30* Gate and the Zion Gate were restored. The remains of the Crusader gate, found a few metres north of the Damascus Gate, were of this period. Excavations carried out here in 1965 disclosed a fortification with towers, built on the principle of the bent entrance; this projects 20 metres north of the present gate and its remains are situated west of the footbridge leading to the modern gate. A church was found attached to the fortifications, identified as St. Abraham.

51

Some scholars believe that Mt. Zion was fortified at the end of the 12th century by an exterior wall surrounding the Church of the Last Supper. A Moslem source states that this was the work of Saladin. Frankish maps of the early 14th century show the hill as walled, and archaeological excavations have disclosed a wall-line which is tentatively ascribed to the period, but the ascription is controversial. The citadel of the Crusader city, "David's Tower", was to the south of the Gate of David (the Jaffa Gate).

gates The city had four main gates, one on each of the four sides of the square enceinte. On the west was David's Gate, today the Jaffa Gate; on the east, the Golden Gate (the Gate of Mercy); on the north, St. Stephen's Gate, (the Damascus Gate); and on the south the Zion Gate, situated east of the present gate. These gates are approached from within by streets at right-angles crossing at the centre of the city. The northern section of the street leading from north to south (from St. Stephen's Gate to the Zion Gate), the main street of the Roman city (the *cardo*), was known in the Crusader epoch as St. Stephen's Street, and its southern stretch as Mt. Zion Street. The western part of the east–west street, or Roman *Decumanus,* was known as David Street and its eastern part as Temple Street. These were the principal thoroughfares of the city.

In addition to the main gates the Crusader city had a number of posterns: the Postern of St. Lazarus was situated near the western corner of the north wall, and not far from the eastern corner was the Postern of St. Mary Magdalene. The Jehosaphat Gate was situated in the northern sector of the east wall (today St. Stephen's Gate). The Postern of the Tannery or Dung Gate was near the eastern corner of the south wall, and at the western end of the same wall was another postern, referred to in several sources as the Beaucaire Gate.

These posterns gave access to streets whose names are detailed in the accompanying map. Apart from the principal streets, which pursued a more or less direct course, the Crusader city was criss-crossed by a tangle of winding alleys.

THE CITADEL—"DAVID'S TOWER"

earlier history At the end of the Byzantine period only one tower survived of the three towers built by Herod at the north-west corner of the city-wall in the Second Temple epoch—the Tower of Phasael. This tower, the most easterly of Herod's three (Phasael, Hippicus and Mariamne), was embodied in the Roman-Byzantine wall, which continued from it north-westward on the present line to the Goliath Tower. It began to be known as "David's Tower" as early as the Byzantine period. Following the Arab conquest a *miḥrab* or prayer niche was placed on the top of the huge solid plinth of the Herodian tower; this perpetuated the allusion as Miḥrab Daud. David's Tower was regarded as the citadel of Jerusalem before the capture of the city by the Crusaders. It was surrounded by a deep moat on all sides and its dressed Herodian blocks were tied together with lead. It had five iron doors, and two-hundred steps leading to the top. Within, grain was stored;

52

it also contained large water-cisterns. After the Crusaders had breached the walls, the Egyptian commandant of the city shut himself into the Tower of David with the remnants of the garrison. Raymond of St. Gilles, who had broken into the city from the south, laid siege to the Tower, and the Egyptian commandant, after negotiations, surrendered and left for Ascalon with his remaining forces. The Provençal count took up his quarters in the Tower of David, refusing to hand it over to Godfrey de Bouillon, though the latter had been made ruler of the city and demanded the cession of the Citadel, because his control of the city would be incomplete unless it were in his hands. Duke Raymond persisted in his refusal, but when the entire Crusader leadership and even a number of his own companions united against him, he ceded the Tower to the Bishop of Albara. The Bishop, who had received it in trust until its fate should be decided, gave it without hesitation to Godfrey. In April 1100 Godfrey promised to hand it over to the Patriarch Diambert with the entire city, should he die without issue. Godfrey died in July and the Tower was seized by Granier de Grey, one of the ruler's close associates, who wished to set on the throne of the Kingdom of Jerusalem Baldwin of Edessa. When Baldwin reached Jerusalem, the Tower was delivered into his hands, and in the years 1101–1104 it was the king's abode, until he left it to dwell in a wing of the Mosque of al-Aqsa. In 1118 the kings took up their quarters in a new palace built to the south of the Tower of David. *quarrels amongst Crusader leaders*

King Baldwin

In 1152 the Queen Mother Melisende fortified herself in the Tower when her son Baldwin III was advancing to take Jerusalem from her. He besieged the Citadel, but despite all efforts and the use of siege engines of all types, was unable to take it by storm. The Queen only left the Tower after negotiations.

During Saladin's invasion of the coastal plain in 1177, the citizens of Jerusalem took refuge in the Citadel in fear of the enemy. After the capture of the city in 1187 the Citadel was strengthened by Saladin, but part of its walls was destroyed by al-Mu'azzam. The emperor Frederick II Hohenstaufen refortified the dismantled structure and during the years 1229–39 it was the only stronghold of the Frankish town. David's Tower was again taken in 1239 by al-Nasir Daud after a six-day siege. The ruler of Karak destroyed it completely and it remained in ruins until the beginning of the 14th century. *1177*

1229
1239

It emerges from the accounts of chroniclers and travellers that at the time of the Frankish conquest the fortress consisted of David's Tower in the restricted sense of the term, that is, the huge Herodian tower. Only in the 1160's was the fortress enlarged by the building of walls and numerous towers. Theodorich (1172) relates that abutting upon the tower was a "solar chamber and palace which adjoins it, and it is strongly fortified with ditches and barbicans."[13] Proof that the fortress was extended is to be found in the fact that in 1177 many citizens took refuge within its enclosure for fear of Saladin. *development from tower to citadel*

The plan of the enlarged Citadel almost coincided with the present-day Mamluk and Turkish Citadel. Only on the south side was the Crusader structure larger and included the area of the "Qishla" (Prison).

THE CITY'S QUARTERS

The city's two main streets divided it into four quarters; the north-westerly was known as the Patriarch's Quarter and coincided with the area of the present-day "Christian Quarter"; it was the only one in the city enjoying judicial autonomy.

Christian quarter   This quarter, in whose centre lay the Church of the Holy Sepulchre, became the centre of the Christian inhabitants in the middle of the 11th century, when it had been abandoned by its Moslem inhabitants. It was defended from the early 11th century by walls on all sides. These were strengthened by the Byzantine emperor in 1063. Within the quarter were, in addition to the Church of the Holy Sepulchre and its priory, the Patriarch's palace, the "Hospital", hostels, churches and monasteries, the grain market, baths, bakeries, piggeries, markets and workshops. The main streets of the quarter were the Street of the Church of the Holy Sepulchre, which branched from St. Stephen's Street to reach the west wall, and the Street of the Patriarch, the present Christian Street. At the southern end of the quarter was the Patriarch's Pool (Ḥammam al-Batraq), one of the city's sources of water.

Armenian quarter   South of David Street, which was the limit of the Patriarch's Quarter, was the Armenian Quarter. This quarter, whose population has not changed ethnically to this day, centred on the Cathedral Church of St. James. The Armenians did not occupy the whole square bounded by the city walls on the south and west and by David Street and Mt. Zion Street on the north and east, but only its southern part. The rest of the area was inhabited by Greeks and also by the Jewish dyers mentioned in Benjamin of Tudela's account. The king's palace lay to the south of the Tower of David, between the Street of the Armenians and the city-walls, in the area today partly occupied by the "Qishla" building (the prison and police-station), and partly by the Armenian Patriarch's garden, where the royal palace of Herod had previously been situated.

Jewish (Syrian)   The north-eastern part of the city had been occupied in the Moslem period
quarter   by the Jewish quarter; abandoned by its Jewish occupants in 1099, it remained deserted. When King Baldwin began to settle Syrian Christians in Jerusalem, in 1115, many of them moved into the quarter, which was still known as the Juiverie or Jewry. Subsequently it began to be called the Syrian Quarter. Its bounds were Jehosaphat Street (now the Via Dolorosa) on the south, and Spanish Street (now Tariq al-Wad) on the west. There were a number of churches in the quarter, some Latin and some of the local Christians (see p. 71).

south-eastern   The south-eastern quarter of the city was occupied before the Crusader conquest
quarter   by Moslems. After the conquest it remained empty and filled up slowly with Frankish settlers. This quarter, which coincided with the area of the present Jewish Quarter, contained a concentration of German-speaking inhabitants. It also contained several churches and in its southern part, near the Postern of the Tannery (the Dung Gate), was the city's cattle market.

The main streets of the city were vaulted and paved. "Almost all its streets are paved with great stones below and above many of them are covered with a stone vault pierced with many windows for the transmission of light".[14]

The houses were all built of stone and their plan was oriental i.e. a square surrounding an open courtyard. Says Theodorich: "The houses, which are lofty piles of carefully wrought stonework, are not finished with high pitched roofs after our fashion but have them level and a flat shape".[15]

THE MARKETS

There were a number of markets in the city, each given over to a particular trade or commodity, or to wares of a specific type. Some were wholesale markets and others bazaars. The markets numbered three: the cattle market, near the Tannery or Dung Gate; the grain market near the Tower of David, and the poultry market in David Street. The first two were in open squares, whereas the poultry market was in a vaulted building which today is used as a vegetable market. The produce sold in these markets was brought by traders from outside the town. The principal bazaar was at the centre of the city, north of the main street intersection. Here also, as early as the Roman and Byzantine periods, was the city's central market-place. The bazaar comprises three vaulted streets running from north to south, with groin-vaults resting on pointed arches. The vaulting is six metres high, the passage-way being three metres wide from wall to wall. The market is lit by square apertures in the uppermost parts of the vaults. The bazaars are not of equal length, the longest being the central one, the shortest the easterly. Internal passages connect the three streets with one another.

The shops are dark, narrow cave-like openings whose area does not exceed four square metres. While the Crusader vaults and shops are preserved, the shop-fronts and street paving have been altered beyond recognition. In the Crusader period stone verandahs were built in front of the shop-openings; these projected from the line of the wall about a metre and stood some sixty centimetres above the street level. The wares were spread upon the verandah, and here the traders received their customers; the verandahs were used also for dicing, in which game even nobles joined. Hugh de Puiset was murderously attacked by a Breton knight and severely wounded while playing dice on a table before a shop in 1132. The western market was known in the Frankish period as the Street of Herbs; the central market as the Street of Bad Cookery (Malquisinat); the eastern market as the Covered Street. In the Herb Market fresh foodstuffs were sold, such as fish, eggs, poultry and cheese, as well as condiments and fruit. Meat was boiled and roasted for pilgrims in the Street of Bad Cookery. The barbers plied their trade in its northern part, and eggs were sold in the Covered Street. The shopkeepers of the market were Franks and Syrians who lived side-by-side and comingled. The Latin traders nevertheless gathered in the Covered

wholesale markets

shops

triple bazaar

traders

55

Street, whereas the Syrians congregated in the street running at right-angles to the market, leading to the Church of the Holy Sepulchre.

The central market, or Street of Bad Cookery, was built by Queen Melisende in 1152, using corvée labour of Moslem inhabitants of al-Bira.[16] Several arches of the market vaulting preserve inscriptions reading: SCA ANNA—evidence that some of the shops belonged to the Monastery of St. Anne. Other shops preserve the letter T, which indicates that they belonged to the Order of Templars.

On the north side of the markets was the Syrian Exchange and on the southern the Latin Exchange. The former was situated in the Khan a-Zeit, a five-aisled edifice of Byzantine or Crusader origin, now partly buried under a heap of debris. The Latin Exchange occupied a vaulted building situated exactly at the central crossing or carfax, where David Street abruptly ceases and where Chain Street (the Frankish Temple Street) begins after a sharp bend. The building, today used as a café ("Café Bashura"), is part of the Tetrapylon of the Roman-Byzantine city.

The town's butchers and tanners foregathered near the cattle market, some in the lower part of the Street of the Temple. The city had twenty-seven bakeries scattered in various localities, twenty-four of them being in the hands of the Church of the Holy Sepulchre. Sources also record the existence of flour mills and "oil mills", that is, olive presses.

THE WATER SUPPLY

use of rain   Jerusalem's water supply has always been based on rainfall. Within the town itself was a ramified system of conduits and drainage channels which brought rainwater to the cisterns and pools. Theodorich says: "The people catch the rain water which falls upon them [the roofs] and store it up in cisterns for their own use—they use no other water because they have none."[16] On the evidence of the Arab historian Yaqut, there was no house without its cistern. This source records that the water's taste was not of the best, for most of it flowed in stone drains, and did not absorb much salt. Within the area of the Temple Mount

pools   there were huge cisterns which held hundreds of thousands of cubic metres. There were three large pools within the walls. That in the Patriarch's Quarter, Hammam al-Batraq, is mentioned also under the name of *Lacus Balneorum* (the "Pool of the Baths"). Near the Jehosaphat (present St. Stephen's) Gate was "the Old Pool", known to the Moslems as the Birket Bani Israil. North of it lay the twin pools known as the "Inner Pool" *(Piscina Interior)* or "Pool of the Sheep" *(Probatica Piscina).* The water in the city was sufficient to supply a considerable number of bath-houses.

Two pools were situated outside the city, one near St. Stephen's (Damascus) Gate, between the Lepers' Colony of St. Lazarus and the Church of St. Stephen, in the low ground west of the Street of the Prophets, known as the Pool of Legerius, and the other, now known as Birket a-Sultan, in the Valley of Hinnom

Jerusalem, Crusader facade in David Street

below Mt. Zion. This was built by the private initiative of a citizen called Germain and was known after him as the Pool of Germain.

The same Germain was responsible for other works for improving the water supply of the city, a chronicler relates:

works of Germain

"In the first year after the death of Baldwin the Leper (1184) it so happened that it rained neither in Jerusalem nor in the territory around, so that there was nothing to drink, or very little. Now in Jerusalem there was a citizen called Germain who was always very ready to do good for the love of God. Because of this dearth of water he had had made, in three places in Jerusalem, marble tanks.

"In each of the three tanks there were two chained bowls, and he had them always kept full of water. Everyone who wanted to, both men and women, went to drink there. When this Germain saw that there was hardly any water left in his cisterns, and that it was not raining, he was much distressed and feared that the good work he had begun would be wasted. Then he remembered how he had heard that men who dwelt there in former days said that close to the pool of Siloam there was an ancient well, the well of Jacob, which had been filled in and covered over, so that now one walked over it and it would be extremely difficult to find. So this prudent man went and prayed to Our Lord that He would give him the Grace to find this well and help him to continue the good he had begun, and that by His Grace the poor people might enjoy the blessing of water. When the next morning came, he arose and went to the monastery and prayed God to counsel him. After that he immediately went and got workmen and went to the place where he had been told the well had been. He had so much tapping and boring done that the well was found. When he had found it he had it emptied and walled anew, all at his expense."

The only source of running water was the spring of Gihon which flows through Hezekiah's tunnel to the pool of Siloam.

THE BUILDINGS OF THE MILITARY ORDERS
THE HOSPITALLERS

Hospital

The buildings of the Order of Hospitallers lay to the south of the Church of the Holy Sepulchre in the area which still bears the Persian name of Muristan, which means "hospital", and where the forum of the Roman city had once been. The area is a square, each side 130 metres long, covering 17 dunams. It is bounded on the east by the triple bazaar, on the south by David Street, on the west by Christian Street and on the north by the street leading to the Church of the Holy Sepulchre. Little remains today of this, one of the most important and splendid edifices of Crusader Jerusalem.

Three churches existed here in early times: St. Mary Latina, in the north-eastern corner, St. Mary Magdalene opposite the Parvis of the Church of the Holy Sepulchre, and St. John the Baptist's at the south-western corner. In the middle of the 11th century St. Mary Latina was restored by Italian merchants of the town of Amalfi and this monastery undertook the care of pilgrims. As the flow of Christian pilgrims to Jerusalem increased in the last decades of the 11th century, and the Hospice of St. Mary became too small to hold them, St. Mary Magdalene's Church, later known as St. Mary Majora, was built, and another hospice erected, consecrated to St. John the Baptist. Just before the advent of the Crusaders this hospice was administered by a knight called Gerard, a subordinate of the Abbot of St. Mary Latina. When the siege of Jerusalem began all the Christian inhabitants were expelled. Gerard managed to remain in the city to guard the property of the hospice, but he was caught and tortured by the Moslems as he was suspected of aiding the Crusaders' entry into the city.

Immediately after the Crusaders captured Jerusalem the hospice was released from the guardianship of St. Mary Latina and became an independent body. The Frankish kings granted it wide lands and much moveable property in the early years of their rule, their generosity arising doubtless from the increase of pilgrims and the expense of their lodging and hospitalization after the conquest.

In 1113 the institution became an independent international order, under the patronage of the Pope, and subject to his exclusive authority. The Order which at first had been engaged solely in the lodging and medical care of pilgrims, gradually became active also in the military sphere, and in the 1160's was one of the main supports of the military power of the Crusader kingdom.

The Hospitaller buildings served both as a monastery where the members of *conventual* the Order, who held various ranks and functions, resided, and as a hostel- *buildings* infirmary for the use of pilgrims. During the 12th century they were enlarged and improved, but the stages of their construction are unknown. The general plan of the buildings was L-shaped and they occupied the western and southern side of the Muristan square. The Hospital is on the west side of the square. John of Würzburg and Theodorich described this structure in the middle of the 12th century. Theodorich wrote:

"And here, on the south side of the church, stands the Church and Hospital of St. John the Baptist. As for this, no one can credibly tell another how beautiful its buildings are, how abundantly it is supplied with rooms and beds and other material for the use of poor and sick people,—Indeed, we passed through this palace, and were unable by any means *contemporary* to discover the number of sick people lying there; but we saw that the beds numbered *descriptions* more than one thousand."[17]

And thus John of Würzburg:

"Towards the south, is a beautiful church built in the honour of John the Baptist, annexed to which is a hospital where in various rooms is collected together an enormous multitude of sick people, both men and women, who are tended and restored to health daily at a very great expense. When I was there I learnt that the whole number of these sick people amounted to two thousand, of whom sometimes in the course of one day and night more than fifty are carried out dead, while many other fresh ones keep continually arriving. What more can I say? This same house supplies as many people outside it with victuals as it does those inside, in addition to the boundless charity which is daily bestowed upon poor people who beg their bread from door to door and do not lodge in the house, so that the whole sum total of its expenses can surely never be calculated even by the managers and stewards thereof."[18]

Jerusalem, St. Mary Latina, cloister

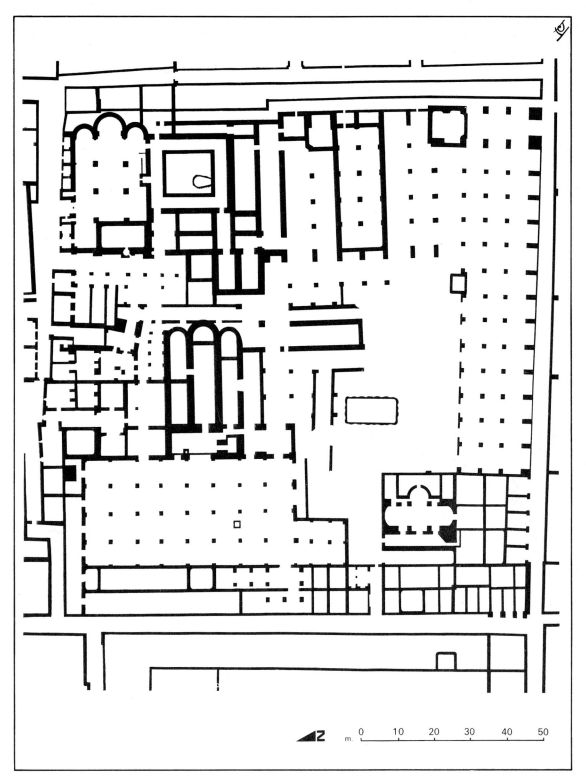

Hospital of St. John (Muristan), Plan from 19th century

Archaeological excavations, carried out in the area before the modern market was built over it, laid bare a huge hall 80 metres long and 40 metres wide, divided into four aisles by three lines of square piers. The height of the arches was 6 metres. The main entry to the hall was in the south-east side. Around the hall were numerous annexes. The Hospital accepted both men and women, being divided into wards, in each of which nine brethren of the Order served under the supervision of physicians, and the sick received treatment of a high standard. The statutes of the Order laid down with precision the details of their diet, their beds and bedclothes, and the duties incumbent upon the brothers and physicians during treatment (see p. 381).

Church of St. John

South of the hospital building was the church of the Order, dedicated to St. John the Baptist. This church, traditionally one of the oldest in the city, was apparently built in the 8th century. After being destroyed several times it was restored just before the Crusader conquest. In the 1100's it became the Conventual Church of the Order. Restored in 1847, it belongs today to the Greek Orthodox. It is of unusual design, with an apse on the east and others on the north and south. An anteroom or narthex leads into it from the west, and below the upper level was a crypt of identical shape to that of the upper church. This was previously at ground level, as can be perceived from the blocked door and window in its walls, but in the course of generations it has become covered with a layer of soil up to its ceiling.

East of the church along David Street were the lodgings of the brethren of the Order. According to Benjamin of Tudela's account, four hundred knights were housed here in the 1170's. When Jerusalem was seized in 1187, Saladin took up his quarters in the palace of the Hospitallers; ten brethren were permitted to remain for a year in order to look after the sick. When Jerusalem was handed over to the emperor Frederick II Hohenstaufen the Hospitallers returned and took possession of the buildings, and the emperor lodged there during his visits to the city. After the Moslem capture in 1244 they were neglected and subsequently demolished; travellers who visited them in the middle of the 14th century describe the size and splendour of the ruins.

St. Mary Majora

The Church of St. Mary Majora lay to the east of the hospital, in the middle of the square, and the street running from the front of the Church of the Holy Sepulchre separated it from the hospital. The street wound eastward and opened into the Street of the Patriarch (Christian Street). There are no remains of the church, but the Church of St. Mary Latina (or Minor—"the Lesser") was situated at the north-east corner, and a remnant of its north entrance-portal is to be found in the entrance to the Lutheran *Erloser Kirche,* built at the end of the 19th century. Attached to the modern church, the Crusader cloister of the Benedictine monks still survives.

THE TEUTONIC ORDER

The Teutonic Order of St. Mary maintained a hospital and a church in Jerusalem. According to one source (Jacques de Vitry) the hospital was established after the Crusader conquest by a German pilgrim, to serve his fellow countrymen. A documentary source,[19] however, described the building as "new" in 1143. It may actually have been established at the beginning of the 12th century, but it is more probable that the building dates from the 1140's. The German traveller John of Würzburg describes the place as follows:

> "As you descend this same street (temple) – – – – on the right-hand side there is a *German Street* kind of passage, through a long portico, in which street is a hospice and a church which has been newly built in honour of St. Mary, and which is called the house of the Germans, upon which hardly any men who speak any other language bestow any benefactions."[20]

German Street (Rue des Alemans), which appears also in other accounts of the city, is today the Street of a-Sharaf, located at the east of the Jewish quarter facing towards the square of the Western Wall. Remains of the church and the hospital exist to this day on the east side of the south end of the street.

Jerusalem, St. Mary of the Germans, east wall

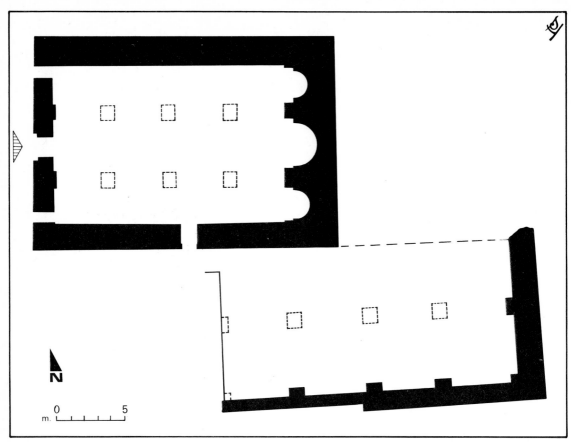

Jerusalem, St. Mary of the Germans (Plan)

St. Mary of the Germans The church had a nave and two aisles ending in three apses, and a straight eastern wall or flat *chevet*. Three apses remain, with traces of pointed windows. The nave and aisles have been partly destroyed and a dwelling built within them. The gate on the west, or street, side is the original gate of the church. South of the church structure was a groin-vaulted hall with two aisles and a line of square piers on the central axis. Some small bent columns remain *in situ,* with a foliage motif on their capitals, which closely resemble the columns of Abu Ghosh, the Church of the Holy Sepulchre, Ramla, Lydda and Gaza. Under the hall there are remains of Crusader vaults.

THE TEMPLARS

This order was founded in 1118 by a Burgundian knight called Hugh de Payns, with the object of protecting pilgrims to the holy places from the peril of attack by robbers. The Order grew from a group of eight knights and became a military organization of great wealth and power. King Baldwin II, who extended his patronage to the Order, gave it a wing of the royal palace, the Mosque of al-Aqsa. Subsequently the royal palace was situated near the Tower of David. The Mosque, called by the Franks the Temple of Solomon *(Templum Solomonis)*, gave its name to the Order. The Templars enlarged the structure westward and built a refectory hall of three aisles, of which only two remain today along the south wall of the Ḥaram. Additional Crusader structures exist on the east side of the Mosque. Beyond them to the eastward, in the south-eastern corner of the Ḥaram area, is the entrance to "Solomon's Stables", which were used as the stables of the Order; these are described on page 261.

al-Aqsa—Templar headquarters

According to historical sources the Templars divided the hall of the Mosque into small living rooms by means of screens, and part of the buildings to the east of the hall also served as dwellings. John of Würzburg relates that during his visit in the 1160's the building of the Church of the Order was not yet finished. It was erected on the east side of the hall of the Mosque and demolished by Saladin, but remains of its apses are preserved outside the wall of the east annex. The buildings on the west side of al-Aqsa are described by Theodorich:

"On another side of the palace, that is to say, on the western side, the Templars have erected a new building. I could give the measurements of the height, length and breadth of its cellars, refectories, staircases and roof, rising with a high pitch unlike the flat roofs of the country: but even if I did so, my hearers would hardly be able to believe me."[21]

contemporary descriptions

A Moslem historian says that "on the west side of al-Aqsa they built a residential building and also erected there all they required for the storage of grains, also privies." Benjamin of Tudela and other sources testify that three hundred

Jerusalem, bazaar, showing old shops' shutters

Jerusalem, al-Aqsa Mosque, central nave

Jerusalem, Church of the Holy Sepulchre

knights dwelt in "the Temple of Solomon". With the Moslem conquest of 1187 part of the Crusader building was pulled down and the Mosque again became a Moslem shrine. In 1243 the Templars returned to al-Aqsa, but were finally expelled from it in 1244.

THE ORDER OF ST. LAZARUS

This order was established early in the twelfth century to care for lepers, and named after Lazarus the Leper (Luke 16:19). Like the Orders of the Hospitallers and the Teutonic knights, the Lepers' Order, by the thirteenth century, fulfilled twin functions, the care of lepers and military duties. The infirmary, known as Maladrerie, surrounded by a lepers' colony, was on the north side of the city outside the walls, where is now the garden of the Latin Patriarch east of the New Gate. The building abutted upon the city wall and near it was a postern known as St. Lazarus' Postern, of which nothing remains.

THE CHURCHES

Jerusalem's churches have been the subject of so much exhaustive research and so many descriptions, that it would seem superfluous to add to them. We shall content ourselves, therefore, with a brief survey in order to round off the subject.

Holy Sepulchre   The Church of the Holy Sepulchre is of course the largest and most important of the churches of the Holy City. The Crusaders found the eastern part of the church (the *Martyrium*) destroyed, but the Rotunda containing the Tomb, destroyed by al-Ḥakim in 1009, had been restored in 1048. After the conquest the Crusaders began a large-scale reconstruction which continued for fifty years. The restored church was consecrated on the 15th of July, 1149, on the fiftieth anniversary of the conquest of Jerusalem, and its general lines have survived down to the present day. It enclosed under one roof all the last stations of the cross and the cave in which St. Helena found the "True Cross". The Frankish conquerors drove the local clergy from the church and Godfrey de Bouillon appointed secular canons. The Latin clergy permitted the local priests to return to the church in 1101, after the Holy Fire had failed to descend on Easter eve. The secular canons were replaced by regular Augustinian canons in 1114. The Patriarch of Jerusalem was its abbot and below him was a prior. A division existed between the income of the Chapter of the church and the Patriarch's revenues, the tithe of Jerusalem belonging to the church, which held extensive landed property in the vicinity of the city, in other parts of the kingdom and abroad. The canons began to work for the colonization and agricultural development of broad tracts in the northern mountains of Judea.

The tombs of the Crusader kings are to be found in the south wall of the choir of the church, below Calvary (Golgotha).

68

Jerusalem, blocked gate to the Holy Sepulchre

The church was not damaged during the Moslem capture of 1187, nor did its rites cease. In 1192 the Latin clergy were allowed to return to the church, which was plundered, but not destroyed, in 1244. The Crusader structure was gravely damaged in a fire in 1808, but at the present time the reconstruction and restoration which are being carried out there are almost completed.

Dome of the Rock   The Crusaders turned the Mosque of the Dome of the Rock into a church and monastery called *Templum Domini,* the Temple of the Lord. The cloister of an Augustinian monastery was erected to the north of the mosque. The changes introduced by the Franks included the paving of the rock with marble slabs and the raising of an altar above it. They enclosed it with a fine grill and encrusted its walls with mosaics portraying events from the Scriptures. They placed Latin inscriptions on its external walls and set up a number of altars and baptistries on the court of the Temple. All these additions were removed or covered up by the Moslems after their capture of Jerusalem in 1187. A great golden cross set on the top of the dome was taken down, dragged through the streets of the city and melted down in David's Tower.

St. Anne's   North of the area of the Temple Mount, near the Gate of St. Stephen, was the Convent of St. Anne. The convent is by the "Sheep Pool" or the Pool of Bethesda. Ever since the 4th century the dwelling of the parents of the Virgin Mary, Anne and Joachim, has been shown here. The church was handed over

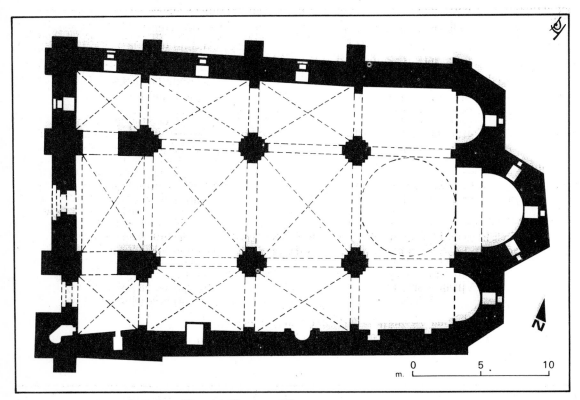

Jerusalem, Church of St. Anne (Plan)

Jerusalem, St. Thomas'

to Benedictine nuns after the Crusader conquest and the present church was built in 1140 with the aid of the royal family. Ivette, daughter of Baldwin II and sister of Queen Melisende, was a nun of St. Anne's until 1144. The church held considerable property in Jerusalem, part of the central market being in its possession. The structure comprised a nave and two aisles of three bays and a non-projecting transept with three apses to the east. The central apse projects from the line of the eastern wall or *chevet*. The building is not symmetrical and its builders obviously used the foundations of the Byzantine church which preceded it.

After the Moslem capture Saladin converted the church into a *Madrasa* or theological college. The building was subsequently used for stabling and storage and in 1856 was given to the French government, by whom it was restored.

A number of churches were situated in the Jewish or Syrian quarter, today the Moslem quarter. St. Mary Magdalene, which belonged to the Jacobites, was near the city wall, with a postern of the same name (St. Magdalene's Postern) not far from it. This church became a mosque, since demolished, and a new school (al-Milawiya) is built on its site. Not far from the Damascus Gate was the

minor churches

71

Church of St. Agnes, now the Mosque of Milawiya. The quarter also contained the Churches of St. Elias and St. Bartholomew. All these churches belonged to local Christian sects, since the quarter was inhabited, as already stated, by Syrian Christians who came to Jerusalem with the encouragement of King Baldwin I. Remains of the Church of St. Abraham, abutting the fortifications of the Crusader gate near the Damascus Gate, were found in 1965. The Armenian quarter contained the Church of St. James, the cathedral-church of the Armenians. It also held the Church of St. Thomas, today in ruins, and the Greek Church and Hospice of St. Sabas, whose remains are now a dwelling (Dar Disse), opposite the Qishla (former prison). At the north end of the quarter near David Street was the Church of James Intercisus, which became the Mosque of al-Yaqubiya. The Church of St. Mark, today belonging to the Syrian Orthodox, is situated on the boundary between the Armenian and the Jewish Quarters. In Jew's Street, called in Crusader times the Street of Judas' Arch, were the Church of St. Martin, today a carpenter's shop, St. Paul's Church, whose whereabouts is unknown, and also the Church of St. Petrus ad Vincula, located between the Synagogue of the Ḥurva and the Mosque to its south, perhaps on the site of the Ramban Synagogue.

The Christian quarter included numerous churches, among them St. Chariton (the mosque of al-Khanqa), the Church of St. George, St. Catherine and others.

Four large monasteries stood without the city walls: The Monastery of St. Mary on Mt. Zion; here the Crusaders rehabilitated a Byzantine basilica, and built a two-storeyed structure above it. The lower part of the building is today known as the "Tomb of David" and the upper as the Room of the Last Supper (*coenaculum*). *monasteries outside the city walls*

The Monastery of St. Mary of Jehosaphat was also a Byzantine building, restored by the Crusaders. The burial-place of Queen Melisende is situated in a niche on the left-hand side of the stairwell descending to Mary's tomb. This monastery was one of the wealthiest and most richly endowed with landed property in the country. Near it were the Church of Gethsemane and the Grotto of the Agony.

The Monastery of the Mount of Olives, the place of the Ascension, formerly a Byzantine monastery which was destroyed by the Persians in 614, was restored in 1152 and became an Augustinian monastery until its destruction by Saladin.

The Convent of Bethany, erected in 1144 by Queen Melisende for her sister Ivette, included a large and beautiful church, and in addition a tower was built to protect the nuns from Moslem attack.

Besides these monasteries in the vicinity of the city stood also the churches of St. Stephen the Protomartyr, north of St. Stephen's (Damascus) Gate; St. Peter Gallicante on Mt. Zion, and on the west side of the Valley of Hinnom not far from the suburb of Yemin Moshe, the church of St. George. Further off was the Georgian Monastery of St. Cross. The rock-cut tombs of the Kidron Valley (Absalom's pillar, the Tomb of Jehosaphat, the Tombs of Bene Ḥezir and the Daughter of Pharaoh) were the dwellings of hermits.

Jerusalem, St. Anne's, north-west corner

MARITIME TOWNS

The Persian traveller Nasir Husru gave an excellent description of the siting of the country's coastal towns:

"The city [of Acre] stands on an eminence, the ground sloping, but in part it is level; for all along this coast they only build towns where there is an elevation, being in terror of an encroachment of the waves of the sea."[22]

The seacoast of the Holy Land divides into three main regions: one, which runs from Jaffa southward, is mostly sandy and shallow, without bays or inlets; the second extends from Jaffa northward and is rocky, falling steeply to the sea, and with no broad sandy areas. Progressing northwards small bays become numerous, the largest being the bay of Acre. North of Rosh Haniqra the limestone mountains of northern Upper Galilee and the Lebanon fall steeply to the sea.

Geographical features have determined the siting of the ports. From Jaffa northward the towns were established on the sandstone *(kurkar)* hills of the seashore, as far as possible in the vicinity of small bays. Their elevation ensured tactical advantage against enemies attacking from the land and against invasion from the sea. From Jaffa southward we encounter the phenomenon of the building of twin towns, the main city being situated on the borderline between the fertile area and the dunes, while its port is built on the shore. Only Ascalon, in whose vicinity the dunes cease and fertile soil penetrates to the actual coast, is exceptional in this respect.

geographical features of the coast

Following a flourishing period which reached its prime in the Byzantine age, a considerable decline took place in the coastal towns of the country after the Arab conquest. The Moslems, lacking seapower and alien to marine craftsmanship, neglected the maritime towns, but the decline was of brief duration. At the end of the 7th century maritime activity was renewed and the population of the coastal cities increased; the Umayyad caliphs strengthened the walls and erected buildings, harbours and docks. After a troubled period, caused by the Byzantine invasion of 975, their prosperity continued to grow. In the mid-11th century there were eight harbour towns along the coast: Anthedon (the port of Gaza), Ascalon, Jaffa, Arsuf, Caesarea, Haifa, Acre and Tyre. Their livelihood was gained from coastal trade and, to a limited extent, also from international commerce. Of the eight, the most important was Tyre, and next to it came Jaffa and Acre.

maritime towns in Arab period

Just before the Crusader advent all the coastal towns were in the hands of the Egyptians, who had taken them from the Seljuks with the aid of their strong fleet. The first port to be captured by the Crusaders was Jaffa, which fell to them without fighting. During the first two years after the fall of Jerusalem friendly

friendly relations during first years

75

relations were maintained between the Crusaders and the coastal towns and armistice agreements were signed between the two sides. But the Crusaders soon felt the urgent need to seize the ports and open them to European shipping, in order to ensure reinforcements and to gain control of maritime trade. At first *capture of towns* they attempted to capture the towns by attacks from the land side, but they were unsuccessful because the Fatimid fleet, which controlled the sea approaches, rushed reinforcements and supplies to the besieged towns. Only after the Crusaders formed alliances with the Italian mercantile cities, and their strong fleets, were they able to mount a successful combined land and sea operation. Thereafter, the coast towns fell into Frankish hands one by one, and all were in their possession a generation later with the exception of Ascalon, which was taken in 1153. The Moslem inhabitants were expelled or massacred and the towns became Frankish centres of population.

Most of the Franks within the Kingdom of Jerusalem lived in the maritime *prosperity during* cities, the largest of which were Acre and Tyre. The main share of the interna-*Crusader period* tional maritime trade was centred on them, while the central and southern coast subsisted on coastal trade. The entire coast indeed now enjoyed a period of economic prosperity such as it had not known for centuries; two ancient coastal towns which had lain deserted for hundreds of years, 'Atlit and Dor (Tantura), were resettled. On the collapse of the Fatimid empire the Frankish fleets became the masters of the Mediterranean. Their power was based on the ships of the maritime communes, for the seapower of the Kingdom of Jerusalem itself was very limited. In 1182, the maximum strength of fighting craft belonging to the realm amounted to no more than thirty-three.

It was Frankish power at sea that saved the last remnants of the kingdom *decline of the* when it was conquered by Saladin's lightning campaign. Although the Moslem *coast* general was able to capture most of the coastal towns, Tyre's resistance to siege, made possible by uninterrupted support from the sea, left in Frankish hands a foothold from which to launch a campaign of reconquest. The lesson was clear to both sides and the Franks, aware of their weakness by land, no longer dared to move far from the coastline or to reoccupy the interior. The Moslems, who in spite of their efforts could not maintain a naval power capable of rivalling the Franks, decided to destroy the coast towns and to block up their harbours. Though they could not prevent a Frankish invasion, the destruction of the ports and fortifications could prevent the invaders gaining a hold in the country. It was Saladin who began the policy of "scorched earth," and his first victim was Ascalon. The Mamluks continued his work of destruction. The ancient prosperous coast towns were wiped from the face of the earth one after the other, their fortifications sundered, their houses burned and their harbours blocked. With the capture of Acre in 1291 the coast of the country was deserted, and remained so until the 19th century.

Despite the work of destruction, sufficient traces remain to enable us to recon-*size and plan* struct the plan of the Crusader coast towns and their ports. All were fortified and all possessed anchorages or harbours. The Crusaders utilized the Byzantine-Arab lines to lay out their walls and harbours, almost without modifications. The walls were set out in a semicircle, an oblong or a trapezoid with a lengthened east side. The cities had four main gates facing the cardinal points, the west gate facing the port. The largest was Acre, with an area of 600 dunams. Ascalon was next with a walled area of 500 dunams, though only part of it was built up. The towns along the central stretch of coast, Arsuf, Caesarea and 'Atlit, were smaller, at 90–120 dunams.

Traces of marine structures survive in various states of preservation at Ascalon, Arsuf, Caesarea and Acre. The only structure in Ascalon harbour, known as a bad and dangerous port, is the broad jetty which joins the south wall of the city below the Citadel. In Caesarea, a narrow mole remains, made of segments of ancient columns laid side by side over a distance of 100 metres at the north end of the ancient harbour. Arsuf's small harbour survives almost intact, with three sea walls. The southern and northern are 30 metres long, closed by a breakwater to seaward about 100 metres long: the area of the anchorage is thus three dunams; the harbour entrance is on the south-west. *marine structures*

The largest of the ports was Acre, whose protected anchorage covered 60 dunams. It was double, with an inner and outer basin, two breakwaters and several jetties. The length of the eastern breakwater, which ran south-west to north-east, was 325 metres, and of the western breakwater, which lay east-west, 240 metres. The harbour entrance was on the south. At right-angles to the western breakwater was a jetty 125 metres in length which divided the anchorage. West of it was the inner harbour or *Darsana*, and east of it the outer harbour or *Portus.* At the north end of the latter was another mole enclosing the dock area (the Arsenal). The plan of Acre port is almost identical with that of Tyre. *port of Acre*

The maritime activity of the Mediterranean ports was considerable, and in the months of the *passagium,* the months of travel falling between Easter and late autumn, the number of ships anchoring in the harbours could be counted in dozens. The ships were of various types, the commonest fighting ship being the galley. This was 30–40 metres long with a six metre beam. The largest merchantman, the "Buze-Nef", was 36 metres long and 14 metres beam, with a displacement of 600 tons. Her maximum complement was a thousand people. *maritime activity*

The navigator received direction to port by written instructions and charts. The entrances to the anchorages were defended by iron chains which were raised in the dark hours to prevent the entry of pirate craft. Ships dropped anchor in the roadstead or tied up to the jetties, and on the shore of the harbour were warehouses, a customs house and a market. Documents concerning customs dues have been preserved, and tell us much of the scale of commerce and what was exported and imported. Nor was maritime activity restricted to the Mediterranean; there is known to have been a lively traffic on the Dead Sea, which was crossed to and fro, from the region of 'Ein Gedi to Karak. In 1152 the Hospitallers obtained right of free passage on the Dead Sea and exemption from import and export dues. There was also a traffic of fishing craft and merchant ships on the Sea of Galilee and in the Gulf of Eilat.

ACRE

This picturesque townlet, situated on a rocky headland north of the bay which bears its name, is today no more than a shadow of the city as described by the writer of the *Itinerarium:*

"If a ten years war made Troy renowned, if the triumph of the Christians ennobled Antioch, then to Acre belongs eternal fame—the city for which the whole world contended."

reasons for being principal port

Acre in the Middle Ages was the principal port of the Palestinian coast. Two factors combined to endow it with this status: the first was the form of the country's coastline, straight and shallow, providing scant shelter from gales. The few inlets along it—Tyre, Caesarea, Arsuf, Jaffa and Ascalon—were all inconvenient for anchorage or disembarkation and dangerous in rough weather. The ancient artificial harbour of Caesarea, which Herod had built with immense effort, had become almost entirely blocked in mediaeval times and no longer provided safe moorings.

Acre harbour, protected on the north, west and east by natural, and on the south by man-made barriers, assured shelter from gales and comfortable anchorage in all weathers. Merchants, and above all pilgrims, reaching the coast of Palestine and desiring to make their way to Jerusalem, preferred to land at the port of Acre, rather than land at the open port of Jaffa, which was shallow, exposed to wind and full of reefs, and thus very dangerous as a harbour for their ships.

The second factor contributing to Acre's pre-eminence as a port was her position at the end of a major trade route leading from the interior of Asia to the Mediterranean shores. This route came from east of Damascus, the great crossroads and mercantile centre, and continued across the plateau of Bashan and Golan to the plains of Lower Galilee (Jezreel and Beit Netofa), reaching the seacoast at Acre. It was used by the commercial caravans which brought the precious wares of the east to Acre and loaded them on ships bound for Europe. Although Acre did not rank with Constantinople or Alexandria in the scope of her commerce, her trade was considerable. Added to these advantages was the great richness of her hinterland; the Plain of Acre was densely inhabited by a rural population which grew various crops including sugar cane, orchard fruits and vegetables, and also herded cattle; the city was a natural market for their agricultural produce.

Acre before Crusader arrival

The Persian traveller Nasir Ḥusru, who visited Acre in 1047, has left us an account of the city. According to his description its area was much larger than that of Acre today, and also larger than the Crusader city as tentatively restored (see p. 93). By Nasir's measurements it was 650 metres wide from north to south and 1,200 metres long.

Acre was destroyed by the terrible earthquake of 1067, but rebuilt and refortified in the 1070's. Immediately before the Crusaders' arrival it had been re-occupied by the Egyptian army which had been expelled from it several years previously by the Seljuks.

The Crusader armies first beheld the walls of Acre in May 1099, on their way to Jerusalem from the north. On their march from Tyre they passed the *Ladder of Tyre* (Rosh Haniqra), and arrived before the city walls on the 22nd of May. They pitched their tents on the banks of the River Na'aman (the Belus) where it flowed into the sea. The Egyptian governor of Acre and its inhabitants brought gifts to the Franks, and provided them with food at moderate prices. The governor behaved in a very friendly fashion to the leaders of the expedition and came to an agreement with them that if the Crusaders captured Jerusalem and were able to remain in the country twenty days longer, and if the caliph of Egypt did not advance to fight them, or if they defeated him, he would hand over the city to them without hostilities. Meanwhile he pledged himself to maintain peace and friendship with them.

first encounter

The Crusaders remained camped near Acre for two days. On Tuesday the 24th of May, 1099, they continued their march southward, along the coast towards Caesarea.

After the capture of Jerusalem and the repulse of the great Fatimid counter-attack near Ascalon on the 12th of August 1099, many of the Crusaders, led by Robert of Flanders and Robert of Normandy, set out for home. Their men passed through Acre, Tyre, Sidon, Beirut and Tripoli, where they were received hospitably and permitted to purchase foodstuffs, and from there embarked for Europe. It may be assumed that the authorities of the coastal cities behaved in this way because of the complete failure of the Egyptian forces.

The hostilities of 1099 and the swift capture of the regions of Judea, Samaria and Galilee by Godfrey and Tancred interrupted the regular conduct of the merchant caravans on their way across the country to the ports. Both sides were interested in the renewal of the country's commercial life, and an agreement was quickly reached with the maritime towns, restoring peaceful conditions. The emirs of Ascalon, Caesarea and Acre sent a delegation to Godfrey in Jerusalem offering to pay five thousand gold bezants together with horses, mules, oil and other products in return for a peaceful settlement. Godfrey accepted the terms and the agreement was signed, but these peaceful relations were of brief duration. A Venetian fleet arrived on the 10th of June 1100, and the Venetians offered their military services on condition that they were allotted a quarter and a market in every town captured with their help. This condition was accepted by Godfrey and the Crusader leaders, and it was agreed that in return for their part in the capture of towns between the 24th of June and the 16th of August the Venetians would receive in each a church, a square and a market. This was the beginning of a long series of privileges granted to the various communes at Acre, even before its capture. They were to remain on paper for the time being.

peaceful relations

After the Venetians had performed their pilgrimage to the holy places in Jerusalem, they returned to their ships in the port of Jaffa. Although Godfrey's health grew worse at this time, the Frankish host, led by Tancred and the Patriarch Diambert, left Jaffa on the 17th of July, 1100, and set out to capture Acre. The Venetian fleet sailed the same day. The plan was to lay siege to Acre by land and sea as the preliminary to its conquest; the Venetian fleet reached the town three days before the Frankish army, which was still on the way when the news arrived of Godfrey's death in Jerusalem. The Venetians thereupon sent messengers to Tancred asking him if they were to proceed with the original plan. Under the conditions of an interregnum a protracted siege, such as was to be expected before a strong city like Acre, was impossible. Tancred decided to select an easier target; the Frankish force and the Venetian fleet altered their plans, attacked Haifa and took it. Thus the first plan to capture Acre came to naught.

The accession of Baldwin I did not at first modify relations between him and the maritime towns. At the beginning of March, 1101, an embassy of the emirs of Ascalon, Arsuf, Caesarea, Acre and Tyre arrived in Jerusalem to renew the peace agreements between them and the Franks. But these agreements were soon rendered worthless: Baldwin determined to gain direct and final control of the ports and of their commercial traffic. To do so it was necessary to assemble a

naval force, and the assistance of the Italian communes was again required. As early as the spring of 1101 he had a favourable opportunity. A Genoese fleet arrived off the Syrian coast in early March and anchored in the harbour of Jaffa in April. Baldwin's aim was first to clear the shore nearest to Jerusalem; he took the towns of Arsuf and Caesarea, and with their capture the entire central coast was in Frankish hands. But he had not yet achieved his objective. The southern and central ports were shallow and exposed to gales; the large secure harbours of Acre and Tyre were still in Moslem hands, and serving as bases for ships which assailed the Christians as they approached the shores of the Holy Land. Thus in the winter of 1101 the inhabitants of Sidon, Acre and Ascalon seized pilgrim vessels that had been wrecked on the coast by storm, butchering many of the passengers and selling the rest as slaves.

Baldwin decided to take Acre in March 1103, although he knew that a precondition of success was the maintenance of an effective sea blockade, and he had no navy. The chronicler, Albert of Aix, relates that after the assault on the pilgrims, Baldwin summoned the entire forces of his kingdom to Ramla—five thousand in all. The king arrived before the walls of Acre with siege machinery, and artillery and catapults in great quantities, and began his siege. The city suffered considerable damage and many casualties from the constant bombardment and the inhabitants, in great distress, determined to surrender on condition that Baldwin spare their lives. A delegation of three men was sent to discuss terms of surrender. While the envoys were still negotiating with the king, twelve Moslem ships reached the harbour from Tyre, Sidon and Tripoli with five hundred troops and much war material on board. With these reinforcements the town's defences were greatly strengthened and the sheikhs at once broke off negotiations. In the renewed fighting the Franks attacked courageously, but

80

when the king realized the strength of the defence he decided, after consulting his nobles, to raise the siege. He burnt his war machines, destroyed the crops in the fields around the city, cut down its plantations, drove away the flocks which he found in the neighbourhood and retired to his own territory.

The siege of Acre failed because of the lack of a naval force to cut off the defenders from reinforcement by sea. This force Baldwin found a year later, in the spring of 1104, when a Genoese fleet reached the country's shores. Hearing of its arrival, he despatched envoys inviting the new arrivals to follow the example of their fellow citizens, who had helped to take Caesarea. After negotiations an agreement was reached whereby the Genoese were to assist in the capture of Acre in return for a third of the town, a third of the port revenues, a third *second siege* of the land for a league outside Acre, a regular yearly payment of three hundred bezants and the right to extra-territorial courts of justice. After signing the agreement, the allies proceeded to besiege the town, completing its investment on the 5th and 6th of May, 1104. This time all possibility of help from the sea was cut off. King Baldwin set up stone-throwers which weakened and destroyed the city walls and the buildings within. Severe illness swept the city, while a large number of the defenders were killed in the operations. After a twenty-day siege the Emir of Acre saw that there was no prospect of holding out. He assembled the inhabitants and proposed that they surrender. They decided to lay down their arms, and the Emir suggested terms of capitulation to the king whereby those who wished to leave the town could do so, taking with them their families and moveable property; those who wished could remain, on condition that they pay a fixed yearly tax to the king.

The king and the Patriarch held a council and decided to accept the terms, calculating that if they rejected them the population would put up a desperate *capitulation* resistance, anticipating that their fate was in any case sealed, so that the town would only be captured with difficulty and at great cost. They considered, moreover, that by consenting to the terms they would save human lives and preserve property destined to be their plunder. The Pisans and Genoese, however, their covetousness aroused, at first refused to accept the agreement on any account, though they finally did so after much dispute, and the capitulation was confirmed on oath by both sides. It was agreed that the gates should be opened on the 26th of May, 1104. The greed of the Pisans and the Genoese was again aroused, on seeing the inhabitants quitting the town with large quantities of possessions. Breaking the terms of surrender, they attacked the citizens as they left the city, robbing them of gold, purple dyestuffs and other valuables and murdering many of them. The king's men, beholding this unbridled plundering, were also roused to lust for spoils and they too began to kill and rob. Some four thousand citizens were slain and innumerable treasures were looted.

Fearing that he would be accused of deliberate deceit, the king wished to punish severely those who had broken the agreement. It was only with difficulty that the Patriarch Evremar prevented him from doing so and thus restored peace. The Genoese received the agreed areas and the extra-territorial rights.

81

Despite the great slaughter, some Moslems resettled in the city. A mixed population always dwelt in the town as long as it existed, and Moslem sources inform us that their coreligionists received complete freedom of worship.

The capture of Acre at last gave the Crusaders a safe harbour, sheltered at all seasons of the year. Despite its distance from Jerusalem all commercial and passenger traffic was directed through the port without delay; further, as William of Tyre noted, "The coast was freed, at least in a measure, from enemy attacks."

But the Moslems had not yet relinquished Acre. In August 1110, while King Baldwin was at Edessa, an Egyptian fleet attacked it and also Beirut, which the Crusaders had taken three months before; although the harbour of Acre was damaged, the Moslems were unable to regain the city.

mercantile communes
Acre's great commercial importance is well reflected in the interest displayed by the communes in obtaining charters and privileges in the city. Although the Venetians were the first to be granted concessions there, even before its conquest, the first actually to obtain property in the city were the Genoese who had helped to capture it. Baldwin later confirmed the privileges he had granted to the Venetians in 1100 and gave certain building sites to the Doge Ordelafo Falieri in 1110. The Commune of Marseilles received privileges there in 1115.

The favoured status enjoyed by the Genoese in Acre ended in 1124, when the Venetians obtained a third of the town by virtue of an agreement signed between them and the Patriarch Gormund. This agreement fixed the reward which they were to receive in exchange for their assistance in capturing Tyre and was signed in the absence of the king—a prisoner in Moslem hands at the time—but confirmed by him upon his release. This well-known *Pactum Varmundi* granted to the Venetians a third of all the towns of the country, whether royal or baronial, regulating the Venetian rights of extra-territorial jurisdiction and their exemption from the local courts except in certain isolated cases. In addition to these general grants and privileges, the treaty recorded precise details of the rights of the Venetians in Acre, including the right to establish there an oven, a mill and a bathhouse and to use weights and measures, and bottles for liquid and dry measures. The exact boundaries of the areas in Acre which had previously been allotted the Venetians were also confirmed.

The Commune of Pisa joined the communes of Genoa, Venice and Marseilles in 1168.

naval activity
The port of Acre became the permanent station of the royal fleet and its allies. At the beginning of the winter of 1110 a Norwegian fleet left Acre on its way to capture Sidon. The Venetian fleet concentrated at Acre at the end of 1123 and sailed in the winter of 1124 to take Tyre. The maritime force of the Second Crusade gathered there in 1148, as did the Crusader fleet in 1169 for the Egyptian campaign. In 1182, when Saladin attacked Beirut, the king ordered the Frankish navy to assemble in the harbours of Tyre and Acre; within a week thirty-three craft, duly equipped, were ranged in the port of Acre. The Frankish forces also assembled there frequently, as in 1182, in 1183, on the eve of the Second Crusade (1148), and before the battle of Hattin (1187).

Soon after its capture Acre became a royal centre of great political importance, virtually a second capital. The king's council *(Curis Regis)* often met there for deliberations and decisions—as in 1123, 1148 and 1184. Acre's position as the kingdom's second capital is evident from the fact that all the taxes imposed in 1182 on the north of the country from Haifa to Beirut, to finance the war with Saladin, were transferred to Acre, while those from Haifa southwards were taken to Jerusalem. *second capital*

The city frequently served as the royal family's winter residence. In the winter of 1143, while the royal family was at Acre, King Fulk was mortally injured in a hunting accident in the neighbouring countryside, and died there three days later.

Acre and its environs were part of the royal domain from the time of its capture. When Fulk reached the country in 1129, the city, together with Sidon, was made over in dowry to him and his wife Melisende, who held it for three years until Fulk's accession to the throne on the death of Baldwin II. When the kingdom was divided between Melisende and Baldwin III, the latter chose the coastal towns of Acre, Tyre and their territories, while Nablus and Jerusalem remained in the hands of the Queen Mother.

In 1157 Baldwin III and the Byzantine emperor agreed that Acre and its land be given to the Byzantine princess Theodora, the king's bride, for life if the king died before her. When Baldwin died, in 1162 or 1163, Acre and its territory passed to her and remained her possession and place of residence until 1168.

Ecclesiastically, the diocese of Acre was under the jurisdiction of the Patriarchs of Jerusalem until 1139. Afterwards it passed into the Archbishopric of Tyre.

We have numerous accounts of the city in the middle of the 12th century. John Phocas, who visited it in about 1185, wrote: *contemporary descriptions*

"[Acre] is a large city and so populous as to surpass all the rest. It receives all the merchant ships, and thither all pilgrims for Christ's sake by sea and by land betake themselves. Here the air being corrupted by enormous influx of strangers, various diseases arise and lead to frequent deaths among them, the consequence of which is evil smells and corruption of the air and the misfortune of the city is beyond repair."[23]

The Moslem traveller, Idrisi, depicted Acre in 1154 as "a large city, spaciously laid out, with many domains round it. The city has a fine and safe port. The population is mixed."[24]

Another account was that of the Moslem traveller Ibn Jubayr in the year 1185:

"Acre is the capital of the Frankish cities in Syria, the unloading place of 'Ships reared aloft in the seas like mountains' and a port of call for all ships. In its greatness it resembles Constantinople. It is the focus of ships and caravans, and the meeting-place of Moslem and Christian merchants from all regions. Its roads and streets are choked by the press of men, so that it is hard to put foot to ground. Unbelief and unpiousness there burn fiercely, and pigs [Christians] and crosses abound. It stinks and is filthy, being full of refuse and excrement. The Franks ravished it from Muslim hands in the first [last] decade of the sixth [fifth] century, and the eyes of Islam were swollen with weeping for it; it was one of its griefs. Mosques became churches and Minarets bell-towers, but God kept undefiled one part of the principal mosque, which remained in the hands of the Muslims as a small mosque where strangers could congregate to offer the obligatory prayers."[25]

In the last days of the first kingdom the centre of political and military events passed to Acre. At the end of August 1186 the child-king Baldwin V died there. After his death Joscelin III, the Seneschal, successfully persuaded the regent of the kingdom, Raymond, Count of Tripoli and Galilee, to leave the city and transfer his headquarters to his own town of Tiberias. On his departure Joscelin seized Acre and proclaimed Sibyl queen in defiance of the last testament of Baldwin IV.

Guy de Lusignan convened his first royal council at Acre late in 1186. Here, too, in May 1187, the entire forces of the kingdom assembled for the battle to be fought at Hattin. After the fight Saladin took Tiberias, which was close to the battlefield, and immediately afterwards marched on Acre. The city was under the command of the Seneschal Joscelin, who sent a citizen called Peter Brice to meet Saladin when he arrived before the city walls on July 10th. The terms of surrender proposed by Joscelin resembled those offered to the Christian conquerors by the Moslem inhabitants of Acre in 1104. According to these, the

fall of Acre city was to be surrendered if the lives and property of the population were spared. Many of the inhabitants, however, regarded the surrender as a shameful act and a brief revolt broke out against Joscelin, but was at once suppressed. Order was restored and Saladin seized control of the city on the same day. The Moslems hoped that the Christian merchants would remain, but they departed, leaving behind them immense stores of goods, silk, metals, precious stones and weapons. These abandoned wares were shared out among the conquerors by al-Afdal, the sultan's young son. The sugar factory outside the city was plundered by the emir Taqi a-Din, much to Saladin's anger. The sultan remained at Acre, while his emirs departed in various directions to complete the conquest of the country. Thus ended the first chapter in the history of Crusader Acre.

Moslem Saladin spent the winter of 1187 in Acre, taking up his quarters in the Templar *settlement* castle, once the palace of the Fatimid governors. The hospital of the Knights of St. John was converted into a theological seminary and received considerable grants from the sultan, drawn from the city's spoils. Much emphasis was laid on strengthening the walls and fortifications, and Karakush, builder of the Cairo citadel, was brought from Egypt to assist with the task. He restored the northwestern sector of the wall and one of its gates was subsequently named after him. The Sultan also passed the winter of 1189 at Acre, again engaged in strengthening its walls, and was careful to station his best troops there.

siege of Acre In August 1189 the curtain rose on one of the most fascinating dramas in the history of war, the siege of Acre. This is not the place to describe in detail all the stages of the three years' siege and the vicissitudes of the belligerents, but an account of the general course of events must be included.

The affair began when a small force commanded by the king, Guy de Lusignan, pitched its tents on the mound of Tel al-Fukhar ("Napoleon's Hill") east of the city walls. This force, which had left Tyre in the middle of August, had not encountered any Moslem troops, who were then occupied in the siege of Beaufort (Qal'at Shaqif). Saladin's units could well have destroyed the Crusaders before they reached Acre, but for reasons unknown to us they did not react to the threat until Guy de Lusignan had entrenched himself strongly before the walls of the city.

Saladin, arriving in the Plain of Acre three days after the Crusaders, set up his headquarters at Tel Ḥaruba near 'Ibillin, on the main road from Acre to Tiberias.

Neither the Crusader movements nor their position on Tel al-Fukhar as yet constituted a threat to the city. They were themselves besieged by a Moslem force moving between the sultan's forward base at Tel Kisan and the city. But within a few weeks the Crusader camp grew stronger until, at the end of August, it was able to maintain a real siege against Acre. While the Crusaders drew their lines and fortified them with ditches and timber palisades, the Moslems stationed their forces in a semi-circle east of the Frankish positions.

On the 15th of September, 1189, when the siege began to affect the defenders of the city, the Moslem right wing broke through the Crusader lines north of Acre, thus opening the road to Tyre. Through the breach supplies were brought into the beleaguered city and Saladin himself came to inspect the arrangements for defence. The Crusaders, realizing that they could not maintain their siege or penetrate the city without a conclusive victory over the force in their rear, decided on a massive assault on the Moslem array. It was delivered in early October 1189. The Crusaders' opening move forced the retirement of the Moslem right wing, and part of the main force was despatched to its aid. The Crusaders charged and pierced the weakened centre, but their initial success was not pressed home and Saladin, concentrating his remaining forces, enveloped the Crusaders and inflicted heavy losses upon them. However, the Moslems also failed to follow up their initial victory, and both sides retired to their previous positions. The winter of 1189 put an end to military operations, and the battle front was quiet for five months.

In the course of the winter Saladin visited Acre and strengthened its fortifications, and in the spring of the new year, 1190, fighting was resumed. This time the Crusaders altered the direction of their attack and renewed their siege on the city, while a covering force kept watch on the Moslem formations which surrounded them. They began with an artillery bombardment of the walls, blocked the moat and undermined the ramparts. The garrison, composed of the sultan's best troops, launched a counter attack, but this was repulsed and the Crusaders were able to reach the foot of the wall (April 1190). At this moment the sultan delivered an assault on their rear, compelling them to retreat from the walls. An Egyptian fleet was then able to enter Acre harbour, bringing fresh supplies to the city. Thereafter the fighting resumed the character of local

*battle of
September 1189*

85

skirmishing, which lasted throughout the summer. The Crusader army was strengthened during the summer and autumn by the arrival of new units from Europe but these were not sufficient to tip the balance in their favour. The second winter of the struggle soon came and the front stagnated again. But the hour of decision was at hand; in the April of 1191 Philip II Augustus reached Palestine, after a long sea voyage, at the head of the French army, followed, in June 1191, by Richard Coeur de Lion at the head of the English host.

arrival of European kings

The arrival of the European kings marked the end of the struggle. The balance of power swung in favour of the Christians as the sultan was unable to raise fresh units. During June the Crusaders carried out a number of rapid assaults upon the city, which was ceaselessly bombarded by their siege artillery. The following is an account of one of the attacks, by the writer of the *Itinerarium:*

"It was about the third hour, i.e., about breakfast time, when these valorous men-at-arms began their work, going forth to storm the tower, which they boldly scaled at once. The Turkish watchmen, on seeing them, raised a shout, and lo! the whole city was soon in astir. The Turkish warriors, hurriedly seizing their arms, came thronging up and flung themselves upon the assailants. The men-at-arms strove to get in; the Turks to hurl them back. Rolled together in a confused mass they fought at close quarters, hand against hand, and sword against sword. Here men struck, there they fell. Our men-at-arms were few, whereas the numbers of the Turks kept on increasing. The Turks also threw *Greek fire* against their enemies, and this at last forced the men-at-arms to retreat and leave the tower, where some of them were slain by weapons, others burnt by that most deadly fire. At last the Pisans, eager for fame and vengeance, scrambled up the tower itself with a mighty effort; but, bravely as they comported themselves, they too had to retreat before the onset of the Turks, who rushed on as if mad. Never had there been such a people as these Turks for prowess in war."

These attacks were repelled by the Moslem defenders with a bravery which gained them the admiration of their foes. Saladin, for his part, did all he could to lessen the pressure on the city: the moment a charge was launched, the garrison would sound its drums as a signal for aid; the Moslem camp would reply and harass the Crusader rear. But the garrison of Acre was at the end of its strength:

last days of Moslem Acre

"So by common consent and counsel, the besieged begged a truce while they sent notice of their plight to Saladin, hoping that, in accordance with their Pagan ways, he would ensure their safety—as he ought to do—by sending them speedy aid or procuring leave for them to quit the city without disgrace. . . . Saladin, meanwhile, having received envoys from the besieged, bade them hold out stoutly in the certainty that he would shortly send them efficient aid. He declared that he had certain news of the approach of a mighty host of warriors from Babylon [Egypt] in ships and galleys."

The promised reinforcements did not materialize and the city's plight grew worse. Three emirs fled during one night, and several Moslems threw themselves from the walls. On the 4th of July the commanders of the besieged Moslems, al-Mashtub and Karakush, asked for terms, but were rejected. Three days later a swimmer brought Saladin the following message from the garrison:

86

"We have sworn to die together; we will fight till we are slain; and we will not deliver up this city as long as we live. Look you to distract the enemy from us and prevent his attacking us. Our turn is over."

On the 12th of July, when no relief was forthcoming, the city capitulated.

capitulation

"On that day, when these famous Turks, of such wonderful valour and warlike excellence, began strolling about on the city walls in all their splendid apparel, previous to their departure, our men gazed on them with the utmost curiosity. They were wonder-struck at the cheerful features of men who were leaving their city almost penniless and whom only the very sternest necessity had driven to beg for mercy; men whom loss did not deject, and whose visage betrayed no timidity, but even wore the look of victory . . ."

The first to enter the town was the Marquis Conrad de Montferrat; taking with him the royal standards, he planted them upon a minaret of the great mosque (the Cathedral of St. Cross), above the Templar castle and on the "Accursed Tower". All the inhabitants were ordered to gather in one quarter and were there divided among the captors. King Richard took up residence in the citadel in the north of the city and Philip II Augustus settled in the Templar stronghold at its southern end. So began a new chapter in the city's history. For a century (1192–1291) Acre was the capital of the kingdom which continued, in name only, to be the "Kingdom of Jerusalem."

After the mosques had been purified and converted into churches, the Franks began to divide the property. Difficult problems arose since the former inhabitants of Acre began to return to their holdings and the European Crusaders still demanded their share. After the matter had been discussed by a special commission, the property of the churches, military orders and communes was restored to its owners, as was that of the inhabitants who could prove their rights to it. Those whose property was restored pledged themselves to billet the European Crusader troops in their homes.

Frankish re-settlement

The town was seriously overcrowded after its capture and Moslems and Jews were prohibited from residing there. The departure of the Crusaders on their march south to Jaffa and Ascalon reduced the overcrowding to some extent, but not enough. The pressure on space within led to the swift expansion of the quarter of Montmusard, built outside and to the north of the city walls, which remained unfortified until the middle of the 13th century.

In 1197 the German Crusader knights landed at Acre; a year later they founded a new military order alongside the older Hospitallers and the Templars. Some time afterwards the Order of St. Thomas of Canterbury was created by the English knights.

In 1197 Henry of Champagne, the ruler and undeclared king of the Kingdom of Jerusalem, fell from a window of the city's citadel and was killed instantly. After his death the crown of Jerusalem was taken by Aimery, king of Cyprus, and thus for the first time the crowns of Cyprus and Jerusalem were united. Aimery set up a separate administration for Palestine which was quartered at Acre, and the king himself spent a considerable part of his time there. On his

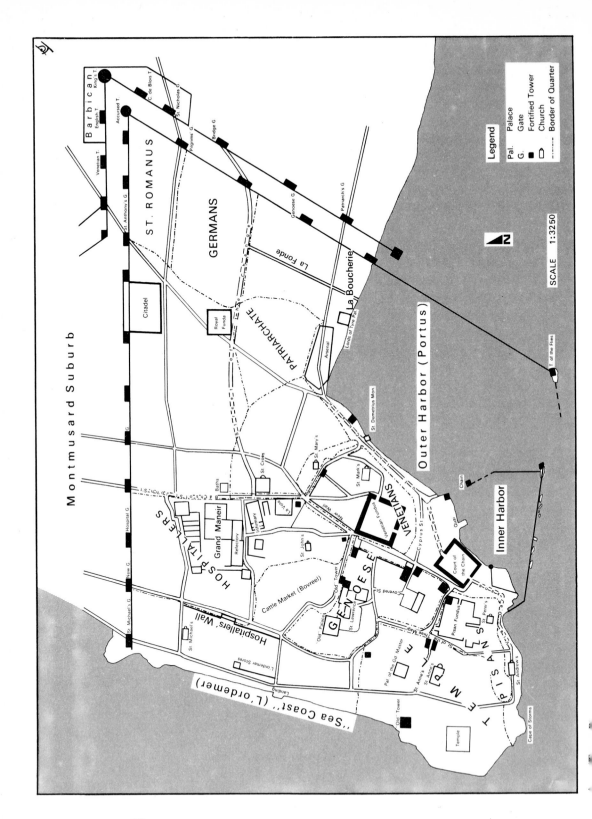

Legend

Pal.   Palace
G.   Gate
▪   Fortified Tower
⌂   Church
-·-·-·-   Border of Quarter

SCALE   1:3250

Barbican
English T
Kng's T
Accursed T.
Venetian T.
C. de Blois T
St. Nicholas G
St. Anthony's G
Pilgrims G
Bridge G
Genoese G
Patriarch's G
ST. ROMANUS
GERMANS
La Fonde
La Boucherie
Citadel
Royal Funda
PATRIARCHATE
Arsenal
Lords of Tyre Pal.
St. Demetrius Mon.
Outer Harbor (Portus)
St. Mary's
St. Mark's
St. Cross
Baths
St. James' St.
Chain
Chain
Gall
Inner Harbor
VENETIANS
Venetian Funda
Cyprus St.
Court of the Chain
New Wall
La Voie
Infirmary
Refectory
Grand Maneir
HOSPITALLERS
St. John's
Old Tower
Covered St.
St. Lawrence
GENOESE
Three Magi
Pisan Funda
St. Peter's
PISANS
St. Andrew's
Montmusard Suburb
St. Michael's G
Hospital G
New G
Cattle Market (Bovreel)
Hospitallers' Wall
Old Palace
St. Michael's
L'ordemer Stores
Pal. of the Grand Master
St. Anne's
St. Anne's
Old Tower
"Sea Coast" (L'ordemer)
Landing
Temple
TEMPLARS
Cape of Storms
T. of the Flies
N

death in April 1205 a regent was appointed to rule over the kingdom until September 1210, when John de Brienne arrived at Acre to be crowned king of Jerusalem.

A number of earthquakes plagued the city in 1202–1204, destroying walls and the royal citadel. The huge buildings of the Order of Hospitallers near the north wall of the city were apparently erected at this time.

As to the atmosphere prevailing in Acre at this period, James of Vitry, who had been called to the bishopric of the city, related:

"Acre is a monster of nine heads, each of which is fighting the other. Nightly men are murdered within the city, men are strangled, women poison their husbands, drug-vendors and whores are prepared to pay high rents for rooms, so that even priests lease houses to them."

Throughout this time disputes stained by bloodshed broke out repeatedly between the Italian communes, and in 1228 the Pisans attacked the Genoese quarter, burning its citadel. *internal strife*

The Emperor Frederick II arrived at Acre in 1228, and his coming ushered in an epoch of feuds and armed conflicts between the imperial army and the baronial forces of the country, known as the "War of the Lombards." At first the emperor lodged in the citadel, but he was forced by the resistance of the local barons, led by the Ibelin family, to leave Acre and camp in a grove of date palms near the estuary of the river Qishon. Fighting broke out in Acre in 1229 between Frederick's supporters and those of the Church, who opposed the excommunicated emperor's sojourn in the city. In the course of these conflicts the imperial forces seized the strategic points in the city and laid siege to the quarters of the Templars, his chief antagonists.

At the beginning of May 1229, the emperor sailed from Acre in secret but his departure had little effect on the internal disputes. Fighting went on continually throughout the years 1231–1235, and the "Commune of Acre" was established around a nucleus formed by the confraternity of St. Andrew. The imperial governor left Acre, and the Ibelin family gained control with the aid of the mobs organized by the "Commune of Acre" with the assistance of the Genoese, who opposed imperial rule. A stalemate had developed by the mid-1230's, with neither side formally conceding claims. In 1242, however, war was renewed between the Ibelins and Filangieri, the imperial governor, the imperial forces assembling in the Hospitallers' quarter, which was besieged for six months.

Louis IX reached Acre in 1250, after his resounding defeat at Mansura and his *St. Louis*
capture by the Moslems. He fortified the northern quarter of Montmusard with walls and towers. In 1253 the Moslems attacked the outskirts of the city, destroyed the flour mills at Kurdani and threatened the city itself. Confronted by a force led by John of Ibelin, which menaced them from outside the city walls, they retired. King Louis left the country in 1254. As long as the French king was at Acre there was comparative peace between the communes, but their struggles broke out again on his departure.

The tension between Venice and Genoa, assisted by Pisa, mounted between 1250–1256 and burst into open hostilities in 1256 when the "War of St. Sabas" broke out. The *casus belli* was a building belonging to the monastery of St. Sabas, located near the Venetian and Genoese quarters, both of which claimed ownership. The Genoese attacked the Venetian quarter, subduing it and destroying its fortifications. This victory won, a feud began between the Pisans and the Genoese who, with the aid of the Regent, John of Ibelin-Arsuf, tore down the towers of the Pisan quarter.

A Venetian fleet which came to avenge the destruction of its quarter was able to break into the port and to capture the entire city, but failed to penetrate the Genoese quarter. The conflict continued for a whole year with the participation of every element in the city, the regent and the Templars supporting the Venetians and Pisans, and joined by the men of Marseilles and Provence. The Genoese were aided by the Hospitallers, some of the barons led by Philip de Montfort, Lord of Tyre, and further assisted by the Commune of Ancona and the Catalans. According to sources most of the buildings in the city were ruined in the war and dozens of ships were sunk in the harbour.

At the end of 1258 the Pope almost succeeded in securing peace, but a Genoese fleet, attempting to bring help to the Genoese quarter, was beaten in a sea battle in the Bay of Acre and wiped out. As a result the Genoese were forced to evacuate their quarter and depart for Tyre. In return for permission to leave the city, the Genoese ceded the whole of their quarter to the Venetians, who plundered and destroyed it completely. By 1258 the Genoese colony at Acre had ceased to exist.

Acre was attacked by Baybars for the first time in 1263. The Mamluks devastated all the orchards, the country houses outside the town and the flour mills of Kurdani, but this was merely a predatory raid and the Moslems deserted the area two days later. A second attack was delivered in February, 1265, to create a diversion from the capture of Caesarea.

The disasters of 1266–1268 left Acre isolated and almost defenceless. Caesarea, Arsuf, Jaffa and Safed fell into the hands of the Sultan Baybars. The truce agreement of 1268 gave the Mamluks half of the territory of Acre. The "Eighth Crusade", organized as a reaction to the news from the Holy Land, foundered in the sands of Tunis and only small forces reached Palestine. Led by Edward (later King Edward I of England), they carried out two limited operations and in 1272 left the country. A new truce was signed which was kept for ten years. Nothing was done to strengthen the defences of the city. The communes continued their quarrels and the ambitious plans of Charles of Anjou to create a new Mediterranean empire came to naught. In 1282 the truce with the Mamluks was renewed.

The last Christian sovereign of Acre reached the city in 1286. Henry II of Cyprus was crowned at Tyre as king of Jerusalem and celebrated his coronation magnificently at Acre, amid evident public rejoicing. But in 1290 riots against Moslem traders in the city's markets were seen by Sultan Kalaun as a pretext for liquidating the last Frankish bastion on the coast of the country, and he officially proclaimed his intention of attacking the city and crushing it. Kalaun began preparations for the siege in the late summer of 1290, giving priority to stocking timber for siege machinery. His troops set upon the forests of Sharon and uprooted many of its oaks. Kalaun died in November of that year, but his son al-Ashraf Khalil continued the preparations, and in the spring of 1291 troops from the whole of the Moslem East began to converge upon the Plain of Acre.

The siege began on the 5th of April, 1291. A Moslem historian related: "The siege of Acre began on the Thursday and warriors came from all lands to fight *siege of Acre* there. The enthusiasm of the Moslems was so great that the number of volunteers exceeded the regular forces. Siege machines were set up against the walls, some taken from the Franks, some so large that they could cast stones of immense weight." There were ninety-two of these. The "Templar of Tyre," one of the Crusader sources for this period, reported that the Moslem forces were deployed over the whole plain "from Toron (Tel Fukhar) to Samariya. The tent of the Sultan was pitched on a hill where stood a fine tower, gardens and vineyards belonging to the Templars."

The Moslems numbered over 66,000 horse and 160,000 foot soldiers. Acre held 40,000 inhabitants, of whom 14,000 were infantry and 800 knights. The Moslems were engaged for eight days in assembling machinery, the four largest engines being directed by al-Ashraf at "the city's principal towers." Preparations completed, the sultan began to bombard the towers, to fill up the moat with faggots and to undermine the walls. He chose the tactic of frontal attack rather than of prolonged siege because he had no fleet at his disposal and the Franks could bring supplies to the city by sea without hindrance. The besieged did not hide behind their ramparts but made several sorties to block the enemy's tunnels before they reached the foot of the wall.

The Moslems' chief efforts at breaching were directed to the north-east corner of the wall, where stood two great round towers. The inner of these was known as the "Accursed Tower" *(Turris Maledicta)*, famous from the siege of 1190–1191, while the outer one, the "King's Tower," had been erected some time before the present siege.

On the 4th of May, under growing Moslem pressure, King Henry II of Cyprus and Jerusalem came to Acre, with a large fleet and a considerable force of Cypriot knights. The besieged were overjoyed at the reinforcements and lit great bonfires of welcome. Henry sent two envoys to the sultan, who received them in a small tent and asked them if they had brought the keys of the city, telling them that he was prepared to permit the evacuation of the inhabitants and soldiery with their property. When the envoys attempted to argue, al-Ashraf replied, "In that case, depart for I have nothing more to say."

Moslem pressure on the King's Tower continued and on the 8th of May the defenders were forced to abandon the barbican protecting it and retreat to the *breaching of outer* exterior wall. The Moslems began to undermine the foundations of the King's *defences* Tower and the towers on either side of it. When King Henry saw that all hope was gone, he left Acre and returned to Cyprus. The King's Tower held out for another week, until Wednesday the 16th of May. The "Templar of Tyre" related:

"The Saracens filled sacks with sand beside the New Tower and every horseman bore with him a sack on the neck of his horse and threw it to the Saracens who were there. When night came the Saracens cast down the sacks and scattered them on the stones till they had made the area as smooth as a floor. On the morrow, Wednesday, towards vespers, they advanced over the sacks and took the said tower."

The following day the Moslems captured the eastern sector of the outer wall. On Friday the 18th of May, al-Ashraf ordered a general assault.

"When Friday came, before dawn broke, the beating of giant drums was heard, and to this sound, so loud and horrible, the Saracens attacked the city of Acre on all sides. The place where they made their first entry was the Accursed Tower, which they took. They came on foot, in numbers past counting; first those who bore great high shields, and after them throwers of 'Greek fire,' then dart throwers and those who shot feathered arrows, so thickly that it was as if rain was falling from the sky."

Moslem penetration

The Franks retreated before this assault from the moat and fortified themselves on the inner wall. But the Moslems burst into "the Accursed Tower" and penetrated the town. A vain effort to check them in the quarter of St. Anthony, which impinged on the north-eastern quarter, failed, and the Moslems reached the heart of the city. The defence collapsed and the Franks fled towards the port. A heart-rending scene occurred on the quays as the soldiers and inhabitants sought to embark in rowing boats and reach the ships lying in mid-harbour or outside the port. The boats were few, and the Moslems, swiftly reaching the harbour, slew everyone they encountered.

last hold

The Templars fortified themselves in their huge fortress at the south-west corner of the city, in company with several hundred citizens. After several days al-Ashraf proposed to the besieged that they yield on condition that they be permitted to leave for Cyprus with their possessions. The Templar commander consented and allowed a company of Mamluks to enter the fortress. But they began to plunder the civilians; the Templars butchered the Mamluks and fighting began afresh. Again al-Ashraf proposed a cease-fire, and when the chief Templars came from the fortress to settle terms, he seized and beheaded them. The "Templar of Tyre" reported of the last moments of Acre in Crusader hands:

"When the brothers within the tower heard that the Marshal and the others had been beheaded, they prepared to defend themselves. The Saracens began to dig a mine beneath the tower, and to shore it with props. Those within the tower surrendered, whereupon the Saracens entered in such numbers that the props collapsed. The stones of the walls fell and the Templar brothers perished together with the Saracens. The tower fell into the street and crushed more than two thousand mounted Turks."

destruction

When not a Frank remained alive in the city, al-Ashraf began its systematic destruction. The markets were burnt, the towers and fortifications dismantled and the harbour blocked with stones. As a sign of victory al-Ashraf removed the portal of the Church of St. Andrew and rebuilt it inside a mosque which he erected in Cairo. Acre became a heap of ruins and remained deserted for hundreds of years.

The remains of the once-handsome city drew the interest of travellers visiting the Holy Land, who recorded their impressions in written accounts, drawings and maps. These show that despite the destruction wrought by man and nature, the traces of Acre's splendour were still recognizable and various structures could still be identified. When it was rebuilt by Dahar al-'Omar in the middle of the 18th century some of the outstanding monuments, such as the Templar castle and the Church of St. Andrew, were destroyed and their stones used to build the city's fortifications. As the new city developed, the process of the obliteration of the Crusader city gathered pace; where the Crusader structures could not be destroyed because of their strength and size, they were filled with soil and the later additions erected on top of them. Mounds several metres in height were thus formed, concealing within them remains of the mediaeval city. *remains of Frankish Acre*

For many years it was thought that hardly a trace was left of the Crusader city, but investigations carried out there, chiefly in the 1960's with the aim of development and restoration, revealed that many fine relics had been preserved. Remains not only of the huge structures of the Military Orders and the Churches were found, but also the gates of the quarters, watch-towers and dwellings. What is more, the city which began to develop in the 18th century preserved the plan and character of the Crusader city, so that it has been possible to identify and restore considerable portions of Acre from contemporary maps and other written sources.

Our information on the mediaeval topography of Acre is very rich. It is based on various sources: accounts of travellers, chronicles, maps of the period, charters, descriptions of the ruins, modern maps and archaeological surveys. These sources include five mediaeval maps of the city, dozens of accounts by contemporaries and about a hundred charters. Despite the abundance of information, every attempt to restore the city's boundaries and fortifications or to identify sites within it is met with numerous difficulties, arising in part from contradictions in the historical evidence and in part from the lack of important links that would permit a systematic reconstruction of all its parts.

THE CITY'S AREA AND DEFENCES

The plan of the defences is well known to us. At the time of the Crusader conquest the city was fortified by a line of walls on the north and east. The length of the wall in this period is not clear. Nasir Ḥusru (1047) did record the city's dimensions, but we do not know if his measurements refer to the city itself— that is, from the tip of the cape to the north wall—or to the perimeter of the ramparts. It is at any rate clear that the north wall was longer than the eastern. These walls, with the cape on which the city was built, formed a square—or more exactly a rhomboid. This plan, which endured until the middle of the 13th *city plan* century, was clearly described by Willbrand of Oldenburg (1212) who wrote that the town had a "four-cornered plan."

size All scholars agree that the ancient city was much larger than the boundaries existing today, but the length of the walls, and consequently the area of the town, remains a matter of dispute. Some would like to transfer the east wall as much as half a kilometre, and the northerly as much as 300 metres, beyond the present ramparts. According to the restored city plan (proposed by us—see p. 88) the length of the eastern wall measures 500 metres and the northern 800 metres.

During the 12th century the landward walls of Acre constituted a single line of defence. At the end of the 12th or at the beginning of the 13th century, however, an additional line was built 30 metres in front of the east wall, crowned with towers 50 metres apart. Between the two lines a moat was dug; another existed in front of the exterior wall. Willbrand's account is enlightening:

fortifications
"This is a fine strong city situated on the seashore in such a way that, while it is of four-cornered plan, the two sides which form one angle are girdled and protected by the sea, and the other two are encompassed by a fine ditch, which is both wide and deep and stone-lined from the very bottom, and also by a double wall which is fortified with towers on an excellent system. Thus the first wall, which together with its towers does not overtop the main wall, is commanded and defended by the second and inner wall the towers of which are tall and very strong indeed. This city has a good safe harbour guarded by a handsome tower."

From the traveller's description it seems that the western (seaward) side of the city was unfortified. This is confirmed by maps of the period. Those who planned the city's defences apparently did not fear a hostile landing from the sea, relying on the rocks and sandbanks which flank the cape.

Unlike the east side, no additional wall was built on the north side, perhaps because from the 12th century onwards the area outside the enceinte was protected by the densely-built quarter of Montmusard. The weakest point of the enceinte was its north-east corner and here a huge tower was erected called the "Accursed Tower" *(Turris Maledicta).* After the outer defence wall had been constructed, the great round tower called "King's Tower" was built in front of "Accursed Tower," and barbicans were raised in front of its exterior ramparts. Despite the strong fortification, it was here that the conquerors ultimately broke into the city. In the middle of the 13th century (1250–1254) the northern quarter of Montmusard was fortified with a double wall 900 metres in length, beginning at a point on the old north wall at a distance of 200 metres west of the "Accursed Tower," and ending on the seashore. The fortification of the triangle of Montmusard converted the plan of the city's defences from a quadrilateral to a "Crusader's Shield." In 1283 the traveller Burchard described it as follows:

"... [Acre] is triangular in shape, like a shield whereof the two sides look upon the Mediterranean Sea and the third upon the plain about it."

gates There were numerous gates in the ancient ramparts: the St. Michael Gate, the New Gate *(Porta Nova),* the Gate of our Lady *(Domine Nostre),* St.

Anthony's Gate, the Gate of Blood *(Sanguinis),* the St. Nicholas Gate, the Bridge Gate *(Pontis)* and the Gate of the Patriarch. There were two gates in the wall of Montmusard, the "Gate of the Evil Step" *(Mallopasso)* and the Gate of St. Lazarus. The main gates of the old city were the Gate of our Lady, situated approximately in the centre of the north rampart, and the Gate of the Patriarch at the south-east corner. These were pierced through square towers 15–17 metres high, like the gates of other Crusader towns. The citadel of the city stood 250 metres west of the "Accursed Tower." We do not know when it was erected or if it existed before the Crusader occupation, but there are grounds for supposing that it was built, or at least enlarged and fortified, by the Crusaders, and that in the pre-Crusader period there had been a citadel in the south-western corner of the town in the area later given to the Templars.

The sources state that the southern citadel was the palace and castle of al-Afdal, the Egyptian vizier and governor of Fatimid Acre. The location of the Moslem stronghold corresponds to the siting of the other citadels of the Pales-tinian coastal towns ('Atlit, Caesarea, Arsuf, Jaffa and Ascalon) which were all *citadel* built on headlands on the seashore near the harbour.

The Crusader citadel *(castellum),* as it appears on maps of the period and in various chronicles, possessed a certain tactical value as it protected St. An-thony's Gate, one of the important entrances to the city. In the 13th century, when the wall of the Montmusard quarter was built, the citadel continued to serve as the royal palace and was also the barracks of the garrison, but lost its importance as an independent defensive unit.

Remains of the mediaeval defences of Acre are barely visible today. The Turk-ish walls, built in the 19th century, have obliterated the Crusader lines which were still clearly discernible at the end of the 18th century. In the area of the Montmusard quarter a ditch can still be traced belonging to the north wall, as well as remains of the wall itself. Many stones from the Crusader fortifications were re-used in the Turkish ramparts. The city's defences were not restricted to the outer enceinte. Due to the constant quarrels between the inhabitants of the various quarters of the city, the bounds of the communes were fortified by walls and towers, which will be described together with the quarters themselves.

THE PORT

The harbour of Acre has been subjected to praise and abuse alike. William of Tyre wrote that: "Its double harbour, lying both inside and outside the walls, offers a safe and tranquil anchorage to ships." Theodorich, on the other hand, observed: "The harbour or roadstead is difficult and dangerous of access, when the wind blows from the south, and the shores trouble from the continual shocks which they receive from the waves . . ." Despite these contrary opinions, there is no doubt that the harbour of Acre was one of the largest and most secure, and in fact the principal port on the eastern Mediterranean coast.

Acre, View from the South (Drawing from 1686)

According to Ibn Jubayr's account it was "second only to Constantinople" and many dozens of vessels anchored there at the peak of the season, just before Easter. Theodorich (1172) related that while he was at Acre the number of ships anchored at the port was eighty.

All sources point to a similarity between the plan of the port of Acre and that of Tyre, some stating that Acre was larger and others that it was smaller than Tyre. The resemblance between the two helps us to reconstruct the plan of the port of Acre, since the remains of Tyre harbour survive and have been mapped, while the remains at Acre are very meagre. Very important additional information about the mediaeval harbour of Acre was obtained by underwater exploration carried out on the shore in the years 1964–1965, even though this was brief and incomplete because the later construction partly cuts the line of the old breakwaters and prevents further investigation.

port in earlier periods The port of Acre was a natural anchorage for craft from very ancient times. Its conversion to a port, by the creation of an artificial anchorage secure in all weathers, took place in the Hellenistic period, when a breakwater appears to have been constructed on the rocks extending eastward from "Storm Cape." At the end of this breakwater an additional sea wall was built, orientated north–south in such a way that the western anchorage was closed on all sides.

At the end of the 9th century the harbour was enlarged by Aḥmad Ibn Tulun, ruler of Egypt. We have an account of the circumstances in which this harbour was constructed, written by the historian al-Maqdisi:

96

"Then Ibn Tulun wished to construct at 'Akka a fortification that should be as impregnable as that of Tyre. From all provinces artificers were brought together; but when the matter was laid before them, all averred that none in those days knew how the foundations of a building could be laid in the water. Then one mentioned to Ibn Tulun the name of my grandfather, Abu Bakr, the architect, saying that if perchance any had knowledge in these matters, it would be he alone. So Ibn Tulun wrote to his lieutenant in Jerusalem commanding that he should despatch my grandfather to him; and on his arrival they laid the affair before him. 'The matter is easy,' said my grandfather; 'let them bring such sycamore beams as be large and strong.' These beams he set to float on the surface of the water, as a prolongation of the [eastern] town walls (seawards), and he bound them one to the other; while towards the west he left the opening for a mighty gateway. And upon these beams he raised a structure with stones and cement. After every five courses he strengthened the same by setting in great columns. At length the beams became so weighted that they began to sink down; but this was little by little, and finally they rested on the sand. Then they ceased building for a whole year, that the construction might consolidate itself, after which, returning, they began to build. And from where it had been left off, continuing, my grandfather made a junction between this and the ancient city walls, bringing the new work right up into the old, and causing the two to join together. Across the western gate of the port he built a bridge, and every night when the ships had come within the harbour they drew across the water gate a chain, even as was the case at Tyre."[26]

The breakwater referred to seems to be that built from the "Tower of the Flies" north-eastward and joining the line of the eastern city wall; its remains are now beneath the sea. Nasir Ḥusru (1047) described the harbour thus: "It resembles so to speak, a stable, the back of which is towards the city, with the side walls stretching out into the sea."

marine structures

With these additions, Acre harbour became a "double port" consisting of the "inner basin," the old western anchorage, and the eastern "outer harbour," resembling the plan of Tyre harbour.

In the Crusader period no important work was carried out on the breakwaters or sea walls, and arrangements at the port remained as they had been at the end of the 9th century. Historical sources, stressing that the harbour was double, distinguished between the outer (eastern) basin and the inner (western) basin. According to Theodorich: "In the inner harbour are moored the ships of the city, and in the outer are those of foreigners." In the northern area of the outer harbour there was an additional anchorage, referred to in the sources such as "La Boucherie." Its position was between the Arsenal and the city wall. The anchorage, visible until recently, served as sailing point of Frederick II in 1229.

The famous "chain" stretched between two towers at the harbour mouth was evidently at the entrance of the inner basin, that is, between the mainland tower and that dominating the terminus of the inner breakwater.

The approach to the port was protected by a strongly fortified sea tower, known as "the Tower of Flies" after Baalzebub, god of the Philistines. This stood on the site of the existing old lighthouse and historical evidence indicates that it was surrounded by water on all sides. Possession of it ensured command of the harbour and of access to it.

97

The shore of the harbour extended in a half-circle 650 metres long and was divided into two areas—the inner shore and the "chain quarter." The first was *foreshore* 250 metres in length from the end of the western breakwater to the entrance tower at the inner basin. Those disembarking entered an iron gate marked on maps of the period *(Porta Ferrea)*. The area beyond the "Iron Gate" was called "Darsana," presumably because the old shipyard of Acre was situated there. The central structure of the inner shore was the *Cour de la Chaine* (Court of the Chain), the customs house and also the seat of the marine court. It was situated where the Khan al-'Umdan now is, and its plan was identical with that of the modern Khan, built at the beginning of the 19th century by al-Jazzar. West of it were warehouses, enclosed courts and other structures. The Pisan quarter abutted on this area on the north.

East of the Khan began the shore of the outer harbour, known as "the Street of the Chain" after the chain closing the harbour entrance. The shore was 400 metres long beginning at a broad square, part of which overlapped the modern "Fisherman's Square." The principal street in Acre crossing the city from north to south terminated at this square. There were warehouses, palaces and dwellings on "the Street of the Chain," and on its north-east was the royal arsenal, guarded by a strong square tower which survives to its full height, the Burj a-Sultan. No merchant commune or corporation with extra-territorial rights had jurisdiction over any part of the harbour shore. Its various structures were the property of the king, sundry nobles, the Orders and the communes. We know of several important structures on the "chain," such as the "Palace of the Constable," situated not far from the harbour square, and the "Palace of the Lords of Tyre," situated east of the Arsenal. Around the port area the chief Italian communes, Pisa, Genoa and Venice, extended in a semicircle.

Maritime activity was not limited to the harbour. On the west shore of the *other landing* city there were two landing points. One was called "L'Ordemer" (in French— *points* "the Sea Coast"), a name used also for the whole length of the western shore of the old city. Somewhere north of the Templar quarter was a quay used by ships when the sea was calm. The sources specify that merchandise imported or exported through L'Ordemer was subjected to lower custom duties than in the harbour.

The other landing point was called "La Cale du Marquis" (The quay of the Marquis), situated on the shore of Montmusard, called in the documents *mare burgi novi* (the sea of the new suburb). Its position is on the small bay just south of the northern wall of the suburb. It was used during several naval operations in the 13th century.

THE PISAN QUARTER

The Pisan quarter was the westernmost and smallest of the quarters of the communes. The Pisans founded the quarter in 1168, when they obtained a char-

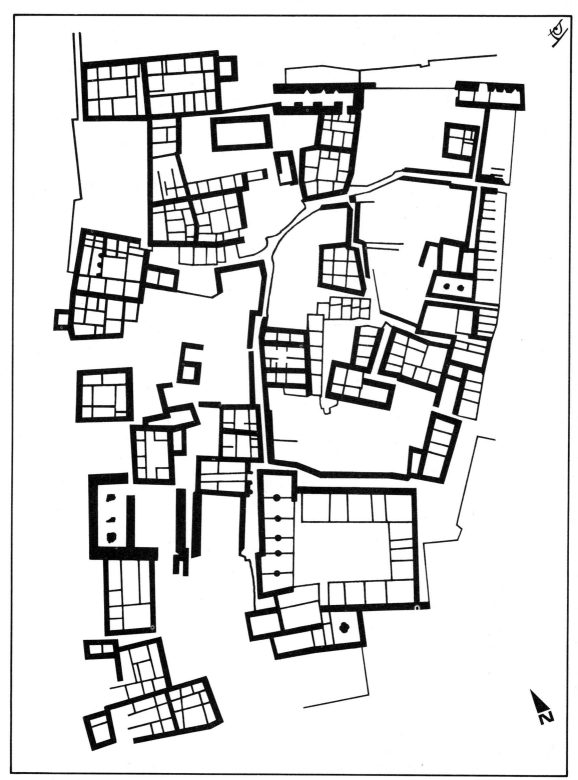

Acre, Crusader structures and streets (General Plan)

ter from King Amalric. The quarter extended from "Storm Cape" on the west to the harbour quarter on the east. Its western limit was the Templar quarter and its northern the Genoese. Most of its area was occupied by a khan-like building (Khan a-Shuna) which served as the store and living-quarters of the Pisan merchants. The sources record that the quarter had a bakery, a bath house, dwellings, a tavern and stores. The Church of St. Peter, Patron of the City of Pisa, apparently lay south of Khan a-Shuna, not far from the Crusader Church of St. Andrew (the modern Church of St. John).

After the capture of Acre in 1191 the Pisans returned to the quarter, but were expelled from it in 1193. In 1195 they came back to settle and fortified it with walls and towers. During the 13th century the quarter suffered in the constant wars waged by the Pisans against the Genoese, their neighbours on the north, and in the course of the hostilities which occurred in 1222, 1258–1259 and 1287, the quarter and its defences were destroyed several times.

THE GENOESE QUARTER

The Genoese quarter was the oldest and largest belonging to the Italian communes, having been allotted to the Genoese in 1104 in return for their active participation in the capture of Acre, and extended over the heart of the old city. Its western limit was the Templar quarter and its southern the Pisan; on the east were the harbour square and the city's main street, and on the north, the quarter of the Hospitallers.

streets Unlike other quarters, it was composed in the main of dwellings and palaces, with few public buildings. Its network of winding lanes and close-set houses gives rise to the conjecture that the Genoese settled in the houses of the old Arab town, doing little to change the character of the neighbourhood. The main gate was on the east, opposite the harbour square and beside the main street of the city. Remains of the gate, and thick walls with typical Crusader stonework, are preserved here to a great height. The gate opened onto the main street of the quarter, which wound in a northerly direction. This was vaulted and was referred to as "the Vaulted Street" (*cooperta*—covered) in the Genoese documents. The street crossed another and, at some distance from the crossing, reached a fortified gate protecting the entrance to the square of the quarter. This gate

gates broadens as it goes, having guardrooms on each side, and was constructed in the unusual late-Crusader fashion, comprising two portals, placed at right-angles to each other (indirect approach). The gate gave access to the main square *(Platea)* of the Genoese quarter, around which all the public buildings were constructed. On the north stood the Church of St. Lawrence, Patron of the City of Genoa, where now stands the Greek Orthodox Church of St. George. On the east was the old tower *(Turris Vetus)* of the quarter and at the corners of

palaces the square stood several palaces. Genoese documents refer to "the Old Palace" *(Palatium Vetus),* where the law court *(Curia)* of the commune met, in this vicin-

100

Acre, crossroad on border of Genoese, Pisan and Templar quarters

Genoese "palace"

ity. This palace may have occupied a two-storeyed building where notably fine Frankish architectural details have been found. Another palace was situated south-west of the square. The communal bakery and bath-house were also in this neighbourhood. Most of the area of the quarter was taken up with dwellings warehouses and shops, some occupied throughout the year and some reserved for the merchants of the mother-city in compliance with the communes' regulations that stores and accommodation be set aside for Genoese traders when they came to Acre, generally between Easter and autumn (the season of the "*Passagium*").

wars and sieges
The quarter was fortified on all sides with walls and towers, and the gateways too were heavily armoured. In fact it was frequently involved in wars and sieges, which often ended in large-scale destruction. In 1258 the quarter was captured by the Venetians during the "War of St. Sabas" and demolished. Columns from Acre were brought to Venice as trophies and are still to be seen there in the Church of St. Mark. The Genoese were expelled from Acre altogether and returned only in 1275, though not all their property was restored to them.

THE VENETIAN QUARTER AND THE STREET
OF THE PROVENÇALS

The Venetians first settled at Acre in 1110, and in 1124 their quarter was enlarged by the terms of the pact of Gormond (*Pactum Warmundi*). The quarter lay

102

along the shore of the outer harbour, although the foreshore itself was not in their possession. The "Street of the Chain", already mentioned, separated them from the sea. The Venetian area was largely taken up by the "Venetian Inn" *(Fundus Venetorum),* which was at the centre of the quarter. The inn was identical in plan and area with the present Khan al-Afranj, the oldest caravanserai in Acre. Remains of the Crusader structure are recognizable in the foundations and columns of the present building. Not far from it, to the north-east, was the Church of St. Mark and beside it the "Palace of the Commune." The rest of the area was occupied by dwellings, storehouses and shops; the remains of these structures are today below ground level.

inn

North-east of the Venetian quarter lay Provençal Street, with the Church of St. Mary of the Provençals. The Provençal communes, whose merchants had reached the country in ships of Marseilles, acquired the street in a charter of 1115, which was renewed from time to time. A special charter was granted to the merchants of Montpellier in 1229 by the emperor Frederick II Hohenstaufen, who had prohibited ships from Marseilles from putting in at Acre.

The street of the Provençals stretched from the main thoroughfare southeastward until it reached the "Street of the Chain." At the intersection near the sea was the Greek Orthodox monastery of St. Demetrius, to be looked for south of the Burj a-Sultan. The monastery is first alluded to at the beginning of the 12th century; it was swept away in 1290 when the sea encroached on the land.

The present al-Ramel Mosque , which has the marble mullion of a window in one of the walls of its court, with a Latin inscription referring to Master Ebule Fazle "who built this church", is assumed to be the old Church of St. Mary: the lettering of the inscription and the name of the man are both southern French.

THE TEMPLAR QUARTER

This quarter occupied the south-west corner of the old city. It was apparently in the 1130's that the Templars acquired the fortified palace of the Vizier al-Afdal, who had resided near the seashore. Contemporary accounts say it was "The strongest place in the city". The building resembled a *castrum* in plan— a square structure with corner towers: "On each side of the citadel there was a small tower and on each one of them there was a shape of a *lion passant* as large as a bull all made of gold". Remains of this stronghold were still visible in the middle of the 18th century, but disappeared completely when Dahar al-'Omar use the building stones to erect the city walls. The Templar citadel was the last Christian stronghold to fall when Acre was captured by the Mamluks (1291). It seems to have been located near the site of the modern lighthouse where there is now a shallow lagoon. In the Crusader period this area was partly above sea level but has become submerged owing to the subsidence of the coastline.

East gate   The principal entrance to the Templar quarter was from the east. It was defended by a gate-tower, mentioned in historical documents and contemporary

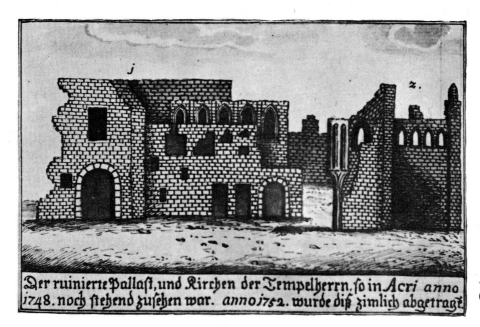

Der ruinierte Pallaſt, und Kirchen der Tempelherrn, ſo in Acri anno 1748. noch ſtehend zuſehen war. anno 1752. wurde diß zimlich abgetragt

Acre, temple. (Drawing from 18th cent.)

maps, the remains of which have largely been preserved. A street leading from the harbour square and forming the boundary between the Pisan and Genoese quarters, continued within the quarter, where it was called the Street of St. Anne *structures* because it passed the nunnery and church of that name. Remains of the church probably exist beneath the present Church of St. Andrew, which has an enormous subterranean vault. Other important buildings are buried beneath modern structures. It is here that we are likely to find the residence of the Grand Master of the Order of Templars, as well as another church, both mentioned in the sources. The "Templar of Tyre" described this neighbourhood as follows:

"On the other side [of the quarter] towards the Pisan quarter stands another tower and near it, above the Street of St. Anne, is a magnificent palace which belonged to the Master of the Order. A little further on, above the Monastery of St. Anne, is another lofty tower containing bells and also a tall and magnificent church."

THE HOSPITALLER QUARTER

This quarter is situated at the northern end of the old city. At the final stage of its development, at the beginning of the 13th century, it was the most extensive of the city quarters, but seems to have been composed only of conventual buildings.

From the middle of the 12th century the Hospitallers maintained a house and *12th century* hospital at Acre. Theodorich (1172) reported: "The Hospitallers likewise have founded a stately house there." The first nucleus of the quarter seems to have

105

Acre, Templar gate tower, second floor

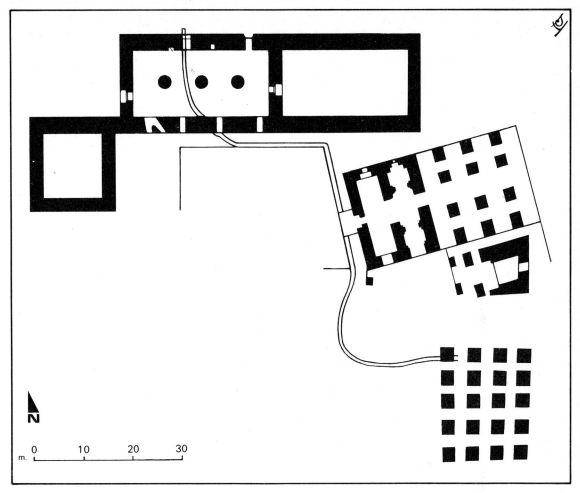

Acre, Hospitaller's Conventual Buildings (General Plan)

been in its southern sector around the *"Posta"* building, whose foundations date from the early Arab period, and the Hospitallers had probably enlarged an old Arab caravanserai. After the Moslem capture of Acre in 1187, Saladin founded a "Maḥkama" or theological college, in the Hospitaller house. The Order recovered its property when the Franks retook the city. With the loss of Jerusalem it became necessary to find quarters for the Master of the Order at Acre and to construct there all the other buildings required for lodging the various ranks of brothers.

In 1193, as the Hospitallers' area was too small for their needs, Guy de Lusignan granted them a large tract extending from the Gate of St. John (the "Hospital Gate") in the north wall of the city to the "Hospital Tower," which stood not far from the sea. In the decade from 1194 to 1204 the Hospitallers erected here a complex of huge and magnificent structures, whose remains include the famous "crypt" and other impressive buildings. In the 13th century

expansion in the 13th century

107

the Hospitallers' quarter contained four blocks of main buildings—the *"Grand Maneir,"* the Infirmary *(Domus Infirmorum),* the Church of St. John, and store-houses *(La Vote).*

The *"Grand Maneir"* was the residence of the Grand Master and also contained offices and a refectory. Its area partly coincides with that of the Turkish citadel, which was later built over its halls after they had been filled with earth. The refectory, situated in the southern part of the complex, has been preserved in its entirety and is today known as "The Crypt of St. John." North of this enormous compound, between it and the city wall, ran a street. South of the refectory a vaulted street, also completely preserved, separated the "Maneir" from the buildings of the Infirmary. The latter's eastern section is probably the *"Posta,"* while the western wing is buried beneath the Turkish baths, today the Museum.

South of the Infirmary was the Church of the Order dedicated to St. John, its location unknown. South of the *"Posta"* is a spacious, sturdily built, groin-vaulted hall, still completely preserved, identifiable as "the Vault" *("La Vote")* or dry-provision store of the Order. An underground tunnel, still intact, connected the supply hall with the refectory, perhaps to facilitate the transfer of foodstuffs.

These identifications are based on maps of the period, as well as on a single document of 1253 which refers to all the landmarks and hints at their location. In addition, the Hospitallers owned another very large building in the new Montmusard quarter, known as the *"Auberge",* or Hostel, which housed the combatant knights of the Order (the Brothers-at-Arms), commanded by the Marshal. According to the sources, the building was 300 metres long and had a spacious courtyard.

OTHER QUARTERS

In addition to these four quarters, there were special quarters on the north-east of the old city for the Teutonic Order, the Patriarch, and the Cathedral Church of St. Cross, possibly the present Great Mosque (al-Jazzar). Their remains are buried just below the surface and their size is indicated by the fact that an archaeological *tel* stands here to a height of over 6 metres above the Crusader level. The excavation and clearing of this mound would probably lead to the uncovering of interesting structures.

The definitely demarcated quarters did not take up the whole of the city's area. A considerable part of it was "neutral" and belonged to the crown or to sundry churches, nobles and burgesses. The royal market *(Funda Regis)* was situated in the north-eastern part of the city, on an important east–west thoroughfare. It was a complex of a market place, customs house, seat of the "Court of the Market" *(Cour de la Fonde),* and an inn. Ibn Jubayr has left us a colourful description of the *Funda Regis* of Acre:

109

Acre, Hospitallers' infirmary

Acre, Crypt of St. John (refectory)

Acre, "La Vote" (Hospitaller stores)

"We were taken to the custom-house, which is a khan prepared to accommodate the caravans. Before the door are stone benches, spread with carpets, where are the Christian clerks of the customs with their ebony ink-stands ornamented with gold. The merchants deposited their baggage there and lodged in the upper storey. The baggage of any who had no merchandise was also examined in case it contained concealed merchandise, after which the owner was permitted to go his way and seek lodging where he would."

THE MONTMUSARD QUARTER

As has been mentioned, a new quarter known as Montmusard developed north of the old city walls and remained undefended until the middle of the 13th century. Scholarly opinion is divided on the meaning of the name and its derivation. Some trace it to the French, interpreting it as "Knaves' Hill"; others see in the name the Arabic word *Mazar* which means a sacred tomb. The quarter has vanished completely. Although the remains of Crusader structures are discovered frequently when modern foundations are dug in that part of Acre which is outside the walls, there is no possibility of identifying the buildings of the quarter. The only reliable sources for determining the general plan are maps of the city

111

and fragmentary 13th-century chronicles. The suburb was surrounded by a double line of ramparts erected by King Louis IX of France between 1251 and 1254. It was inhabited *inter alia* by Christian Syrians and most likely also by Jews. Large portions belonged to the Hospitaller and Templar Orders and here there were palaces, markets and cattle sheds. Another part belonged to the Bishop of Bethlehem. Various religious houses and churches were also situated there, and a special area was occupied by the Franks of English origin.

CHURCHES AND MONASTERIES

The sources award Acre no fewer than thirty-eight churches. The cathedral church, the Church of St. Cross, was located in the north-east of the city on the edge of the Hospitallers' quarter. Among the city's parish churches, St. Michael's, in the north-west of the city on the shore, gave its name to the nearby city gate, and St. Andrew's, situated on the shore near the south end of the head-

St. Andrew's church (Drawing from 1681)

112

land (Cape of Storms), was apparently the church of the Commune of St. Andrew, which played a prominent part in the history of the kingdom in the 1230's and 1240's. Its location at the tip of the cape made it one of the prominent landmarks of the city, and it is referred to in navigational instructions.

St. Andrew's

Remains of the church were seen by many travellers who visited Acre after its destruction. A drawing of 1681 enables us to reconstruct the building. It was a fine Gothic structure with a nave and two aisles, lit by lancet windows and surrounded by blind arcades of pointed arches. It had three portals, one of which was pulled down after the Moslem capture, taken to Cairo and re-erected in a mosque. The remains of the church disappeared at the end of the 18th century. At the beginning of the 19th a small Greek Orthodox church dedicated to St. John was built on its ruins, which are near the modern lighthouse. Under it, Crusader crypts belonging to the old church have been found.

The Military Orders also maintained churches, while numerous religious orders had houses at Acre—the Carmelites, the Benedictines, the Dominicans, the Augustinians and the Franciscans. The Franciscan monastery was founded by St. Francis of Assisi, who was at Acre in 1219. There were also nunneries belonging to the Augustinians, the Sisters of St. Claire, St. Lazarus, St. Anne, St. Catherine, St. Brigit and others.

Acre, Crypt of St. John (vault)

ASCALON

geographical features

Throughout its long history Ascalon was one of the most wealthy and flourishing maritime cities of the country, because its geographical position is superior to that of the other coastal cities south of Jaffa. A belt of shifting sand reaches far inland to cover wide areas of the Judean plain (Philistia). As the lack of fertile soil and water prevented the establishment on the coast of large towns supporting themselves by trade and agriculture, all the ancient cities of the Judean plain—Yavne, Ashdod and Gaza—were set up on the edge of the dunes, some miles from the shore, and connected to a daughter-city with a port on the coast. Only at Ascalon does the belt of shifting sand cease, giving place to fertile soil with abundant water on the coast itself. This phenomenon is caused by the broad bed of the River Shiqma (Wadi al-Ḥesi) which here flows into the sea, bringing with it large quantities of rich alluvium. Thus Ascalon was the only locality where a city could arise on the triple basis of agriculture, commerce and maritime activity. As an Arab geographer puts it: "At Ascalon there is the conjunction of an excellent site, natural defensibility and the combined advantage of soil and sea."

Despite these advantages Ascalon never developed into a great port; the sea is dangerous with currents and high winds, and the shore is low. Nevertheless, much maritime activity went on there and, in the Roman and Byzantine periods, a special harbour known as Ascalon-Maiumas was constructed in the estuary of the River Shiqma.

prosperity in earlier periods

Ascalon's sandy soil was excellently suited to the growing of fruit trees and a variety of vegetables which acquired a wide reputation, such as the Ascalon onion or Ascalot (Shallot). Water is found in numerous wells within the city walls and its location on the caravan route to Egypt further augmented its commercial wealth. On the eve of the Crusaders' arrival the city was described in these words:

"Ascalon on the sea is a fine city, and strongly garrisoned. Fruit is here in plenty, especially that of the sycamore tree, of which all are free to eat. The Friday mosque stands in the market of the clothes-merchants, and is paved throughout with marble. The city is spacious, opulent, healthy, and well fortified. The silkworms of this place are renowned, its wares are excellent, and life there is pleasant. Also, its markets are thronged, and its garrison alert."[27]

At the time of the Crusader capture of Jerusalem, Ascalon, like all the maritime towns of the country, was held by the Egyptians, whose control there was based on their superiority at sea. They made great efforts to fortify and defend the city because of its location and its strategic value as a bridgehead and supply base across the desert of Sinai, and as a barrier against raids and invasions into Egypt.

The Crusaders first saw the walls of Ascalon during the decisive battle with the Egyptians, which was fought near the city in August, 1099. Victory gave the Crusaders control of Jerusalem and the northern part of the Judean plain. After the Egyptian defeat the city faced capture by the Christians. Its inhabitants offered to hand it over to Raymond of St. Gilles on condition that he permit all those who wished to leave the city and go to Egypt. The Moslems also proposed paying a tribute of twenty thousand dinars. These offers led to a quarrel among the Crusader leaders, since Godfrey de Bouillon, now sovereign lord of the realm, would not consent to deliver the city to Raymond. As a result the Crusaders withdrew, neither capturing the city nor taking the money.

In 1100 the country's maritime towns, which remained in Moslem hands, came to an agreement with the Franks, but the friendly relations did not last long. In the years 1101–1104 all but Ascalon were captured. While the assistance and shelter offered by the coastal towns was valuable to the Egyptians, they were not vital to the defence of their own country. On the other hand the loss of Ascalon, whose importance lay not in her trade, but in her strategic position, would lay the way open for the invasion of the Land of the Nile; hence the Egyptian defence of it was staunch and courageous. The city's garrison was relieved *key military* four times a year; a military stipend was paid to all its inhabitants, even to *stronghold of* women and infants. The Egyptian fleet kept watch over the city and its surround- *Egyptians* ings and prevented invasion by sea.

"That monarch [i.e. the Caliph of Egypt] and his princes felt the utmost solicitude for Ascalon, realizing that if it should fall and come into the power of the Christians there would be nothing to prevent our leaders from invading Egypt. They regarded Ascalon as a bulwark---As long as Ascalon held out and our people exhausted their zealous efforts upon it, the Egyptians themselves might enjoy the coveted peace."[28]

The Crusaders, for their part, could not suffer with equanimity the presence of an enemy base so close, for the Moslems used Ascalon as a base for dan- *skirmishes* gerous long-range raids, which sometimes reached the walls of Jerusalem. The struggle for the city, so vital to both sides, dragged on for decades. Battles and sharp clashes occurred in its close vicinity in the years 1101, 1115, 1123, 1125 and 1128. These devastated the surrounding area, for the Crusaders uprooted and destroyed all the plantations and fields outside the city walls before retiring. On several occasions the city was in danger of falling, but at the last moment something always occurred to prevent a Crusader victory; so they came to believe that the city was protected by sorcery, and that it could not be captured. It is interesting that, despite constant hostilities, orderly commercial relations con- tinued between Ascalon and the Crusader kingdom. It is related of one of the *continuation of* governors of the city, Shams-al-Khilafa, that he was "more desirous of trading *trade* than of fighting, and inclined to peaceful and friendly relations and the securing of the safety of travellers."

When the Crusaders saw that they could neither take the city by storm nor prevent the Egyptians from carrying out sorties and raids which were ravaging southern Judea and even imperilling traffic on the highways, they determined to establish a chain of fortresses at strategic points about Ascalon. In the years *encirclement* 1136–1141 they built castles at Beit Govrin on the Ascalon–Jerusalem road, at Yavne on the road from Ascalon to Jaffa, and at Tel Tsafit on the road to Ramla. The function of these castles was twofold; to prevent sorties by the Egyptian garrison and to serve as bases for attacking and besieging Ascalon. This chain of fortresses sharply reduced the Moslem raids and restored peace to the entire region of southern Judaea and the Shephela. At the beginning of 1150 an additional castle was established in the city of Gaza, which had been in ruins for two generations. The building of the Gaza fortress completed the ring of investment about Ascalon, for it cut the land route from Egypt. Henceforward reinforcements and supplies could reach the city only by sea.

In 1153 the Crusaders braced themselves for a renewed effort. The siege and capture of Ascalon are described in detail and dramatic fashion by William of Tyre, who was probably present when the events took place.

The siege began before the Crusaders had intended. At the beginning of January, 1153, they had started a limited raid whose purpose was to destroy the plantations still remaining in the neighbourhood of the city, in retaliation for *siege (1153)* the Ascalonite forays into areas of Judea. But upon seeing the city walls and the panic which seized its inhabitants and defenders, the Franks decided to exploit the unexpected opportunity and to lay siege to the city. When the decision was taken, all the knights of the kingdom were summoned to report for service. With them came the citizens of various cities. The dignitaries of the Church also appeared with the "True Cross." Each unit set up its own separate camp, with the king's tent at their centre. The Crusader fleet under the command of Gerard of Sidon sailed into the offshore waters to beleaguer it from the sea. Ascalon was amply supplied with food and war materials, and its defenders were numerous and well-trained. The garrison defended the walls loyally and tirelessly, and at night kindled great glass lanterns which shed light on the ramparts and assisted the guards. The siege lasted two months.

At the end of the second month, at Easter, a caravan of pilgrims arrived in the country. These were mobilized by royal order and the mariners were prohibited from returning to Europe, all being summoned to take part in the siege and receiving remuneration from the king. The ships then in the ports of the country were purchased and brought to the coast near Ascalon, where they were dismantled, their timbers used for war machines and palisades, and their masts for battering rams. The most important of the war machines was one known as "the tower." The Crusaders attacked the walls with renewed energy and, with the help of "the tower", managed to scale one sector and to shoot from it into the town and upon the adjoining walls; but they lacked sufficient strength to force a decision.

In May, 1153 events took an unfavourable turn for the Crusaders. A diversionary attack from the direction of Damascus indeed failed, but an Egyptian fleet was able to run the blockade from the sea by scattering the Crusader fleet and capturing several of their ships. The city's food supply was renewed and part of

116

the garrison relieved. The struggle began afresh, the spearhead of the Crusader attack being directed against the eastern part of the walls by the Jerusalem Gate. "The tower," made of wood covered with hides, continued to be their most effective and terrible weapon. News of it reached distant Damascus, where a Moslem chronicler called it "the cursed tower." As William of Tyre said, "In comparison with the ills which assailed them from this tower, all the trials which the citizens endured at other points, however hard, appeared light." The besieged determined to set it on fire by throwing down huge piles of faggots to cover the area between the wall and the tower and pouring inflammable materials upon them. The burning faggots kindled part of the tower, but an east wind blew the flames upon the walls, which burnt the night through and then collapsed. Part of the tower fell with them. The Franks saw in this the hand of God and arrayed themselves to storm the breach. But the Templars, who reached it first and wanted to keep the city's plunder for themselves, seized the breach and permitted entry only to their brethren. When the Moslems saw that no more than forty Templars had penetrated and that no other soldiers were following them, they attacked the Franks, driving them from the breach by a supreme effort, and blocked it with a strong palisade. The Knights Templar were butchered and their corpses hung on the walls.

abortive breakthrough

The king summoned his nobles to a council in which most of those present, including the king himself, expressed the view that the siege must be raised. But the Patriarch and the Hospitallers, who were for the continuation of the siege, were able ultimately to convince the meeting, and it was resolved to persevere. This was the decisive point, for the Moslems were at the end of their strength. When they saw that the Crusaders were about to renew their attack, they asked for a truce in order to bury their dead, and handed over to the Franks the bodies of their coreligionists which had been hung upon the walls. During the truce a meeting of the citizens was held, during which one of the notables implored his people to surrender: "For fifty years [we have] waged a dangerous and difficult struggle against this redoubtable people, so persistent in their purpose. The hope of preserving this spot whence we derived our origin and of defending our wives and children, and that far greater privilege, liberty, has ever led us on. Even now, not one among us has less inclination to resist. But the army is wasted away, the supplies are exhausted and the burden of hardship is unendurable."[29]

He proposed, therefore, to cede the city to the king on condition that the inhabitants be permitted to leave with their families and property. The offer was accepted, and a deputation from the city obtained the king's oath to carry it out. On the 19th of August, 1153, a three days' truce was proclaimed. The inhabitants left so speedily that, two days later, Ascalon was empty. The refugees wound their way slowly along the road to Egypt, escorted by the king's horsemen as far as al-'Arish on the Egyptian frontier. Meanwhile, the Franks entered the city with shouts of victory. The great mosque was consecrated as the Church of St. Paul and the king divided the lands within and about the city among those worthy of reward. He turned the city and the surrounding territory into a sep-

capitulation

117

arate seigneurie, which he gave to his brother Amalric, Count of Jaffa. The borders of this seigneurie were almost identical with those of Byzantine Ascalon and with the *kura* (territory) of the Arab city.

Frankish town

The conquest of Ascalon brought the frontier of the Crusader kingdom to the Sinai Desert, between Rafaḥ and al-'Arish, the city being separated from the frontier by two fortresses, Gaza and Darom. The danger of an Egyptian invasion had passed, for Egypt's forward position had fallen; the way was now open for intervention and the attempted conquest of Egypt, in which the Franks were to be engaged for fifteen years. Ascalon became a Christian city, but it may be supposed that a considerable number of Moslems resettled there. We know that there were Jewish, Samaritan and Karaite inhabitants. The Crusaders also settled large numbers of Christian Syrians there. Very little is known of the thirty-four years of Frankish rule in Ascalon.

After the battle of Hattin (1187), Saladin reached Ascalon. At the time of his arrival he already held all the towns on the northern coast of the country. The sultan determined to capture the city before conquering Jerusalem, for he wished to open the direct route to Egypt, and as long as Ascalon was not in his hands this road was closed to the Moslems. Before laying siege to the city, Saladin captured all the castles in the vicinity. In order to hasten its surrender, he brought to the city the king, Guy de Lusignan, and the Master of the Order of Templars, who were in captivity in Damascus, promising them their freedom if they succeeded in persuading the inhabitants to yield. The king and the Master of the Templars appealed to the inhabitants of the town (there were no knights there

siege (1187)

at the time), and begged them to lay down their arms, but the burgesses of Ascalon answered the entreaties of their hapless king with curses and imprecations. After this disgraceful scene the Moslems began the siege, which lasted a fortnight. The valiant defence by the city's inhabitants inflicted heavy losses upon the Moslems, and only after their sappers had been able to breach the walls and an Egyptian fleet had besieged the city from the sea, did the burgesses of Ascalon beg for terms. Those of the inhabitants who wished were permitted to leave with their possessions for Jerusalem. A number remained behind, including the Syrian Christians whom the Sultan persuaded to stay and, apparently, part of the Jewish community. Mosques that had served as churches for thirty-four years now reverted to their original use, while the city walls and towers were repaired and manned by a Moslem garrison.

Ascalon's vicissitudes did not end here. In 1191 the wheel of fate turned once more. Richard Coeur de Lion, at the head of the Third Crusade, inflicted a heavy defeat upon the Moslems at Arsuf (September, 1191). The Moslems faced the danger that Richard, who had meanwhile reached Jaffa, would at once march upon Jerusalem. Knowing that he could not defend both Jerusalem and Ascalon

Saladin's decision to destroy Ascalon

against Richard, Saladin was forced to decide which of them he must abandon. At the council which met in his tent it was clear that for all the strategic importance of Ascalon, the Moslems could not permit the Holy City to be sacrificed in its stead. Saladin decided the issue with the words: "I take God to witness I

118

would rather lose all my children than cast down a single stone from the walls. But God wills it; it is necessary for the Moslem cause, therefore I am obliged to carry it through."

The work of destroying Ascalon began at once and was carried out under the personal supervision of the sultan, the commandant hiring labourers and builders in the city markets to carry out the destruction of their own large and beautiful city. Saladin's biographer, Beha a-Din, who was present, described the *destruction* terrifying scene: "When these people [upon whom the work of destroying the city had been imposed] entered the town, there arose a wail of grief and a terrible weeping, for the city was comely and pleasant to the senses; its walls were strong and its buildings beautiful." The inhabitants, who had been sentenced to expulsion, began to sell their property for next to nothing and went into exile in Egypt. Some of them, chiefly the Jewish community, left for Jerusalem, thus renewing its Jewish settlement, which had been prohibited under the Franks. When tidings came of the renewed Christian advance, the sultan ordered the city's buildings to be burnt. Those inhabitants who had not managed to leave lost all their possessions. The walls and towers were filled with wood and burnt down. Part collapsed, but the work of demolition was difficult, since the walls were very thick and resisted the fire and the hatchets of the labourers. The city burned for twelve days, during which the sultan and his sons supervised the work in person. Ascalon's principal fortification, the "Tower of the Hospital" or "Tower of Blood," withstood all attempts to destroy it and fell only after repeated onslaughts. The collapse of the tower marked the end of the work of destruction, and the sultan left behind him a heap of smouldering debris. The city lay in ruins for the second time in a generation. At this time Richard Coeur de Lion was in Jaffa, where his knights were taking their fill of the city's delights. Rumours of the destruction of Ascalon did not reach him at first, and when at length the news was brought he determined to set out immediately; but his knights refused to abandon their pleasures.

The full impact of the destruction of Ascalon, which prevented the Crusaders from occupying it, cutting the road to Egypt and setting up a strong base for the march against Jerusalem, was understood by the far-sighted amongst them. One chronicler wrote: "Had they tried to save Ascalon, the whole land would have fallen into their hands." The decisive importance of the city was thus clear.

In January, 1192, after the Crusaders had despaired of winning the Holy City, Richard Coeur de Lion set forth with Henry, Count of Champagne, to fortify the deserted Ascalon. When they arrived, they found the town utterly destroyed. *Frankish* The country had suffered a severe winter that year; rain had turned the soil of *rebuilding of* the coastal plain into a quagmire, the sea was stormy and the supplies which had *Ascalon* left Acre did not arrive, while a number of ships that did were wrecked by the heavy gales. Despite these difficulties the Crusaders worked assiduously to rebuild the ruins, Richard and all his nobles labouring with their own hands. Reconstruction went on for four months, at the end of which the walls stood once more. But the results of their labours were destined to be ephemeral.

119

In the summer of 1192 both sides, weary of constant fighting, negotiated for peace. The principal point of dispute which prevented an agreement from being reached was the city of Ascalon. The Moslems' chief condition was the destruction of the city and the castles built around it (Darom and Gaza had been captured in the spring and refortified by the Crusaders). Richard could not agree to this but, anxious to obtain peace without giving up the city, he made an unprecedented proposal: that Ascalon be held by him in fief from Saladin and that he, the Christian King of England, be regarded as a vassal of the Moslem ruler. The sultan, who could on no account tolerate a Christian garrison in the town, replied with the counter proposal that the Christians accept Lydda and its surroundings in exchange. The Franks replied: "We cannot by any means permit that one stone of its fortifications be dismantled. We cannot suffer that it should be said of us in this land [that we had consented to so shameful a deed]." Negotiations reached a stalemate and hostilities began anew, but talks continued simultaneously, with Ascalon as the issue. The Moslems even agreed to cede the Church of the Holy Sepulchre in Jerusalem to the Christians, but to no avail.

peace negotiations

By August, 1192, Richard, wanting to go home, was willing to sign a peace treaty at almost any price. Ascalon faced destruction less than three months after its resurrection. According to one of the conditions of the treaty, the destruction was to be carried out by the Moslems, accompanied by a force of Frankish observers. When the Moslems arrived at Ascalon, the Christian garrison refused to leave the walls, not because they wished to prevent the destruction, but because they had not received their pay. Only when the king's envoy arrived with part of the money due to them did the garrison evacuate the city. The Frankish contingent aided the Moslems in the work, each side being allotted its share of the wall for demolition. The ruins of the hapless city remained in Moslem hands, and no effort was made to resettle them.

second destruction

More than fifty years later the Franks returned to Ascalon. Theobald, Count of Champagne, began to build a castle on the ruined site, but the restoration of the city and its walls was no longer considered since there had been no settlement there for over two generations. On Theobald's departure Richard of Cornwall continued the work of raising "a castle with double wall, many towers and a moat." A formal peace-treaty was signed between Richard and the Sultan of Egypt, restoring the whole of southern Judea and the Shephela, including Ascalon, to the Franks.

Upon completion, the castle was handed over to the governor appointed by Frederick II Hohenstaufen, titular ruler of the Kingdom of Jerusalem, who transferred it to the Order of Hospitallers. But by October, 1244 the Crusaders had been defeated in the battle of Hirbiya *(La Forbie)* and all the southern parts of the country had fallen into the hands of the Egyptians. The castle of Ascalon held out against an attack mounted by land and sea, and, after a short siege by the Moslems, was left in peace. In the summer of 1247 the Mamluks laid siege to the castle, again investing it by land and sea. A Frankish fleet was able to break the naval blockade, drop anchor near the quay of the castle and bring in

Mamluk siege (1247)

vital supplies while the Moslem craft were wrecked off the coast. When the Frankish fleet had returned to Acre, however, the Moslems renewed the struggle, building siege engines from the wrecks of their ships. Their engineers were able to mine beneath the walls and to penetrate the castle. Part of the Hospitaller garrison managed to escape by sea but the rest died. The Mamluks seem to have stationed a garrison in the castle, but in September, 1270 Baybars ordered the fortress to be destroyed and the nearby anchorage blocked up.

final destruction

This was the finale of the long and tragic history of the beautiful five-thousand-year-old city. Its fertile and well-watered land became the plantation of the Arab village of Jora which rose to the north of its ruins.

For a general description of the city and its fortifications little need be added to the account of William of Tyre:

description

"It lies upon the seacoast in the form of a semicircle, the chord or diameter of which extends along the shore while the arc or bow lies on the land looking toward the east. The entire city rests in a basin, as it were, sloping to the sea and is surrounded on all sides by artificial mounds, upon which rise the walls with towers at frequent intervals. The whole is built of solid masonry, held together by cement which is harder than stone. The walls are wide, of goodly thickness and proportionate height. The city is furthermore encircled by outworks built with the same solidity and most carefully fortified. There are four gates in the circuit of the wall, strongly defended by lofty and massive towers. The first of these, facing east, is called the Greater Gate and sometimes the Gate of Jerusalem, because it faces toward the Holy City. It is surmounted by two very lofty towers which serve as a strong protection for the city below. In the barbican before this gate are three or four smaller gates which one passes to the main entrance by various winding ways.

"The second gate faces the west. It is called the Sea Gate, because through it people have egress to the sea. The third to the south looks toward the city of Gaza, to which reference has been made above, whence also it takes its name. The fourth with outlook toward the north, is called the Gate of Jaffa, from the neighbouring city which lies on this same coast."[30]

Even today the city's line of defence can be followed in detail with the aid of the chronicler's description. The walls are built on an artificial mound which rises on the north and east to a height of seven to ten metres above its surroundings. This *tel* has a sloping masonry foundation topped by piles of stones, which have been covered during the centuries by a thick layer of wind-blown sand. The slanted medium-sized blocks at the base of the *tel* have been exposed for some seventy metres to the north of the wall, west of the Jaffa Gate. Facing the sea there are sections of a sloping stone wall which supported the sandy hill and prevented its collapse. At the top of this small artificial mound rise the walls and towers of the city. The circumference of the land wall is about one and a half kilometres and that of the sea wall some twelve hundred metres. The course of the wall can be followed throughout its length, although its remains are not always visible on the surface. The outer wall is two metres wide with casemates in various sections. Judging from drawings of the 17th and 18th centuries, it is probable that the top of the wall was crenellated. At irregular intervals along the

defences

121

Ascalon, glacis at north wall

walls stood round towers of varying sizes, each solid throughout, which protected keypoints such as gates, wall-corners and approaches. According to one historical source, the city wall had fifty-three towers, meaning that they must have been built at a distance of thirty metres one from another. Walls and towers were constructed of medium-sized blocks of local sandstone *(kurkar),* laid with very hard mortar compounded of broken potsherds, sand, lime and a great deal of ash, giving it a dark hue. Harder than the soft *kurkar* blocks of which the walls are built, the mortar survives after the masonry has crumbled, in the form of large lumps. The masonry courses are strengthened at weak points, such as angles and towers, by marble and granite columns taken from the Roman buildings. The barbicans or outworks described by William of Tyre are situated on the east and west sides of the wall, and compose part of the defences of the *Porta Major* or Jerusalem Gate and the *Porta Maris* or Sea Gate, shortly to be described.

gates

The city had four gates which created two axes of traffic, from north to south and from west to east. These intersect at the city centre, as is customary in Roman and Byzantine town planning. What remains on the surface today enables us to reconstruct the general plan of the gate areas. The access is not directly to the gate but runs along and at the foot of the main wall. The route passes a number of gates or secondary obstacles, constantly altering its direction but continually under the surveillance of a large tower placed at right angles to it, till it makes a sharp turn to the main gate and enters the city. On the east is the main or Jerusalem Gate, on the south the Gaza Gate, on the west the Sea Gate and on the north the Jaffa Gate.

At the Jaffa Gate the approach is from the west, parallel to the main wall. A gigantic square tower was placed at right angles to the road, projecting northwards from the line of the wall and the gate. The remains of this tower have largely disappeared, but are still discernible at a sharp turn of the mound, east of the entrance road to the Ascalon Antiquities Park, which encompasses the area of the ancient city.

main gate

The main or Jerusalem Gate was fortified strongly and with the utmost skill. A gigantic round tower was erected here, its remains surviving to a considerable height on a high sandstone hill at the edge of the modern camping area. From this tower a barbican turned south-eastward, descended the hill slope and, extending some thirty metres from the main wall, continued in a straight line southward. Remains of the barbican, in the form of giant wall blocks and a complete round tower, are piled by the road leaving the park. The course of the outer wall can be traced for some distance. The barbican seems to have ended opposite a large round tower, strengthened with grey granite columns, which is situated on the main wall. Here there appears to have been a wall which linked the barbican with the main rampart and contained an exterior gate. The approach into the city was thus from the south, parallel with the main wall and at its foot. By the exterior gate the road passed between the two walls, dominated by the walls and towers on both sides and by the great tower in front. Where the modern road

Ascalon, barbican and east wall

emerges today, in a small gulley at the foot of the great tower, a sharp turn westward, apparently past an additional gate, led to the central gate in the main wall.

According to William of Tyre, the Jerusalem Gate was defended by two very high towers and three or four gates in the barbican. The more northerly tower is visible today. The second was opposite the round tower to the south of the gate. This gate, which was square in form and which contained rooms, was still extant in the mid-19th century, but today has disappeared completely. The gate is identical with the one drawn on the Byzantine Madaba map of the 6th century. Its towers are the strongest fortified points in Ascalon and William of Tyre called them *"Quasi Praesidium"*,—(quasi citadel). Their strength and tactical advantages have caused various scholars to identify them as the citadel of Ascalon. But locating the citadel here would be in strange contrast to the plans of the fortifications in the other maritime towns, where the citadel was situated on the shore, close to the harbour. We are inclined to locate the citadel of Ascalon near the huge series of buildings at the south-west corner of the wall, since this corresponds more closely to a citadel site both when compared with the plans of the other coastal towns and in the light of historical references mentioned below.

sea gate   The Sea Gate is also heavily defended. In front of the main rampart, at a distance of three metres, a barbican or outwork wall stretches along the seashore. The south corner is still visible, near the famous wall into which projecting grey

124

granite columns were inserted to strengthen the courses. The barbican continues northward, parallel with the main wall, and terminates with a tower. The approach was from the north, the road entering the gate between the walls, then turning sharply eastward and reaching the main gate, which was built in a tower. This is located near the modern steps going down to the shore.

The Gaza Gate, situated on the south side of the wall, is also preserved and is recognizable by the huge blocks from its tower walls which lie on the hill slope. This tower may have had a defence system similar to the others, but if so the remains have been covered by sand driven by the frequent south-westerly winds.

As well as this system of fortified gates there were, as stated above, a large number of small towers some thirty metres apart along the line of the wall. Some of them are still visible, as well as casemates and posterns. In addition to the gate bastions there were two other large bastions, one, polygonal in form, at the north-west corner of the wall, the other between the Gaza Gate and the south-west corner.

It would be well to deal at greater length with the southern bastion, which was apparently the citadel of the city. The remains of several towers and thick walls are to be found at this point, extending eastward from the scarp of the seashore. *southern* Two central towers can be identified. One is at the very edge of the scarp and *bastion* includes half of a large barrel-vault supporting traces of a second storey. A wall continues from this tower across the beach to join the jetty built of many granite columns and coursed masonry blocks. Some distance east of this tower are the remains of a second tower, whose wall is preserved to a considerable height. Parts of other buildings are buried beneath the thick layer of shifting sand. On the north, within the city, is another rise, lower than the hill with the towers, and here also are segments of buried walls.

The "hill of the towers" is the highest point within the city's walled area. Judging by the height of the mound and the strength of the fortifications, there can be no doubt that here is one of the strongest defence points in the city, if not the strongest. A number of historical details encourage us to believe that this is really the most important fortified point in the city. Typically, these towers are the only ones known to us by name, doubtless because of their importance.

The eastern tower was known in the Crusader period as the "Tower of the Maidens" *(Turris Puellarum)*. It is mentioned by this name in a document of 1177, in which Sybil Countess of Jaffa-Ascalon bestowed it upon the Spanish Order of Knights of St. Mary de Montjoie (the Frankish name for Nabi Samwil near Jerusalem). The name appears again in the chronicles of the Third Crusade and has survived down to our own time among the Arabs, who call it in their translation *Burj al-Banat*. The western tower on the seashore is also mentioned in the Countess Sybil's grant, but its name is not indicated. The Arab historians, however, give us one more detail: describing it as "a building that commanded the sea and was as strong as a castle," and it was called the "Tower of the Hospital" *(Burj al-Isbitar)*, the "Tower of the Order" *(Burj a-Dawiyya)* or the "Tower of Blood" *(Burj a-Dam)*. The last name recurs in the Crusader chronicles of the Third Crusade as *Turris Sanguinum,* and according to a Moslem historian this was its name before the Crusader conquest; it was built in the Fatimid period at the end of the 11th century. Its strategic value is indicated by the fact that Saladin, while supervising the work of destruction at Ascalon, was urgently needed in the north at Jaffa, but decided to remain two full days longer in order to witness the destruction of the Hospital Tower. The structure was so strong that the labourers' hatchets made no impression upon it, and they were forced to fill its walls with faggots and set them alight in order to soften them. Only after two days and nights could the workers proceed to break up the tower, under the personal supervision of al-Afdal, son of the sultan. The completion of its demolition marked the end of the work of the city's destruction. That such attention was paid to this tower is proof that it was the chief fortress of Ascalon, even though it may not have been known as the citadel.

If we compare the plan of the Ascalon fortifications with those of the other maritime towns of the country, it is clear that the location of the citadels of Arsuf, Caesarea, Tyre and Sidon all sited at the end of the enceinte on the sea-shore and in close contact with the harbour, strikingly resembles the location of the "Tower of the Hospital," and the "Tower of the Maidens." It is therefore our conjecture that Ascalon, too, had a citadel which was part of its defence system, but was also an independent defensive unit. Surrounded by its own moat and with its own harbour close by, it was designed to receive assistance from the sea, both for aid against invasion and to facilitate flight when necessary.

The bastion concerned was apparently rebuilt by Richard Coeur de Lion and later destroyed in accordance with the peace terms signed by Richard and the Moslems. But while the walls of Ascalon remained in ruins after the destruction of 1192, the towers of the south-western corner were rebuilt in the years 1239–1240 by Hugh, Duke of Burgundy, and subsequently by Richard of Cornwall. The accepted view is that the entire circuit of the city walls was rebuilt in those years. But Crusader sources explicitly mention the erection of the *castrum,* meaning the castle, and not the fortification of the city as a whole. Hospitaller sources, which are particularly precise in their use of the terminology of fortification, leave no doubt of this. This was, according to the accounts, "a castle with excellent towers and moat" or "a castle with double wall with numerous towers and a barbican." There was naturally no point in fortifying the entire perimeter of the walls of Ascalon, which encompassed 500 dunams, when the city had lain uninhabited for forty years—since 1192.

In the account of the second siege, which took place in 1247, the location of the 13th century Crusader castle emerges beyond all doubt. The Egyptians invested it from the sea, assistance reached the Christians from Acre by sea, and it was from ships that the Crusaders brought supplies and reinforcements into the castle. This could only have been done by utilizing the shallow anchorage and jetty at the foot of the "Hospital Tower." The garrison's flight in boats after the citadel walls had been breached also shows that the area was the last Crusader fortress of the city of Ascalon.

126

Ascalon, Hospitaller tower.

The walls surround the area of Ascalon as it was at the height of its prosperity, and there is no doubt that their foundations and much of their construction belong to the period before the Arab conquest. Byzantine influence is seen in the town plan, in its gates and barbicans, and even in details of building. It may be recalled that the main or Jerusalem Gate, as shown on the Madaba Map of the 6th century, was built between two large towers exactly as in William of Tyre's account, and this is confirmed by the remains. On the testimony of Arab historians, the Byzantines destroyed the city walls and expelled the inhabitants when they evacuated the city in 640. The Umayyad Caliph 'Abd al-Malik rebuilt them in the middle of the 7th century, evidently on the Byzantine plan. The Fatimids, who captured Ascalon in the mid-10th century, repaired the fortifications, at least in the case of one tower, the "Tower of Blood" already referred to. When the place was captured, the walls were found in good condition and it is improbable that the Crusaders added much to the fortifications or altered them. After Saladin had recaptured the city, the walls were destroyed. We do not know the actual extent of the rehabilitation by Richard Coeur de Lion, but even if he rebuilt all the walls, which seems doubtful in view of the total evacuation of the town's population, the peace of 1192 followed and they were demolished again.

Ascalon's walls basically Byzantine

walls built by the Franks

As mentioned, the Crusaders did not restore the city walls after the reconquest of 1239, but built a castle in the south-west corner of the perimeter. This fortress was destroyed by Baybars in 1270. The remains of the city's fortifications as they appear today are therefore chiefly Moslem, on Byzantine foundations, the contribution of the Crusader builders being limited to small sections. The latest building period of the walls, apart from the south-west corner, is the end of the 12th century. After the destruction of the last Crusader fortress built by Richard of Cornwall, the city and its walls remained ruined and empty. In the middle of the 19th century the Egyptian Ibrahim Pasha made an attempt to fortify the city, but left the wall unfinished.

inhabitants

The total number of inhabitants in the area enclosed by the city walls is unknown to us; we only know that the Jews, Samaritans and Karaites, as noted by Benjamin of Tudela in the 1170's, numbered some 540—200 Jews, 300 Samaritans and 40 Karaites. According to our own estimate (see p. 27) the maximum population of Ascalon in the Crusader period was ten thousand. There is no doubt, therefore, that a great part of the city's walled area was not inhabited, but contained orchards and gardens, as was usual in the Middle Ages. Its buildings were apparently concentrated in the southern and central part of the enclosed area.

economic condition

The city apparently flourished before the Crusader period. It had important markets and most likely benefited from the caravan trade that passed along the *Via Maris* to Egypt. But the period of Crusader rule, which began after the town was almost completely abandoned, lasted too short a time to produce real economic prosperity such as it had enjoyed in the Byzantine epoch and at the end of the 10th century, according to the accounts of the Moslem geographers. As mentioned above, Ascalon's harbour was notoriously bad. Despite this there was

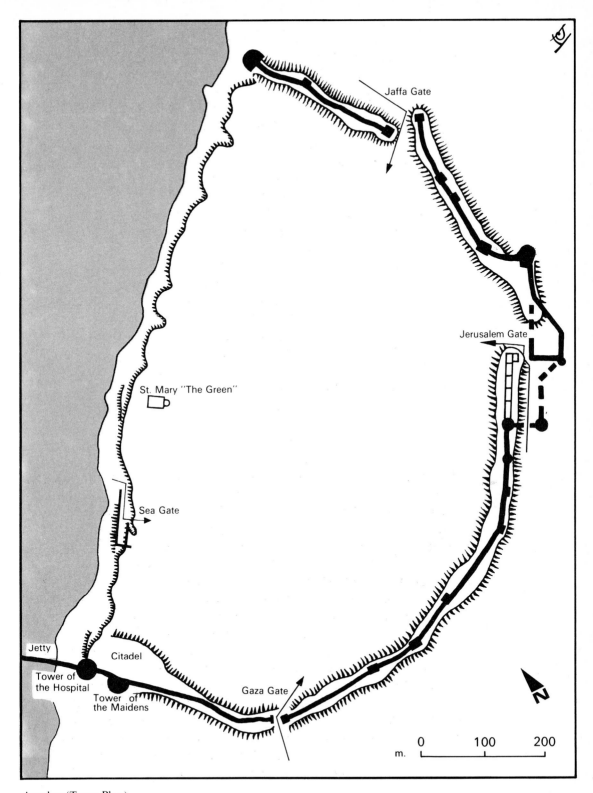

Jaffa Gate

Jerusalem Gate

St. Mary "The Green"

Sea Gate

Jetty

Citadel

Tower of
the Hospital

Tower of
the Maidens

Gaza Gate

0   100   200
m.

N

Ascalon (Town Plan)

considerable maritime activity; indeed the city held out at various times only thanks to its maritime connection. This was the case at the end of the Byzantine era, during the years of the Crusader blockade, and on several occasions in the Frankish period. There are remains of two jetties of Ascalon's harbour, one continuing the southern wall of the city, the other north of the Sea Gate.

jetties

Sources tell us of several important buildings within the city area. The spacious markets were situated near the intersection of the main streets. The city also contained a considerable number of places of worship, consecrated to the religions of its conquerors. In the Crusader period there were five churches, four Latin and one Syrian Christian. Only one of these can today be identified with certainty, that of St. Mary the Green *(Mahomeria Chatara, St. Maria Viridis)*, the al-Ḥadra or Green Mosque. The church, which existed in the Arab period, became a mosque under the Fatimids, and was restored to its previous function with the Crusader conquest. Its name and remains still survive in the Maqam al-Ḥadra on the western hill, the highest hill within the walls, adjacent to the sea wall. This *maqam* (a Moslem holy tomb) was abandoned and already in ruins in the middle of the 19th century. Remains of other churches were still to be seen at the beginning of the 20th century in the north and centre of the town. A church in the north wall was excavated during the 1920's and a three-apsed structure was found. These remains have almost completely disappeared today and traces of the Middle Ages within the city are extremely scarce compared with the proud relics of more ancient times.

structures within the city

ARSUF

The town of Arsuf, of Tel Arshaf, as it is now called, is one of the country's most ancient maritime cities, and was called after the Canaanite deity Reshef, god of fertility and the underworld, the Greek Apollo. A city called Rashpunah is mentioned in the victory list of King Tiglath-pileser of Assyria. In the Hellenistic period its name was changed to Apollonia and it underwent another transformation in the Byzantine age, when it became Sozousa ("the town of the Saviour"). After the Arab conquest, it reverted to its original, ancient Semitic name, as did most of the localities of Palestine, and was known as Arsuf. The Crusaders altered the name slightly to give it a French sound—Arsur. In their usual arbitrary fashion where the identification of ancient places was concerned, they decided that Arsuf was the Herodian Antipatris. Another Crusader source identified it with Ashdod (Azotus), city of the Philistines.

earlier history

Before the Crusader conquest Arsuf was a small fortified town and the centre of a district *(kura)*. Its vicinity was fertile and rich in plantations. Its woodland, which extended north-east of the town, was destined to be a battlefield between Richard Coeur de Lion and Saladin (the battle of Arsuf). The harbour of Arsuf was the scene of some mercantile activity and served as an intermediate port of call for coastal shipping plying between Acre and Jaffa.

130

After the capture of Jerusalem and the battle of Ascalon (1099), Arsuf offered to surrender to Raymond of St. Gilles, one of the Crusader leaders renowned for his chivalry, for he alone had kept his word at the capture of Jerusalem, harming none of the inhabitants who had yielded to him but letting them go in safety. For this he became known throughout the country, so that Ascalon, too, had offered to surrender to him. But at Arsuf, as at Ascalon, Godfrey, the un-crowned king of Jerusalem, refused to agree to Raymond's receiving the town. When their offer of surrender failed, the people of Arsuf begged Godfrey for terms. He demanded that a tax be paid and that his governor be received into the town. The governor appointed was a Flemish knight called Gerard d'Avesnes. *situation after conquest of Jerusalem*

Friendly relations did not last long. At the end of the summer of 1099 Arsuf ceased to pay taxes and Godfrey advanced upon the town to take it. The towns-people pinned their unfortunate governor to the walls and he was transfixed by his comrades' arrows. But Gerard was not killed and was ultimately able to re-turn to the Crusader camp. The Crusader knights failed to capture the town because they had no fleet with which to maintain an effective investment, while Arsuf's needs were supplied by the Egyptians. When the siege engines he had brought up were burnt, Godfrey, retiring, ordered the surrounding fields to be ravaged. *first attempt to seize Arsuf*

Considerable naval forces, chiefly those of Pisa, were concentrated off the shores of Palestine in the winter of 1099–1100, and with their assistance Godfrey was able to blockade the maritime ports, so that their supply situation became grave. In an attempt to run the blockade the Egyptian fleet broke into the har-bour of Arsuf and reinforced its garrison, which also attempted to deliver a counter attack towards Jaffa but fell into an ambush and most of its men were slain. After this disaster the people of Arsuf asked the Franks for a truce; a dele-gation sent to Jerusalem brought the keys of the city and a pledge to resume the yearly payment of taxes.

The people of Arsuf were not the only ones to come to an agreement with the Franks. At the end of April, 1100, similar agreements were signed with the other maritime towns. These friendly relations were, however, short lived, and the Crusaders accepted them only because they knew that without a strong fleet they could not capture the coastal cities, which enjoyed the protection of the Egyptian fleet. In the spring of 1101 the Genoese fleet appeared and furnished the Franks with the seapower they needed. King Baldwin I, Godfrey's brother and succes-sor, entered into negotiations with the Genoese in order to enlist their help in the war. These Italian merchants could only be persuaded by the promise of an "honourable compensation."

The first campaign jointly conducted was the capture of Arsuf. Baldwin laid siege to the town on the land side while the Genoese fleet closed in from the sea. The king ordered a moving tower to be built and brought up close to the walls. Owing to a fault in its construction, the tower collapsed under the weight of the Franks who manned it and about a hundred men fell from a great height, some upon the city walls. Those who fell into Moslem hands were crucified and exhib- *siege of Arsuf*

131

ited upon the ramparts. The Franks, incensed by the torments of their comrades, threw themselves upon the walls and scaled them with ladders. This desperate assault was successful and the walls were taken; the siege had lasted three days in all. When the Moslems saw that hope was gone, they asked for and were granted terms, according to which they were permitted to evacuate the entire population, though taking nothing with them. The inhabitants departed unscathed for Ascalon and the Frankish host entered the town. Baldwin left a garrison and proceeded immediately to Caesarea, which was also taken.

Arsuf captured

Arsuf and its territory remained in royal hands under a governor. The Genoese obtained their agreed share of the town in 1104, the king granting a third of it and of the agricultural area in the immediate vicinity. Arsuf continued to be a crown domain until approximately 1168, when "the Lord Johannes of Azotus," or in another document "Johannes of Arsur," appears in the grants for the first time. As the same man still appears without title in 1163, it must be supposed that the lordship became independent in the middle 1160's. The territory of Arsuf embraced the coastal plain from the Yarqon on the south to the River Poleg (Wadi Faliq) on the north. The seigneurie reached the foothills of Samaria on the east, and included Qalqilia and Jaljulia. At Arsuf, as in most other districts, the seigneurie included the same tracts as had belonged to the Arab *kura* before the conquest.

seigneurie

Arsuf was captured by Saladin at the end of August 1187, but reverted to the Crusaders after the famous battle of Arsuf in September, 1191 and was included in the renewed Crusader kingdom by the peace treaty signed between the Crusaders and Moslems in 1192, so that the town and lordship returned to their lords, the family of Arsur. Frankish civilian population was apparently renewed in Arsuf.

1187–1191

In the last decade of the 12th century, John d'Ibelin, constable of the kingdom, who was to be "the old sire of Beirut" *(le vieux sire de Baruth)* and leader of the country's barons, married Melisende, heiress of Arsuf. The seigneurie thus fell into the hands of the Ibelin family, which already held all the seigneuries in the southern coastal plain. After the death of the old lord of Beirut in 1236, the estate passed to John d'Ibelin-Arsur, who strengthened the walls of Arsuf in 1240. After his death in about 1260, the seigneurie passed to his son Balian, but he was unable to hold it as its rich lands lying to the east were already in Moslem hands. He therefore rented it (the castle, town and seigneurie) to the Order of Hospitallers (1261) in return for a yearly payment of four thousand bezants.

Arsuf passed to the Ibelins

As soon as they took over the town, the Hospitallers began to fortify it, walling the undefended suburb which had developed east of the town. At the time a truce was in force between the Franks and the Moslems, and Baybars saw in the work of fortification an infringement of the armistice, which prohibited the strengthening of defences. These were the last days of Arsuf. In the spring of 1265, after the capture of Caesarea, the Moslem army advanced upon the town under the direct command of Baybars, surrounding it completely. Their main efforts were directed to breaking through on the north-east, where the town moat

fortified by Hospitallers

was close to the inner ditch surrounding the citadel and was divided from it by a narrow tongue of land. The Hospitallers, who maintained a considerable garrison, conducted a gallant defence but were forced after a forty-day siege to abandon the town and fortify themselves in the citadel (26th April, 1265). There they were joined by the civilian population, some thousand people. After the capture of the town, Baybars opened the attack from the south, where the hill on which *Mamluk siege* the town stood reached almost to the same height as the citadel. The Crusaders dug a counter mine to the Moslems' mine and succeeded in setting it on fire, so that it caved in before reaching the foundations of the citadel wall; but the brave effort was in vain. Baybars dug a new mine and, after three days, the barbican near to the gate to the south of the citadel collapsed, and the Moslems reached the inner wall. The commander of the citadel, who had now lost ninety knights— a third of his force—saw that further defence was pointless, and asked Baybars for terms. The sultan agreed to release the surviving Christians, but after he had seized the citadel he broke his pledge and took the Hospitallers prisoner; they were sold as slaves in Cairo after they had been led in the victory parade.

Baybars gave the eastern part of the seigneurie to several of his emirs, and Arsuf itself remained a crown possession. The traveller Burchard, who visited it in 1283, described Arsuf as a village, and wrote that although the Hospitallers had lost the town, they were still paying its lord thirty-eight thousand gold bezants. The city remained in ruins. In the Mamluk period the Maqam (shrine)

Arsuf (Town Plan)

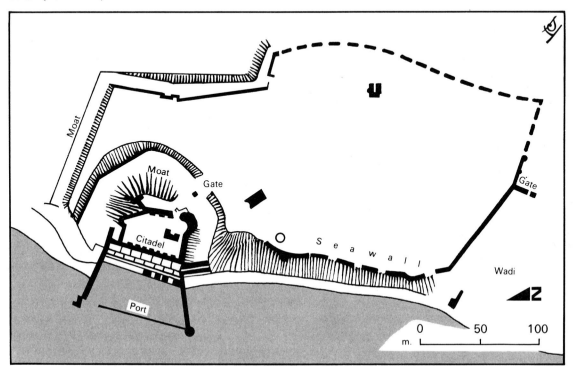

of Sidna 'Ali was built, in honour of Abu'l-'Alim who, according to Moslem tradition, was killed during the capture of Arsuf.

description of the ruins

The remains of Frankish Arsuf are amongst the most impressive on the coast of the Holy Land, especially the citadel, which rises like an eagle's nest over the seashore and the little harbour at its feet. The plan of the town's fortifications is identical with that of the other coastal towns of the country; a curtain wall encloses it on the north, east and south, and it is fronted by a masonry-revetted moat. The citadel is inside the wall at the corner commanding the harbour, but separate from the walls and has its own moat. The town had four gates at the cardinal points: one near the south-eastern corner, a second in the middle of the east wall, and the third, the Sea Gate, near the south-west corner of the wall on the seashore. The northern gate has not been found but is thought to have been situated at the north-east corner of the wall.

The approach to the south gate, near the entrance to the area of the ruins, was by a drawbridge over the moat; remains of the piers are partly preserved. A similar drawbridge existed at the east gate. The approach to the east wall and gate is now fenced off. The south wall survives to a height of several courses along the moat, at some distance from it. At the south-west corner the gigantic remains of towers are visible; a 19th century survey records that there was a spring here, but there is no trace of it today. The foundation of the sea wall also remains for the whole of its length.

The citadel is situated at the north-west angle of the town. Here a deep moat was dug between it and the city wall. The two walls join near the beach, forming between them a compact fortified triangle. The area of the citadel is two dunams; it has a glacis and curved barbican on its south side. The gate is to its east, approached over the moat by a drawbridge; some of the piers can still be seen. The citadel's east wall retains a number of vaulted chambers. The west wall is particularly massive and is built on supporting walls on the *kurkar* slope to prevent the collapse of the soft sandstone. Steps lead from the top of the wall to the harbour.

Arsuf, citadel, north side

134

Arsuf, harbour, north breakwater

The corners of two square towers have survived to a considerable height at the north-west and south-west angles of the citadel. Its north and south walls, continuing westward, adjoined the two jetties of the port. This is of small dimensions, but is better preserved than the other harbours of the period, and consists *breakwater* of two jetties, 30 metres in length, and a breakwater 100 metres in length which joins the northern mole. The entrance was from the south-west. Huge blocks of wall which have rolled down from the citadel lie on the narrow strip of beach near the harbour. The town area is 90 dunams, much similar to that of the town of 'Atlit. It contains some poor remains of vaulting. It may be assumed that the walls of Arsuf, like those of the other towns, were built on early Arab foundations, the plan of the Crusader fortifications corresponding to that of the ancient Arab and Byzantine works.

CAESAREA MARITIMA

It might be said that George Adam Smith summed up the entire mediaeval history of Caesarea in two brief sentences when he said: "As long as the land was held by men with interests in the west, the town triumphed over the unsuitable-

135

ness of its site. But when Palestine passed into the hands of an eastern people with no maritime ambitions, it dwindled and was finally destroyed by them."

Mediaeval Caesarea was no more than the shadow of the wealthy and populous city built by Herod "The Great" in the years 22–10 B.C. The capital of Palestine in the Roman and Byzantine periods, it was the last city to be taken by the

earlier history

Arabs. With the Arab conquest its population dwindled and its importance diminished; Herod's gigantic project, the port of Caesarea, already decaying at the end of the Byzantine period, became blocked and fell into ruins during the Arab era. The Arab geographers do not even mention its existence while the Frankish chroniclers, familiar with the works of Flavius Josephus, wrote that the city was practically without a harbour. William of Tyre reported: "This city has great advantages, but it is without a port. We read, indeed, that Herod, at great expense, endeavoured, without success, to construct a harbour there."

Despite its decline as a port, Caesarea was still a rich and beautiful place at the end of the Arab period, and the Arab geographers praised it. Al-Maqdisi wrote: "There is no city more beautiful nor any better filled with good things. Plenty has its wellspring here." Its main source of wealth was agriculture; nearby plantations yielded dates, oranges and lemons, and it was also renowned for its

decline of port

wheat, from which excellent white bread was baked, and its milk from the numerous buffaloes which lived in the swamps of the Crocodile River. The Roman aqueducts which brought water to Caesarea seem still to have been in working order at that time, and supplying abundant water for drinking and irrigation.

Although its trade had declined, Caesarea retained a certain commercial importance at the end of the Arab era, as can be deduced from the various spices found there, and especially the large quantities of pepper plundered by the Crusaders after its capture. These spices were mentioned in the account of the traveller Fetellus: "In the circuit of the city, among gardens, were various small caves, constructed of sawn stones . . . in which spices and aromatics were mingled in the fire, so that the whole city was redolent of the combining wafted odours."[31] Traces of a copper industry were found during the archaeological excavations on the site, and the hoards of gold and silver coins and fine gold ornaments then discovered point to the city's wealth at the end of the period.

The city was surrounded by a strong wall with iron gates, beyond which lay an open suburb. Its area in the Arab period is unknown, but it was probably not much more extensive than in Crusader times. In 1099, when the Crusaders were encamped before the walls of Caesarea on their way to Jerusalem, a considerable number of Jews were living in the city, which was under Egyptian rule and held a large garrison. The Franks made no attempt to capture it, as they were in haste to reach the Holy City, but after they had taken Jerusalem they began to harass the inhabitants of the Moslem coastal towns, by cutting off their food supplies and disrupting the orderly conduct of their trade.

In April 1099 the emirs of the coastal towns signed an agreement with the Franks and friendly relations were established. When Godfrey passed through

136

Caesarea, he was invited to a great banquet held in his honour by the emir of the city. After the banquet, upon reaching Jaffa, he fell ill, and his knights suspected that he had been poisoned at the feast; he never recovered.

After the capture of Arsuf in 1101, the Frankish army, led by King Baldwin I and supported by a Genoese fleet, advanced upon Caesarea. The fleet blockaded the city from the sea while the army attacked its walls and, after a fortnight of fierce fighting and intensive bombardment, scaled them. Organized resistance ceased and the Christians massacred the inhabitants indiscriminately. A large number of the citizens sought refuge in the mosque, which stood in the ruins of a Roman temple, now overlain by the ruins of the Crusader cathedral, but the sanctity of the place did not protect the fugitives, almost all of whom were butchered by the Franks in the intoxication of victory. Only the emir and the qadi of the city, and a number of women and children, were spared by the king and held for ransom: the qadi was ransomed by the Moslems of Acre, for a thousand bezants. The city was plundered and the stores of pepper found there were shared among the troops. The Genoese took from the great mosque a large goblet which was brought to Genoa and declared to be the Holy Grail, the emerald goblet used by Jesus at the Last Supper, and in which Joseph of Arimathea gathered the blood that flowed from the wounds at the crucifixion. The goblet is still at Genoa. This may be the grail mentioned by the Persian traveller Nasir Ḥusru, who saw it in 1047 in the great mosque of Caesarea. *capture of Caesarea*

After its capture, a third of the city was given to the Genoese, for it was on this condition that they had agreed to take part in its conquest. As befitted Caesarea's position in the ancient ecclesiastical hierarchy, it became the see of an archbishop, and the great mosque was converted into the cathedral church. The city and the adjacent countryside remained in the hands of the crown for seven years. In about 1108 it was made over to Eustace Garnier and became an independent lordship, one of the largest and most important in the Kingdom of Jerusalem, for its territory extended from a point north of 'Atlit to the River Poleg in the south. On the east it included the whole area of the coastal plain to the foot of the Carmel range and the mountains of Samaria. *seigneurie*

After the Crusader conquest, not only Franks but also eastern Christians and Moslems settled in the city. Its population was estimated at about five thousand (see p. 27). From accounts of travellers who visited the city in the 12th century it would seem that it had declined, in comparison with the pre-Frankish period, although its orchards and great fertility were still referred to. In this period the high-level aqueduct bringing water from springs north-east of the city ceased to function, although the low-level aqueduct which conveyed water from the Crocodile River appears still to have been intact. Commerce was largely underdeveloped, as may be deduced from the little interest shown by the maritime communes in obtaining commercial privileges in Caesarea. Apart from Genoa, only Pisa acquired privileges there. *economic conditions*

The city was captured by Saladin in the summer of 1187, evidently without fighting. In the summer of 1191 it was retaken by the Franks during Richard

Coeur de Lion's march from Acre to Jaffa. The Moslem inhabitants fled, and the Crusaders found it empty. We have no clear information as to what had become of the fortifications of Caesarea, yet even if they were dismantled by the retreating Moslems—which is not specifically stated in the sources—they had not been destroyed systematically as in other places, such as Ascalon. In a document of 1206 the city walls are referred to explicitly, although they may not have been complete or manned. Many of the orchards and vineyards in the vicinity were uprooted or neglected, as is indicated by another document of the same year, which mentioned most of them in the past tense.

1187–91

After its recapture by the Crusaders, a number of inhabitants returned to the city, and the property of the Frankish notables was restored to them. Although Richard Coeur de Lion attempted to give Caesarea and Jaffa to the brother of Guy de Lusignan, the deposed King of Jerusalem, the heiress of the lordship of Caesarea, Juliana, was able to annul the transfer and regain her ancestral inheritance.

King Jean de Brienne began to refortify Caesarea in 1218, with the help of the Hospitallers and of Duke Leopold of Austria. The work was carried out chiefly on the citadel, which lies on the seashore, but it is likely that the outer walls were also repaired. The work of reconstruction lasted for a month, and during this time the cathedral church was also repaired. The new fortifications were attacked by the Moslems some three years after their completion, at the end of 1220, when al-Mu'azzam, ruler of Damascus, advanced upon the city with a large force. The outer walls probably fell at once and the inhabitants fled to the citadel. The small Frankish garrison appealed urgently to the royal capital at Acre for help. As most of the Crusader force was occupied at the time at Damietta in Egypt, the Genoese forces at Acre came to the aid of Caesarea, agreeing to take responsibility for the citadel and to send it supplies and troops. But the Genoese were unable to hold out against the Moslem attack and evacuated the citadel by sea after a four-day defence, taking with them the inhabitants of the city. When the Moslems entered the citadel, they found it empty, and demolished the building. Even after this fresh destruction some of Caesarea's inhabitants returned to the town. In 1228 during the Crusade of Frederick II Hohenstaufen, the city walls were rebuilt by German pilgrims under the command of Heinrich of Limburg, but an Arab geographer describes the place at the end of the 1230's as "more like a village than a city."

1218–1230

The last revival of Caesarea was the splendid enterprise of Louis IX, the canonized King of France. The king, who had arrived in the country after his defeat and capture in Egypt, began to restore the ruins of Caesarea on the 29th of March, 1251. The fortification took a year to complete, and Louis remained throughout this period, taking a prominent part in the work of construction. The chroniclers relate that the king carried sand and soil on his back to build the moat and the ramparts. The magnificent walls of the city, as they appear today, are the result of this gigantic undertaking, and will be described below. It is not known how many inhabitants there were after its walls had been rebuilt,

St. Louis rebuilds walls

138

but it may be assumed that they were few. The city remained in the possession of the Lords of Caesarea.

The bitter end came for Caesarea in March, 1265. Sultan Baybars attacked on the 28th of February; the few Frankish defenders were unable to man the full length of the outer walls and the Moslems were able to scale them in a frontal attack, using ladders and ropes. The Franks retreated into the citadel, rebuilt by King Louis, which was surrounded by a moat filled with water from the sea. Baybars set up his headquarters on the artificial "acropolis" on whose summit stood the remains of the cathedral, and directed the siege operations from there. The efforts of his sappers to undermine the foundations of the walls failed because seawater seeped into the tunnels and because the walls had been reinforced with granite columns. A number of attempts were made to storm the citadel from the sea under cover of a heavy barrage by stone-throwing artillery. After a week's siege, the Crusaders gave up hope of saving the city and abandoned the citadel, retreating by sea to Acre. Baybars resolved to destroy Caesarea completely, fearing that if he left the walls and citadel intact, the Crusaders

end of Frankish Caesarea

Caesarea, capital at north gate

would have a base for renewed invasion against which he, without a fleet, would be powerless. The demolition of the city and its walls was systematic, and Baybars took part in it personally. When he left Caesarea, only miserable traces remained of the splendid city which had been continuously occupied for thirteen hundred years. As a traveller described it: "Now all of this has come to nothing," and the heap of ruins was hidden by deepening drifting sand.

description of ruins

The Crusader city, whose imposing remains were cleared and partly restored in the years 1960–1962, covered 120 dunams, in fact only the harbour area of the Herodian city. The ruins of Byzantine Caesarea, extending eastward far beyond the Crusader city walls, had been covered by sand drifts and the area was under cultivation in the Middle Ages. The Roman hippodrome near the Byzantine city wall was in the heart of the mediaeval orchards. The great obelisk, now

Caesarea Maritima (Town Plan)

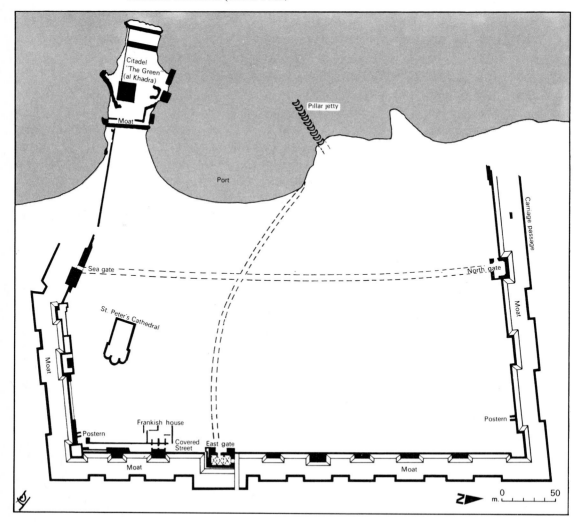

140

broken, stood to its full height of three metres in the centre and was known in the Crusader documents as *Agullia Sancti Petri,* "St. Peter's Finger." A contemporary guide book described it as "a very fair stone of marble, great and long . . . and there are two little stones which are round, large below and pointed above, which are called the candlesticks of our Lord"[32]. The small stones were the goal posts of the hippodrome, one of which still survives; the great obelisk is made of granite and not of marble.

The walls of the Crusader city as they appear today are the work of the masons employed by St. Louis. They are trapezoid in shape, the eastern side being 650 *walls* metres long and the northern 275 metres. A moat, 7 metres wide at the bottom, was dug in the sand and has a masonry counterscarp. At the foot of the walls is a battered glacis, 8 metres high at the point where it joins the wall. A wall rose 10 metres above the edge of the glacis, with sixteen towers, three on the north, nine on the east and four on the south. These towers projected seven to eight metres from the line of the curtain wall, which was pierced along its entire length *towers* with loopholes. With the exception of a small sector on the south side, the wall had been completely demolished to the lip of the glacis. It was built of small stones, tooled in the 13th century fashion and secured with strong white cement. As in all Crusader structures, the walls were of ashlar inside and out, with a rubble and mortar core.

Caesarea, east wall and moat

The city had three gates and three posterns. The main gate was on the east, in the middle of the wall, and was reached by a bridge over the moat. The gate plan was based on the principle of indirect approach. Its outer portal was at right-angles to the gate south of it; thus anyone crossing the bridge was confronted by a great tower rising above him. At the foot of the wall the entrance road turns south by the outer portal into the gatehouse. This large and magnificent hall, 15 metres long and 4.5 metres wide, is roofed with rib-vaulting. Anyone entering had to change direction by ninety degrees as he advanced, and turn to the right (westward). He then encountered another portal, and only when he had passed through this, did he gain access to the city. Both the outer and the inner entrances possessed defensive devices such as a portcullis, and a slit through which oil could be poured. *East gate*

Another gate is situated in the middle of the north wall. Here, too, a bridge crosses the moat, supported by a pier in the moat and by arches on the glacis. *other gates* The entrance gate is to the west; to enter the city at this point it was necessary to turn southward inside the gatehouse. The gate-chamber was rib-vaulted; the vaulting has collapsed but the corbels of the ribs are preserved and carry carved leaf designs which are among the most beautiful Crusader carvings in the Orient.

There are traces of another gate in the south wall. For reasons not clear to us, it was never completed. The gate-house and the outer portal facing westward were begun, but only the inner portal of the entrance was actually erected. The wall also had three posterns, one near the east gate and two more near the north-eastern and south-eastern corner towers. These two posterns led to the bottom of the moat; their purpose was to facilitate surprise sorties and the despatch of messengers and spies. The openings of these sally-ports had been blocked with good masonry, evidently before the last siege of 1265. There was an additional entrance to the city, not in the form of a gatehouse, at the west corner of the north wall; this was used for loaded carts.

Two phases of building can be distinguished in the city walls. The rampart and gates were built in 1251 by St. Louis, but in several places there are indications that the French king's masons utilized sections of the older walls.

As in all the Crusader coastal towns, a citadel was built on the shore of Caesarea at the corner of the city wall. It is separate from the wall and constitutes an independent defensive unit, sited so as to protect the city from sea-borne invasion, to secure unimpeded maritime communication in time of siege, to provide a refuge after the walls had been taken and to facilitate evacuation if no alternative remained.

The citadel of Caesarea is built on the southern breakwater of the ancient Herodian harbour. A broad water-filled moat separated the tongue of land from the mainland; on the other side a wall of massive blocks was erected, with square *citadel* towers on each side. The tongue is surrounded by walls on all sides. In the centre of the area rose a gigantic tower, apparently of three storeys, entered from the north-east and containing halls at ground level, now almost completely blocked up with sand. The walls were strengthened by a row of marble and gran-

143

Caesarea, east (main) gate

Caesarea, citadel and pillar jetty

ite columns laid between every three or four courses, a form of construction found in numerous Moslem and Crusader buildings. The citadel was built at some time prior to the city walls, probably as early as the 12th century.

port While the splendid ancient port was for the most part destroyed and blocked before the beginning of the Crusader period, there is no doubt that some maritime activity went on in the small bay formed by the two huge breakwaters of the Herodian harbour. To facilitate the access of ships to the shore, a jetty made of granite columns taken from the ruins of the Roman city was built on the northern side of the artificial bay. It is not clear when this primitive mole was built but it probably dates from the Crusader period.

structures within
the city Several important Crusader structures lie within the city area. On the east side of the wall runs a street of a type already referred to, and common in Crusader towns: it was provided with stone arches which carried a groined vault, or between which linen awnings were stretched. Holes were provided in the piers of the arches for tethering animals. In this covered street is a Frankish house built in eastern style, its rooms leading off from an inner court with a cistern in the centre; below ground level are silos and cellars. This type of building is also common in other Frankish towns. (See p. 373).

cathedral The cathedral church of the city stands on the top of the artificial hill raised by Herod to serve as the city's acropolis and on which a Temple of Jupiter formerly stood. Here lay the Arab city's great mosque, later converted to the Cathedral of St. Peter. We do not know when it was destroyed and when the church was built whose ruins are visible today. Excavations show that the re-

144

mains of the fine apses belonged to a church which was never completed; its builders evidently stopped work after the north wall they had erected began to bulge owing to the collapse of the ancient vaulting over which it was constructed. A smaller church, apparently with nave and one apse, was put up in place of the large unfinished structure. According to the authors of the *Survey of Western Palestine,* there was another church in the west of the town, not far from the jetty referred to above. No traces of this church, perhaps that of St. Lawrence mentioned in documents, remain today. From the documents of the period we know of other buildings such as a market *(funda),* shops, houses belonging to the Hospitallers, the Abbey of Mount Zion, the Church of Bethlehem and the Abbey of *Templum Domini.*

TOWNS OF THE INTERIOR

There were seven towns in the interior of the country in the Crusader period: Hebron, Ramla, Jerusalem, Nablus, Beit Shean, Tiberias and Banias. Five of these were walled on the eve of the Crusader advent, namely Jerusalem, Tiberias, Ramla, Beit Shean and Banias. Two, Hebron and Nablus, were left unfortified. All except Jerusalem were taken without fighting, as they lacked garrisons. The Fatimids, who theoretically ruled the entire country, maintained real control only in the maritime towns, with the help of their strong fleet. The populations fled from them on the approach of the Crusaders, but some returned in the course of time. Unlike the coastal cities, those of the interior remained inhabited by indigenous peoples, but during the Crusader period a decline took place in the populations of Hebron, Ramla and Beit Shean, while those of Jerusalem and Tiberias increased. Bethlehem and Nazareth, only small townships in the *townships* Arab period, grew and became towns. All the towns of the interior became the centres of seigneuries in the 12th century. After the battle of Hattin the Franks lost control of the interior of the country and, for a few years during the 13th century, held only Jerusalem (1229–1244) and Tiberias (1241–1247).

Caesarea, Covered Street

BANIAS - BELINAS

Located at the foot of Mt. Hermon, Banias lies on the most important road in the north-east of the country, commanding the main route from Damascus to Tyre at the point where it descends to the Hula Valley.

Control of Banias and its citadel not only secured passage over this important route, but also directly threatened the capital of Syria; the steep ascent is the *location* only natural obstacle, and beyond it the road follows a direct and easy path until it reaches Damascus. Likewise, Banias is the last obstacle for any army attempting to invade Western Palestine from the east. Indeed, throughout its history the location of Banias has been of such strategic importance that possession of it has continuously been disputed by rivals to the east and west.

Two fortified positions guarded this strategic area during Crusader times. One was the city of Banias and the other the castle of Subeibe, situated three kilo- *is Subeibe a* metres (1.6 km. as the crow flies) from the city, on a lofty spur. Most experts *Crusader castle?* assert that Subeibe was the citadel of Banias and that it was built by the Franks after the city was captured by them in 1129. However, a thorough examination of the sources shows that this assertion is not firmly based; the sources do not mention the existence of a separate citadel in the vicinity of Banias, but always refer to a citadel within the walls of the city, specifying a separate defensive unit within the city defences. William of Tyre described its position clearly: "There was a citadel in one part of Banias well equipped with arms and men with sufficient food for a short time."[33] Ibn al-Qalanisi left another clear indication when he reported: "The Franks who were in the town took refuge in the citadel and the bastions,"[34] showing that the citadel was connected to the bastions of the city wall. The position of the citadel becomes clearer if we follow the chronicler Ibn al-Qalanisi's account of the siege of 1157. The Franks "fled to the citadel" after the city was captured and the Moslems besieged them there. Later, when the Frankish relieving army approached and took by surprise "the two [Moslem] armies, that which was encamped before Banias to besiege it and that which was holding the road in order to prevent access to it, policy necessitated their withdrawal from thence and the Franks reached the fortress and relieved those who were holding it."[35] In 1157, Lord Humphrey gave "one half of the city of Banias"[36] to the Hospitallers. The royal confirmation mentioned "*Medietatem castelli Paneadensis.*"[36a] The castle of Banias is therefore identical with the city of Banias and, again, there is no mention of a separate castle. The citadel of Banias was thus a separate defensive unit, within the fortifications, and resembled the defensive arrangements of Jerusalem, Arsuf, Caesarea and Tyre. It is possible that Subeibe was indeed not the citadel of Banias, but an independent Frankish castle, though this is doubtful since no such castle is mentioned in the sources. True, a late Arab source (Ibn Shaddad) related that Subeibe was built by the Franks in 1129–1130 (H. 524), but it is significant that no Frankish chronicler or even contemporary Moslem mentioned the construction of such a great castle, or its whereabouts, until the end of the 13th century. The first Frankish source to mention the name Subeibe was Joinville, in his account of the attempt to capture it in 1253. It has already been pointed out some years ago that the name l'Assebebe mentioned in the Frankish list of seigneuries referred not to Subeibe, but to Ḥasbeya in Marj 'Ayun. Archaeological material available today cannot illuminate the problem because, apart from a superficial survey, no archaeological excavations have been carried out there. The only thing which is clear today is that Subeibe was not the citadel of Frankish Banias and that in its present form it is an Ayyubid-Mamluk structure.

earlier history   This is not the place to recount the history of Banias-Caesarea Philippi in the Roman and Byzantine periods. In the early Arab era it was a flourishing and well-populated city. Among its agricultural products were cotton and rice, and it was called "the granary of Damascus". The dense woods surrounding it were a famous hunting ground. The city seems to have been fortified, but its walls were destroyed or neglected. The chronicler of Damascus, Ibn al-Qalanisi, was the first to give specific information about the fortifications and citadel of the city, relating that Banias was given by the ruler of Damascus to the Isma'ili sect in 1126—the sect later known as the Assassins. Its leader, Bahram, began to fortify the city and the stronghold: "When he had established himself in Banias, he set about fortifying it and rebuilding what was in ruins or out of repair."

Banias taken by   In 1129 a great massacre was perpetrated against the members of the Isma'ili
Franks   sect living in Damascus. Their leader, Isma'il "the Persian", who succeeded Bahram after his death, seeing that he could not defend Banias, sent messengers to the Franks offering them the city and citadel in return for asylum to members of his sect. His offer was accepted by King Baldwin II, and the Franks seized control of the city.

1129–1132   No sooner had the Franks occupied Banias than it became a base for Frankish raids against Damascus. Baldwin II attempted to besiege Damascus in 1129 but was forced to retire. The area was handed over to a knight called Renier Brus and became the capital of a seigneurie. Between 1129 and 1132 the Franks strengthened the fortifications of Banias and its citadel. A truce came into force between Damascus and Jerusalem in 1132, but Shams al-Mulk of Damascus exploited the fratricidal conflict which broke out among the Franks and attacked Banias. It is clear from the account of the hostilities that the city was fortified to a very high degree. Its garrison was substantial, although the knights were at
Banias taken by   that moment with Renier Brus at Jaffa. William of Tyre reported that King
Moslems   Baldwin endeavoured to come to the aid of the city which, however, fell before he could reach it. The Moslems mined beneath the walls and were able to penetrate them; the Franks evacuated the outer defences and escaped to the citadel, but they soon surrendered and were taken prisoner. Shams al-Mulk sacked the

148

city and returned to Damascus, leaving a garrison. Among the prisoners was the wife of Renier Brus. The capture of Banias restored this strategic keypoint to the people of Damascus. With this grave menace to the Syrian capital removed, they now possessed a base for attacking the regions of the Kingdom of Jerusalem in the Ḥula Valley and the mountains of Naphtali.

At the end of the 1130's, decisive changes took place in political relationships in the East. Zengi, ruler of Mosul, grew stronger and began to threaten the *alliance between* Frankish principalities and the independence of the Moslem cities of Syria. He *Damascus and* captured Ḥama and Ḥims in 1138 and cast covetous eyes upon Damascus it- *Jerusalem* self. The ruler of Banias, Ibrahim Ibn Turgut, rebelled against the Emir of Damascus and capitulated to Zengi. Threatened with the loss of its independence, Damascus appealed to the Frankish infidels, offering to sign a formal treaty against Zengi, their common foe; after conferring with his court, King Fulk of Jerusalem consented to the proposed treaty. One of the principal conditions imposed by the Franks was that Banias should be captured from Ibn Turgut and ceded to them. Unur, the regent of Damascus, agreed to this condition, for, as William of Tyre explained, the Moslems "preferred that Banias be restored to the Franks whose favours they enjoyed, rather than to behold it in the hands of a hated and disloyal enemy."

In May 1140 a combined Moslem-Christian host advanced upon Banias to take it. This was an exceptional event in the history of Frankish-Moslem relations and both the Moslem and Christian chroniclers were keenly aware of it. William of Tyre reported: "Then might have been witnessed a strange and novel sight; a hostile people encouraging an enemy to the fiercest warfare and, as an ally, actually in arms for the destruction of a common foe . . ."[37]

The Frankish-Moslem armies operated in absolute harmony and unity. The siege lasted a month and was heavy and brutal. The besieged defended themselves desperately against the continued assaults of the besiegers, who maintained a ceaseless bombardment of artillery. Seeing that they could not subdue the city's defenders with such means as they had, the Franks erected a high tower of timber brought from the forests near Damascus. From the top of this tower, edged close to the wall, the besiegers commanded the outer fortifications and the buildings within and so made defence impossible. The besieged, losing hope, appealed to the Moslem commander, Mu'in a-Din, for terms. Comparatively moderate conditions were offered: the commandant of Banias was compensated for the loss of his city by the grant of another domain, while the inhabitants were permitted to leave with all their movable possessions. Mu'in a-Din per- *returned to the* suaded King Fulk and the Frankish leaders to agree to these terms, and the *Franks* defenders of Banias evacuated their city. Fulk restored it to its lord, Renier Brus, and a bishop was appointed to the see.

In the new political situation of the 1140's Banias had a different role to play. A close military alliance now prevailed between Damascus and Jerusalem and the citadel, though so near to the Syrian capital, no longer threatened it, but instead provided security and deterred the common enemy, Zengi and his son

149

and heir Nur a-Din. In this period Banias became a meeting place and hunting lodge for the Frankish and Moslem nobles. A description of such a hunt at Banias has been left by the Syrian noble Usamah.

Second Crusade

The alliance of Damascus with the Franks, which was maintained almost for a decade (1140–1148), was unilaterally broken by the Franks when the Second Crusade (1148) advanced upon Damascus, but retreated without capturing it. After the campaign, the treaty was renewed, but was again tested in 1151, when a body of Turkmens attacked Banias. The lord of the city sallied out against them and was defeated; the Damascus government, hearing of the raid, arrested the Turkmens and forced them to restore their plunder to the Franks. But the days of peace between Franks and Damascenes were drawing to a close: the slogans of a Holy War and the demands to unite the forces of Islam against the infidels began to influence the inhabitants of Damascus.

Moslems attack Banias

In 1153, while the Franks were preoccupied with the siege of Ascalon, the Emir of Damascus, Mujir a-Din, was impelled by public opinion to join Nur a-Din in a combined operation against the Franks; a Damascene force advanced on Banias, then without knights. The siege was raised on this occasion, when sharp feuds broke out between the Moslem commanders, but the period of calm on the north-east of the Kingdom of Jerusalem had ended. Nur a-Din captured Damascus in April 1154. With it, the Moslem counter offensive had gained a key position and jumping-off point against the Kingdom of Jerusalem, so that Banias again became a frontier fortress of supreme importance. In the first years of his rule in Damascus Nur a-Din refrained from direct attacks upon the Franks, and signed a truce with King Baldwin III, but the agreement was violated in 1152 by the king, when he conducted a raid against some Turkmen tribes east of Banias. Nur a-Din awaited an opportunity for revenge.

The renewed threat from across the frontier laid upon the lord of Banias, Humphrey of Toron (Tibnin), a burden too heavy to be borne. The gallant knight, who had acquired Banias by marrying the daughter of Renier Brus, was unable to carry it alone; William of Tyre wrote of him that he was "weary of the constant responsibility and the expenses which fell upon him on account of the care of the city of Banias." In the middle of 1157, therefore, he gave half of Banias and its territory to the Hospitallers, simultaneously transferring to them half the stronghold of Hunin (Chastel Neuf). In return, the Order undertook to pay half the cost of the city's defence and to keep a strong garrison there.

half of Banias given to Hospitallers

siege of 1157

The Hospitallers soon discovered how costly were the obligations they had assumed. Nur a-Din, determined to punish the Franks for their perfidy, fell upon a convoy of Hospitallers moving towards Banias and annihilated it. After this defeat the Hospitallers withdrew from their agreement with Humphrey and he was left to bear the burden of frontier defence on his own. His trial soon came. In May 1157 Nur a-Din moved upon Banias. At first the Franks defended themselves behind the city ramparts, but the Moslems swiftly penetrated them, so the defenders, with Humphrey at their head, shut themselves in the citadel. When King Baldwin learned of the desperate plight of Banias, he gathered a large

150

force and set out northward. Nur a-Din raised the seige on the approach of the Franks, but remained encamped in the neighbourhood without dispersing his troops. Upon reaching Banias, Baldwin ordered the rebuilding of its walls; the ramparts and buildings were restored in a short time and, the work complete, the king set out southward. As he was encamped near 'Einan ('Ein al-Malaḥa), Nur a-Din fell upon the Frankish army and slew the greater part of it. Only the king, with a small bodyguard, survived.

After this victory Nur a-Din returned to Banias and renewed the siege (June–July 1157). The defenders again shut themselves in the citadel and Baldwin summoned reinforcements from Tripoli and Antioch, fixing Hunin as the point of assembly. In face of this move, Nur a-Din raised the siege and returned to Damascus.

The end of Frankish Banias came in 1164. While the Franks were preoccupied with the adventure of conquering Egypt, Nur a-Din seized the opportunity to attack the city, left without troops while its lord, Humphrey of Toron, as Constable of the kingdom, was commanding the Frankish army in Egypt. After a brief resistance, which gave rise to rumours amongst the Franks that the commanders were bribed by the Moslems, Banias and its citadel at last fell to the Moslems (October 1164), and never returned to Frankish hands. The loss of this stronghold was regarded by the Franks as a major defeat, and King Amalric sent a delegation to Europe to stress the danger to the kingdom, and to appeal for help. *Moslems take Banias*

In the twenty-four years between the loss of Banias and fall of the Kingdom of Jerusalem (1164–1187), the frontier passed through the middle of the Ḥula Valley, as described by the traveller Ibn Jubayr: "The cultivation of the vale is divided between the Franks and the Moslems, and in it there is a boundary known as the 'Boundary of Dividing.' They apportion the crops equally, and their animals are mingled together. Yet no wrong takes place between them because of it."[38] Nur a-Din, and Saladin after him, fortified the city and kept a strong garrison there. Ibn Jubayr described it as "small but [it] has a fortress below the walls of which winds a river." It was probably at that stage that the castle of Subeibe was built, or at least enlarged considerably. *1164–1187*

The Franks from time to time endeavoured to recapture Banias, but without success. The most serious attempt was in 1174, when King Amalric attacked the city on hearing of the death of his old enemy, Nur a-Din (May 1174). Nur a-Din's widow offered the king a large sum of money to raise the siege. At first he refused, but realizing after fifteen days that he could not overcome the defenders, he agreed, took the money and raised the siege. It was during this time that he fell ill with the dysentery that led to his death (July 1174). A further attempt was made in April 1179. In this attack Humphrey II, the lord of Banias, was mortally wounded. In June 1179 another attack was repulsed.

Banias and Subeibe became a part of the frontier defences of the Ayyubid kingdom, and were given by Saladin to his son al-Afdal. They passed in 1196 to the sultan's brother, al-'Adil, and from him to his son, al-'Aziz 'Othman *Banias under Ayyubids*

151

(1212). In 1219 al-Mu'azzam, sultan of Damascus, destroyed Banias and Subeibe as part of the wholesale destruction wrought upon the country's strongholds, including that of Jerusalem, to prevent their falling into the hands of the Franks. At this time the forces of the Fifth Crusade had just captured Damietta in Egypt and it looked as if they were about to be victorious. Subeibe was rebuilt by 'Othman in the years 1226–1230, and additional building was carried out at the end of the 1240's.

St. Louis   The Crusader forces of St. Louis, King of France, made an unsuccessful attempt to capture Banias and Subeibe in 1253, but in 1260 they were captured by the Mongols, who in turn lost them to the Mamluks after the Battle of 'Ein Jalut ('Ein Ḥarod).

Sultan Baybars was the last to conduct any building activity at the castle of Subeibe. In the Mamluk period the castle was used as a prison at first, but was ultimately neglected and abandoned.

description of   The city is situated near the source of the large spring of Banias, on a flat area which is bordered on the south and west by the steep banks of the Banias *ruins*   and 'Ein Qunia streams. The curtain wall is rectangular in plan, each side being 270–280 metres long. The steep slopes form a natural defence for the southern and western walls. On the east side a moat, 15 metres wide, was dug. The north side has completely gone, but it was probably defended by a similar moat. Eight wall towers defended the curtain wall. They were built at irregular intervals, and project only slightly from the wall-line. The citadel was situated at the north-western corner of the curtain, the most vulnerable point in the defences. It faced the flat high ground north of the city, which is admirably situated for siege operations. The position of the citadel is similar to those of other citadels and,

Banias, main gate
and south wall

152

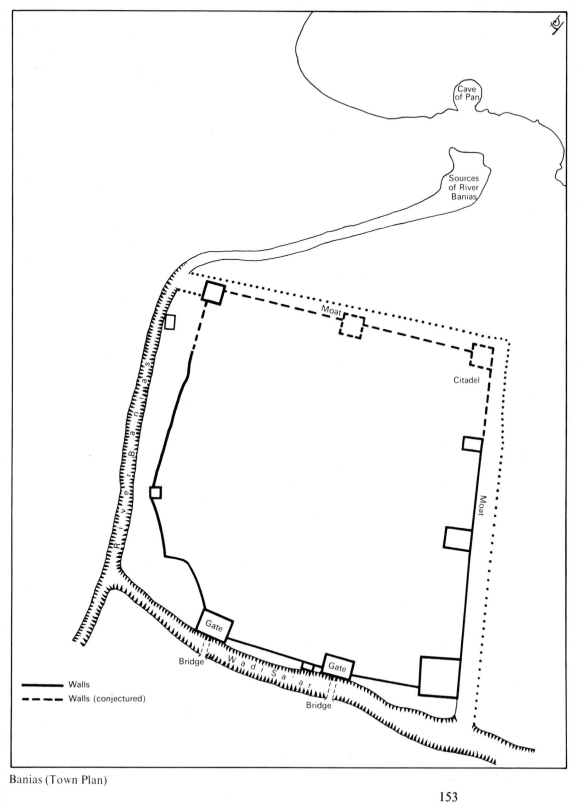

Banias (Town Plan)

notably, the "Tower of David" in Jerusalem. It was a rectangular structure. Its *citadel* eastern and northern walls, respectively 15 and 20 metres long, were incorporated into the defences of the city wall. The west and south walls, facing the city, were defended by a moat. The gate was on the southern side. Remains of the Crusader period can be seen in the lower parts of a modern house, situated near the Kuneitra road.

main gate The main city gate, the best preserved mediaeval fortification in Banias, is in the south wall. The gate is built on the principle of direct approach, its outer and inner portals being parallel. The gate hall is groin-vaulted. Two rooms are situated on either side of the hall, with entrances from the north. A staircase leads to the gate-tower roof. The approach to the gate was over a large single-arched bridge, now destroyed. From the style of the wall constructions, the building material and especially the plan of the gate, it may be surmised that the fortifications of Banias date from the early Arab period and that the Crusaders probably made only minor repairs. As in other instances, we do not have to take the chroniclers literally when they refer to the total destruction and later the complete rebuilding of the walls of Banias.

Subeibe The castle of Subeibe (Qalát Namrud) is built on a spur of the mountains three kilometres east of Banias, the easiest approach being by a mountain path leading directly westward from the village of 'Ein Qunia. It was erected on a long east-west spur which slopes from east to west. The slopes of the spur are very

Banias, main gate from inside the town

steep on the north and less so on the east and south, though still difficult to climb. A rock-cut moat separates the castle area from the rest of the spur on the west. The plan of the stronghold is long and narrow because of the narrowness of the spur: the castle is 450 metres long and 60 metres wide at the narrowest point; the length of its eastern side is 70 metres and of its western 160 metres. The interior area is divided into a lower bailey on the west and an upper bailey and keep at the highest point on the east. The main entrance was at Tower 3 on the south; it led to the upper bailey and the keep. There is another entrance at Tower 8, which leads to the lower bailey. The present approach is from the west, through a breach in the wall between Towers 9 and 10.

description

Owing to the topography of the area, the east, south and west sides were fortified with walls and numerous towers, while a wall almost without towers was built on the north, which is protected by a deep chasm. As will be recalled, Subeibe was built or enlarged at the beginning of the Ayyubid régime, and destroyed by al-Mu'azzam in 1219. The castle was restored by 'Othman in 1228–1229, by a-Sa'id (1239–1240) and by Baybars (1260). At this time not only were the older fortifications restored but a considerable number of towers and structures were added, greatly increasing the strength of the castle's defences.

As the visitor approaches the area today, he reaches the castle from the west, where a wide and deep moat separates the castle area from the rest of the spur. To the west of the moat are remains of an outer tower or barbican. Crossing the moat, the visitor climbs over a heap of ruins remaining from the western wall, between a corner-tower, 9, and Tower 10. Another tower, No. 11, is built on the western wall. Towers 11 and 9 were enlarged and strengthened after 1219. Tower 9 was built on the foundations of the glacis. The original portion of this tower is of relatively small dimensions, with eight loopholes. It was enlarged considerably on the north-east and south sides. Three building periods can be discerned in Tower 11; here two Moslem inscriptions were found, one recording the name of

Subeibe, Castle (General Plan)

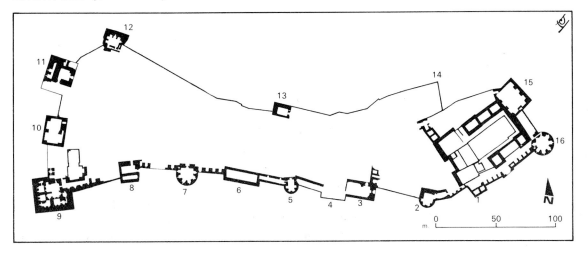

Subeibe, approach road and south ramparts

'Othman and the years AH 627 (1229–1230 A.D.) the other that of Baybars. Another stairway leading to a postern is built at the western corner.

A huge vaulted water cistern is attached to Tower 9; nearby is a Moslem inscription bearing the name of a-Sa'id and the year AH 637 (1239–1240 A.D.).

Progressing from Tower 9 along the south wall, we reach Tower 8, the gate tower of the lower bailey. The outer gateway is in the east wall of the tower and approached by several steps. Its arch is protected by a portcullis. The inner gateway is in the south wall, that is, at right-angles to the entrance, the usual bent entrance principle. Seven towers, three circular and four square, were built alternately along the southern wall. In the surrounding curtain wall connecting them are loopholes and, above, a *chemin de ronde* linked to the tops of the towers. Although the defences on the south side date from various periods, they are of uniform appearance.

The main gate of the castle is in Tower 3, and has been almost completely destroyed. The keep is placed at the highest point of the castle, near the east wall. A moat divides it from the lower bailey. It is in the shape of an elongated rectangle, surrounded by walls with six towers, four at the corners of the rectangle and two on its longer sides. The space between the walls of the central tower and the surrounding rampart is very restricted. On the west a cistern is built between the central tower and the two rectangular corner towers in front of it. On the north-west side is the entrance to the keep, consisting of a series of three gates

156

built at right-angles to one another, defended by loopholes and commanded by the corner towers. Inside the keep there are remains of Moslem wall paintings. East of the central tower and abutting onto it is a large hall with two aisles, each containing three bays. The vault is supported on two square central pillars. There is a small door in the eastern wall which is also pierced by six loopholes. The north side of the castle is protected, as already noted, by a very steep slope, so that its wall is strengthened only by two square towers (12, 13). Within the walls are the remains of various buildings of unclear plan and purpose.

BETHLEHEM

The town of Bethlehem was inhabited on the eve of the Crusader period as it is today, by a large Christian population. Throughout the generations the Church of the Nativity had been an important centre for pilgrimage, even after *earlier history* the Arabs had conquered the country and the Christians were subjected to religious persecutions. The church, whose structure was renovated in the 6th century by Justinian, had been preserved in its entirety, almost unmarked by the waves of destruction which obliterated so many contemporary churches. The building remained unscathed during the Persian occupation in 614, when all the churches of Jerusalem were laid in ruins, and was not damaged in 1009 when the Egyptian Caliph al-Ḥakim burnt down the churches of that city.

When the Crusaders reached the vicinity of Jerusalem in 1099, the Church of the Nativity in Bethlehem was again in danger of destruction, as the Moslems had set about systematically demolishing all the settlements around Jerusalem in order to deny the Crusaders foodstuffs, water, and timber for making siege-machinery. The Christian villages in the Jerusalem area suffered during this *Crusaders take* period and the people of Bethlehem, fearing for the fate of the church, sent a *Bethlehem* deputation to the Crusader camp at Emmaus (Abu Ghosh), begging the leaders of the Crusade to despatch part of their force to its defence. In the words of William of Tyre: "The faithful of Bethlehem were in terror lest these infidels invade their city and pull down the church which the Christians had repeatedly redeemed from destruction."[39]

The Crusaders responded to the request, and a troop of a hundred horsemen commanded by Tancred and Baldwin of Le-Bourg (later King Baldwin II) set out on a night march to Bethlehem. They reached the town in the morning, were received by the inhabitants with boundless rejoicing, and led in procession to the church, where prayer was offered by the Greek priests. Tancred raised his standard on the roof of the church as a mark of victory. After a brief sojourn he set out at the head of his knights for Jerusalem and rejoined the main body of the Crusaders, which had in the meantime arrived before the walls of the city.

Within the hierarchy of the Byzantine Church, Bethlehem was subject to the Bishop of Ascalon, but after the conquest the Greek ecclesiastical hierarchy was

157

Bethlehem, Church of Nativity and Cloister (Plan from 17th Century)

Bethlehem, cloister

*coronation of
Baldwin I*
replaced and a Latin prior was appointed to the church, subject to the Church of the Holy Sepulchre. Baldwin was crowned at Bethlehem in the Church of the Nativity on Christmas Day 1101, thus becoming the first Crusader king to wear a crown. He chose to be crowned at Bethlehem rather than in his capital because "he had not the presumption to adorn himself with a royal crown or to deck himself with gold and precious stones and to proclaim himself King of Jerusalem, in the place where the Lord Jesus, King of Kings, Lord of Sovereigns, debased and humiliated unto death for the sake of the world's redemption, had been crowned with a crown of sharp thorns."[40]

bishopric

Bethlehem was made a bishopric in 1110 and the Church of the Nativity then became a cathedral. Baldwin, who had proposed this change to Pope Pascal II and obtained his authorization, gave the town of Bethlehem to the bishop as a feudal fief, also granting him villages in the vicinity and others near Acre and Ascalon. A cloister was built north of the church; here dwelt the Augustinian canons who served in the cathedral.

*description of
Frankish remains*

The main Crusader influence to be noted in the cathedral is the extensive ornamental and decorative work. Impressive mosaic designs still adorn the walls of the nave and transept. According to a Greek inscription in the apse of the choir, the work was executed by Ephrem the Monk during the reign of Amalric I and in the time of Ralph, Bishop of Bethlehem. The subjects and style are Byzantine.

Over the site of the manger are remains of a mosaic portraying Jesus and Mary with the shepherds. On the south wall of the nave are mosaic pictures, under each of which is a Latin inscription; paintings of prophets and saints, also bearing Latin inscriptions, appear on some of the marble columns of the nave. The columns of the basilica bear other inscriptions, and graffiti left by Frankish pilgrims of the 12th century.

The Crusader cloister has been restored on the north side of the basilica, where the modern Church of St. Catherine is situated. It includes a court surrounded by an arcade which is supported on double columns, as well as a number of halls and chambers.

1187–1244

The relatively tranquil life of Crusader Bethlehem ended in 1187, when Saladin took the town a few weeks before the capture of Jerusalem. The Church remained untouched, but the Latins were expelled. The Latin clergy returned to the Church in 1192 by permission of Saladin, in response to the request of Hubert Walter, Bishop of Salisbury, one of the leaders of the Third Crusade. Eastern Armenian and Greek clergy also found their way into the Church. Bethlehem reverted to Frankish control in 1229 under the peace treaty between the emperor Frederick II and the Sultan al-Kamil.

The Franks were finally expelled from Bethlehem in 1244, but the Latin rite continued, uninterrupted, throughout the 13th century.

HEBRON-ST ABRAHAM

Hebron, city of the Patriarchs, was captured by the Crusaders shortly after the conquest of Jerusalem. Situated in the heart of a rich agricultural region, it was also a centre of trade. The Crusaders expelled the Moslem and Jewish inhabitants, and some of the Syrian Christian citizens went to live in Jerusalem. Although the population of the city dwindled, considerable numbers remained and travellers who passed through at the beginning of the Crusader conquest praise the fertility of the area.

The Crusaders set up and garrisoned a fortified tower here. The "Haram", a Herodian-Byzantine building over the Cave of Machpela, was converted from a mosque to a church served by Augustinian canons. The city and its region remained a crown domain until the 1160's, though various knights received extensive tracts in the mountains of Hebron. The city and its fort were entrusted to castellans, some of whom took its Crusader place-name as their surname *(de St. Abraham)*. The Frankish population which gathered there was small, but a burgesses' court was nevertheless set up, and wayfarers of the 1150's record Hebron as a city.

In 1119 a crack appeared in the floor of the church built over the Cave of Machpela. Frankish canons making their way into the cave, discovered bones there which were declared to be the relics of the Patriarchs. This entry into the sacred place became widely known among Franks and Moslems.

Hebron was separated from the royal domain in 1161 and made over to Philip de Milly together with the seigneurie of Transjordan. Henceforward these seigneuries were linked, but their independence was preserved and each had full seigneurial rights. In 1168, a bishop was appointed to Hebron, whereupon the erection of a new church was begun in the precincts of the "Haram." This church is still used as the "Mosque of Haram Ibrahimi," and occupies the south side of the square of the huge Herodian structure, whose general orientation is north-west–south-east. The interior is divided into a nave and two aisles by two lines of columns; it is roofed with rib-vaulting.

Hebron was taken by Saladin in 1187. He reconverted the church to a mosque and brought there from Ascalon a *minbar* (pulpit) ordered by Nur a-Din. Hebron was the capital of a district in the Mamluk period. Baybars replaced Christian decoration from the Haram with Mamluk ornamentation.

NABLUS-NAPLES

The capital of Samaria, set between the mountains of Ebal and Gerizim, was an opulent and flourishing city before the advent of the Crusaders. Its main livelihood was olive-growing and the making of oil and soap; the city was surrounded

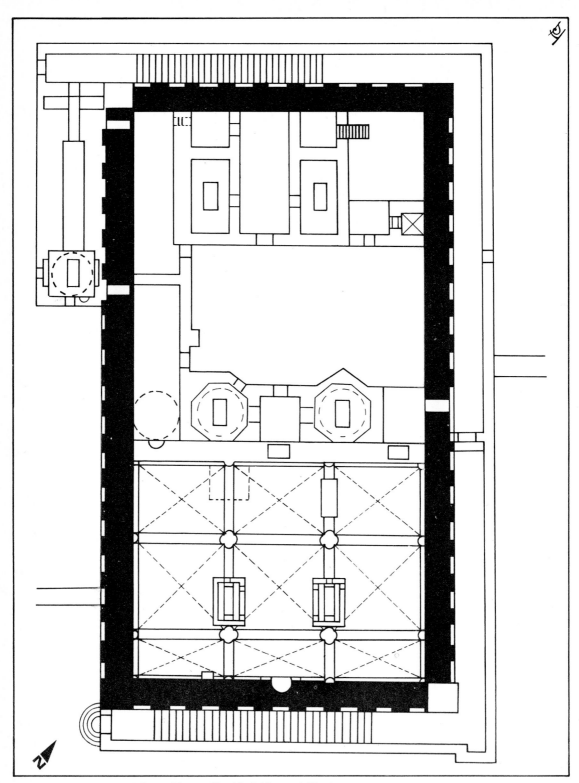

Hebron, Ḥaram Ibrahimi (General Plan)

by orchards and olive groves, its houses fine and spacious, so that the Moslems called it affectionately "little Damascus."

Nablus was captured by Tancred in July of 1099, a few days before Jerusalem. The city was without defences, so that its capture presented no difficulty, and its inhabitants surrendered, unresisting, to the Norman noble who arrived at its gates at the head of eighty knights. Nablus remained in Tancred's possession handed by until he left the country on his way to his principality of Edessa, when he handed Tancred to the it over to King Baldwin I. The city and its territory continued as royal domain king until the 1170's.

Christian travellers who passed through Nablus after the Crusader conquest praised the city and its surroundings. Daniel the Russian reported:

"The land of Naples is very rich in various fruit trees, figs, nuts and olives. The planta- conditions after tions resemble dense forests surrounding the town. The territory also has fertile fields Frankish conquest of wheat. The entire region is notable for its beauty and its rich produce includes oil, wine, grain and fruit. The city of Jerusalem obtains its foodstuffs from Naples."

Its inhabitants were Samaritans, Moslems and Franks. According to the testimony of Benjamin of Tudela (c. 1170) there were a thousand Samaritans in the city. A considerable number of Franks settled there, some of them members of the nobility who held estates in the region and some Frankish merchants engaged in the wine trade (see p. 378).

The wealth of the city attracted the churches and the Military Orders to it. The Hospitallers obtained grants there from 1108, and in 1114 the Church of the Holy Sepulchre and the Patriarch of Jerusalem received tithes from Nablus. Ecclesiastically the city was subject to the monastery of Templum Domini (The Dome of the Rock), but, as has already been mentioned, it remained within the royal domain and a viscount administered it on behalf of the king, presiding also over the burgesses' court.

As an open city Nablus suffered on several occasions from Moslem razzias (1113, 1137, 1183 and 1184). In some of these the Moslem inhabitants joined the raiding forces and helped them to rob and slaughter the Franks. In these times of distress the Franks found shelter in the fortified tower *(Turris Neapolitana)*, erected on the west side of the city, a typical feature of the open towns and villages (see p. 275). Because of its central geographical position Nablus was the meeting-place of the king and his court on several occasions. Many charters were signed in the "royal palace" of Nablus, and in 1120 a council met there which discussed and decided on steps for the improvement of the ecclesiastical discipline of the Kingdom of Jerusalem. The city was the administrative centre administrative of an extensive district bounded on the south by the frontier of the mountains of centre Samaria, on the north by the town of Jenin, on the east by the Jordan River Valley and on the west by the hills bordering the maritime plain. This area contained a considerable number of feudal estates, both large and small. The military obligations of Nablus amounted to three hundred sergeants and eighty-five knights.

In the 1150's the city and its area became an estate passing to the queen mother on the death of her husband, the first to receive it being Melisende (in 1152). When she died, in 1161, Nablus reverted to the king, but in 1174 it was given to Maria Comnena, the widow of King Amalric. After her marriage to Balian d'Ibelin, Nablus passed from the possession of the crown and became an independent seigneurie held by the Ibelin family.

passed to Ibelins

Nablus was captured by Saladin after the battle of Hattin; its Frankish inhabitants left and the peasants of the vicinity destroyed their houses, plundering the abandoned property. Thereafter, it never returned to Frankish hands.

Remains of the Crusader period at Nablus are few and negligible; most of the buildings described by explorers of the 19th century have disappeared, either in consequence of the severe earthquake of 1927 or because of the construction of modern buildings over the ruins. The following Crusader structures were recorded as late as the 1920's: a) the Tower of Nablus; b) the Hospital of the Order of Hospitallers; c) the Church of Templum Domini, and d) the Church of the Passion and Resurrection, which belonged to the Church of the Holy Sepulchre.

description of Crusader ruins

Of the Tower of Nablus, the fortified stronghold of the open city and the supposed seat of the viscount, only a few courses of dressed and bossed blocks remain, and a modern dwelling has been built over the battered plinth of the wall. The tower, in which Roman and Byzantine stones are discernible, is located in

Tower of Nablus

Nablus, Hospitaller vault

the western part of the town, near the Mosque al-Yasmin in the street of the same name.

The Hospital of the Order of the Hospitallers was founded in 1180, and an inscription found on the site as long ago as 1592 testifies to the date of its construction and purpose. On the site, where lepers were housed at the end of the 19th century, and which was called after them *Jam'a al-Masakin* (the Mosque of the Lepers), there stands today a modern apartment-house in the street of the Prophets (Tariq al-'Anbia), not far from the Mosque of the Sons of Jacob (Jam'a Awlad Ya'aqub). The Crusader building, in so far as its general plan can be reconstructed, was a square of halls and rooms surrounding a central court, whose length from north to south was 80 metres. On the south side of the square is a pointed barrel-vault, 12 metres long and 6 metres wide, now used as a store for building materials; the north-east corner of the square also survives and contains a ribbed vault. The other sides have been largely destroyed but the new structures have preserved the original form of the court. *Hospital*

The Church of the Templum Domini, where according to the evidence of scholars the mosque of a-Nasser was located after the Moslem conquest, was completely destroyed in the earthquake of 1927. The mosque has indeed been restored, but is built into the second storey of a commercial building with shops on the ground floor. Of the Crusader structure, only a few dressed embossed blocks remain, incorporated into the wall of the modern building. *church of Templum Domini*

The fourth relic, the Church of the Passion and Resurrection, was built in 1168 by the canons of the Church of the Holy Sepulchre, with the sanction of King Amalric. The Crusaders revived an ancient Byzantine church and added to it a number of bays and apses. After the Moslem conquest this church became the great mosque of Nablus (Jam'a al-Kbir). The Moslems demolished the apses, arranging the entrance to the building on the east side. A very beautiful Gothic portal was preserved in the outer gate of the mosque, but this was completely destroyed in the earthquake of 1927, when the entire Crusader structure—the eastern part of the mosque—was destroyed. However, the three western bays which had survived from the Byzantine church were not damaged. The destroyed portion has been restored since 1927 with crude concrete columns, and a new portal has been constructed, but the remains of the Gothic gate have vanished. *Great Mosque*

NAZARETH

At the time of its conquest by Tancred in 1099, Nazareth was a small ruined village whose population was mostly Christian. Seawolf (1103) described it as a "town completely devastated." There were two Greek churches, the Church of the Annunciation and the Church of St. Joseph. True to his policy, aimed at establishing bonds of friendship with the Christian population of Galilee, Tancred confirmed the title of the Church of the Annunciation to its landed *conquest*

165

property, which extended around the town. He also repaired the churches, contributing ornaments and furniture.

Archbishopric of Galilee Shortly after the conquest, the Nazareth churches, like the monastery of Mt. Tabor and other churches in Palestine, passed into the hands of the Latin clergy, and in 1112 there was already a Latin bishop in the town. The Archdiocese of Galilee was transferred from Beit Shean to Nazareth in the middle of the 12th century and the Church of the Annunciation became the cathedral church of the Archbishop of Nazareth. The bishopric of Tiberias was subordinated to him and he possessed certain episcopal rights over the church of Mt. Tabor.

During the 12th century the Crusader settlement increased and travellers who visited Nazareth in the 1170's described it as "a large village" or as "a town." The Archbishop of Nazareth held full seigneurial rights, including a burgesses' court. He was bound to furnish the Frankish army with a hundred and fifty serjeants, an obligation identical to that laid upon the large monasteries and the Archbishop of Tyre.

rebuilding of Church of Annunciation About the time of the elevation of Nazareth to an archbishopric the rebuilding of the Church of the Annunciation was begun. A structure 75 metres long and 30 metres wide, its plan was basilical with nave and two aisles, terminating in three apses. The eastern wall or *chevet* was straight, but the square containing the central apse projected. The nave was roofed with a pointed barrel vault and the aisles were groin-vaulted. The Grotto of the Annunciation was in the crypt of the church, and extended below the two eastern bays of the nave and the northern aisles. The main portal was in the western front; the columns of this portal had five carved capitals which are amongst the best examples of romanesque sculpture. These capitals were not set in their intended positions, as the building of the church was never completed. They were concealed in a flanking recess

capitals and it is assumed that the artist who carved them hid them on the approach of the Moslem army in 1183. Their style is identical with that of mid-12th century romanesque art in Burgundy and in the vicinity of Paris, and it is supposed that they were carved by an artist who came from France. The carvings portray scenes from the life of Jesus and the apostles, and are today kept in the Franciscan museum in Nazareth. The smaller Church of St. Joseph was rebuilt at the same time as that of the Annunciation, being 29 metres long and 15 metres wide with a nave and two aisles. The construction of the new cathedral of the Annunciation was interrupted by a terrible earthquake which occurred in 1170 and destroyed most of the houses in Nazareth.

1183–1187 In 1183, Moslem units raided the district of Nazareth, attacking unsuccessfully the Monastery of Mt. Tabor. The population of the township, chiefly the women and children, fearing the approach of the enemy, crowded into the cathedral, then still being built, and many were crushed to death in the ensuing panic. Nazareth was captured by the troops of Saladin in July 1187; the Frankish inhabitants again sought refuge in the Church of the Annunciation, but were butchered by the Moslems. For nearly twenty years no Christian entered the place, until 1204, when a peace treaty was signed between al-'Adil and the

Franks, one of its conditions providing freedom of pilgrimage to Nazareth.

In 1219 the town and its churches were destroyed by al-Mu'azzam, with the castles of Galilee and the walls of Jerusalem. The town was restored to the Franks by the treaty signed between Emperor Frederick II Hohenstaufen and the Sultan al-Kamil. In addition, a corridor leading to Acre was ceded to the Christians. The churches of the town were partly rebuilt and a small number of Franks returned to live there, but Nazareth was largely desolate.

13th century

St. Louis visited the town in April, 1254, and prayed for the whole day in the Grotto of the Annunciation, fasting and wearing sackcloth *(cilice)*. In the same year Henry Archbishop of Nazareth rented what seems to have been his entire landed property to the Order of Hospitallers.

The end of Frankish Nazareth came in the spring of 1263. Moslem troops moved upon the town, annihilating its inhabitants and destroying its churches completely. In 1283 the Franks acquired the Church of the Annunciation and four houses nearby, but possession remained theoretical, as nobody seems to have returned to care for them.

The churches of Nazareth remained in ruins until 1620, when the Franciscans restored the Church of the Annunciation and the Church of St. Joseph, using building materials taken from the ruins of Crusader structures. The churches were extended and enlarged on a number of occasions. A large modern church has recently been erected on the site of the old Church of the Annunciation.

RAMLA AND LYDDA

Just before the arrival of the Crusaders, Ramla was a large city and the capital of southern Palestine. It had been founded in 717 by the Caliph Sulaiman ibn 'Abd al-Malik, who was unwilling to place the centre of authority in Christian Lydda. When it was founded most of the inhabitants of Lydda migrated to it and the ancient city, former capital of a district and an important commercial centre, dwindled to a village.

earlier history

Ramla was well populated in the 10th and 11th centuries, splendidly adorned with public buildings and gardens and surrounded by a strong wall. Most of its inhabitants were Moslems or Christians, but there was also a large community of Samaritans. The Jewish population grew in the 10th century and reached its peak at the beginning of the 11th. In the century preceding the Crusader occupation the city suffered both natural and human disasters: it was devastated by Bedouin tribes in 1025, and in 1033 an earthquake destroyed most of its buildings and caused much loss of life. The whole city was ruined again in 1067 by a further earthquake in which, according to sources, over twenty thousand people perished. In 1071 Ramla was taken by the Seljuks. On the arrival of the troops of the First Crusade all its inhabitants fled and the city was found abandoned.

The seizure of Ramla gave the Crusaders a strategic point of prime importance, since the city lay at the central crossroads of the maritime plain and from it the routes went up to Jerusalem, but it was threatened from the flank by Egyptian military concentrations which had as yet not been engaged by the Crusaders. The latter, in haste to reach their destination, the Holy City, were in grave danger lest the Egyptian force, advancing northward, should retake Ramla and so block their vital supply lines from the coast. Realizing the value of Ramla, the Crusaders left a garrison there before setting out for Jerusalem (6th June, 1099).

situation of Ramla in first years

During the first five years of the Crusader kingdom, Ramla was the rear base for its armies in the life-and-death struggle which they waged with the Egyptian host. Godfrey de Bouillon concentrated his army there for the decisive battle with the Egyptians near Ascalon in August 1099. In May 1101, an Egyptian force advanced towards Ramla to cut the road to Jerusalem. The garrison of the city stood its ground desperately until reinforcements from Jerusalem, commanded by King Baldwin I, put the Egyptians to flight and drove them back to their base at Ascalon. At the end of August in the same year the Egyptians again laid siege to the city, but retreated on the approach of a Crusader force from Jerusalem. In the spring of 1102 the Egyptians were able to capture both Ramla and Lydda after defeating the Crusaders in a fierce battle near Yazur, but the Crusaders succeeded in driving the Egyptians out of Ramla at the end of May. The city faced similar ordeals in the years 1105, 1106, and 1110.

development of civilian population

Despite frequent hostilities, civilian settlements developed at Ramla and Lydda, with the encouragement of the lord of Ramla and Lydda, Robert of Rouen, who was elected bishop of Lydda and received the town as his feudal domain. The inhabitants included Syrian Christians who lived in Ramla before the conquest and had fled; others were of Frankish origin. There must have been a considerable civilian concentration at Ramla as early as 1102 because the chronicles relate that the inhabitants fled from the city in that year, before the short-lived Egyptian occupation.

After hostilities had died down in 1106, the population further increased. At this time Ramla passed into the hands of a lay seigneur, a certain Baldwin, so that the ecclesiastical seigneurie of Lydda became restricted to the town itself and to a few of the villages in its vicinity. Syrian and Frankish inhabitants, settling in Lydda, renewed its ancient status as a city; its market, which had been famous of old, again became an important commercial centre. The inhabitants gained their livelihood from agriculture, trade, and the furnishing of services to the pilgrims passing through on their way to Jerusalem. As in every centre of Frankish settlement, there were burgesses' courts at Lydda and Ramla. The seigneurie of Ramla extended over the eastern maritime plain from Shafrir on the west to Yalu in the east. In 1148 the seigneurie passed to Balian the Elder, the husband of Helvis, the heiress of Ramla. Balian already held the two neighbouring lordships on the north and south, Mirabel and Ibelin.

1177–1187

After a long period of tranquility, war returned to Ramla, Lydda and the surrounding area; in the autumn of 1177 Saladin invaded the territory of the Crusader kingdom. Having besieged Ascalon for some time, he penetrated to the heart of the country and reached the gates of Ramla and Lydda. The inhabitants fled to Jaffa and Mirabel, and the Moslems destroyed the Church of St. George of Lydda. The Frankish army commanded by King Baldwin IV reached Ramla and, in a battle which was fought out on the hills of the Shephela between the city and Tel Gezer (Montgisart), the Moslems were soundly beaten and retreated to Egypt in disarray.

Third Crusade

After the battle of Hattin, Ramla and Lydda were taken without resistance, their civilian inhabitants fled and the Moslems burnt the Church of St. George for the second time within a decade. During the Third Crusade, Ramla again became a base for the Crusader armies, this time those of Richard Coeur de Lion, moving from Jaffa eastward to Jerusalem after the battle of Arsuf (September 1191). Saladin, based on Mirabel, ordered the destruction of all the fortresses of the Shephela and its towns, including Ramla and Lydda. Richard, who had left Jaffa on his way eastward, reached Ramla in November of 1191, to find it empty. His forces stayed there six weeks and left only at the end of December for Latrun and Beit Nuba. There they paused for two weeks before returning to Ramla. At the beginning of the summer of 1192 the Crusaders again endeavoured to advance upon Jerusalem, only to retire defeated to Ramla once more. In the peace treaty which was signed in September 1192 it was determined that the district of Ramla be divided equally between the Moslems and the Christians. The Crusaders rebuilt the Church of Lydda and a few Franks also returned to Ramla. Al-'Adil made his base there in 1198 for an attack on Jaffa. It reverted to the Crusaders in 1205 and remained in their hands till 1268, when it was taken by Baybars. The Mamluk sultan reduced the church of Lydda to ruins yet again, and in the Mamluk period Ramla reverted to its position as a provincial capital and important commercial centre.

Lydda

The Frankish population of Lydda in the 12th century was concentrated around the Cathedral Church of St. George which, built over the tomb of one of the Christian martyrs, and patron saint of warriors, was founded on a Byzantine basilica dating from Justinian's time. When the Crusaders first came to Lydda they had found it demolished; rebuilding it, they added a monastery, and fortified the entire complex. The church was the seat of the bishop of Lydda, whose diocese included the whole territory of the seigneurie of Ramla and also Ibelin, Mirabel and Blanchegarde. As has been mentioned, the first Latin bishop, Robert of Rouen, received Ramla and Lydda as his feudal domain, but he only held the area for five years. From 1105 onwards the fief of the bishops of Lydda included only the town of Lydda and a few villages in its vicinity. A large number of canons ministered in the Church of St. George, and four monasteries situated near the town were subject to the bishop, namely, St. Joseph and St.

St. George's

Habacuc (Al Knisa near Lydda Airport); St. Jean Evangelista (whose location is unknown); St. Catherine de Montgisart (evidently Gezer); and St. Maria Trium Umbrarum (St. Mary of the Three Shades, location also unknown).

remains

The remains of the Crusader church of St. George are to be found in the old city of Lydda. It consisted of a nave and flanking aisles, ending in three apses.

169

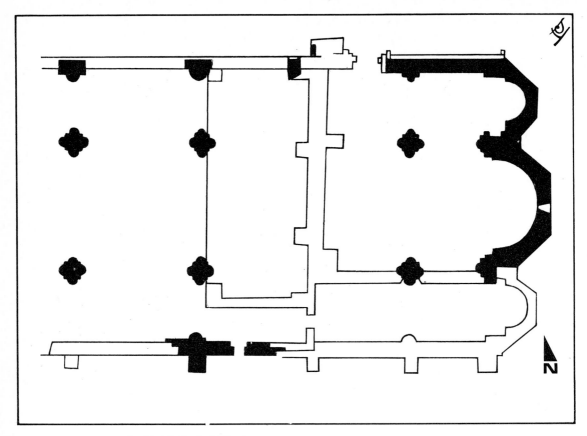

Lydda, Cathedral (Plan)

The eastern ends of these projected to create a polygonal *chevet,* quite unusual in Palestine. The interior of the church was divided into six bays by five lines of cruciform piers, each of which was engaged with four columns. The whole building was groin-vaulted, and 30 metres long. A Greek Orthodox church was built in the north-east corner of the Crusader structure in 1874 and contains the left and central apses, as well as two bays of the nave and the north aisle. The *tomb of* right-hand apse and south aisle have been completely destroyed along the entire *St. George* length of the southern wall of the Greek church. The western part of the Crusader building is today used as the courtyard of the great mosque of Lydda and the bases of the piers can be seen within it. Byzantine capitals and columns from the church have been used again in the mosque. The tomb of St. George is in the crypt of the Greek church. Phocas reported of his visit in the 1180's: "A very great church of the great and holy martyr George—the church is oblong and in the apse, under the place of the holy table, one sees the mouth of his sepulchre, faced all around with white marble."[41]

The Frankish settlement at Ramla occupied only part of the Moslem city within its walls. Other parts appear to have consisted of cultivated fields and

170

Ramla, church

farms, Frankish Ramla resembling in this respect Ascalon. In the 12th century, both places had smaller populations than in previous epochs and their walls, which remained in their entirety, enclosed areas which were partly unoccupied. As a result it was difficult to defend the long perimeter, and the walls served as no more than an obstacle against raids. They were useless against any regular force that set out to breach them, and in such cases the inhabitants escaped to neighbouring strongholds, as during the attack by Saladin in 1177. The Frankish population concentrated on the south-east side of the town; the only relic remaining is a church, which was converted into a mosque by Baybars on the capture of the city in 1268. The Crusaders erected the church over the foundations of a Byzantine basilica and made secondary use of the columns and capitals of the ancient edifice.

description of Frankish Ramla

The church is divided into a nave and two aisles, terminating in three apses built in the thickness of the east wall, which has a flat *chevet*. The interior contains seven bays divided by square piers the capitals of the columns being ornamented with foliage motifs. The nave has a pointed barrel vault supported by arches of unequal span. The aisles are groin-vaulted; between them and the nave

171

are arcades of pointed arches. The vault of the nave is higher than that of the aisles, and the clerestory is pierced with narrow pointed windows lighting the nave. Similar windows in the north and south walls of the building light the aisles. There are also windows in the three apses. The original main entrance was on the west, where there is a marble portal with three pointed arches. On the north side of the west entrance was a square bell-tower, on whose foundation, when it was destroyed, a round minaret was erected. On the north are side-entrances leading from a paved court. There was another entrance in the south wall, but this was blocked when the Moslems erected the *Miḥrab* (prayer niche) in front of it, and is now visible only in the exterior wall of the building.

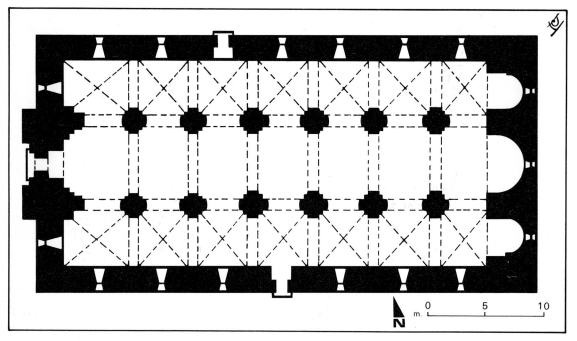

Ramla, church (Plan)

TOWNSHIPS

As has been indicated, the Frankish population concentrated in the large towns in the initial period of occupation (see p. 26) and all the centres of military and administrative control were located there. But the need to defend the frontiers *creation of secondary administrative centres* of the kingdom, and to control the feudal domains administratively, led to the definition of territories and to the foundation of territorial *chefs-lieux*. From these royal and seigneurial centres the administration of the financial and juridical affairs of the domains and counties was conducted. Secondary administrative centres were also established in the more extensive seigneuries. The setting up of centres outside the cities was not confined to the secular nobles, but extended also to the churches and the military orders, which gathered very extensive tracts of land into their hands. In every selected spot a fortified stronghold was erected which served a dual purpose, military and administrative. The function and form of the castle are dealt with elsewhere (see p. 277). The same process is well known from Europe; there the establishment of seigneurial centres with *same process as in Europe* military and administrative functions began in the 9th century, when fortified structures were set up throughout the continent. These contained quarters for knights, a house to accommodate the lord on his visits, a chapel, a hall of judicial assembly, and barns and storerooms for the collection of crops from the serfs. Around the centre grew a settlement which was called *Bourg*.

There were eighteen military-administrative centres in Palestine, namely Beit Govrin, Tel Tsafit, Deir al-Balaḥ, Gaza, Yavne, Hunin, Migdal-Afeq, Mi'ilya, Yoqne'am, Qalansuwa, Qaqun, Dor, Tsipori, Safed, 'Atlit, Tibnin, Karak and *eighteen bourgs in Palestine* Shaubak. They can be divided into two types: the first were frontier fortresses whose primary function when erected was military; Beit Govrin, Tel Tsafit, Deir al-Balaḥ, Hunin, Karak, Shaubak and Tibnin. A few of them retained their military function throughout the period, but the majority lost it because of later developments. Following the conquest of Ascalon, the military importance of Beit Govrin, Tel Tsafit, Deir al-Balaḥ and Yavne declined, while the *military raison d'être* conquest of Tyre changed the function of Tibnin. William of Tyre emphasized this change when describing Toron (Tibnin):

"Consequently, this site not only offered its founder advantages well suited to his needs at the time, but even now, because of its rich soil and the excellence of its famous fortifications, it is of the greatest benefit to the city of Tyre and indeed to the whole locality."[42]

These frontier castles thus became important administrative centres and the nuclei of semi-urban settlements.

Centres of the second type were established initially for administrative-feudal *administrative* purposes, whether as the *chefs-lieux* of seigneuries or as the secondary centres *raison d'être* of large fiefs. To this category belonged Migdal-Afeq, Mi'ilya, Yoqne'am,

173

Qalansuwa, Qaqun, Dor, Safed and 'Atlit. They did not continue for long as mere fortified strongholds. Frankish civilian settlements gradually grew up around them composed of peasants, traders and craftsmen who earned their living by furnishing services and produce to the administrative centre and the neighbouring villages. These settlements are called in the contemporary sources *suburbia (suburbani loci), villae* or by the European term—*Bourg (Bourc)*. William of Tyre described the colonization of Deir al-Balaḥ *(Darom)*. After the castle was built, "a few cultivators of the fields nearby united with some traders and formed a little settlement. They built a village and a church not far from the castle and took up their abode there."[43]

development of faubourgs

The same process was repeated in Tel Tsafit (Blanchegarde): "A great many suburban places grew up around it. Numerous families established themselves there and tillers of fields as well."[44] We know of similar developments in all the above mentioned *bourgs*. Gaza was a large urban centre, a mere decade after the erection of a castle there. Even in a frontier fortress like Hunin we know of a civilian Frankish population and the documents mention private dwelling houses outside this castle. There was a considerable difference in the extent to which the *bourgs* developed. Some did not thrive because of unfavourable economic conditions, while others became sizeable towns. The great majority were not defended by walls and relied for their defence on the ramparts of the castle. Only a few (Gaza, 'Atlit, Karak and Montreal) were fortified and thus exactly resembled the European *faubourgs*.

The process of the development of a civilian settlement around the nucleus of the feudal-military castle as described above is almost identical to that so well known in Europe, but there is an important difference worth mentioning: while the European castle was the nucleus of settlement, most of Frankish *bourgs* in Palestine were established in ancient, decayed or abandoned Byzantine-Arab urban administrative centres. Continuity of settlement is a permanent phenomenon in the Holy Land, and arises chiefly from the need to be in close proximity to the few sources of water supply. The Frankish chroniclers indeed describe these settlements as if they had been ruined and deserted prior to the Frankish reoccupation, but indirect evidence shows that the destruction had not been complete, and that even if the Moslem inhabitants had left these townships on the eve of the conquest, they soon returned.

most bourgs in Palestine built on ancient settlements

We do not know whether the Frankish inhabitants mingled with the local residents or established their own quarters, but it may be assumed that they concentrated in close proximity to the castle. The Frankish inhabitants of the *bourgs* were burgesses and enjoyed the same rights and legal status as their fellow burgesses in the large towns. The lord's viscount was the chief administrator of the area under the jurisdiction of the *bourgs* and the head of the burgesses' court, discharging municipal and juridical functions. He was also sometimes castellan of the castle. Nor do we know what the physical form of the Frankish civilian settlement was, nor what the dwellings looked like, since no such suburb has been the subject of an archaeological investigation, with the exception of 'Atlit,

174

which has been partially surveyed. However, since it was built in the 13th century and was the last *faubourg* to be developed in Palestine, it cannot serve as an example of the *bourgs* of the 12th century. The only structure in the township that we know of, apart from the castle, is the parish church. Such churches were found in Gaza, Beit Govrin, Yavne, 'Atlit, Tsipori and Migdal-Afeq. The economic life of the Frankish population was based on agriculture, crafts and, to a lesser extent, on trade. There are townships which remained as rural settlements, no more than large villages, but others, like Gaza and Safed, developed into real administrative and commercial centres.

'ATLIT - CHASTIAU PELERIN

The impressive and formidable ruins of 'Atlit, jutting out from the Mediterranean shore between Haifa and Caesarea, are much more than a proud example of the diligence, devotion and architectural genius of the Crusaders. 'Atlit's magnificent fortifications, huge storerooms, graceful chapel, sculptural and ornamental relics are a majestic monument to the concept of strategy and colonization on which they were founded—and in which they failed—a concept which held that stone walls could take the place of men, that fortresses could guarantee sovereignty over a hostile population. This concept was criticized by the arch-enemy, Baybars: "A state cannot be defended by wall-building nor its inhabitants by the digging of moats."

The walls of 'Atlit crumbling in the waves symbolize the beginning of the end of the Crusader attempt to settle in Palestine. The Franks, having failed to secure a firm foothold in the land, were expelled after the battle of Hattin. When they attempted to reconquer their kingdom, they no longer ventured far from the coast. Fearful of the open spaces and of the Moslems, they clung to the sea, the only safe lifeline to their lands of origin. In the words of John de Joinville, the biographer of St. Louis, writing of an inland castle, "The barons of Outremer did not think it advisable to have the walls of this castle rebuilt, because it was five leagues from the sea, so that no provisions could be sent from the ports without the risk of their falling into the hands of the Saracens who were stronger than we were," and when the supreme ordeal came, the knights of 'Atlit abandoned their mighty fortress without a fight, and the Moslems did not even trouble to occupy it for some weeks after its evacuation.

Chroniclers of the epoch and modern historians have given varying answers as to why the Crusaders chose to fortify the cliff of 'Atlit: to counterbalance the Moslem fortifications of Mt. Tabor; to serve as a springboard for the capture of Jerusalem, as it was the only fortified point between Acre and the Holy City; or to enable the Templars to avoid the filth of the town of Acre and seclude themselves in this monastery-like spot. But it appears that the *raison d'être* of the fortress lay in the Franks' desire to gain an additional foothold in the narrow coastal belt of their kingdom, and this desire culminated in the simultaneous erection of the castles of 'Atlit and Caesarea. 'Atlit is situated in the Carmel Valley, on a small rocky cape which forms two shallow bays, north and south, providing shelter from gales to the ships of the period. Why they selected this particular spot, apart from its natural advantages, we do not know.

12th century

A small fort called Destroit was erected at 'Atlit as early as the beginning of the 12th century and entrusted to the charge of the Templars. The fort guarded the narrow passage between the *kurkar* (sandstone) ridge to the east and the sea-shore, which was a place of ambush for robbers. Building began on the castle of 'Atlit at the end of the winter of 1217–1218. King Jean de Brienne, together with the local knights and Crusader leaders from abroad, decided to fortify two points along the coast south of Acre, 'Atlit and Caesarea. The available strength was divided in two; in February 1218, under the Flemish knight Gautier d'Avesnes, the companies of the Templars and the Teutonic knights, with some of the European knights, began the fortification of 'Atlit. Many details concerning the building of the castle are known to us, mainly from the letters of Oliver of Paderborn. In his chronicle, known as "The History of Damietta," he relates:

building of
'Atlit (1218)

"The Templars, with the Lord Gautier d'Avesnes and with the aid of companies of pilgrims, and of the Teutonic Order, began to build Pilgrims' Castle, formerly known as Districtum, which is situated in the Diocese of Caesarea, between Haifa and Caesarea. It is located on a broad high promontory projecting into the sea naturally fortified by rocks on the west, north and south. For a period of six weeks while the fortification of Caesarea proceeded, the Templars dug and laboured on the cape, until they reached foundations and an ancient wall of great length and thickness. They found coins of a kind unknown to the men of their time, given by the son of God to his knights to alleviate them from their labour and expense. Later, while digging the sandy area inside, in order to clear it, they came upon another shorter wall, and abundant fresh water flowed in the level area between the walls, and the Lord gave amplitude of stones and cement.

"Two towers were built at the front of the castle, their stones being squared and cut to such a size that one stone could be hauled with difficulty by a yoke of oxen. Each of the towers was a hundred feet long and seventy-four feet in width. They enclosed within their breadth two vaults, and their height exceeded that of the cape. A high new wall with an external rampart was built between the two towers, and thanks to admirable skill, armed horsemen could go up and down [using a staircase.] Another wall was also [built] at some distance from the towers, continuing from one side of the sea to the other and so enclosing a spring of fresh water. The cape was surrounded on both sides by a high new wall on the rocks. Between the south wall and the sea there are two springs of sweet water which supply abundance of water to the castle. The castle contains within it a chapel, a palace and many houses. The chief use of these buildings is to enable the Templars to escape from the sinfulness and filth that fill the city of Acre."[45]

The work was completed by the Easter of 1218 (April 15th). The first test for the new stronghold came in the autumn of 1220. At that time the Christian and Moslem armies were locked in the battle of Damietta in Egypt, and the hostilities in Palestine were mere skirmishes in comparison. Al-Mu'azzam, ruler of Damascus, attacked Caesarea and destroyed it, and then turned north to

Mu'azzam attacks
'Atlit (1218)

attack 'Atlit. At his approach the Templars destroyed the castle of Destroit and concentrated at 'Atlit. The Crusader garrison numbered four thousand men. The Moslem force entrenched on the plain between the shore and the *kurkar* hills, deploying from Naḥal Oren (Wadi Falaḥ) on the north to the salt-pans south of the castle, were protected by wooden palisades and a ditch. An artillery duel developed, the Moslems firing missiles from eight pieces of mangonels and the Crusaders replying with missiles from engines mounted on the castle walls. The duel went on for a fortnight. The Moslems, who were in the open, suffered heavy losses while their missiles made no impression on the fortifications of 'Atlit. Crusader reinforcements began to arrive from Beirut and Cyprus to aid the besieged, and after a month had elapsed, al-Mu'azzam, seeing that he could not capture the castle without prolonged fighting and further weakening of his forces, decided to raise the siege. However, the Moslems destroyed all the plantations around 'Atlit before returning to their base at Damascus.

Following this ordeal, 'Atlit enjoyed relative peace for some years, and a suburb *(faubourg)* with a considerable Frankish population grew up in the shadow of the castle walls. This urban concentration is comparable in size to other Crusader towns such as Banias and Arsuf. The number of inhabitants is indicated by the Crusader cemetery, containing as many as seventeen hundred graves. Many buildings have been found in the town area, including a church and large barns and stables. 'Atlit was also the seat of a burgesses' court.
development of faubourg

At the end of 1228 the Emperor Frederick II attempted to seize the castle, but was unsuccessful. Another European ruler, Louis IX of France, strengthened 'Atlit's walls, and his wife Margaret of Provence bore a son there.

In 1265 the Mamluks, commanded by Baybars himself, attacked 'Atlit. They breached the town wall and destroyed all its houses, and the inhabitants sought refuge within the walls of the castle. Traces of this destruction are still discernible in the buildings of the town.
Baybar's attack (1265)

After the fall of Acre (1291), 'Atlit alone remained, the last Frankish stronghold in the country. The castle was not attacked, but its defenders decided to evacuate it without a fight, since with the loss of the Crusader capital, there was no point in defending it. On the 14th of August, 1291, the Crusaders abandoned the fortress and set sail for Cyprus. With the embarkation of the last of the knights of 'Atlit, Christian rule in the Holy Land came to an end. The Moslems took the castle six weeks after the evacuation and their commander ordered its gates and towers to be demolished.
last stronghold in Palestine

In the Mamluk period 'Atlit was the capital of a district *('Amal),* and at this time parts of the castle walls were rebuilt. The castle became a source of stone which the country's Turkish rulers, al-Jazzar, Sulaiman and the Egyptian Ibrahim Pasha, used for building the cities of Acre, Haifa and Beirut. As late as the 1880's the Turkish governor of Haifa sold fifty thousand stones from the castle to the governor of Jaffa to build the mole and the customs house of the port. Large parts of the castle were destroyed by an earthquake in 1837.
later history

The general plan of the town of 'Atlit is identical with the plans of the other

'Atlit, east town wall, from south-east

'Atlit town Crusader coastal towns (see p. 273); the town was walled and the citadel was situated on the seashore as a separate defensive unit. But, unlike the other coastal towns, the castle was here the nucleus around which the civilian settlement developed.

'Atlit was protected by two exterior and three interior lines of defence. A chain of forts was established on the crest of the *kurkar* ridge two kilometres *Destroit* from the shore, the northerly and the principal fort being Ḥ. Qarta (Destroit), built in 1103 and destroyed in 1220. Its plan is that of a Norman keep. The *kurkar* on which it was founded was levelled and parts were removed in such a way as to leave a square foundation a metre high, on which the walls of the tower were built. It had two storeys, reaching a height of 20 metres. It was surrounded by a wall and its inner court contained two cisterns, and mangers for horses. Remains of additional forts are to be seen a kilometre south of Ḥ. Qarta.

outer defences of The outer line of fortifications of 'Atlit itself is the town wall. The eastern *town* face was 600 metres long, beginning with a tower built in the sea on the northeast and terminating on the south-east with a square corner tower whose plan resembles that of Ḥ. Qarta. The tower is older than the wall and seems to have been used in the 12th century as an independent fort which was annexed to the wall when it was built in the 13th century. The southern town wall, 200 metres long, begins here and ends with a tower in the sea south of the castle. The town wall is fronted by a moat two metres deep. The walls rose 7.5 metres above the moat and were built of large stones tooled in a style identical with that of the

178

masonry of the castle. There were four wide gates into the town, three in the east wall and one in the south, all built within gate towers two storeys high.

The area of the castle begins 250 metres west of the town itself. It is built on a rocky headland, described by Oliver of Paderborn, its main fortification being concentrated at the narrow neck of the peninsula. A moat 6 metres deep was dug across it, revetted with large dressed ashlar blocks which rose above the lip of the moat to form an exterior wall or barbican. The bottom of the moat, which was below sea level, could be filled with water. There are two gates on the counterscarp, a narrow one on the north for pedestrians and a broad one on the south for wagons. The outer walls of the castle, built within the moat to a height of 16 metres, had three projecting towers. A vaulted corridor ran along the wall, opening onto loopholed casemates, and the top of the wall was edged with battlements. Thus the defenders had two rows of firing positions, one from the loopholes two-thirds of the way up the wall, the other from the battlements. Both positions covered the area in front of the moat. But the moat itself, at the foot of the wall, was dead ground from these positions, and the duty of covering it devolved upon the three wall towers. Although these were little higher than the top of the wall, their projection enabled enfilading fire to be directed from them. Each had two gates, to the north and south respectively.

defensive concept of castle

'Atlit, town, south-east corner tower

'Atlit, castle, east
curtain wall

Within the outer wall was a second line of defence, based on two huge square towers built opposite the spaces between the three projecting towers. These rose to a height of 30 metres, 16 metres above the outer wall and its towers. As the height of the outer wall above the revetment of the moat was also 16 metres, the relative heights were identical along all three lines of defence; the fortifications rose 16 metres, one above the other, along the whole length of the castle front. An enemy approaching from the east was thus within shooting range of three walls and five towers, as the defenders of each line fired over the heads of those below them.

conformity to Byzantine plan 'Atlit's fortifications conform to the classic Byzantine plan. According to Procopius, the 6th century historian whose works became the classic textbooks of Byzantine military architecture, a fortress should have three defensive lines, a moat at least the depth of the foundations of the wall to prevent sapping, an outer rampart or barbican, and an inner wall with two lines of defensive positions and square towers, each of three storeys. The Franks improved upon this design by installing passages and stairs linking the defence-lines and facilitating rapid reinforcement of threatened points. They also added numerous loopholes and machicolations. The flanks of the promontory which face the sea were fortified by a single wall with square towers; the Crusaders apparently did not anticipate an attack from this direction.

main gate The main gate of the castle was on the south and linked the outer and inner walls. It led into the inner courtyard as well as into a long corridor built into the thickness of the inner wall (see below). The gate itself has been completely destroyed. An additional gate was built on the north of the castle, likewise between the inner and outer walls.

outer wall The south tower of the outer wall, entered from the inner bailey, is preserved in its entirety. Its outer gates were evidently blocked at the end of the Crusader period. The upper sections of this tower, as well as part of the wall to its north,

180

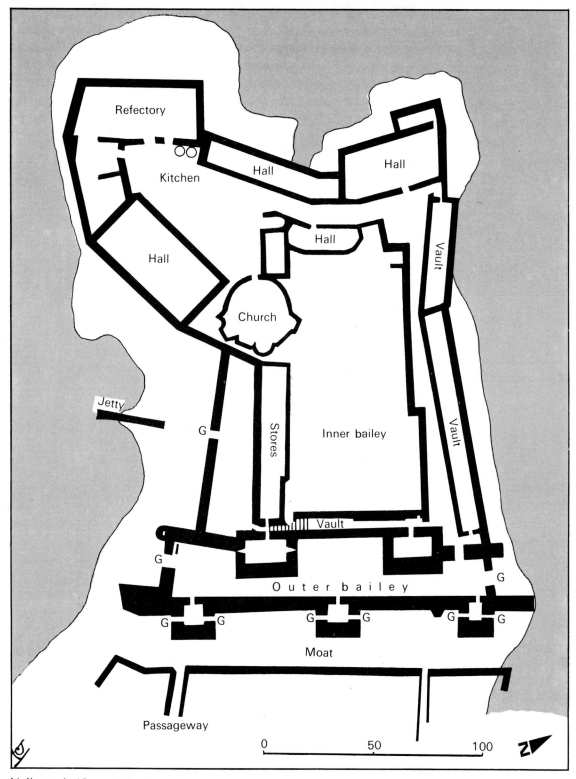

Refectory

Kitchen

Hall

Hall

Hall

Hall

Vault

Church

Jetty

G

Stores

Inner bailey

Vault

Vault

G

G

Vault

Outer bailey

G

G

G

G

G

G

G

G

Moat

Passageway

0   50   100

N

'Atlit, castle (General Plan)

'Atlit castle, vault at north-west side

were constructed by the Mamluks of small stones. They contained small loop-holes for muskets.

The outer wall contains traces of concealed staircases which connected it with the inner rampart. These stairs, found near the north tower and also near the south (main) gate, seem to be those of which Oliver of Paderborn declared, "thanks to admirable skill armed horsemen could go up and down."

second line   The castle's inner wall with its two huge towers constitutes the eastern end of the principal block of structures. A long corridor built in the thickness of the east wall connects the two giant towers. This corridor leads also to vaults and to the rooms on each side of it, and to a broad staircase providing access to the upper level of the block. The huge north tower, whose east wall is preserved to a great height, was the central hall of the castle. It had three storeys: a basement entered from the east corridor, a middle storey and a main storey, rib-vaulted, as high as the two lower storeys together. Corbels still remain on the inner side of the wall, bearing figures sculpted in the Gothic style which testify to the hall's splendour. The south tower, which apparently resembled the northern, has been almost completely destroyed, only its basement and part of its middle storey remaining. The south side of the main block is occupied by an immense hall which was used as a storeroom. This opened towards the eastern corridor and also southward towards the southern courtyard.

the castle   The castle chapel, polygonal in shape, is a graceful Gothic structure, almost *chapel*   entirely in ruins, but traces can be seen of the columns which stood at the corners of the building and of a decagonal apse on the east. According to the account of the English traveller Pococke, there were three apses. The roof vaulting

182

'Atlit castle, east vault

'Atlit castle, north main tower

survived until 1837, when it collapsed in an earthquake. Immense sections of the walls, with their windows, lie overturned in the middle of the chapel. To its *west hall* west is a magnificent hall with rib-vaulting. Entry to the hall, which has four bays, is from the south end which is built diagonally to the main axis. West of the hall, on the edge of the promontory, along the entire western and southern side of the castle, vast halls were built. These have almost entirely disappeared. There are some interesting buildings in the town area. About a hundred metres *church in town* from the south-east corner of the wall, flush with the eastern sector, the remains of an unfinished church in the Gothic style have been found. Built within a courtyard, it had a pentagonal apse, one square bay and a temporary wall to its west. Also to the west are the remains of additional bays, once under construction but never completed. Stone benches survive inside the church and fragments of stained glass windows within lead frames have also been found. On the south side of the town, near the wall, vestiges of barns and stables which were burnt in 1265 have been discovered; these are described elsewhere (see p. 259). On the north side are traces of a street, dwellings and a bath-house, which has been reconstructed. Outside the town walls, at the north-east corner near the seashore,

184

was the cemetery of the town. Carved tombstones were found here, bearing
crosses as well as symbols denoting the crafts of the deceased.

      cemetery

    Archaeological excavations were carried out at 'Atlit in the years 1930–1935
by the Department of Antiquities of the British Mandate Government.

BEIT GOVRIN - BETHGIBELIN

In the heart of the Shephela, on the crossroads leading to Jerusalem, Hebron,
Gaza and Ascalon, lies the settlement of Beit Govrin, "the house of the giants"
or "the house of the men." Beit Govrin reached the height of its prosperity in
the 4th–6th centuries A.D. when it was a large and populous walled city. In the
Byzantine period it was known as Eleutheropolis ("free city" or "city of free-   *earlier history*
men") and its territory embraced the entire south-eastern Shephela and the
southern Judaean Hills.

    The city declined during the Arab period and the number of its inhabitants
dwindled, as the Arab geographer al-Maqdisi related at the end of the 10th century: "It is the emporium for the neighbouring country, and a land of riches
and plenty, possessing fine domains. The population however is now on the
decrease, and impotence has possession of its men." Administratively the city
retained its position throughout the Arab period as the capital of a district *(kura)*

185

known as al-Darum. During the Crusader conquest its population decreased further, but, despite the testimony of William of Tyre that it lay desolate, there is no reason to suppose that all the local inhabitants had deserted it.

The Frankish settlers had settled in Beit Govrin as early as the first generation of the Crusader occupation. In this period it belonged to the territory of Hebron (St. Abraham) and a Greek monastery of St. George existed there throughout the Frankish period. Beit Govrin was identified by the Crusaders as the site of Beersheba, city of the Patriarchs, and this name (Bersabee) appears in the sources together with that of Bethgibelin. During the generation of the Crusader conquest the region of southern Judaea, including Beit Govrin, suffered much from the raids of the Egyptian garrison of Ascalon. In order to prevent these raids and to tighten the ring of investment surrounding the last Moslem stronghold on the coast, the Crusaders built a chain of fortresses around Ascalon, the first of which was at Beit Govrin. The fortresses of Tel Tsafit, Yavne, and Gaza were added subsequently. William of Tyre described the circumstances under which the castle at Beit Govrin was built:

building of castle

"The Christians perceived that the bold incursions of the enemy showed no signs of ceasing; their forces were constantly renewed. Hence after long deliberations, our people resolved to erect fortresses round about. Within these strongholds forces could be easily assembled which, from their very proximity could more readily check the enemy's forays. Twelve miles from Ascalon they built a strong fortress surrounded by an impregnable wall with towers, ramparts and a moat."[46]

handed to Hospitallers

The building was finished in 1136, the first Hospitaller castle to be erected. Before its completion, the city and a wide surrounding area including ten villages were handed over to the Order. Here the Hospitallers founded a settlement populated by peasants of European stock and conducting itself according to defined custom *(consuetudo)*. These rules determined penalties for crimes such as murder and adultery. The settlers were freemen who could, therefore, with certain restrictions, sell their property and leave the settlement. Each received a house and a plot of 700 dunams, part for irrigated cultivation and part composed of olive groves. For these the settlers paid a tenth of the crop and an additional fixed payment. The settlers owed military service and received a share of the spoils taken from the Moslems. Thirty-two families settled in Beit Govrin, some of them of the second generation in the country and some of the first. Frankish offenders were tried before a burgesses' court. The city had a mixed community which, apart from the Franks, local Christians and Moslems, included three Jewish families.

civilian settlement

The strategic value of Beit Govrin declined with the capture of Ascalon in 1153, but it continued to be an important crossroads where, according to a Moslem traveller of the time, taxes were levied on passing caravans. It was captured in 1187 by Saladin without fighting, and four years later its castle was destroyed to prevent its falling into the hands of the Franks. In 1240 it was restored to the Crusaders following the peace treaty between Richard of Corn-

13th century

186

wall and a-Saliḥ Ayub, ruler of Egypt, and the area returned to the ownership of the Order of the Hospitallers, who had assumed control of the whole area between Beit Govrin and Ascalon. In 1244 Beit Govrin was recaptured by the Moslems.

The Tel of Beit Govrin is rich in archaeological remains, chiefly of the Byzantine period. Traces of the Crusader castle lie west of the road from Beit Shemesh to Qiryat Gat, near the approach road leading to Kibbutz Beit Govrin. Here there is a series of ruined structures, called by the Arabs al-Qal'a (the Fortress). The Crusaders built their castle at the north-west corner of the Byzantine city wall and added a sector of wall on the south and east. Within the square enceinte was a structure with four towers, one at each corner. The plan of Beit Govrin castle thus resembled that of Belvoir, which also belonged to the Order of the Hospitallers. South of the interior structure was the chapel of the castle. The church had a single nave ending in an apse, and the hall was divided into four bays. The vaulting is supported on columns with Byzantine capitals taken into secondary use by the Crusaders. The first bay leads to a long narrow room with barrel-vaulting. From the second bay a corridor opens into an excellently preserved stair-well ascending to the second storey. At the end of the room a window looks down upon the courtyard, the court of the castle, and the exterior ramparts, which survive on the north to a considerable height.

South of Tel Beit Govrin are remains of the Church of St. Anne (Kh. Sanda-ḥannah), mentioned by the chronicler of Richard Coeur de Lion in his account of Richard's march through the area in 1192. The Franks utilized an ancient structure, of Byzantine origin, and erected a chapel by walling off the nave and central apse, leaving the aisles and side apses of the old basilica in ruins.

description of ruins

castle

St. Anne's

Beit Govrin (Bethgibelin), chapel in the castle (Plan)

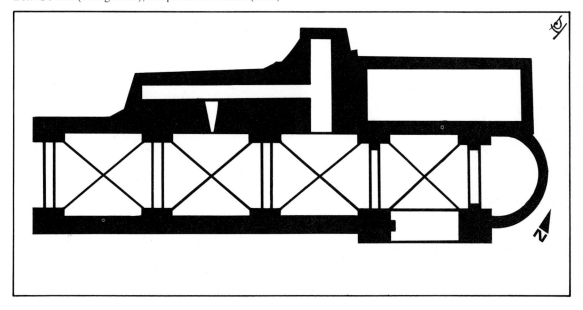

Beit Govrin, chapel in castle

DOR - MERLE

The double bay of Dor is called in Arabic Tantura, "peak of the cape," after the small cape which divides the bay into two, and in Talmudic literature "the tooth of Dor." It is one of the few natural anchorages on the coast of Palestine, *earlier history* and for this reason the Sidonians founded here, as early as the second millennium B.C., a large mercantile town, the southernmost of their cities. We hear of maritime activity on the coast of Dor as early as 1115 B.C., and Sidonians, Egyptians, Jews, Assyrians, Greeks and Romans used the port. In the Hellenistic period Dor was a flourishing town whose many remains, including walls, the port, a theatre and tombs, survive to this day. It declined in importance when Caesarea was established ten miles away, and fell into ruins in the 4th century A.D., remaining desolate throughout the Arab period, so that even its ancient name was forgotten.

The Crusader conquerors sought the site of ancient Dor, whose name was known to them as the seat of a bishopric in the early Christian period. Unable to verify its location, they identified it with Caesarea. As an anonymous traveller wrote, "Caesarea was first called Dor, then Strato's Tower, and is now called Caesarea."

The Crusaders built a castle on the small cape on the coast of Dor and named it after the family of de Merle, which received the area from the lords of Cae- *Frankish Merle* sarea as their domain. Hardly any information has come down to us about the history of Merle in the Crusader period, though it is known that a Frankish settlement with a burgesses' court existed there at the time. Merle was captured by Saladin in 1187. The chroniclers then referred to it as *Merla Templi,* signifying that it had previously passed into Templar possession. The Crusader fortress was abandoned just before the fall of 'Atlit in the year 1291. Sketches from the 19th century show a high wall which was apparently part of a Norman keep. The remains of the structure are meagre and the exact plan of the castle cannot be reconstructed.

GAZA - GADRES

From earliest times, the city of Gaza has been the key to the gateway of Egypt. The last large town on the border of the Sinai desert, it was situated on the *Via Maris* (Way of the Sea), the historic route traversed by all the peoples on their *earlier history* way to and from Egypt. To every generation Gaza was an important commercial centre and a strong fortress town.

Under Arab rule Gaza retained her status as a populous commercial centre. When the Holy Land was conquered by the Crusaders, the city remained in Egyptian hands as a transit point on the road to their main base at Ascalon. The

Crusaders seized Gaza and fortified it only in 1149, after they had completed the encirclement of Ascalon from the north and east by the castles of Beit Govrin, Tel Tsafit and Yavne. The object of the city's capture and fortification was, in the words of William of Tyre, "so that Ascalon might be hemmed in on the south just as it was on the north and east by the fortresses they had built there."[47]

According to William, the Crusaders found the city destroyed and completely deserted, but the words of the Frankish historian are apparently not to be taken literally: he wrote that other places where the Crusaders built fortifications were also derelict, whereas we know from other sources that this was not the case. It may therefore be supposed that, despite his explicit statement that the city was in ruins and abandoned, Gaza was not completely empty and that occupation had not ceased there, although it must certainly have dwindled. Five years after the renewal of its fortifications Gaza was visited by the Moslem traveller Idrisi, who wrote that the city was "very populous." We can hardly assume that this large population had gathered again in so short a time. The Moslem noble Usamah also testified indirectly to the continuity of the city's occupation when he referred in 1154 to the quality of the saddles manufactured at Gaza.

Crusaders rebuild Gaza The Crusaders began the work of fortifying Gaza in the winter of 1149–1150. "On the appointed day the entire people assembled as one man at the place designated. They attacked the work with concerted efforts and each vied with his neighbour in assisting to rebuild the place."[48] The Crusaders decided not to repair the ancient wall of the town, but to build a castle on the top of the hill at its centre, as they considered that they had not the strength to defend the whole area. On completion, the castle was handed over to the Templars.

The work of refortification caused great concern among the Moslems, who saw that the encirclement of Ascalon would thus be completed, and that it would no longer be possible to send supplies and reinforcements there by land. They therefore attempted to interrupt the building of the castle by diversionary attacks from the direction of Galilee and by raids from Ascalon. Although they failed, and the Crusader hold on Gaza interrupted the relief of the Egyptian garrison at Ascalon, it could not completely seal the roads to the movement of small mobile Moslem forces. Nevertheless, during the siege of Ascalon (1153), the castle of Gaza served to stop the speedy arrival of Egyptian reinforcements. After Ascalon had been captured, Gaza's functions changed and it became a frontier fort on the edge of the desert of Sinai, and an advanced base for Crusader campaigns aimed at the conquest of Egypt.

growth of Gaza In the 1150's and 1160's Gaza's population grew. Its inhabitants, mostly Moslems and Syrian Christians with a few Franks, settled at the foot of the Templar castle and rehabilitated the old city walls. A burgesses' court was set up. As elsewhere in Palestine, the development of the urban settlement of Gaza in the 12th century was very like that of the urban settlements *(faubourgs)* in Europe, and its livelihood came from its trade and crafts. Gaza's ancient port of Anthedon, three kilometres from the town, was used and its name was transformed by the Arabs into "Tida."

190

In 1170 Amalric built the castle of Darom (Daron) at Deir al-Balaḥ, south of Gaza, but immediately after its completion it was besieged by Saladin in the winter of the same year. A Crusader army went to the help of the fortress, making its rear base at Gaza. Seeing the superior strength of the enemy the Franks decided not to join battle, but to keep close formation. Saladin, unsuccessful in *siege of 1170* drawing the Franks, decided to seize their base at Gaza, where the town and castle were commanded by Milo do Plancy. At sight of the enemy approaching the civilian population sought refuge within the walls of the castle, but its commander prevented them from entering, in order to force them to defend the outer walls of the *faubourg*. The Moslems, arriving at the foot of the wall, which was low and weak, began to penetrate the town. Fierce hand-to-hand fighting developed, in which sixty-five Frankish youths of al-Bira *(Magna Mahomeria)* distinguished themselves, fighting desperately against the Moslems until most of them were slain. The enemy broke into the town and the wretched citizens, refused entry into the castle enclave despite their hopeless plight, were butchered with their wives and children. The *faubourg* was destroyed and plundered and the Moslems returned to their own territory laden with loot.

In November 1177, Saladin again attacked Gaza, but its Templar defenders held their ground. The Moslems decided not to waste time and continued on *1177* their way to the battle of Gezer (Montgisart), where they were defeated. Five years after that battle, in 1182, a Moslem force again invaded the country; this time it was a coordinated attack on the kingdom from the north and the south, the northern force advancing upon Beirut and the southern towards Gaza. The invasion from the north was the more threatening, and the Frankish army set out to meet it, leaving the southern frontier to be defended by the Templar garrisons of Gaza and Darom. In spite of considerable losses, the Templars were able to prevent a Moslem encroachment on Crusader territory again.

After the battle of Hattin and the conquest of the north of the country, Saladin arrived in the southern coastal plain in mid-August. The key to control of the area was the great fortress of Ascalon, and during the siege there Egyptian forces *Third Crusade* captured the castle of Darom. Gaza held out for some time, but its Templar defenders were ordered to surrender by the Grand Master, Gerard de Ridefort, who had been captured at the battle of Hattin and was set free by the Moslems in return for the surrender of Gaza. During the Third Crusade Saladin ordered the destruction of Gaza and the other fortresses of the southern coastal plain, in order to deny the Franks all possibility of finding bases in the area.

The city was destroyed in September 1191, but Richard Coeur de Lion reached it six months later. He repaired the walls of the castle and restored it to the Templars, but the renewal of Frankish rule was short-lived; by the peace treaty of 1192 Gaza remained outside Frankish control. Furthermore, Richard himself undertook to demolish its walls. The city was restored by the Moslems and became an administrative, military and commercial centre. Severe fighting between the Crusaders and the Moslems took place around Gaza in the years 1239 and 1244, ending in the defeat of the Crusaders.

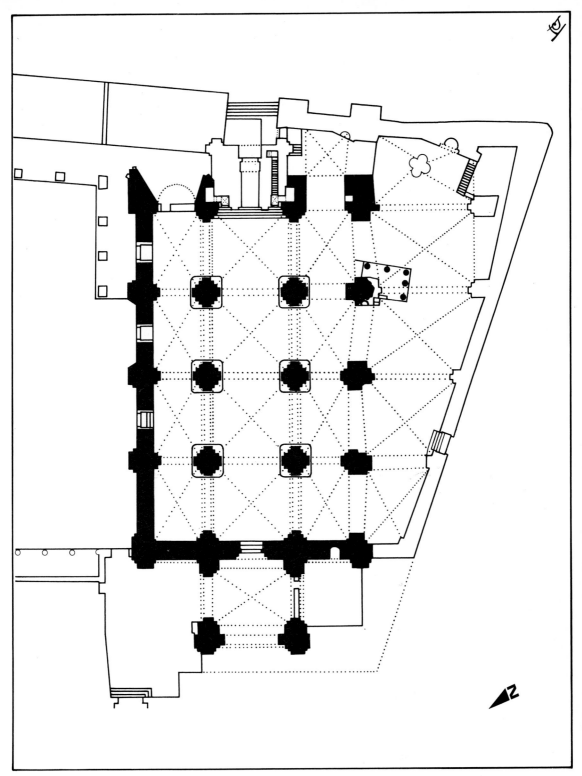

Gaza, Church of St. John

Relics of the Crusader occupation were severely damaged during the First World War, when Gaza was heavily bombarded by the British army, and the remains of the Crusader castle, still visible in the middle of the 19th century, were destroyed at that time. Another survival, the Church of St. John, which had become the great mosque of Gaza, was also hit in the bombardment of 1916 and its eastern part demolished, but this was afterwards restored.

The Church of St. John stands in the centre of ancient Gaza, on the edge of the old market. The Crusader building was extended southward, and its original walls have been preserved on the west (the entrance portal) and the north. The interior was divided into a nave and two aisles, terminating in three apses, the nave being loftier than the aisles. The building is roofed by a groined-vault resting on square piers joining four columns with Corinthian capitals. The columns and other building materials came from the Byzantine basilica which preceded the Crusader church. One column also shows a decorative relief from a synagogue. The main entrance was from the west, where there is a fine marble portal, composed of three pointed arches on either side resting on twin columns.

Another mediaeval building at Gaza is the Greek Orthodox Church of St. Porphyrius. This consists of a chapel with nave divided into two bays ending in a single apse. During the Crusader period Gaza was the centre of a Greek bishopric which included Beit Govrin.

MIGDAL - AFEQ - MIRABEL

From the top of a chain of hills at the foot of the mountains of Samaria, Mirabel commands one of the most important natural passes in the coastal plain, the Pass of Afeq. Here, more than a mile west of the hills, rise the rich sources of the River Yarqon. Although it is not broad and its banks are low, the Yarqon once constituted a sizeable natural obstacle because of the tangled vegetation which lined its banks and the swamps through which it passed on its way to the sea. The narrow defile between the foothills and the headwaters of the river had therefore always been one of the most important passes on the *Via Maris*. Owing to its strategic position, it was fortified in most periods. The fortifications were situated on each side of the pass—Migdal-Afeq on the east and Tel-Afeq on the west. Many battles have been fought in the pass—in the biblical period, in the days of the Hasmoneans, in the early Arab period, in Crusader times, during the First World War and during Israel's War of Independence.

Two keypoints, west and east of the pass, were fortified in the Crusader period. On the east the castle of Mirabel was erected, and on the west a small fort was established on the hill of Antipatris, with the picturesque name of *Turon ad surdos fontes* (the Fort at Deaf Springs), which is mentioned in a document of 1160 as being within the domain of Mirabel. The exact date of the construction of Mirabel is not known. In 1122 Mirabel already appears as the centre of a fief, whose lord was Balian the Elder, the founder of the Ibelin family. Balian, who was the Constable of Jaffa, received Mirabel from the *centre of fief* Count of Jaffa, in whose domain it was before it became an independent seigneurie. In 1143 Balian also received Yavne, and in 1148, Ramla. Upon Balian's death. Mirabel passed to his widow, who married Manasses de Hierges.

In 1152 rivalry over the control of Jerusalem broke out between Baldwin III and his mother, the Lady Melisende. The army of the queen mother, commanded by Manasses de Hierges, withdrew to Mirabel, but surrendered to the force of Baldwin III after a short siege. At a later period Mirabel was in the hands of the Ibelins, but it ceased to be an independent seigneurie, and was subordinate to Ramla. An urban-agricultural settlement developed around the castle, with houses, vineyards and orchards belonging to various churches *faubourg* and to the Hospitallers. Mirabel was the seat of a viscount, indicating that it was an administrative centre, and that there was probably a burgesses' court.

In 1187 Mirabel was captured by the Moslems and the Frankish inhabitants were allowed to proceed to Jerusalem. Thereafter, Saladin's army used it as a base for raiding and overrunning the maritime plain, and following the defeat of

Migdal-Afeq (Mirabel) north-west corner tower

the Moslems in the battle of Arsuf (1192), Saladin pitched his camp in and near the castle. The Moslem general correctly gauged the strategic value of Mirabel, its usefulness as a base for attacking the Franks, who were advancing south-ward, and as a vantage point commanding the roads ascending eastward towards Jerusalem. But after Richard Coeur de Lion had crossed the Yarqon near its mouth, and taken Jaffa, there was no further point in holding the base in the Afeq Pass, and the Sultan, fearing that Ascalon would be captured, left Migdal-Afeq to make his way there. The Crusader castle was destroyed by the Moslems as part of the "scorched earth" policy carried out in the towns of the maritime plain, to which Lydda, Ramla and all the castles of the district fell victim. In the peace treaty between Richard Coeur de Lion and Saladin, Mirabel was ex-cluded from Crusader territory and does not seem to have been recovered by the Franks.

ruins Remains of the fortress are today embodied in the huge structure of "Sheikh Sadiq" on the summit of the hill of Migdal-Afeq. The castle is of the *"castrum"* type. The Crusader remains consist of the north-western corner tower, the foun-dation of the southern curtain wall and a square keep with walls two metres thick, with loopholes. A Greek inscription is to be seen in secondary use on the entrance of the keep.

In the Mamluk period the castle of Mirabel remained in ruins and the western flank of the Afeq Pass was fortified instead. The small Crusader fort on the hill of Antipatris was enlarged and became a fine fortress whose remains survive in greater part to the present day.

MI'ILYA-CHASTIAU DOU REI

This fine castle and township was built on the ancient Tel of the biblical city of 'Aloth (I Kings 4, 16). The hill is occupied today by the Arab village of Mi'ilya,

position whose population numbers some fifteen hundred, all members of the Greek Orthodox church. The village was formerly built entirely within the ancient walls of the Crusader castle and in its immediate proximity. Most of the villagers have now left their old houses and built modern dwellings for themselves to the north and west of the fortress.

At present, as in the Crusader period, the villagers cultivate the fertile lands of the Vale of Me'ona, of which the traveller Burcardus wrote in 1283: "[It] abounds with all good things and with fruits which even in that land are rarely found elsewhere."[49]

description The castle is oblong, its north and south sides being shorter than the eastern and western. Square towers are built at the corners of the rectangular walled enclosure; hence the castle is of the *castrum* type. The north side is completely preserved today, with two corner towers surviving to their full height. The east-ern and western walls are also preserved in greater part. The corner towers have

Mi'ilya, north wall

loopholes directed towards the moat and also towards the curtain wall between the two towers. The stones of the fortifications are cut with drafted bosses characteristic of the 12th century and many carry masons' marks. Within the oblong walled enclosure are additional Crusader structures which have been utilized, with alterations, in the Arab peasant dwellings. The stones of the castle were used to build the old mosque of the village, which dates from the Mamluk period.

We have no information concerning the fortification of this site during the period preceding the Crusaders, nor is the date when the Crusaders built the fortress known. They called it by its Arab name (both the name Mhalia and that of *Castellum Regis,* "The King's Castle," appear in the documents). Probably captured in 1104, when Acre was taken, it belonged to the royal domain of Acre during the first years of the Crusader occupation. As early as 1160 the king granted certain rights to one John of Haifa at "my castle called Mhalia". During the 1160's it was no longer part of the royal domain but came into the possession of a noble named Henri de Milly. This family was one of the oldest in

centre of seigneurie

197

the Kingdom of Jerusalem and had been connected with the region of Acre since the conquest. The domain of the "King's Castle" was extensive, including not less than thirty-six villages throughout western and central Galilee, and also Naḥal Keziv, where the castle of Montfort was built. (On the connection between Mi'ilya and Montfort, see Montfort.)

The domain of the "King's Castle" possessed full seigneurial rights, including a seigneurial court as well as a burgesses' court. Around the nucleus of the castle a sizeable Frankish settlement grew up. In the 1170's *Joscelin III* of Courtenay, a kinsman of the king of Jerusalem, married the heiress to the "King's Castle" and received the domain as dowry, adding to it a number of neighbouring estates. In 1179 he purchased the domain of Chamberlain in the Plain of Acre and that of St. George, Montfort, Manueth and others, so that, by the end of the 12th century, the Joscelin estate was one of the largest in the kingdom. But in 1187 the domain of the "King's Castle" was taken by Saladin. When it was restored to Joscelin's family, in 1192, it was divided among Joscelin's three daughters and their husbands. Mi'ilya itself came into the possession of Otto of Hanberg. It was sold in 1220 to the Teutonic Order, who transferred the administrative centre to Montfort in 1228, after that castle was also bought by them.

The castle was captured by Baybars in 1265.

Joscelin III

Teutons

QALANSUWA-CALANSUE

In the middle of the Arab village of Qalansuwa are remains of a Crusader tower and church. The latter, partly rebuilt, is today used as the village mosque. Its southern and western portions retain their original form to a height of six metres. The south wall, two and a half metres thick and built of large blocks tooled and drafted, has an entrance at its centre leading to the vaulted cellars.

West of the church are the remains of one wall of the Crusader tower, now used as part of a dwelling. The Crusader wall is some 13 metres high.

Calansue was a Frankish township and an administrative centre in the lordship of Caesarea, and the seat of a viscount. Part of the village was transferred to the Hospitallers in 1129. It was captured in 1187 by Saladin and restored to the Franks five years later, but in 1265 it was taken by Baybars, and granted as a fief to one of the Mamluk emirs.

QAQUN-CACO

The remains of a Mamluk castle built on Crusader foundations lie in the centre of the abandoned village of Yikon (Qaqun) on the highroad from Caesarea to

Nablus. In the Crusader period Qaqun, known to the Franks as Caco, was a small townlet with a number of inhabitants of Frankish origin. It belonged to the lords of Caesarea and was the seat of a viscount. The Hospitallers owned tracts of land, and water rights, at Qaqun and in its vicinity. On the eve of the battle of Hattin the existence of a Templar force at Qaqun is mentioned, but it is not clear whether it was stationed there temporarily or whether the castle was the property of the Templars.

Qaqun was captured by Baybars in the 1260's. After conquering Caesarea in 1265, the Mamluks began a systematic destruction of the region of the maritime plain. Caesarea, and with it the remainder of the castles and villages of the littoral, fell victim to this policy, and the Mamluks transferred the administrative centre inland to Qaqun. In 1267 the castle was enlarged, a market and trading centre were established there and tribes of Turkmens were settled nearby, charged with the defence of the coastal plain.

In November 1271, Edward (subsequently Edward I of England) raided Qaqun, but decided to retreat when he realized that he could not take it. The plan of the castle is not clear, but the remains suggest that the Crusader fortification was of the "Norman Keep" type.

SAFED

Safed today is a small picturesque town on the top of a high hill (840 metres above sea level), with an inspiring view over the hills and the Sea of Galilee. The old houses and tortuous lanes of the town are piled one above another over the steep slopes of "Citadel Hill," upon which the great Crusader stronghold was erected.

The name of Safed does not appear until the first century A.D., when it was fortified by Flavius Josephus during the great rebellion against Rome. Despite *earlier period* its comparative youth, Safed is regarded, with Jerusalem, Hebron and Tiberias, as one of the four sacred cities of the Jews of Palestine, owing its sanctity to the Jewish community which flourished there in the 16th and 17th centuries, when it was the centre of the great mystical school of Kabbala. Strangely enough, this flowering of Jewish Safed was made possible to no small degree by the fact that a Christian order of knights and a Christian bishop fancied the town as a dwelling place and erected a castle there. When it was captured by the Mamluks, it became the capital of a province, and gradually developed into a great commercial centre in which many Jews settled.

Today only scanty remains survive of what was one of the largest and greatest Frankish castles in the Orient. Wars and, more than wars, severe earthquakes, *scanty remains* such as visit Safed every century (1759, 1837, 1927), have destroyed the stronghold completely. Small forts were built over its ruins in the 18th century, and after the First World War a large park was laid out there. The stones of the

Safed, keep

castle have been used as building blocks in the houses of Safed, and its halls as water reservoirs. All these have almost entirely obliterated the outline of the gigantic structure. Thanks only to the accounts of travellers and scholars who visited Safed in the 16th and 17th centuries, and to drawings made late in the 19th century, do we know the plan of the castle and the details of some of its inner buildings, though a brief archaeological excavation in 1962 added a little to our knowledge.

description of
castle
The fortress was elliptical in shape, comprising three concentric lines of defence with a common centre. The first line was an outer wall with ten circular towers defended, apparently, by a rock-cut moat. This wall was built along the main street of Safed (Jerusalem Street) and today has completely disappeared, although a number of courses were found near the bridge crossing the street. A tower which comprises part of the gate area remains on the south-west side of the hill, and as late as the beginning of the 19th century a vaulted passage, which apparently led under the moat to the gate in the inner wall, could be seen there.

Within the outer wall was a second rock-cut moat, and behind it an inner wall with a number of circular or polygonal towers. Remains of this wall have been partly uncovered south of the Citadel Garden area, to the right of the road which encircles it; here a section of the moat can also be seen. Remains of an additional tower of this wall are visible on the north-west side of the garden, further along the road.

A huge central keep of polygonal plan occupied the summit of the hill, and

200

by its great height commanded the whole castle area. The western part of this tower has been excavated and cleared. Its interior and exterior walls are visible, as are remains of a vault, mostly collapsed, which connects them. In the centre of the keep, buried beneath the modern observation point in which stands a war memorial, is a gigantic polygonal hall, today a water reservoir. The inner bailey of the castle once lay to the north of the keep.

The main gate of the fortress was on the south-west side, and is partly ex- *gate*
posed not far from the section of the inner wall near the approach road to the citadel. Remains of an arch, a paved area and a number of steps are visible. The plan of the entrance has not yet been clarified, nor has the gate in the outer wall been found. Various interior structures have been discovered in the area between the keep and the inner wall, in the southern part of the castle; here the foundations of a wall have been excavated, apparently the base of a roofed corridor which led through various twists and turns from the gate to the interior of the castle. Such a corridor is indeed alluded to in a traveller's account of the 16th century, and also in the descriptions of Arab travellers and historians of the Mamluk period.

A subterranean water tunnel, partly rock-cut, partly masonry-built, has been disclosed in the area of the keep and to its south. It is known from accounts of *water supply* Arab historians that the castle had a remarkable water-supply system, which they regarded as one of the wonders of the world. Two sources stated that it consisted of wells, another that it was a channel. This system supplied the inhabitants of the castle with running water within its walls. The exact plan of the water system has not been traced. Remains have also been found of an aqueduct which carried water from the north, but its source of supply is unknown. It may be noted, however, that a number of springs exist north of the castle, rising at a higher altitude than that of Citadel Hill, and from these water could have flowed to the fortress. Halls, storerooms, stables and living quarters are buried beneath the park, but it is doubtful if they will ever be uncovered, for this would involve the destruction of the delightful garden that had been planted over them.

The citadel of Safed belongs to the type known as the concentric fortress, which is a modification of the "Spur-Castle" type. The remains exposed enable us to date a number of building periods identical with the historical information we possess concerning the castle. Details have been found which belong to the first period of building, namely the 12th century, and there are numerous remains of the period of its greatest glory, the mid-13th century; details of its plan and measurements have been preserved in numerous accounts and these will be noted as we proceed. Remains have also been found of the period after the Crusader conquest, when the castle was in the possession of the Mamluks.

Before we pass to an account of the castle's history, something must be said of its position and strategic importance. The Crusader historians called Safed *strategic* "the key of Galilee", a well-deserved epithet. The town dominates the whole *importance* region between the Ḥula Valley and the Sea of Galilee, once traversed by such important routes as the Damascus–Tiberias highway, on which was the important "Jacob's Ford" (Gesher Benot Ya'aqov). Safed also commanded the mountainous and densely populated region of central Upper Galilee. The stronghold further acted as a vital link in the Crusaders' network of beacons (see p. 294).

built in 1102–3   Although the exact date of building is not clear, it may be assumed that the first fortifications were raised in 1102–1103, judging from a document of 1103 which mentions Safed as a fortified place. A Moslem historian puts the date of building in the year 1102. If so, it was built by Hugh of St. Omer, Prince of Galilee, who wished to extend the bounds of his principality northward and in 1105 went on to build the castles of Tibnin and Hunin. At all events, in the first quarter of the 12th century the castle seems to have belonged to the prince of Galilee. It was subsequently transferred to the ownership of King Fulk in unknown circumstances, and was probably enlarged by him in the 1140's. A burgesses' court sat at Safed, and its presence shows that a considerable European population lived there at the time.

faubourg   King Amalric sold the castle to the Order of the Templars in 1168. A large urban settlement, which included a Jewish community, began to flourish in the shadow of its walls. When Saladin marched upon the castle of Chastelet in 1179, the Moslems raided the *Faubourg* of Safed and destroyed it, uprooting its orchards and laying siege to the castle to prevent it from rendering aid to the neighbouring Chastelet. After the battle of Hattin, the Crusaders held out at Safed for over a year, but surrendered at the beginning of December 1188, after a two months' siege conducted by Saladin himself. The latter was not unappreciative

Safed, castle (General Plan from 19th Century)

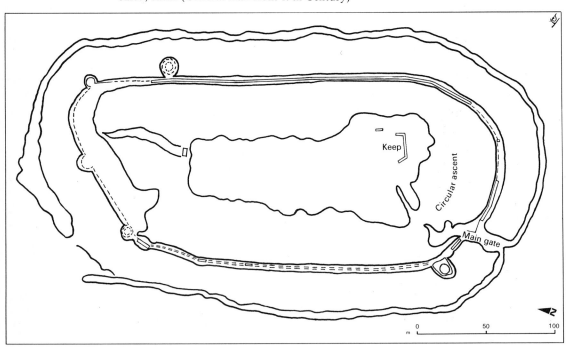

of the bravery of the defenders, and as a token of his esteem allowed them to go unmolested to Tyre. The Moslems fortified Safed in their turn, making use of the Crusader castle.

The stronghold was destroyed by the sultan al-Mu'azzam in 1219 when, following the landing of the Fifth Crusade in Egypt, he feared a Christian victory and demolished many Crusader fortresses to prevent them from falling into Frankish hands again. When the crusade against Egypt failed Safed remained in ruins, but still in Moslem hands. *destroyed in 1219*

In 1240 the whole of Galilee was ceded to the Crusaders by the peace treaty signed by Richard of Cornwall. The ruined castle was restored to the Templars *rebuilding* and occupied by a small garrison. Its rebuilding was begun under the aegis of Benoit d'Alignan, Bishop of Marseilles, at the end of the same year. The history of the rebuilding of the castle, together with its description and measurements, was given in great detail in a work entitled *De constructione castrum Saphet,* written in 1264 by the Bishop himself.

While visiting the country with the Crusade of the Count of Champagne in 1239, Benoit d'Alignan had perceived the importance and strategic value of *Benoit d'Alignan* Safed, above all for the protection of Christian pilgrims visiting the holy sites in Galilee. He proposed to the Master of the Templars that he rebuild the ruined fortress of the Order. After hesitations and delays arising from lack of money and shortage of manpower, the Bishop was able to persuade the Master to accept his plan, and it was decided to begin work immediately. The decision spread joy among the knights of the Order and the inhabitants of Acre. A force of knights and archers was enrolled to protect the workers, money was collected for the building, labourers and beasts of burden were assembled and supplies brought up for the builders' needs. In December 1240 the knights and workers gathered at the appointed place and the Bishop performed the ceremony of laying the corner-stone. Moslem sources state that a thousand Moslem prisoners of war were employed in the work of construction. When they saw that the Franks numbered no more than two hundred, they determined to mutiny and communicated their plans to the ruler of Damascus. He, wishing to maintain good relations with the Christians, informed them of the conspiracy, whereupon the Christians retaliated by putting to death all the Moslem prisoners.

The castle was the largest Christian fortress in the east. According to the Bishop of Marseilles' account, it extended over an area of 40 dunams, a figure that corresponds to modern measurements of the ruins. The circumference of *largest Frankish* its exterior wall was as much as 850 metres, the height of its ramparts 28 metres *fortress* and the depth of the moat 15 metres. The outer wall had seven large towers, each 24 metres in height (in the 19th century plan of the site, ten are marked on that wall). The fortress was equipped with all the engines of war in use at that period.

The rebuilding of the castle of Safed was completed within two and a half years, by the middle of 1243, at a cost of more than a million gold bezants. The castle was so planned that it could be defended by a relatively small number of people. In peacetime seventeen hundred people lived there, but in time of war the number grew to two thousand. In normal times the garrison comprised fifty knights and their squires, thirty Brothers-at-Service, fifty light horsemen with their mounts, three hundred operators of the military engines, eight hundred and twenty workers for current maintenance and four hundred slaves.

A flourishing town with a population of several thousand developed under the castle's walls, and became the trading centre of all the surrounding villages. It is called in the documents *Burgus sive Villa*. Historical sources state that the domain of Safed included two hundred and sixty villages comprising ten thousand families. Near the town twelve water mills were functioning. Sources mention orchards, vineyards, olive groves and pasturage in the vicinity. Safed's prosperity, which reached its peak at the end of the Middle Ages, thus received its impetus from the Crusader castle. The Jewish community grew steadily during the 13th century and Safed became an important Jewish centre.

The town did not remain in Frankish hands for long. In June 1266, the Mamluk Sultan Baybars marched on Safed with a large army and laid siege to the town. But the gigantic fortifications resisted all attempts at breaching, although the walls suffered damage at several points, and the strong garrison threw back the Moslem assaults. The morale of the besiegers sank so low that Baybars was forced to imprison forty emirs for defeatism. After six weeks of siege, when the Moslem general saw that he could not win by force, he chose cunning. He appealed to the Syrian Christians within, promising to spare them if they would open the gates of the castle. The attempt to create discord among the defenders was successful; in the ensuing disorder the besieged decided to send a delegate to Baybars to discuss terms, hoping that the Sultan would allow them to leave the castle peacefully and proceed to Acre. The delegate, a certain Syrian by the name of Leon, was bribed by the Moslems and betrayed the Franks. Upon returning to the castle he told them that the Sultan had accepted their terms; the gates of the castle were opened on the 23rd of July 1266, the Moslems surrounded the Christians and took all of them prisoner. The women and children

were sold as slaves, while the men were taken to a nearby hill and decapitated. The sources relate that over a thousand Christian warriors were put to death in this fashion. Baybars spared two knights, one of whom was sent to Acre to recount the story of the siege and of Moslem brutality, in order to spread alarm and despondency.

In 1267 Baybars began the work of rebuilding the castle, a project which lasted two years and cost a considerable sum. Safed became the capital of a Mamluk province which stretched from Jenin in the south to Tibnin in the north, and from 'Atlit in the west to Tiberias in the east.

TEL TSAFIT - BLANCHEGARDE

Frankish Blanchegarde was situated on the hill of Tel Tsafit, at a crossroads in the Judaean foothills. From the summit of the hill a wide view extends over the entire region of the Judaean Plain and foothills, from Ramla in the north to the northern Negev in the south and from the hills of Hebron in the east, westward to the sea.

The castle of Blanchegarde was built in 1142, by King Fulk of Jerusalem, as one of the border strongholds erected to face Egyptian Ascalon. William of Tyre wrote:

"Accordingly, in the following spring, it was resolved to build another fortress. By increasing the number of fortified places round about, they could harass the people of Ascalon.---Workmen were called, the people were furnished with all necessary materials, and a stronghold of hewn stone, resting on solid foundations, was built. It was adorned with four towers of suitable height."[50]

The same writer went on to sum up the significance of the castle of Blanchegarde as a colonizing influence:

"The result was that those who dwelt in the surrounding country began to place great reliance on this castle as well as on the other strongholds, and a great many suburban places grew up around it. Numerous families established themselves there, and tillers of the fields as well. The whole district became more secure because the locality was occupied and a more abundant supply of food for the surrounding country was made possible." *suburban development*

Blanchegarde was held by the King until Ascalon was captured. After 1153 it apparently belonged to the Count of Ascalon, and subsequently to Amalric I, King of Jerusalem. A Frankish township developed around the castle, and a burgesses' court was established. In 1166 the region about the castle became an independent seigneurie which was handed over to the Brisbarre family, the former lords of the city of Beirut. *seigneurie*

The township was taken by Saladin in 1187. On Richard Coeur de Lion's advance into the south of the country in 1191, the castle was destroyed on Saladin's orders, but was recaptured and garrisoned by the Franks in 1192. After the peace treaty of 1192 Blanchegarde was returned to the Moslems. In 1241, it came back into the hands of the Franks, but was captured and destroyed by the Moslems in 1244. *1187–1244*

Very scanty Crusader remains have been found on the site and the plan of the castle cannot be reconstructed although, according to William of Tyre's account, it was of the *castrum* type, with four corner towers. *remains*

205

TSIPORI - LE SAFORIE

Just before the coming of the Crusaders, Tsipori was a large township and the capital of an Arab district (kura). Information about the town after the arrival of the Crusaders is very scanty, although it is clear that it was occupied throughout the 12th and 13th centuries. Travellers described it as a "fortified town" and a "fair town with a castle above it," although in 1185 John Phocas referred to it as "almost entirely uninhabited." It belonged to the Archbishop of Nazareth and it seems that it had a small Frankish population. Tsipori lay at an important crossroads on the pilgrim route from Acre to Nazareth and its fertile lands extended over the Plain of Beit Netofa to the north. The springs of Tsipori ('Ayun al-Qastal) south of the town were the point of assembly for the Crusader

small Frankish population

Tsipori, church (Plan)

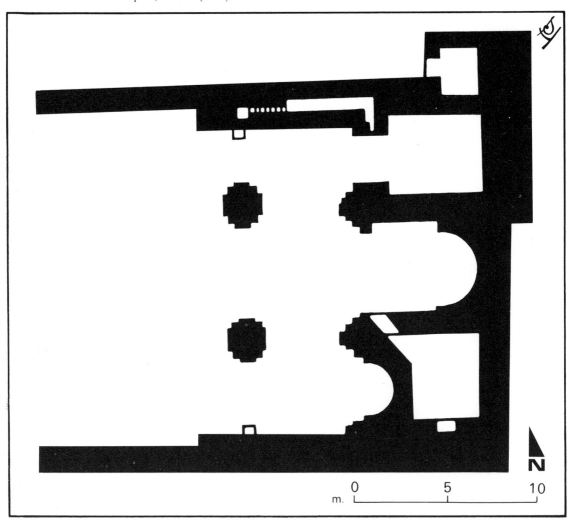

armies mobilized by the king in the years 1171, 1183 and 1187, and the Crusader host set out from there for the Battle of Hattin.

Tsipori was captured by Saladin in 1187 and restored to the Franks in 1240. In the 1250's the castle of Tsipori was in the hands of the Templars, as is recorded by John de Joinville, the biographer of St. Louis, who visited it in 1251 while on a pilgrimage to Nazareth. In 1255, a Rayis (see p. 218) of Saforie, John Semes, is mentioned in a charter. The town and castle were captured by Baybars in 1263.

The castle stands on the top of the hill of the ancient city; its remains form *castle* the south-western corner of the more recent Arab fortress, built at the end of the 18th century by Aḥmed, son of Dahar al-'Omar. Masonry courses of Crusader date survive to a considerable height in this portion. The second storey of the structure was built by the Turks in the 1880's as a school for local children.

West of the fortress are remains of the Crusader church of SS. Anne and Joachim, the parents of Mary, mother of Jesus, who lived at Tsipori according to Christian tradition. The church has a nave and two aisles. The nave and southern aisle terminate in apses. There are sacristies behind the apses. The church, *SS. Anne and* to judge by the pillars and capitals, is 12th century work. It was probably de- *Joachim* stroyed by Baybars and only its eastern portion is completely preserved today, incorporated into the modern monastery of SS. Anne and Joachim.

YAVNE - IBELIN

A small castle crowning the hill of the town of Yavne, the refuge of the Jewish sages after the destruction of Jerusalem by Titus, was the home of the most noble Frankish family produced by the Holy Land—the Ibelin family. The Euro- *home of Ibelins* pean origin of the House of Ibelin, called after its first castle, is obscure. When the first member of the family came to the Holy Land, he was probably no more than a simple knight without lineage, but within twenty years of its settlement at the castle of Yavne, the family had become one of the largest and wealthiest landowners in the Kingdom of Jerusalem, allied in marriage with the royal house of Jerusalem and even with the emperors of Byzantium.

The members of the House of Ibelin were not only the political leaders of the kingdom, but some of its greatest jurists, arbiters of taste, and experts in Arab language and culture, admired throughout the Orient, by Moslems and Christians alike, for their wisdom and courage.

At the time of the Crusader conquest Yavne was a small town famous for its fine figs, known as damascenes. The Crusaders identified it with the Philistine city of Gath. Some fierce battles were fought nearby, between the forces of the Franks and the Egyptians, mainly in the years 1105 and 1123. In 1141 King Fulk erected a castle there, one of the frontier strongholds aimed against Egyp- *building of castle* tian Ascalon. William of Tyre related: "---they built a fortress of very strong masonry with deep foundations and four towers. From the old buildings of which many vestiges remain to the present day, an abundant supply of stones was obtained. The walls of olden times that existed in large numbers in the vicinity of the ruined city also afforded an abundance of water . . ."[51] According to this description the castle of Ibelin was of the *castrum* type; after its completion it was handed over to "a certain nobleman of great wisdom, Balian the elder." This Balian was the constable of Jaffa and the lord of Mirabel.

civilian settlement   After the construction of the castle, Frankish elements began to settle around it. In the middle of the 12th century it was referred to as a village by travellers. Like every Frankish *bourg,* Ibelin had a burgesses' court.

In 1187 Yavne was occupied by Saladin. Richard Coeur de Lion spent a night in the ruined castle in 1191 during his march to Ascalon. In the peace treaty between the Moslems and the Franks, Ibelin remained outside the territory of the reconstituted kingdom of Jerusalem, but in the 1240's it returned to the Franks and was in the hands of the lords of Caesarea.

Yavne (Ibelin) church (Plan)

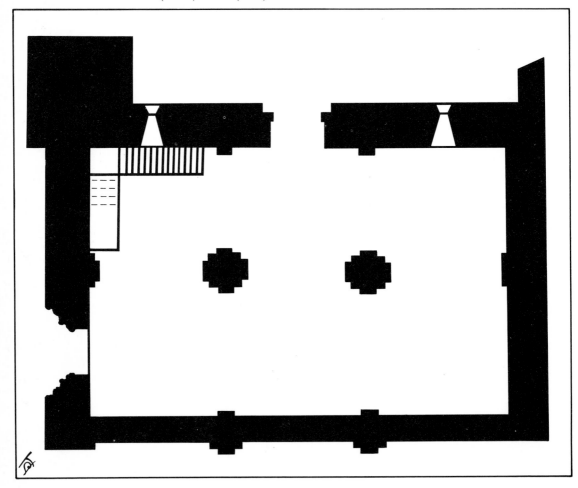

We have no further information on the history of Yavne, or the area of its domain, as the archives of the family, like the records of all the secular seigneurial families, have been lost.

The ruins of the castle are situated above the abandoned Arab village, near a water reservoir. Remains of a wall and square tower with the arch of a window *ruins* can be seen. South of these remains stands a minaret, all that is left of the village mosque, which was built on the foundations of the Crusader parish church. The church was destroyed by artillery bombardment during the First World War. According to a survey carried out at the end of the 19th century, the Frankish structure was of the simple basilica type, consisting of a nave and two aisles, terminating in three apses. It was 20 metres long, 12 metres wide, and groin-vaulted. The entrance was from the west, through an impressive portal.

Part III THE COUNTRYSIDE

The majority of the population of the Holy Land was engaged in agriculture, which formed the economic basis of the Frankish regime.

The most fruitful period of the country's agriculture had ended centuries before the Crusader conquest; its dense population, its abundant woodlands, its magnificent system of water supply, its rich crops and ample exports of agricultural produce, all belonged to the distant past. The decline had begun in Palestine in the 5th century A.D., and its main causes were rooted in the weakening of the central authority, in constant wars and in the incursions of nomads. The Arab conquest intensified the neglect of agriculture and its installations. At the end of the 10th century and during the 11th the process was further accelerated as a result of the internal conflicts which broke out in the 'Abbasid Caliphate and of the invasion of the country by the Seljuk Turkish tribes. The country became a battlefield between the Byzantines and the Moslems, and between the Seljuks and the Egyptians, and also suffered from Bedouin raids. Natural disasters compounded the damage done through human agency; in the 11th century there were a number of earthquakes, floods, and plagues of locusts. Just before the Crusaders' arrival large tracts of country had been laid waste and orderly cultivation had been interrupted. Thousands of Moslem peasants fled as a result of the Crusader conquest, many villages being burned down and many fields ravaged. *decline of agriculture after Byzantine period*

Despite the long and continuous decline of its agrarian system and the dwindling of its population, the land was still fertile and relatively densely populated. The accounts of the country in the writings of European travellers and chroniclers who sojourned there, during the First Crusade and immediately after it, are full of praise of the land, of its abundant water, its yields, and its numerous trees (see p. 389). The consolidation of the Frankish regime and the long periods of relative internal peace and security brought about the renewed prosperity of agriculture. The extent of cultivation and the degree of settlement can be gauged by three criteria: the development and maintenance of the water supply systems, the population density in the region of the desert frontier and the general density of settlement-sites. We deal elsewhere with the subject of water, and the settlement of the desert frontier (p. 305) and shall see that, despite the decline, these criteria point to a relatively high agricultural prosperity. The density of agricultural settlement in various parts of the country will now be examined. *agriculture level in Crusader period still relatively high*

THE DENSITY OF THE AGRICULTURAL SETTLEMENTS

Topographical records of the country's settlements in the Crusader period are more comprehensive than those for any other period in the country's history before the 19th century. This is due to the supreme importance ascribed by the Franks to the recording of landed property and the documentation of its ownership. The number of documented grants, sales, leases, tenures and usufructs of property amounts to many hundreds; and the number of such documents is a mere fraction of those which originally existed. Those which have survived relate to the property of churches, monasteries and military orders with branches in Europe, in which copies of the Palestinian documents have been preserved. The inventories of the royal house and the secular seigneurs, on the other hand, have mostly been lost or destroyed.

recording of landed property

Such importance did the Crusaders ascribe to the recording and confirmation of their landed properties, that they continued to document them even after the areas concerned had been lost to them for decades. At the end of the 13th century, when their control did not extend beyond the walls of Acre, they still busied themselves with the drafting of grants confirming the proprietorship of individual houses in Transjordan or Hebron which had been in Moslem hands for over a century.

Some twelve hundred inhabited places and geographical features are detailed in the documents, and of these about nine hundred have been identified. The term "village" *(casale)* was applied to six or seven hundred of the settlements and there were in addition some two hundred *gastinae,* or dependent villages (see below). The resultant picture of settlement-density in the various regions of the country is to some extent arbitrary. Numerous place-names have disappeared from the map owing to the loss of many documents and, if a whole area happened to belong to an order or lord whose records have disappeared, the entire region will appear to have been uninhabited. We may note as an example Safed, which belonged in its entirety to the Order of Templars. Because the Templar records have not come down to us, hardly any Frankish settlements are marked in this area. A Frankish chronicle nevertheless observes that the region had no less than two hundred and sixty villages. This figure is doubtless exaggerated, but it does nevertheless indicate an area of dense settlement.

settlement-density

If we ignore these difficulties and assume that the distribution of the missing villages was even throughout the country, we shall arrive at the following picture of rural density: In the area of western Palestine from Beirut to Beersheba, which amounts to 18,000 square kilometres, there were seven hundred villages. The highest settlement-density is in the region of Tyre, where sixty-five villages are recorded in an area of 340 square kilometres, or 5,200 dunams per village. In the Acre area, which covers 970 square kilometres, eighty-three villages have been counted, or 11,700 dunams per village. In the Nablus area where ninety villages existed in an area of 1,500 square kilometres, the ratio is 16,600 dunams per village. In the Jerusalem area, on the other hand, extending over 2000 square kilometres, a hundred and four villages have been identified, giving 24,000 dunams per village.

average village areas

It is worth comparing this density with that of periods prior and subsequent to the Crusader epoch. The number of settlements counted in western Palestine in the Byzantine period exceeds two thousand; in the Mamluk-Turkish period their number was between seven and eight hundred, which included many temporary settlements *(khirba)*. The number of villages in 1931 was nine hundred and eighty-one. Archaeological researches in limited areas show that the number of settlements in the Crusader period was only slightly smaller than that of the Byzantine period. The remains of fifty-three Byzantine settlements have been found in the Plain of Acre and in western Galilee, and fifty-three settlements of the early Arab and Crusader epochs have been traced in the same area. The sites of thirty-two Byzantine settlements have been listed in Upper Galilee, compared with twenty Arab-Crusader, and fifteen Mamluk settlements. Twenty-nine Byzantine and seventeen Arab or Crusader settlements have been enumerated in the northern Jordan Valley. The number of Byzantine settlements in south-western Judaea was twenty-nine, compared with thirty Arab-Crusader settlements.

settlement density throughout the ages

This examination of settlement-density, according to such data as we possess, confirms the conclusion drawn from various sources, namely that the agricultural population in the Crusader period was dense and the level of agriculture relatively high. This flourishing condition continued throughout the First Kingdom, but a grave deterioration of internal security occurred towards the 1180's. The invasions of Saladin in 1177 and 1182–3, and the decisive battle of 1187, wrought much destruction upon the country. Thereafter battles, raids and razzias became a recurring phenomenon. The resulting destruction increased and reached its climax in the raids of the Ḥwarizmians in 1244 and in the wars of the Mongols and the Mamluks (1260). If the destruction of agriculture was an unavoidable by-product of warlike operations at that time, the Mamluk conquest made destruction a deliberate and systematic policy. The "scorched earth" wrought by the Mamluks dealt a final blow to the population of the country, from which it recovered only at the end of the 19th century.

deterioration of agrarian system since 1187

The overwhelming majority of the village population were native Moslems, though some villages were occupied by local Christians and several Jewish villages survived in the region of Upper Galilee, while in the region of Samaria a Samaritan rural population continued to dwell. The number of villages whose inhabitants were of Frankish origin did not exceed half-a-dozen.

The total rural population of the Crusader kingdom amounted to some half a million, so that the average number of inhabitants per settlement was between seventy and eighty.

THE INDIGENOUS VILLAGE

The village was known by the Crusaders as the *casale,* the plural form of which was *casalia.* The Arab village did not alter in terms of its appearance, methods of cultivation and mode of life, from Crusader times down to the end of the 19th century. Built on the top of a hill to command a broad view, its elevated site was chosen for economic reasons, as well as for reasons of security and health. For threshing and winnowing the peasant needed the light breeze that blows more strongly in high places. The winds also eased the burden of oppressive heat. Elevation also to some extent avoided the scourge of the malarial mosquito which bred in the pools and swamps of the valleys, while the commanding view guaranteed early warning of Bedouin incursions or the attacks of neighbours.

The village houses were crowded together on the slope of the hill; among them wound paths defined by high walls through which apertures led into the yards. A homestead comprised a farmyard and the dwelling, which was also used as byre and poultry-house.

cultivated area Part of the cultivated area was concentrated in the immediate proximity of the village and part at a considerable distance away. It is a frequent phenomenon that the landed property did not constitute a continuous tract, but was split up, with neighbouring plots belonging to different villages. The village lands were divided into plots according to related clans *(ḥamula);* parts were private property in the permanent proprietorship of the *ḥamula* and part undivided property *(mush'a);* the undivided lands were allocated according to a fixed system of sharing, each farmer working his share for an allotted period. Peasants to whom a distant plot was allotted, left their village homes in the seasons of ploughing and harvest and dwelt in "secondary villages." Since the temporary settlements remained empty and forsaken for most of the year they were called, in the singular, *khirba* (deserted place). These were generally the remnants of ancient settlements, and less often temporary places established by the peasants as seasonal habitations. The number of secondary villages varied from place to place, and was conditioned by the distribution of cultivable soil and its distance from the parent-village. In certain hill villages only a very small part of the cultivated land was situated near the main village and most of it was scattered a long distance away, in the areas of the secondary villages.

size of plots There are very considerable differences in the size of the village-areas. Some amounted to less than 1000 dunams while others ran to several thousand. The minimal amount of land required for the subsistence of a *fallaḥ* (peasant) family, and which it could cultivate in conditions of unirrigated agriculture, is some 160 dunams. This unit is known as a *feddan,* and is defined as an area workable by a yoke of plough oxen in the course of the agricultural year.

The Arab villages in the Crusader period differed little from the modern ones. The village lands were divided into *carrucates,* whose area was evidently twice that of the *feddan,* and covered some 320–350 dunams. The *carruca* was the land unit worked by the Arab peasant family and was the basis for calculating the scales of income and taxation, although there were peasants who cultivated more than one *carruca. Casalia* whose areas were fragmented and far removed possessed secondary villages known as *gastinae* (waste), a term used in Europe *the* gastina to denote uncultivated land, woodland and pasture. In Palestine the *gastina* is the precise translation of the Arabic term *khirba,* both in its etymological and in its topographical sense. The name of the place called khirbat al-Asad—the Khirba of the Lion—is translated into Latin as *Gastina Leonis.* A ruined house in the Christian quarter of Jerusalem is also called *gastina*. Secondary villages in all areas of the country are likewise known by this name. The village *gastinae* were not areas of fallow land or pasture but of cultivated land, worked, owing to remoteness from the mother-village, by peasants who lived temporarily in a makeshift settlement. The lands of the *gastina* formed an integral part of the land of the parent-village and were included in the assessment of its income and taxes.

There were villages with very small areas of cultivable land in their immediate vicinity, and most of whose lands were at a distance in the *gastinae*. The village of Batiole near Tyre, for instance, had only one *carruca* of land, but no less than 36 *carrucae* in its *gastinae*.[52]

The village area in the Crusader period varied from village to village and from region to region. In the Tyre region it ranged from 2000 to 12,000 dunams; in the Ascalon region the scale averaged 16,000 dunams. In Upper Galilee we find villages whose areas vary from 10,000 to 26,000 dunams. In this matter, too, there is no difference between the situation in the Crusader period and that in the 19th century.

The population also varied from place to place; there were villages in which only ten to twenty families lived, and others whose population exceeded five hundred. The cultivable soil was allotted to various crops. Market gardens were situated near the village, while the orchards included figs, pomegranates, peaches, apples, lemons, almonds, bananas and the other fruits which are still usual in Palestine. Especially important were the olive groves and vineyards. In areas of abundant water-supply sugar cane was grown, as well as flax, cotton and sesame. Most of the cultivated area was devoted to crops such as wheat, barley, oats, sesame, durra and vegetables. *cultivation and produce*

Cultivation was conducted on a two-year cycle, the fields being divided into two parts. On one half winter cereals were sown, while the other remained part fallow and part sown to vegetables. In summer both parts were sown with summer crops such as durra and sesame. The following year the first part was left fallow and the second sown with winter cereals. The ratios of seed and yield were identical with those normal in the traditional Arab *fallah's* farm. Winter cereals were sown at seven kilograms per dunam. The yield was 35–49 kilograms per dunam or 5–7:1.

The village, with its inhabitants, land and livestock, was the property of the feudal lord and the peasants were regarded as serfs who held and worked their land in return for payment of part of the crop. The Franks made no change in tenurial arrangements. The peasants paid a quarter to a third of the crop, usually in kind. They also paid the lord a supplementary tax three times a year. In the royal lands around Tyre, for each carrucate they paid one hen, a dozen eggs, 1.3 kilogram of cheese and twelve gold bezants. Corvées were minimal owing to the absence of demesne land worked by the lord himself, but the Franks did utilize corvée labour of the peasants to mend roads and put up public buildings. The scale of such obligatory labour in the royal domain was a day per year for each carrucate. The burden of taxes imposed on the local inhabitants was *property of feudal lord* not insupportable, and compared favourably with the conditions of the peasants in Moslem countries (see p. 20).

There were villages which were divided among several lords, while others belonged to one domain. In the large domains the Crusaders set up centres where produce was collected and stored until it could be transferred to the cities (see p. 221). The feudal lords left the management of their estates in the *administration* hands of the Moslem village-headmen, who were known to them by the Arab term of *rayis*. These were responsible for the village administration and the collection of taxes, and also held police and judicial rights over the inhabitants. Their status was traditional and preceded the Crusader conquest. The *rayises* owned big estates and lived in large well-appointed houses which will be described below. Several such *rayises* could be found in large villages inhabited by several clans. The *rayis* held an honourable position in relation to the feudal lords; he was consulted by the Franks, who lodged with him and discussed with him the problems of the village; he took part in the ceremonies when property was transferred and swore fealty to the new lord; this oath was taken in Arabic as he laid his hand on an unsheathed sword according to the local custom.

The native villages contained the greater part of the population of the countryside, whereas the number of villages inhabited by Franks was very small. The failure of the Franks to settle and populate the rural areas was one of the main factors weakening the fabric of the Crusader kingdom. Despite their comparative rarity, however, it is worthwhile devoting a special place to the Frankish villages, since their buildings and organization are of considerable interest.

FRANKISH VILLAGES AND DEPOTS

The townships which sprang up, or were established, around the primary nuclei of the military strongpoints and administrative centres have already been described. *village and* As we have seen, these *bourgs* developed in different ways; some, like 'Atlit *township* and Gaza, became real towns while some, like Beit Govrin, remained as small settlements of rural character. Despite the difference we dealt with them together, because in all cases the establishment of a military stronghold or seat of administration was the decisive factor leading to their foundation and their subsequent development. In addition to the towns and townships, there was another type of Frankish settlement, defined here as a "village"; that is a settlement whose inhabitants were Franks and which was set up primarily and preponderantly to provide agricultural produce.

The distinction between the "township" and the "village" is difficult and sometimes impossible, since some of the villages grew into townships, most townships were agricultural and both contained strongholds. The historian will regard the distinction as artificial, for the same historical processes affected both types of settlement, and their character and way of life were in most cases similar. The distinction itself is foreign to the period, as is evident from the fact that the

218

sources used the same name—*villa*—for the village of Qubeiba and for the town of Gaza. The distinction is nevertheless of interest to the student of the historical geography of the Holy Land, as it helps him to arrive at the root, the *raison-d'être,* of these settlements, also clarifying for him the purpose and function of the various buildings to be found in them.

The number of Frankish villages was very small; less than ten can be found among the hundreds of permanent settlements within the territory of the Crusader Kingdom. Of some no history survives except their Frankish names and their meagre remains, but of others we know the history and even the names of their inhabitants. Scattered throughout all the regions of the country from the Plain of Acre to the border of the Hebron Hills, some grew up through private enterprise, while in other cases the source of initiative is not known, but it is clear that the majority arose as part of a planned effort at colonization, owing to the shortage of manpower which followed the flight of thousands of Moslem peasants before the advance of the Crusaders. An additional factor in the programme of colonization was the need to introduce intensive cultivation and specialized crops, for consumption by the feudal lords and also for sale and export, as a means of increasing the revenues of the kingdom. *colonization activities*

The progressive institutions, both in the Holy Land and in Europe, were the Church and the Military Orders. Most of the experiments in colonization were made, therefore, in their domains, but we also know of such activities on royal and seigneurial lands. Similar colonizing initiative is well-known in western Europe: in many places secular and ecclesiastical lords set up *villes neuves,* new village settlements, on their lands with the object of enlarging the revenues from their domains. To attract settlers they would grant a charter known as *Carta Puebla,* and would assist the settlers by building houses and donating land. It is of interest to note that the same term, *ville neuve,* was used also to identify some Frankish villages in the Holy Land. In 1160 Frankish settlers were granted "plots for the construction of houses, lands to plant vines and trees, carrucates of arable land, olive groves . . . , an oven and a mill"[53] in Nova Villa.

The settling agency would allot tracts of land to the settlers for cultivation and the erection of homes; in some places they would even put ready-built dwellings at their disposal. The settlers, some of them newly-arrived from Europe, some of them old hands in the country who had come from the towns or other villages, were freemen, at liberty to leave the village and to transfer or mortgage their property. The land was tilled by the settlers individually or in common, according to the locality or type of crop. The mode of life of the village community and the rights and the duties of the settlers were settled by "custom" (*consuetudo*) or charter. In addition to material rights and duties the charter included rules of conduct and penalties for crimes. The landowner was represented in the village by a steward or curator, whose function was to supervise the work of the peasants, to collect the taxes and to look after the settlement's administrative affairs. The peasants paid a tax fixed as a percentage of the crop, to be delivered in kind, and other taxes and imposts. *internal administration*

The number of inhabitants in the Frankish villages varied from forty families or so in the smallest up to something over a hundred in the largest; if we use a demographic multiple of five per family, the number of inhabitants per village would have amounted to something between 200–500 people. Sometimes the Frankish settlers were called in contemporary documents *habitatores*[54] (settlers), and sometimes *burgenses*[55] (burgesses) or *cives* (citizens).[56]

All the villages were situated in fertile, well-watered areas, and most seem to have been established at crossroads or on main highways, not far from centres of consumption. With such advantages they appear to have flourished, and we know that several of them doubled their populations in the course of two generations.

physical plan

Very little is known of the physical plan of these villages as only two have been investigated archaeologically—Qubeiba and Akhziv. The discoveries at these places enable us to determine the general lines of their lay-out. The buildings of the Frankish village were placed in two long lines on each side of a broad central street. The dwellings were built in groups, adjacent houses sharing party walls. A house consisted of one large square room which may have been divided into smaller rooms by partitions. It had two entrances, one from the street and one from the rear, leading to farm buildings or services in the yard. The houses were cross-vaulted like Arab dwellings, and the exterior walls were two metres thick. The symmetrical plan of the village as found at Qubeiba and Akhziv was doubtless influenced by the European custom and had nothing in common with

houses

the oriental village, which was built as a triangular network of alleys with houses piled up and abutting one upon another. The symmetry of the Frankish plan also indicates that the buildings were erected simultaneously by a central authority. A number of public buildings, the most important being the church and the

public-buildings

fortified tower, stood in the centre of the village. In those villages which were administrative centres a building was also placed near the tower, serving partly as a store for the collection of agricultural produce and partly as the quarters of the steward and his staff. In addition to these central buildings, there were service buildings such as a bakery and a bathhouse, these being a seigneurial monopoly. Most of the villages also had an olive press, a wine press and a flour mill and some villages had other public buildings, such as hostelries. The village church was of the simple basilical type, with nave and two aisles ending in three circular apses with straight *chevet*. A more detailed account of this type will be given elsewhere (see p. 346).

The churches were subject to the authority of the diocese, but if the village belonged to one of the religious orders, the building was under its authority.

churches

The Hospitallers were permitted to set up churches and cemeteries independently of the authority of the local church in certain areas. Such village churches were to be found at al-Bira, Qubeiba, Beit Nuba, Sinjil, and Jezreel. They do not differ from the churches to be seen in such townships as Yavne, Beit Govrin and Tsipori.

The tower *(turris)*, built in the centre of the village or at a point of natural strength, was the fortified stronghold of the village, to be used as a refuge in time of trouble. These structures are described elsewhere (see p. 275).

The third public structure of the Frankish village was the rural administrative centre. As has been explained elsewhere, the feudal lords, whether lay or ecclesiastical, left the peasants of their estates very much to themselves. The responsibility for collecting taxes and rents devolved upon the *rayises,* and the feudal lords generally received them in kind and not in money. The churches and orders actually preferred this, since the crops were required to feed their monasteries and hospitals. But the collection of agricultural produce from the villages in the domain required a ramified organization, with the establishment of collecting points to which the crops could be brought, and where the quantities could be recorded and the produce stored until it was transferred to the centres of consumption. *administrative centres*

These depots had to be located in a central place within the territory of the domain, which was both easy of access and well-protected from the attacks of robbers. The depots were sometimes located at castles, as in the case of Belvoir, Tsova and Fula, and sometimes in Frankish villages like al-Bira, or in Arab *casalia* such as Qula. The historical evidence on these centres and the way they worked is scanty and fragmentary, but there is no doubt of their existence and development along lines similar to the depots in Europe at this period. The archaeological remains of those in Palestine are located in three places: Qula, Ḥ. Manot and Qubeiba. While the Crusader buildings at Qula and Ḥ. Manot were units separate from the native villages in which they lay, the centre at Qubeiba was an integral part of the Frankish village. At Qula and Ḥ. Manot we find a combination of storage buildings and an adjacent watch-tower of the "Norman keep" type, while at Qubeiba the depot was built opposite to the church and a watch-tower was attached to it. These centres will be described in detail below. According to the sources al-Bira had a collection centre similar to that at Qubeiba; it was managed by a *dispensator* (steward) and the centre was called the *curia.* Isolated towers in other places, such as those at Burj a-Tot *(Tour Rouge)* and Beit Tsur *(Beithsur),* may well also be the remains of such centres, but if so the storehouses have been destroyed. *depots*

AKHZIV - CASEL IMBERT

The remains of the Frankish village of Casel Imbert are situated in one of the most picturesque corners of the northern plain of Acre, near the ancient city tel of the biblical Achzib (Josh. 19:29). The village was called after the knight Humbertus (Imbert) de Paci, who received it from the king after its capture in 1104. The Semitic name was preserved by the Franks, who called it Ziph *(Castellum Ziph).*

In the 1140's the village reverted to the royal domain. In the middle of the

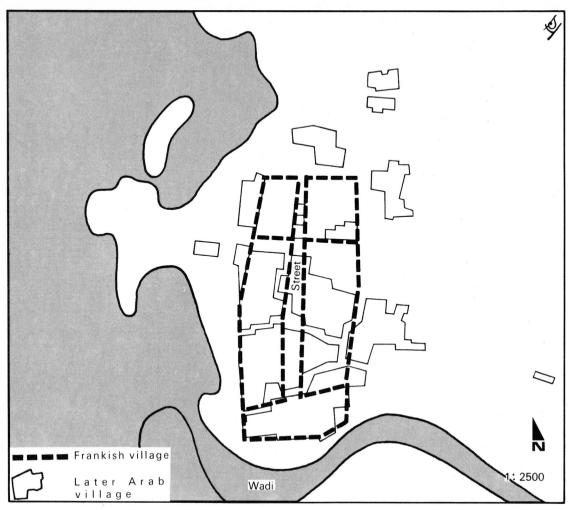

Street

Wadi

■■■■ Frankish village

Later Arab
village

N

1 : 2500

Akhziv (Casel Imbert)

century an attempt was made by King Baldwin III to settle peasants of European origin there; by a document of 1153 he gave every inhabitant a plot of land for growing wheat and another for vegetables, fruit trees (vineyards and olive groves). Each settler also received a dwelling free of rent. The unirrigated tracts *free dwelling* on which wheat was grown were worked in common and the crop shared, two thirds going to the peasants and one third to the king. The settlers received rights to use manorial monopolies such as the bakery, mill and bathhouse, in return for a smaller payment than usual, and were exempt from paying taxes on the sale of bread, wine and meat. A royal steward was placed in charge of the village and was responsible for administration and the levying of taxes.

Akhziv was captured by Saladin in 1187 but returned to Frankish possession in 1191. In 1232, a battle took place near the village between the army of the Emperor Frederick II and the Frankish nobles headed by Jean d'Ibelin-Beirut,

222

who was then lord of the village. Jean d'Ibelin leased it to the Teutonic Order in 1256 and the lease became a permanent proprietorship in 1261. It appears that Akhziv was captured by Baybars in 1271.

The village was on the summit of the hill and built parallel with the shore. The houses were set out on each side of a central street, each with a small back yard. The village lay-out resembles that of the village of Qubeiba and shows that it was centrally planned and that the houses were all erected at the same time. This is further confirmed by the documents, which record that all the settlers received houses from the king.

Traces of a tower have been found here. It is to be supposed that Akhziv also possessed a church, but it has not yet been identified.

AL-BIRA-MAGNA MAHOMARIA

This village was the centre of an agricultural district which was occupied by Frankish peasants on the initiative of the canons of the Church of the Holy Sepulchre. The village, today a township of some size, is situated 15 kilometres *initiative of the* north of Jerusalem on the main road to Nablus. Its soil is fertile and its vicinity *church of the* rich in springs. In 1100 it was given to the Church of the Holy Sepulchre by *Holy Sepulchre* Godfrey de Bouillon, with a number of additional villages nearby.

Al-Bira was occupied by Moslem and Syrian-Christian farmers. About the 1120's, the canons of the Church of the Holy Sepulchre initiated a planned population of the village by Frankish inhabitants. By 1155 there were ninety-two Frankish families, and these subsequently increased to a hundred and forty-two. The size of the village is indicated by the fact that no less than sixty-five young men from there took part in the battle for Gaza in 1170. Most of them fell "fighting bravely for their country and their freedom."[57]

Theodorich (c. 1172) described Mahomaria as "a large village".[58] The Frankish inhabitants came there from the towns and villages of the Holy Land and from various parts of Europe. The Hospitallers also held lands at al-Bira.

The Frankish settlement appears to have been established apart from the old village and it may be supposed that, as at Qubeiba, its planning was European *description* and symmetrical, rather than Oriental. In the centre of the village a tower was erected, later to be enlarged and made into the *curia* or *castellum*. One source even mentions a wall around the village, but this is doubtful. The *Castellum* was the seat of the steward *(dispensator)* appointed by the canons of the Church of the Holy Sepulchre, and here the dues were collected and stored. The village had a church, built in 1146, and an inn. Two pools *(berquilia)* were constructed in the plain to the south of al-Bira, one belonging to the village and the other to the Hospitallers. The inhabitants' main source of livelihood was olive-growing and viticulture. Each received a dwelling rent-free and a tract of land on which to grow olives and wheat. The settler paid a quarter of his crops in kind for the land, and also a tithe to the Church. The Church of the Holy Sepulchre had a particular interest in vine-growing, for there was a great demand both in the country and abroad for sacramental wine; hence very extensive vineyards were developed at al-Bira. These were worked collectively and every settler received a plot to cultivate under the supervision of the canons. In return for the plot he paid half the crop plus tithe. The mill and bakery were, as elsewhere, the monopoly of the lord.

"custom of Mahomaria"
The settlers were subject to a special "custom" (*consuetudo*), referred to in the documents as the "custom of Mahomaria," which determined their rights and duties. They were all freemen, whose property passed to their heirs, and were permitted to leave the village, but the Church retained pre-emption rights. The Church of the Holy Sepulchre exercised jurisdiction over the settlers and the custom of Mahomaria seems to have applied to the other Frankish settlements set up in the region, such as Qubeiba and Beit Suriq.

The fertile settlement of al-Bira was destroyed by Saladin in 1187, but was apparently resettled by Moslems near the end of the 12th century. In 1229, when the emperor Frederick II received Jerusalem from the Moslems, the administrative headquarters of the Ayyubid district of Jerusalem were transferred to the village of al-Bira.

No vestige remains of the dwellings of the Frankish settlement. The ruins of the Church, which was destroyed in 1915, and the inn and the tower described by
remains travellers at the end of the 19th century, have disappeared almost completely. Remnants of the church are to be found in the centre of the old portion of the townlet of al-Bira, consisting only of the bases of the piers, which are cruciform, a few stones of the south wall and a small part of its southern gateway.

On the evidence of explorers who visited the place in the 1860's and 1870's, the Church was of the simple basilical type, a nave and two aisles terminating in three circular apses. The interior was divided into four bays; the stones of the interior were smooth-tooled, but the exterior wall was built of roughly-dressed blocks with asymmetrical joints into which gravel chips were packed. The plan of the church was thus identical with that of the church of Qubeiba. South of the church and close to it was the inn. A few stones of the tower survive northwest of the church. Not far from the parish church, on the Jerusalem highway, stood another church, St. Mary's. Theodorich related that "close by a church dedicated to St. Mary stands a great cross of hewn stones, raised upon seven steps; which steps are ascended by pilgrims who from thence behold, not without groans, the tower of David."[58]

QUBEIBA-PARVA MAHOMARIA

The Arab name Qubeiba means "Little Dome" and the Frankish name is an exact translation of this. The Crusaders applied the name to every Moslem sacred site because of the domes built over them. The Frankish village seems to have been the first permanent settlement on the spot and was situated on the shoulder of a western sloping hill. A Crusader document related how Qubeiba came to be built on the lands of the village of Beit Suriq (Beitsurie). The area formed part of a large estate belonging to the Church of the Holy Sepulchre. This estate extended over the whole area north-west of Jerusalem and was granted to the church as early as the reign of Godfrey de Bouillon.

history

In the 1120's a settlement of Frankish peasants was set up at Qubeiba. The remains suggest that this was a planned project and that all the structures were built at the same time according to a uniform plan. The circumstances attending the establishment of the settlement, its character and arrangements, are unknown to us, but were probably identical to those of the large village of al-Bira (Magna Mahomaria). A document of 1169 describes Qubeiba, al-Bira and Beit Suriq in the same way, "as villages built by the Church and settled by Latins."[59] The settlement was situated on the main road from the coastal plain to Jerusalem and was thus on the pilgrim route. Benjamin of Tudela mentions the place by its Spanish name, *Mahomaria Lapetita*.

on the main road to Jerusalem

The Frankish inhabitants were driven from Mahomaria in 1187. A clash between the Crusader vanguard, whose base was at Beit Nuba, and a Moslem force took place near Qubeiba in 1192 during Richard Coeur de Lion's campaign. The village was not resettled by Moslems, and remained in ruins. Willbrand of Oldenburg described "ruined villages and empty churches" in this area in 1212. In 1241 the village was restored to Crusader control under the peace treaty obtained by Richard of Cornwall, according to which the region between Beit Ḥanina on the east and Latrun on the west was ceded to the Crusaders.

After the final expulsion of the Crusaders from Jerusalem and the mountains of Judaea in 1244, Christian pilgrims were forced to reach the Holy City by a defined route, which went through Beit Nuba, Qubeiba and Nabi Samwil; furthermore, they were not permitted to visit the holy places around the city. The

Qubeiba, Frankish village (General Plan)

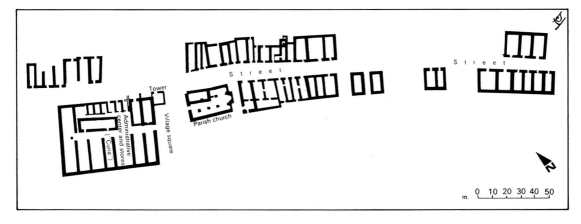

225

Qubeiba, Frankish
village and church

difficulties of access resulted in the "transfer" of ancient traditions to points on the line of the permitted routes. In consequence of this process, known elsewhere in the Holy Land, the castle of "Emmaus" began to be shown at Qubeiba from the middle of the 13th century, this tradition having been transferred from Abu Ghosh (see below).

On the capture of Jerusalem by the Turks in 1517 most of the stones of the ruined church at Qubeiba were taken to build the walls of the city, and thus only its foundations remained. In 1872 its site was acquired by the Marquise Nicolay; *remains* a church was erected on the foundations of the Crusader structure, and near to it a monastery. The Franciscans, who were resident here, carried out numerous archaeological excavations which disclosed the Frankish settlement in its entirety. The village is built on either side of the wide Roman road which ascends from the plain to Jerusalem. Within the monastery area are the remains of some forty peasants' dwellings with party walls, set out in two long lines along the road. The houses, however, are not of uniform size, some having an interior *houses* area of 70 square metres and others of 150 square metres. Some have stone-built back yards. The remains show that there was no internal room division, the dwelling space consisting of one large room. Each house had two entrances, a main entrance from the street and a rear door from the yard. The buildings were cross-vaulted after the manner of Arab buildings, and the walls were 2 metres thick. A bakery was found in one of the village houses, and in another an olive press.

public buildings Public buildings were situated at the west end of the rows of houses and consisted of the church, the *curia* and the tower, with a small square between them.

226

The planning is European, and the lay-out had nothing in common with that of the Arab village. The original church, on whose foundations the modern one was built, was 31 metres long and 17 metres wide. It was divided into a nave and two aisles with four bays, which terminated in three apses, built into the east wall. The piers supporting the roof were cruciform. The roof was a groined-vault with pointed arches. The north line of piers had only one member, the western part of the roof resting on a wall 14 metres long which divided the interior of the church into two. Tradition holds that the closed north-western part was the house of Cleopas, mentioned in the New Testament as one of the disciples whom Jesus met at Emmaus (Luke 24:18). Traces of half-obliterated frescoes were found near the lateral apses.

church

South of the church, on the spot where the present monastery stands, was the *curia,* a square building 68 metres from west to east and 48 metres from north to south. The entrance was from the village square on the east side of the structure. A square tower stood at the north-east corner of the structure, commanding the main street and the square in front of the church. Within the *curia* were long chambers lying at right-angles to the south wall and opening into the central courtyard, where there was a cistern. The middle of the building was occupied by a long hall lying east-west. Here dwelt, it would seem, the *dispensator* appointed over the village by the Church of the Holy Sepulchre, and the agricultural produce paid as tax was stored in the building. This combination of *curia* and *turris* is mentioned in several Frankish documents and can be seen in a number of ruins, throughout the country.

"curia"

QULA-CHOLA

The Crusader structures at the abandoned village of Qula, north of Lydda, constituted until recently the sole remaining example of a perfectly preserved rural depot. The Hospitallers purchased the village in 1181 and soon afterwards erected a storehouse and watchtower there.

The storehouse, 38 metres long and 11 metres wide, had walls 2 metres thick. The structure, part of which was two-storeyed, was roofed with a pointed barrel-vault. All the openings were on the south, while the entire north wall was blank. There were three entrances, two broad and one narrow, and also three loopholes on the south and one on the east. The outer walls were fashioned of roughly tooled blocks, while the arches and apertures were of smooth dressed stone with incised mason's marks. There was an underground cistern on the north-west side of the storeroom and another 150 metres to the north-east. Ten metres to the south stood a rectangular tower, 17.5 by 13.5 metres, 8 metres high; it had three loopholes, in its northern, western and eastern walls. The entrance was in the south side, and beside it were steps leading up to the roof.

storehouse

The exterior walls were built of rough-hewn stones of various sizes; the joints

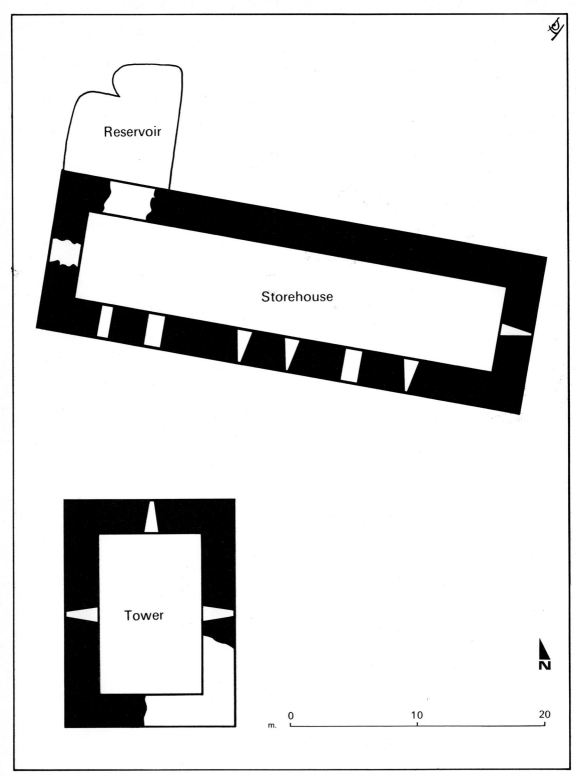

Reservoir

Storehouse

Tower

0   10   20

m.

N

Chola, storehouse and tower

were not levelled and were filled with gravel. The quoins were of square blocks with bosses.

TSOVA - BELMONT

On the lofty hilltop of the village of Tsova are remains of a large Hospitaller fortress. The place appears under two names in the sources: here pilgrims located Modi'in, the birthplace of the Maccabees, apparently because of its nearness to Abu Ghosh, which was identified with Emmaus; in several documents the place was called Belmont. The castle was the administrative centre of a Hospitaller domain which commanded wide areas, including Qaluniya, Qastal, Aqua Bella and Abu Ghosh. Responsibility for the domain rested with the Castellan of Belmont, who is mentioned in a document of 1170. In records of the same period the Commander of Emmaus is also referred to, but we prefer to locate the Hospitaller Commandery of Emmaus at the village of 'Imwas, as will be explained elsewhere (see p. 349).

identification with Modi'in

Castellan of Belmont

There are remains of a walled enceinte built on a battered plinth. These are especially prominent on the north-west and west, where traces of a rock-cut moat are also to be seen. On the east are remains of a gate built of huge smooth-dressed blocks and numerous building blocks, once belonging to Crusader structures, lie strewn within the castle area. The ruined castle was used as a stronghold by the peasants of the vicinity down to the 19th century. In 1834 it was completely destroyed by the cannons of the Egyptian Ibrahim Pasha in the course of suppressing a peasant rebellion.

remains

ḤORBAT MANOT - MANUETH

This Crusader ruin, situated in Naḥal Keziv (Wadi Qurayn), where the gorge leaves the mountains of western Galilee and opens into the maritime plain, was the centre of a small fief which extended through the fertile well-watered countryside.

In the 1160's the domain passed into the hands of one of the prominent knights of the Kingdom of Jerusalem, Godfrey le Tor, who also held fourteen villages in central Upper Galilee, his estates being scattered rather than contiguous. In the 1180's the domain was transferred to the possession of Joscelin de Courtenay and attached to his estate, whose centre was at Mi'iliya (the "King's Castle"). In 1187 Ḥorbat Manot was captured by Saladin, but was restored to the Courtenay family in 1192. Joscelin's daughter sold it to the Hospitallers in 1212 and they turned it into an administrative centre for the collection of agricultural produce.

history

229

Manueth, storehouse

The history of Ḥ. Manot is obscure from the middle of the 13th century; historical sources relate that in 1260 it was taken by Baybars, who converted it into a base for attacking Safed. But it was in the hands of the Hospitallers as late as 1270, when they leased it to the Teutonic Order, owners of Montfort, to furnish food for the castle, which was short of supplies at the time owing to Moslem raids. Yet another document shows that the castle was in Frankish hands even in 1278, after the capture of the neighbouring Montfort.

remains The ruins of Manueth consist of an elongated storehouse with very thick walls and an entrance on the eastern side, a flour mill adjacent to the store, and a small square tower higher up the slope. All are the remains of the Hospitaller centre built at the beginning of the 13th century.

SINJIL - ST. GILLES

The village was a royal administrative centre on the border of the mountains of Judaea and Samaria and also the centre of a small fief. In the village are remains of a church and a tower (Kh. al-Burj). The former is used today as the village mosque. The church had a single nave divided into four bays. The tower is of the "Norman keep" type.

230

Sinjil was a centre of vine-growing. In 1186, a settler *(habitator)* named Adam Magnus donated a considerable quantity of wine to the Order of St. Lazarus in Jerusalem; in the same source other Frankish settlers were mentioned.[59a]

The village was captured by Saladin on his march from the north to Jerusalem. Its Frankish name survives among the Arab inhabitants down to the present day and so constitutes an exception in the toponymy of the Holy Land.

Beit Ḥoron
(Beit 'Ur)
Manorhouse

Burj Bardawil, vault

MANORHOUSES AND FARMS

Among the many remains left in the countryside from the Crusader period, rural buildings of various types occupy a notable place both in terms of number and of quality. One group has been discussed above, namely the buildings of the Frankish villages. However, many structures are to be found in settlements or areas where no permanent Frankish occupation is recorded. There is hardly a large village in the regions of Jerusalem, Ramallah or central Samaria without isolated remains of Crusader structures. The following list, which is not exhaustive, is enough to afford a striking illustration of the extent of their occurrence. Frankish structures are to be found at Beit 'Itab, Sifla, Beit Safafa, Lifta, Beit Iksa, al-Jib, Jabá, Upper Beit Horon (Beit 'Ur al-Fouqa), Beituniya, Jifna, Tappuh, Zababida, Rama, Rantiya, Lubban-Sharqiya and Rabba. In addition to the buildings to be found in Arab villages, there are remains of isolated structures in the centre of small fertile valleys and on the flat tops of high plateaux, notably at H. Tannur, Aqua Bella, Burj Bardawil, Kh. Bir-Zeit and Kh. Baubariya near Sabastiya. *extent of phenomenon*

Closer examination of these relics shows that their size, their quality and their style far surpass those of the village buildings in whose midst they stand. Although they possess defensive elements such as arrow slits their planning leaves no doubt that they were not constructed for military purposes but rather as residences. Were we to discover such civilian rural buildings in Europe, we would not hesitate to define them as manorhouses, the houses of the lesser knights who resided with their families at the centre of the villages which constituted their domains, engaging in farming and in supervising their peasants' labours. But we must bear in mind the unequivocal conclusion of the historians, who maintain that the Frankish lords in Palestine, great and small, did not live on their domains, but in the large towns, where they felt safe among their brethren, fearing to settle on their estates, which were populated only by Moslem peasants. There was moreover no point in their residing in the villages, since they neither held demesne land nor worked it themselves; nor, to be accurate, did they work it by the obligatory labour of their serfs. All contacts and business between the feudal seigneurial class and their peasants were conducted by means of a village headman. *difficulty in establishing raison d'être*

Our knowledge of the life of the small knights who stood on the lowest rung of the nobility is very limited. Though conclusions of scholars are therefore based on scanty historical evidence, they are convincing in general terms. This being so, what were the buildings and what was their purpose? Their existence has not escaped the notice of some scholars but, loyal to their doctrine, which sees in every Crusader building a fortification or a church, they have identified them as forts, churches, or monasteries, although on closer scrutiny of the build-

233

ings themselves, they were obviously not appropriate to any one of these purposes. We therefore have to look for the civilian occupants of such buildings.

The standard of building in relation to the other rural dwellings forces us to seek the inmates among the upper strata of society, and it is a reasonable assumption that they were functionaries holding posts on behalf of the feudal lords. Two types of rural functionaries appear in the sources, the *Rayises* and the *Dragomans*. We already know the function of the former. As to the *Dragomans,* we know very little of their duties, but it is clear that they were men of dignity and means. The functionaries were mostly Moslems, but among them were also Franks. By virtue of their rank and the means at their disposal, these men could have erected and maintained large and imposing rural buildings. The Moslem traveller Ibn Jubayr told of a reception given him by a Moslem *rayis* in his home north of Acre: "We alighted at a farmstead, a parasang distance from Acre. Its headman is a Muslim, appointed by the Franks to oversee the Muslim workers in it. He gave generous hospitality to all members of the caravan, assembling them great and small, in a large room in his house, and giving them a variety of food and treating them all with liberality."[60] In 1254, when the Hospitallers bought Kafar Kanna (Casale Robert) from Julian of Sidon, the formal ceremony of transfer was held at the house of the local *rayis,* which must have been a large and luxurious establishment.

probably houses of Rayises *and* Dragomans

Some of the rural dwellings, then, were the homes of the Moslem *rayises* and the dragomans. But there is some evidence to suggest that there were also Franks among the inhabitants. The way the name "Boverie" (Kh. Baubariya) took root to denote part of these buildings (see p. 259), points to their occupation by French-speaking people. These Frankish residents might have been functionaries of the lord of the domain. Some of them might have been minor knights, living on their estates rather than in the nearby towns, and thus exceptions to the general rule. Such an instance is perhaps to be found in the case of the manor of Jifna, where there was a large and splendid manorhouse. The only occasion on which the village is mentioned in the sources is in 1182. In that year one Raymond de Jafenia signed as last witness to a royal document. It is quite possible that this same Raymond lived in the manorhouse of Jifna.

proper manorhouses

The surnames of several knights were applied to small villages in the vicinity of Jerusalem and Nablus. Most of the manorhouses are found at no great distance from the towns and from the centres of the Frankish rural settlements at al-Bira, Qubeiba and Sinjil, in areas which belonged to the royal domain. We know that dozens of nobles lived off the royal domain, holding very small fiefs consisting of a village or two, in exchange for which they were bound to serve the king personally. Such nobles comprised the lowest stratum of the aristocracy. Some of them apparently elected to settle in manorhouses in the centre of their villages, where these were situated close to the capital or a large town. In so doing, they were no more than exceptions to the majority of the knighthood, who dwelt in the towns and visited their villages only for business purposes. Even so, these exceptions were important and should not be ignored.

234

As we have indicated, the rural buildings fall into two groups. One consists of buildings situated in inhabited village centres and the other consists of isolated structures. The first group we may call manorhouses. To judge from their plan and location, those belonging to the second class were farmhouses. Here too we cannot be certain to whom they belonged, and who lived in them. The possibility that they were occupied by Frankish farmers seems remote, despite the fact that *farmsteads* some of them are still called today by the Frankish name of Kh. Baubariya. Without doubt most of them were occupied by Moslem estate owners. The farms are referred to in Crusader documents as *curtile;* their Arabic name, also frequent in Frankish documents, is *Mazra'a.* According to sources it would seem that these farms were numerous near Jerusalem, Hebron, Caesarea and other cities.

Descriptions follow of four farmhouses and one manorhouse which may be taken as examples of buildings of this type.

ḤORBAT TANNUR

The ruins of a large farm are to be found near the village of Mat'a ('Allar) in the Judaean Hills, north of the road from Bethlehem to the Valley of Elah. The farm is built in a small fertile valley planted with fruit trees, and the waters of a large spring gush forth about 300 metres to the east of it. The building is divided into two parts, a hall with dwelling rooms on the eastern side and a farmyard on the west. The hall is 15 metres long and 10 metres wide and was

Kh. Tannur,
farmstead, general view

235

roofed with a ribbed vault of three or four bays. Remains of the ribs survive in the north wall, which still stands to a considerable height, and includes two loopholes with rounded tops. Another is situated in the eastern wall, which also remains to a considerable height.

remains   The hall is very beautifully constructed, being also plastered and limewashed; notable are the corbels and the cornice. The hall has an entrance in the south wall, while its west wall adjoins the wall of the farmyard, which is 40 metres long and 35 metres wide and surrounded by farm buildings. The east side of the yard was occupied by three or four barrel-vaulted rooms, one of which is completely preserved. A narrow gate was located in the north-eastern corner of the yard. There were three small cells on the south side of the farmyard, which seem to have been used as byres or sheep folds. At the south-west corner is a long groin-vaulted chamber, and a wide entrance to the yard appears to have been located near it. On the north side was an elongated structure without internal subdivisions.

The exterior walls of the farm are built of roughly dressed blocks; gravel chips
not mentioned   of varying size were inserted into the joints.
in sources   As might have been expected, the place is not mentioned in contemporary sources. The entire area for some miles around it belonged to John Gotmann, and was sold by him in 1161 to the Church of the Holy Sepulchre. The farm resembles Aqua Bella in its building style and site.

Kh. Tannur, farmstead, interior of hall

KH. BIR-ZEIT

This Frankish farm building stands on the top of a round hill some distance from the little town of Bir-Zeit, north of Ramallah. This is also constructed on a square plan, measuring about 35 metres on each side. The inner structures are ranged along the southern and western sides, while the north and east sides are *two barrel* formed by a thick wall only. The principal buildings comprise two barrel-vaulted *vaults* halls, 20 metres long and 4 to 6 metres wide. Whether they were internally divided by party walls cannot be ascertained. In the south-eastern corner of the yard is a barrel-vaulted chamber with a loophole in its south wall.

Kh. Bir-Zeit,
farmstead (from east)

BURJ BARDAWIL

This relic has been identified by investigators as a road fort, built to guard one of the important and dangerous passes on the Jerusalem–Nablus highway, namely Wadi al-Ḥaramiya or "Robbers' Gorge", a name which testified to the peril which lay in wait for wayfarers who passed through it. The Crusader name was *Vallis de Cursu,* or "Valley of Running," in reference to flight from robbers. *location*

The location of Burj Bardawil was suitable, as it was on the spur of a hill bordering southward on the Robbers' Gorge, commanding a view of the whole length of the gorge, and two kilometres from its centre as the crow flies. Its Arab name, which means "the tower of Baldwin," also indicates its period and function. But examination of the surviving remains reveals the interesting fact that among the numerous remains of this large structure there are hardly any fortifications. The general plan of the building is square, with a 90 metre side. There are traces of vaulting along the east and north sides, but on the south a pointed barrel vault 4 metres high is preserved intact. The western part of the vault has

237

been completely destroyed, but the foundations show that it continued along the whole south side of the square. A blocked aperture is today visible in the surviving wall of the hall and to the north of it is a gate, likewise blocked. On the eastern side of the building, there remain the foundations of another vaulted hall, which appears to have been divided into rooms. The north wall of the square, on which remnants of another vault can be seen, survives to a considerable height. At the north-east corner of the structure is a gate leading to a long corridor with a pointed barrel vault.

The exterior walls are built of undressed stones of varying sizes laid without symmetry. Only the corners, chiefly near the south vault, are built of dressed blocks. There are no loopholes in the long exterior walls, except one which lights the northern vault. The walls are without towers. The only fortification would seem to be the tower situated some distance from the north wall, within the yard. Here a barrel vault survives. Above it is a small square tower, but this seems to be mostly a late addition. These remains would appear to indicate that Burj Bardawil was mainly used for civilian and agricultural purposes, as a farm cultivating the fertile soil of the flat hilltop.

We have no information about the history of the place, but the valley at its foot is mentioned in several documents. In one dated 1114, *Aineseins* ('Ein Siniya), in the valley of *Valdecours* is referred to as part of the domain of the Church of the Holy Sepulchre, whose centre was at al-Bira (Magna Mahomaria). Andrew *de Valle Cursu* is also mentioned in connection with this domain. The area to the north-east of the Wadi al-Ḥaramiya belonged to the Bishop of Bethlehem.

JIFNA

A large manorhouse, almost complete and still occupied, is to be found in the middle of the village of Jifna, north of Ramallah. Its general plan is that of a square enclosing an inner court. The monumental entrance-gate is on the east, and within it is an arcade supported by columns. This is today blocked by modern walls and divided into rooms. On the south of the court are the living quarters of the manor, and on the west various farm buildings. The north wall is taken up along its entire length by a large barrel-vaulted hall which has been completely preserved. The present entrance to it is simply a loophole which had been widened and converted into a doorway. Additional rooms survive on the west and at the north-east corner. The hall is called "Baubariya" by the villagers and the name may still preserve a tradition that it was used as stables and byres. The original entrance was from the court, on the south wall of the hall, but it is now blocked. In addition to the main entrance to the manor there was apparently another for livestock at the north-west corner of the court, between the arcade and the "Baubariya."

238

Jifna, entrance to manorhouse

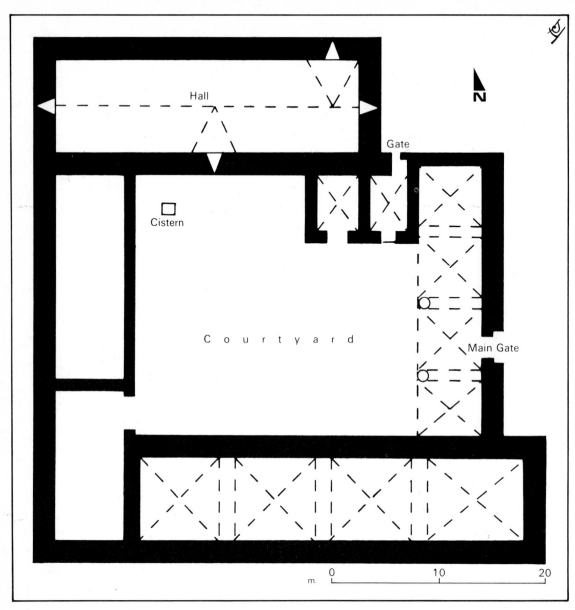

Jifna, manorhouse (Plan)

The building is rich and elegant in character. Raymond *de Jafenia* is referred to in 1182, and he may have been lord of the manor and resident there. We have found no further historical information about the place in the Frankish period.

There are other interesting relics of the Crusader period in the village. Not far from the manor, there are remains of a Crusader church, and also ruins of what is probably a tower.

Jifna, east arcade

AQUA BELLA

The considerable remains of Aqua Bella are situated on the bank of a well-watered stream bed clothed with tangled undergrowth. A grove of stout and ancient oaks stands nearby, preserved thanks to the sanctity accorded to them by the Moslem inhabitants of the neighbourhood. The site and its surroundings are among the loveliest in the Jerusalem Hills. The Crusaders, indeed, found a highly appropriate name for this delightful corner, calling it "Aqua Bella" or "Fair Water."

The accepted identification of the ruin is that of a nunnery. This derives mainly from its Arabic name—*Deir al Banat,* "Convent of Women"—but, the Arab name is probably an abbreviation of the name *Deir bint malik Fenis,* "The home of the daughter of the king of Phoenicia". Identical names appear in other parts of the country in connection with ancient and splendid buildings for which the local inhabitants invented fanciful attributions; one such can be found near Tiberias. In the case of Aqua Bella the Arabs also kept the Latin name, Kh. 'Iqbala.

accepted identification probably wrong

241

Aqua Bella, general view

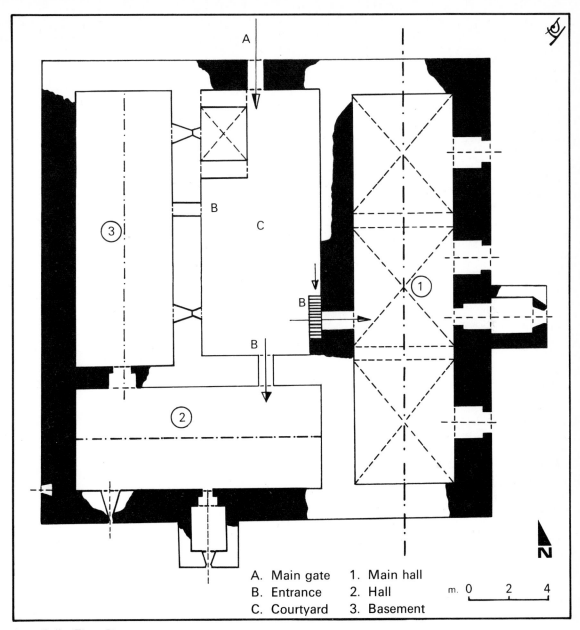

A. Main gate   1. Main hall
B. Entrance   2. Hall
C. Courtyard   3. Basement

m. 0   2   4

Aqua Bella (Floor Plan)

Neither a nunnery nor a monastery are mentioned in the Frankish documents. The name Aqua Bella appears in a solitary document,[61] dated 1168, in which a large tract of land that belonged to the Hospitallers was offered by them to the Duke of Hungary. The places included in the area were *Castellum Emmaus* (Abu Ghosh), *Aqua Bella, Belveer* (Qastal) and *Saltus Muratus* (Qaluniya). This document shows that, at least until 1168, it was not a religious house because,

offered to secular ruler

243

structure probably
a manorhouse or
farm

if it had been, it would not have been offered to a secular ruler. From the style of the buildings it was definitely erected before 1168; the arches and vaulting ribs testify to that. The structure, which is a self-contained unit of which all the architectural parts are known, has no chapel, an indispensable part of a convent. Hence we must conclude that Aqua Bella did not serve as a nunnery or a monastery. It is very hard to decide what its function was, but judging from the general plan and from structures situated in similar locations at H. Tannur and Jifna, we can tentatively assume that it was a Frankish farmstead or a manorhouse.

description

The structure is rectangular, its length from north to south 40 metres, and from east to west 30 metres. The approach is from the north, from the direction of the water source. A narrow pointed archway is situated in the middle of the northern wall. The entrance gate leads to a rectangular courtyard, 12 metres long and 6 metres wide, around which rooms and halls were built in two storeys. Entrance to all rooms was from the courtyard, except for one door in the eastern wall. There are three rooms at ground level, two of which, the western and the southern, are dug into the ground because of the slope. The eastern room, with a gate to the stream, served as an olive press, and all its parts remain *in situ*. All the rooms on the ground floor are barrel-vaulted. An outer staircase leads from the courtyard to the upper storey, where there are three rooms, equivalent in size to those of the ground floor. The eastern room in the upper storey is the main hall of the manor. It is roofed with a rib vault of three bays, which has collapsed and is completely ruined except for the corbels in the east wall, the only wall that remains intact. The other two halls are smaller, and barrel-vaulted. Above the north-western corner of the building a small corner tower with a loophole is preserved. We can assume that a similar tower existed in the north-eastern corner.

Aqua Bella,
courtyard and
main hall

244

These towers defended the vulnerable flank of the building, which is unprotected by the sloping bank of the stream. The outer walls of the structure are two metres thick, their exterior faces built of irregular rough-tooled blocks with a thick layer of mortar and gravel between the joints. Only the corners of the walls are built with dressed stones. There are numerous loopholes. The gates and arches are flat-pointed with a very narrow keystone. There are numerous mason's marks on the voussoirs.

Arab peasants crushing olives

MILLS

The mill *(molendinum)* was one of the central institutions of the mediaeval agrarian system. The tenant or the serf, after exhausting himself in tilling his lord's lands and setting aside for him a considerable proportion of his produce, brought his own grain for grinding to the mill located on the river bank.

While waiting his turn at the mill, the peasant met his friends from near and far, exchanged information with them and heard what was going on outside his small world. Even there he did not escape the exploitation of the feudal lord, for the mill was a seigneurial monopoly. In return for grinding his corn the peasant had to pay part of his flour, and illegal grinding was punished even if it was done in the peasants' home. The Crusaders brought to the Holy Land the customs regarding mills that prevailed in Europe. Here, too, the mill was a seigneurial monopoly, and the king or the barons were jealous of their rights in this respect. In some documents the owner of the monopoly granted vassals or peasants the right to use the mills, either free or for a fixed payment.

central institution in Mediaeval agrarian system

The principal difference between the Crusader mills in Palestine and the mediaeval mills in Europe was a technical one. The Franks, used to large broad rivers which flowed slowly over level plains, were faced with the geographical reality of an arid land with few perenially flowing waters, a land in which "large rivers" were only tiny streams in comparison with the rivers of Europe. The installations which had worked in Europe were not suited to these conditions, and the Franks had to adjust themselves to the technique of exploiting water power which had been developed in the country. This technique was by no means backward; quite the contrary, from various points of view it was more advanced than that of Europe.

difference between Palestinian mills and European mills

The exploitation of water in the service of man, which began in the Near East in ancient times, had attained considerable technical advancement before the 12th century. When the Crusaders arrived in the Holy Land, they found an elaborate system of mills of various types serving varying needs; there were flour mills, water-driven oil presses and tanneries. But while the vertical water wheel was common in the lands from which they came, here the horizontal wheel was used.

In Europe, a vertical wheel was set up over the flowing water and partly immersed in it. A stream of water flowed onto the fins fitted along the rim of the wheel and so propelled it. The rotary movement thus created was transferred to a horizontal axle-shaft on which the wheel was fixed. Simple cog transmitter wheels attached to the end of the axle altered the direction of propulsion from vertical to horizontal in order to set the millstones in motion. The vertical wheel was very large; its characteristic form and the sight and sound of the millrace have often been portrayed in art and literature. This type of wheel was well-adapted to the slow-flowing and abundant rivers of Europe. In the Holy Land, however, where most of the streams are scant in water and swift-flowing, the horizontal wheel had been developed. The wheel itself was small and concealed in the lowest part of the mill, and better-adapted to harnessing the available water power.

Crusader mills

The surviving Crusader mills are of the chute type. A stream would be dammed across its entire width by a high wall built of mortared masonry, to raise the water level to the maximum height of the stream at its source. Near the dam sluices were built, through which the water flowed in stone channels to plastered masonry chutes. On the larger streams the water fell into the chutes from a height of two to three metres. The chutes were constructed at a gradient of 35–40 degrees, wider at the top and narrower at the bottom, and from there the water was directed onto the wheel through an adjustable wooden spout. The jet of water flowing with great force down the gradient of the chute struck the fins of the horizontal wheel, causing it to revolve. The wheel was fitted to the lower end of a verticle axle, with the runner millstone connected to the upper end. The motion of the wheel was thus transferred to the runner which revolved upon the nether millstone or bedstone.

The grain was poured from a funnel into the hopper mouth of the runner and ground between the upper and lower stones. The mills were two storeys high. At the lower level was the elongated wheel-tunnel, two metres in height and barrel-vaulted, which held the water wheel. The chute was in the wall facing the dam. The vertical axle passed from the wheel-tunnel through a square or round hole in the ceiling to the chamber above, containing the mill-stones. After propelling the wheel, the water flowed over the slightly sloping floor of the wheel-tunnel and returned to the stream, or used to drive a second mill further downstream.

Wheel-pit and
chute, Kurdani mill

248

Frankish sources indicate that there were many water mills in all parts of the country except southern Judaea, which lacked streams to operate them. Mills are mentioned on Naḥal Ga'aton at Umm al-Faraj (the mill of *Ferge*), at Nablus, Lajjun, near Caesarea, on the River Na'aman *(Belus)*, on the Yarqon, near Jericho, on the banks of the Sea of Galilee, near Shaubak *(Montreal)*, at Tyre, Sidon, Banias and Ascalon. The sources mention twelve mills on the water-course near Safed. Most of the mills were for grinding grain, but a few were used for sugar. We have no information about the use of water power for any other similar purpose, such as olive presses or tanneries. Most of the Crusader mills have been completely destroyed, but the majority of those that survived are built on the large permanently flowing rivers of the coastal plain: the Na'aman and the Yarqon. It should be noted that besides water-driven mills, the Franks also used windmills (in Jerusalem, Ascalon and Safed) and mills turned by animals.

THE NA'AMAN MILLS

KURDANI (RECORDANE) AND DA'UQ (DOC)

These mills exploited the waters of the River Na'aman or Acre River *(Flum d'Acre)*, the Belus of the ancients. The river, fed by the springs of al-Bass, flows *River Belus* in a semi-circle in a general south–north direction before entering the sea, not far from the walls of the city of Acre, at a distance of some twelve kilometres from its source. As the difference in land-level from its source to its estuary does not exceed a few metres, the stream was very sluggish, and wide marshes were formed along its course in winter.

The southern part of the plain of Acre, where the Na'aman flows, was fully cultivated in the Crusader period, being particularly well known for its crops of sugar and grain, and supported numerous villages. Two groups of mills were established along the course of the river, one near its mouth at the foot of Tel Kurdani, the other some two miles north of Kurdani not far from Tel Da'uq.

The village and mills of Kurdani, *Casale Recordance cum molendinis,* were first referred to in 1154 in a list of the Hospitaller domains, the mills being al- *history* ready in existence when the Order took over the locality at about this time. Sources do not mention Kurdani until 1235, but the style of building leads to the conclusion that the Hospitallers fortified the mills when they were restored to them after the conquest of Acre in 1191. The second group of mills near Da'uq is first heard of in 1235, when it was in Templar hands, but we do not know when or how it was acquired by the Order. The name Da'uq is indeed mentioned in the sources, in the description of one of the battles fought during the siege of Acre in 1190; but it merely refers to the bridge over the Na'aman near Da'uq, not to the mills themselves.

Fortified mill, Kurdani (north side)

dispute between
Templars and
Hospitallers

In 1235 a dispute broke out between the Templars, who owned the mills of Da'uq, and the Hospitallers, lords of Kurdani; the account of the dispute and its vicissitudes sets forth many of the problems encountered in exploiting water power for driving mills in Palestine.

The Templars had erected a dam across the river in order to raise the height from which the water dropped into the chutes of their mills. After prolonged negotiations, in which the Pope intervened, the Hospitallers agreed to the erection of the dam, but on condition that the river level so raised should not exceed the line marked on the wall of their mill at Kurdani. The higher water level was apt to cause damage to the Hospitallers, as swamps might be formed further upstream and their mills were in danger of being flooded. The erection of the dam right across the stream also created difficulties for the Hospitaller boats sailing upstream from Acre to the Kurdani mills. The Hospitallers therefore undertook not to harm the dam and to repair any damage inflicted as a result of the movement of their boats. Both sides bound themselves not to erect any further structures across the river.

In the middle of the 13th century 'the mill of Da'uq' is mentioned on the map of Acre attached to a work of Matthew Paris; south-east of the wall of Acre, as marked on the map, is written: *"Co est La Porte u(ez)s le Mol (in) de doke."* The Da'uq mills, like those of Kurdani, were fortified at this period by a strong tower. In 1253 the Moslem forces raided the Plain of Acre, destroyed the Kurdani mills and the tower of Da'uq with its mills and also burnt the neighbouring fields.

The agreement of 1235 did not put an end to the dispute between the Orders over the waters of the Na'aman. In 1262 the Hospitallers accused the Templars of raising the height of the dam, alleging that the water level had consequently risen over the agreed line, making the movement of boats upstream still more difficult and damaging the mills at Kurdani. The Templars in turn accused the Hospitallers of digging a channel to divert the river to their sugar plantations, thus preventing the mills of Da'uq from working for lack of water. Only after the intervention of high-ranking mediators was a compromise reached.

The agreement between the Orders was reached only a few months before the end came for the Na'aman mills. Baybars advanced upon the plain of Acre in 1263 after capturing and destroying Nazareth and Mt. Tabor. He overran Kurdani and reached Da'uq, where four Templar Knights and thirty foot-soldiers were stationed. The place was destroyed after a short battle. We do not know the fate of the mill of Kurdani or when the Hospitallers ceased to operate it.

The Kurdani mills were concentrated in one structure which has been pre- *description of* served in its entirety, though it is no longer used as a mill but as a barn and *Kurdani mills* granary, and the mill installations have mostly disappeared. The local inhabitants testify that the mill was working down to 1925. The great dam, 325 metres long, which blocked the river survives: with the addition of walls and iron locks, the area of the ancient pond was utilized for fishponds, but these have dried up since the river was drained.

The mill building, which is north of the dam, is composed of three parts. To the west is an elongated structure which contained four units of millstones. The chutes, most of them choked with rubbish and cattle manure, were in the south-east wall. On the northwest side, at a lower level, are four tunnels for the water wheels, but these are almost completely choked up. To the east of the elongated building with the four millstones stands a square tower of two storeys, which was used as the fortified stronghold of the mill. Its walls are loopholed; only some of the holes are preserved in their original form, for most have been en-larged and converted into windows. The entrance to the tower is on the north and is largely blocked by later building; it is defended by a machicolation. The masonry of the tower is drafted and close-jointed with only a thin layer of mortar between the stones. Adjacent to the tower is another mill with the wheel-tunnel preserved to its full height; here the stone chute is visible at the far end. Kurdani mills are very similar in plan and appearance to fortified mills in Europe.

While the Kurdani mills are completely preserved, only the tower remains at *description of* Da'uq. There was once a spring at the foot of the mound on which the ruined *Da'uq* tower stands while cisterns and structures survive which may have served as a mill. But even if there was once a mill here, this cannot be the Templar mill indi-cated in the sources; that must have been on the River Na'aman, over a kilo-metre from Tel Da'uq. No traces of the mills or of the bridge reported by the

251

documentary and historical sources now remain in the old river bed near Tel Da'uq.

pointed barrel vault

On the top of the tel are remains of a substantial and largely ruined structure, which was used as a *Khan* (Khan al-Da'uq) in the Middle Ages, and was a station on the road from Acre to 'Ibillin-Tsipori (Darb al-Ḥawarna). Here the foundations of a wall surround a rectangular yard. The length of the east and west walls is 70 metres and of the northern and southern 40 metres. A Crusader pointed barrel vault survives in the north wall of the court, 35 metres in length and 6 metres wide. This hall, to judge from its shape, was used as a storehouse.

THE YARQON MILLS

The Yarqon mills are alluded to in a number of Crusader documents. In 1158 or 1159 a grant made by the Lord of Mirabel to the Hospitaller Order mentions "the Mill beneath Mirabel", close to which is the "thorny land" *(terra spina)*. Downstream on the Yarqon, near the road leading to Arsuf, the mill of "The Three Bridges" *(Molendina Trium Pontium)* is noted; half of this mill was transferred to the Hospitallers by John d'Ibelin in 1241.

Hospitaller control

The Hospitallers, according to the documents, had considerable economic interests in the area and seem to have controlled all its mills. The importance of the region to the Order is proved by the fact that it saw fit to appoint a special command, the *Praeceptor de Spina.* The Crusader mills are both upstream, near the source of the river, and also not far from the estuary. In both places the structures survive. The first lies about half a mile north-west of Tel Antipatris, the Crusader *Surdi Fontes,* at a place known as the mill of al-Mirr. The remains show that the mill already existed in the Roman and Byzantine periods and was restored and repaired by the Crusaders. A dam diverted the river into a pond, whose water drove the mill, which was of the chute type. Like all such mill structures, that at al-Mirr is two-storeyed.

The second Crusader mill is on the boundary of the city of Tel Aviv, not far from the Tel Aviv–Hadar Yosef road, at the spot known as "The Ten Mills". Here was a three-arched bridge (hence the mill's Crusader name), preserved down to the First World War. The dam across the full width of the river diverted its waters into an artificial bed from which it flowed to the mill chutes. Five or six pairs of millstones were operated here.

SUGAR PRESSES

Sugar cane originated in the Far East but had reached the Near East early in the first millennium A.D. Detailed descriptions of peeling the cane, boiling the sweet sap and crystallizing the sugar are given in the Jerusalem Talmud. The sugar industry was perfected in the centuries preceding the Crusades and developed chiefly in Persia and Egypt. Sugar was exported in considerable quantities from these centres to Europe, but it was to be found only on the tables of kings and nobles in the south, being quite unknown in central and northern Europe, where the only sweetener was honey. *earlier history of sugar production*

The Holy Land was suitable for the growing of sugar cane, and extensive plantations flourished there as early as the 9th and 10th centuries. Best known were the plantations in the Plain of Acre (Kabul), around Tyre and in the Jordan Valley. The Crusaders quickly learned the economic value of this branch of agriculture. It is not surprising that, a short time after they had settled in the country, they began to grow sugar cane and soon became expert in the processes of sugar manufacture. Sugar was known as *zuccarum* and the cane as *cannemeles,* that is, "honey canes". Jacques de Vitry explained: "Of honey I have seen an abundance in those parts, in sugar canes. Sugar canes are canes full of honey—that is, of exceeding sweet juice—from which by crushing them in a press, and then thickening the juice over the fire, men make first a sort of honey and then sugar. These are called cannameles, a word compounded of *canna,* a cane, and *mel,* honey, because these canes are like reeds or rushes."[62] *sugar production by Franks*

The chief centres for growing sugar cane in addition to those already mentioned, were Sidon, Caesarea, Nablus, Jericho, Tsoar (a-Safi) and Shaubak (Montreal). As the cultivation of sugar cane requires abundant water, the plantations were either close to ample sources of water for irrigation or in swampy areas; the documentary material concerning this crop always mentions irrigation installations such as channels and aqueducts. In addition to plantations the sources also record installations for sugar production. Sugar presses are referred to at Tyre, at Yannuḥ near Acre, and near Caesarea.

The Arab name for a sugar press, *Ma'asera,* was taken into European languages, and a *"masera qua efficitur zucharum"* is mentioned in a Venetian document of 1243. A sugar factory was situated near Acre, and was plundered by the Moslem Taqi a-Din after the capture of the city from the Crusaders in 1187. The sugar of Nablus was sold "throughout the kingdom" and that of Transjordan was exported to Cyprus.

The Franks' expert knowledge of the production of sugar became renowned in Europe, and the emperor Frederick II sent a group to set up a sugar industry in Sicily. The production process was described by Burchard of Mount Sion: "The canes are gathered, cut in lengths of half a palm, and so are crushed in the press. The juice squeezed out of them is boiled in copper boilers, and when thickened, is collected in baskets made of slender twigs. Soon after it becomes dry and hard, and this is how sugar is made."[63]

The production of sugar had several stages. The canes were cut and taken to the press. Here they were peeled, cut into pieces, chopped and pulped; the juice was collected and boiled in copper pots. The liquid sugar ("honey") was placed in earthenware vessels or in wicker baskets to dry. After drying, the lump of sugar was the shape of a hemispherical cake.

operation of sugar mills

The Franks utilized water power to crush and pulp the sugar cane. For this purpose sugar mills similar to flour mills of the chute type were constructed, the only difference being in the millstones. An elongated upper millstone with pointed lugs capped the lower stone, which was larger than the bedstone of a flour mill, and resembled the basin of an olive press. The waterwheel turned the upper stone, and the peeled and cut sugar canes were inserted between its lugs, whose movement crushed and pulped them. The pulp collected in the concave bedstone and was taken to the press to extract the juice. In Palestine only two sugar-product installations have been preserved, one at Tawaḥin a-Sukkar near Jericho and the other near a-Safi.

TAWAḤIN A-SUKKAR ("THE SUGAR MILLS")

history

These mills are situated a kilometre from biblical Jericho (Tel a-Sultan) at the foot of the monastery of *Deir Quruntul,* the Crusader *Quarantene.* The mills were referred to as early as 1116, although the document of that year does not specify that they were used to manufacture sugar. They were in use throughout the Crusader period and subsequently. Burchard saw them at work in 1283 and they were also recorded by Felix Fabri in the year 1484.

Three mills could still be seen at this site at the beginning of the century, and the archaeological survey of the British Mandatory government of Palestine mentioned "an Arab inscription and knight's coat of arms" on one of them. One mill remains intact today, as well as a Crusader building where the sugar was apparently boiled.

In the 12th century the whole area was at first in the possession of the Patriarch of Jerusalem, who received from it an annual income of 5000 bezants. The place was given to the convent of Bethany by Queen Melisende in 1138. The area at the foot of the mountain of Quarantene was very fertile and noted for its crops of dates, bananas and sugar cane.

description

The mill was driven by water brought by one of the aqueducts from the springs of Nu'eima and Duyuk to the Jericho plain. This magnificent supply system, established in the time of King Herod, was still in working order, and was also repaired by the Crusaders. A stone chute with a plastered channel 40 centi-

254

Sugar factory,
Tawaḥin a-Sukkar

Aqueduct and sugar mill, Tawaḥin a-Sukkar

metres in width was built on the slope of a hill and conveyed water from it to the waterwheel of the Frankish mill.

The wheel pit is completely preserved in the mill structure; it is ten metres long, three metres wide and two metres deep. It is roofed with a barrel vault, and the giant basin remains over the pit. In the centre of the basin is a round hole with a raised lip, through which once turned the shaft of the waterwheel. The upper millstone has disappeared.

The aqueduct, supported by a circular arch, runs along the slope where the mill stands with the opening of its wheel tunnel facing east. To the north-east of the mill house, close by it, stands the ruin of a groin-vaulted hall, where the sugar was probably boiled.

OLIVE PRESSES

The cultivation of olive groves and the production of olive oil have always been one of the chief branches of the economy of the Holy Land. Olive groves covered wide areas of western Palestine, and still do. The centres of cultivation are the mountains of Judaea, Samaria and central Galilee. Remains of olive presses have been found at numerous ancient sites throughout the land, so that the Crusaders, when they reached the country, found olive-growing and the oil industry well developed.

The cultivation of olive groves and arrangements for rental payments are referred to in several documents of the Crusader period in connection with villages in all parts of the country. Oil presses, however, are noted only in isolated instances. An olive press in the language of the Franks was an "oil mill" *(molendina olivarum)* and the production of oil in the presses of the Crusader period was simply a continuation of the ancient process: crushing the olives, pressing out the oil and straining it.

The olives are placed on a large circular stone basin with a raised rim and a vertical shaft in its centre. A crushing wheel sits vertically on the basin, with a horizontal ploughshaft fixed in its centre and attached to the vertical shaft of the basin. A draught-animal harnessed to the shaft pulls it around the basin. The olives are placed on the basin, pounded by the weight of the crushing wheel, and then put into baskets lying on a basin-like shelf on the wall. A thick beam fastened to the wall operates a weight stone, which extracts the oil from the crushed olives. The oil is collected in a stone vat and the pressing is repeated three times.

description of olive press

The Crusader olive presses do not seem to have been installed in special quarters but were part of farm buildings or large manorhouses. This is perhaps the reason why they are not mentioned separately in the sources. Another reason may be that the production of olive oil, unlike the grinding of grain, was not a seigneurial monopoly.

Oil-producing installations, clearly identifiable as Crusader by the building style of their walls, have been discovered in three places, all near Jerusalem. A large Crusader structure has been found at Mei-Neftoah (Lifta), at the lower end of the village near the junction of Naḥal Lifta with Naḥal Soreq (Wadi Tulma). This structure, which was apparently a manorhouse, is very strongly built, its outer walls partly made of drafted and bossed blocks. On the west side of the building, in the cellar, is an olive press with all parts, except the wooden ones, preserved. The village of Lifta is mentioned in a distorted form (*Clepsta*) in a document dating from the 1240's. There are also remains of an olive press at Aqua Bella in the eastern room on the ground floor. Here a medium-sized basin lies on the ground near fragments of a crushing wheel. The pressing shelf for the olives is in the wall of the same room.

examples of Frankish installations

257

Olive press, Aqua Bella

A large structure, also a manorhouse, is to be seen in the village of Beituniya, which lies south of Ramallah. In one of its cellars are the remains of a basin, and the building is known locally to this day as "Badd al-Balad" (the village oil press). The building is notable for its gate with pointed arch and embossed blocks. Beituniya, called Beitiumen by the Franks, belonged to the Church of the Holy Sepulchre.

STABLES AND BYRES

The Crusader period made a poor contribution to the toponymy of the Holy Land. It is interesting and characteristic that the only Frankish term to be absorbed throughout the country, and used to the present day by the inhabitants to denote a locality, is the term for a stable or byre—*boverie,* or in Arabic, *baubariya.* There are no fewer than nine places today called "Kh. Baubariya," in the mountains round Jerusalem, in the neighbourhood of Nablus, in the She-phela, in the coastal plain and in the Plain of Acre, in each of which the name relates to the remains of Crusader buildings. "Baubariya" is to be found in or near the villages of Ḥ. Manot, Jifna, Fahma, Ḥ. Tannur, near Sabastiya, Zaba-bida, Tayiba near Ramallah, Yazur, Sarafand al Kharab and Rantiya.

baubariya

We do not know for certain whether all these buildings were used as stables or byres, but there is no reason to suppose that any of them were not. In three of the villages (Ḥ. Manot, Tayiba and Yazur) the buildings are situated near castles. In other places they are near churches, manorhouses, farms or administrative centres. The absorption of the name "baubariya" into the Arab language seems to confirm that the Crusader stable, in which the beasts enjoyed a building especially adapted to their needs, was an innovation in the country, where it had been the practice to lodge the livestock in cellars or temporary structures.

The heavy chargers on which the Frankish knights rode to war were not easy to obtain and were brought with much difficulty from Europe. The climatic conditions of the country, the rockiness of the ground and the constant fighting led to a high percentage of losses. As a result the Franks took great care of their horses. The statutes of the Hospitallers stipulated that they might not be put to the full gallop without the commander's sanction. The Knights Templar were duty-bound to visit their mounts twice every night—after Vespers and before they retired to sleep. A special statute of the Kingdom of Jerusalem laid down that the Crown and local lords should pay compensation to those of their knights whose horses were slain or wounded in battle *(Restor).* Besides the European chargers, of which every knight used two in battle, local breeds were also put into service by the mounted auxiliary forces.

Franks take great care of horses

Since the horses of the Franks were valued so highly, their owners spared no effort to build special quarters for them. The Baubariya, however, were used not only to lodge horses, but were designed for all sorts of livestock such as cows, oxen, mules and even sheep. Remains of buildings for housing livestock have been found at 'Atlit and at two places in Jerusalem, on the Temple Mount and in the Citadel, the "Tower of David."

Frankish stables

The Baubariya of 'Atlit has been subjected to careful archaeological investigation by the excavator of the citadel and the town, C.N. Johns. The building was in the *faubourg* near the south-western corner of the town wall, abutting

'Atlit

259

Stables, 'Atlit town

upon its southern sector. It is square in plan like an Oriental *khan* (caravanserai), the stalls being arranged round three sides of the square to open onto the inner yard. Rooms for the use of the grooms, stores and a barn are built on the fourth side of the square, which contains the entrance.

There was room in the building for two or three hundred beasts of which no more than a small part, not more than fifty, were horses. The rest of the accommodation was for sheep, cows or oxen.

accomodated horses and other beasts The halls which housed the stock were divided according to the type of beast, being long and narrow for horses and small for sheep. There were individual troughs for horses, but those for sheep were long and common to the flock. The walls of the building were of local stone; the roof, made of brushwood covered with quarry sand and lime coated with plaster, rested on pinewood beams brought from Mt. Carmel. Each hall, with a span of over 4 metres (the maximum length of the local pine-beam), had a square pier in the centre to support the roof beam. The timber roof was so light that there was no need for thick walls or vaults. The grooms' quarters, the stores and the yard yielded tools, horseshoes, coins, gaming pieces and various other objects. This Baubariya was built in the 1220's and was evidently burnt down by the Templars themselves in 1265, when Baybars destroyed the *faubourg* of 'Atlit. It was used, apparently, not to stable the chargers of the knights of 'Atlit but for the horses of the auxiliary forces and the castle livestock. The stables known as the "Boverie", which appear on the old maps of Acre and in city documents, probably resembled the stables of 'Atlit, in function if not in structure.

260

The great stables of the Templars have survived in their entirety on the Temple Mount of Jerusalem. Theodorich described them as follows:

Solomon's stables

"They have below them stables for horses, built by King Solomon—a wondrous and intricate building, resting on piers and containing an endless complication of arches and vaults, which stables we declare, according to our reckoning, could take ten thousand horses with their grooms."[64]

John of Würzburg, whose account was a little more modest than Theodorich's, wrote that the stables contained room for two thousand horses and one thousand five hundred camels. The stables of the Order are underground, in the south-eastern quarter of the Temple Mount. Here are large subterranean halls, 83 metres long from west to east and 60 metres from north to south. These are divided into thirteen tunnel-vaulted aisles resting on twelve lines of piers, eighty-eight in number, the arches of the arcade being semi-circular. The piers are huge Herodian blocks laid on their sides, in which holes for tethering the horses' reins are visible. A blocked entrance, the "Single Gate", is situated in the south wall of the sixth vault from the east. This blocked aperture, visible from outside in the south wall of the Temple Mount, not far from the south-east corner of the wall, seems to have been used as the entrance to the stables. West of the thirteenth vault a gate, today blocked, opened onto a series of vaults leading to the "Triple Gate" in the south wall of the Temple. Remains of stables containing *Tower of David* stone mangers have also been found in two places within the "Tower of David", both on the south-east side of the bailey and west of the tower today used as a mosque.

WATER SUPPLY

A supply of water for drinking and irrigation is of supreme importance in the semi-arid conditions of the Holy Land. In every generation the country's rulers and inhabitants have engaged in the construction of installations for storing rainwater, for utilizing sources of fresh water and for transferring it to points of need. Water installations hold an honoured place among the country's antiquities, from the magnificent underground water-tunnels of the kings of Judah to the elaborate aqueducts of the Roman period. The technical level of construction, maintenance and repair of the water installations is an accurate yardstick of the standard of material culture, density of population and conditions of security in various epochs throughout the country's history. The decay and neglect of the installations similarly witness to the deterioration of population and agriculture, to the decline in material culture and to the fecklessness of the country's rulers in other periods.

water works in Palestine

As in all other spheres of material civilization, the water supply and installations of the Holy Land reached the peak of their development in the Roman and Byzantine periods. The well-constructed aqueducts, the regional and local supply systems and the dams and wells, whose remains are to be found throughout the country, were sufficient to sustain a dense population and render fertile entire regions which are arid desert from the climatic point of view.

With the Arab conquest, a period of decline and decay began. However, when the Crusader armies reached the land many of the ancient installations were still working, in spite of neglect and reduced capacity. As with the rest of agriculture under the Franks, water installations continued to be used and maintained. Complete decay and destruction of the ancient civilization began again only after their expulsion, in the Mamluk period. Documents and historical sources show that the most elaborate water installations in the country, namely those at Caesarea and Jericho, were still in partial working order. The high-level Roman aqueduct, which brought the water from Ras a-Nabá at the foot of Mt. Carmel over a distance of 12 kilometres to Caesarea, had indeed fallen into disuse, but the second source, the "low-level" aqueduct which began at the Crocodile River, was still working and supplied running water to irrigate orchards and gardens near the city walls and for the fountains of Caesarea. The houses of Acre also had running water.

decline and decay begin with Arab conquest

There is further evidence that the Crusaders possessed the technical knowledge necessary to repair the conduits and restore them to working order. Lord Hugh of Caesarea reserved for himself (in 1162) the right "to repair the ancient water-line and to bring the [waters of the] spring to grow sugar cane."[65] The system of conduits, reservoirs and distribution channels erected in the Plain of Jericho by Herod, and improved by his successors, was still partly working. Re-

Crusaders possess technical knowledge to maintain and repair works

263

Antiliya

mains have been discovered in a section of the conduits bringing water from the springs of Wadi Qilt, Duyuk and Nu'eima which show that they were repaired in the Crusader period, and the sugar mills elsewhere described were driven by the water from one of these conduits.

The monks of Quarantene were allowed by Emma, the widow of Eustace Garnier, to use the water of the aqueducts for their mills "every Saturday and the night before it."[66] The entire region, indeed, was a flourishing garden, referred to by Frankish travellers as the Garden of Abraham.

Some of the local water systems were also still working. Thus Solomon's Pools, called by the Franks *Majus Stagnuum* (the great pool), were still supplying water to Bethlehem although the aqueducts of Jerusalem were dry. The installations of the Roman epoch built by the inhabitants of the neighbouring Jewish town at the spring of 'Ein al-Ḥilu, near the foot of Belvoir, continued to function.

There are several types of waterworks mentioned in Crusader sources or discovered in connection with remains of the period: the cistern or well, the pool and the aqueduct. Like the Arabs, and in contrast to the ancient Hebrews, the Crusaders did not differentiate between the well and the cistern. The same name *(cisterna)* is used by the sources, both for a cistern hewn to collect rainwater and for a well from which subterranean water was tapped.

The water was drawn from larger wells and cisterns by means of a "Wheeled machine"[67] and a contemporary chronicler ("Eracles") wrote: "Then he had a wheel made above it, with a bar which an animal turned. And stone tanks were put in place where the water drawn from the wheel poured out." This "machine" is the age-old *"antiliya"*, as still used by some Arab peasants. It consists of three wheels. A small wheel is placed above the well's pit. On it, square buckets are suspended, tied to each other by a rope or chain. By the wheel's motion, the

types of waterworks

cisterns

265

Duyuk, Aqueduct

buckets are lowered into the water, filled, drawn out full, and poured into an open reservoir situated beside the well. The small wheel is connected to a large wheel by a thick beam which serves as an axis. The large vertical wheel is turned by another, horizontal, wheel which is rotated by an animal plodding round it.

conduits   Many settlements subsisted on cisterns only, lacking springs or wells of fresh water. Fortified places posed a special problem, and here every effort was made to ensure a water supply within the enceinte. Elaborately ramified systems to channel rainwater were installed in many castles, such as those discovered at Montfort and at Belvoir. In these castles earthenware ducts, catchments and stone channels have been found, by means of which all the rainwater falling upon the ramparts, roofs and courts was drained into large plastered tanks. All the large castles and most of the small ones had cisterns of various sizes, some bottle-shaped and some circular shafts. In places built on a rocky foundation the cistern was hewn from the rock. In others a deep excavation was made and the walls of the cistern were built of masonry lined with non-porous plaster. Jerusalem's water supply was based almost entirely on the storage of surface water, and no house was without its cistern, the rainwater being drained into them from the streets and the roofs (see p. 56). Stormwater and the water of small springs was concentrated in pools known by the Arab-Frankish name of *birke* or *berquilia*. These are to be found throughout the country and provided water both for drinking and for irrigation.

pools   Some of these pools were replenished with the help of dams which caught and collected the flood waters running down the wadi slopes, while channels hewn in the rock or constructed of masonry drained the slopes of seasonal torrent-beds and guided the water into the pools. Others served as catchment basins for small or large springs rising in their vicinity, the water being drained into the pools by

Kh. Kurmul,
reservoir (Berquilia)

266

channels or earthenware pipes. The first class includes the pools at Qula and al-Bira, the Jerusalem pool of Legerius and the Sultan's Pool (Germain's Pool). To the second type belong the pool of Siloam outside Jerusalem, Solomon's Pools and the pool at Carmel (Kurmul) in the mountains of Hebron. The arrangements for the supply of fresh water to castles are worth emphasizing. Apart from the catchment of rainwater, special efforts were made to safeguard the flow of subterranean or springwater in such a way that it could not be interrupted by an enemy in time of siege (see p. 289).

Ramified irrigation systems were developed for agricultural crops needing ample water—sugarcane, for example. Such systems existed near Tyre, where *irrigation* the water of the spring of Ras-al-'Ein, the Frankish Raseline, was carried by channels. Channels were also used to bring water power to mills, as described earlier (see p. 248). Not far from Acre the Hospitallers diverted the Na'aman water to their fields of sugarcane near Yannuḥ. Irrigation channels are also alluded to in the vicinity of Caesarea, at Nablus and at Jericho.

The water sources were the property of the feudal lords and were granted either together with the land near them or separately. Their owners kept strict *water—property* watch on their rights, and the permission to water livestock at a well was re- *of feudal lords* garded as a grant worthy of inclusion in a written, sealed charter. In 1177 the Master of the Hospitallers confirmed the permission granted to the inhabitants of Qalansuwa to water their livestock at the well of the Order. Numerous disputes took place between feudal lords over the ownership of water sources and over the right of using water from channels and pools.

Most of the water installations were lost as part of the systematic destruction carried out in the coastal plain following the Mamluk conquest, and the total ruin of the works at Caesarea and Tyre occurred at that time. In the inland areas, where the Mamluk 'scorched earth' policy was not put into operation, the systems remained in use but fell gradually into decay when all centralized government in the country ceased.

MEANS OF COMMUNICATION

The Crusaders were ignorant of ways and means to arrange rapid and reliable means of communication, resembling in this respect the governments of the European kingdoms of their time. Organized systems of communication for military or administrative purposes were therefore undeveloped in the Crusader epoch.

In this respect an obvious regression occurred in the Crusader period, com- *regression in* pared with the Arab period that preceded it. The Arab authorities had main- *Crusader period* tained a number of means of communication: the royal mail or *barid,* the pigeon-post and smoke-signalling. The royal mail was the continuation of the Byzantine imperial mail or *veredus,* and was in operation for most of the period of the Umayyad empire. Official correspondence was carried between the centres of government, the horses and messengers being changed at stations dispersed at fixed intervals along the routes. The pigeon-post also operated throughout the 'Abbasid and Fatimid empires. Zengi introduced it into Mosul in 1160. In 1171 Nur a-Din established a royal pigeon-post between Damascus and Cairo, also based on a system of stations where the pigeons were changed. Signalling by beacon or smoke existed in the country at the end of the 10th century. Al-Maq- *earlier periods* disi related: "At the stations . . . they sound the horns, also, if it be night, they light a beacon there on the tower, or, if it be day, they make a great smoke. From every watch station on the coast up to the capital there are built at inter- vals high towers. [They] kindle the beacon on the nearest coast station, and then on that lying next above it and onwards, one after another, so that hardly an hour elapses before the trumpets are sounding in the capital . . ."[68] In contrast to these organized and very efficient means of communication, the Franks used primitive methods which operated sporadically. Important information was sent by messengers who rode the whole distance without reliefs. In isolated cases pigeons were used to carry information, chiefly from besieged fortresses, but *Frankish* this was mere improvisation. The only organized form of communication ap- *improvisations* pears to have been fire-signalling. Ernoul wrote that "there was a custom in Outremer that when the Saracens were known to have entered any part of the country, the first who had seen them lit a fire, till it was seen all over the country."

It is interesting that the use of fire-signalling is mentioned only once in Cru- sader chronicles. This was in 1183, when the Franks besieged in Karak of Moab lit a fire to summon help. The beacon was seen in Jerusalem and the king set out to help the besieged fortress. It may be asked why the use of signalling is not mentioned in other cases if it was really an accepted means of communication. It should also be remembered that fire-signalling is limited by its very nature, *fire-signalling* and cannot convey detailed information.

Most Crusader fortresses and some of their towns are notable in that there is intervisibility, such as make fire-signalling practicable. We shall see (p. 294) that there was intervisibility between all the castles on the frontier of Galilee. Most of the mountain centres and some of those on the maritime plain are also within sight of one another.

Mamluk period   When the Mamluk kingdom was set up the state systems of communications were re-organized. In 1261 Baybars re-organized the royal mail, which operated twice weekly and by means of which letters reached Damascus from Cairo in four days. The pigeon-post was also organized on a regular basis and acted as a swifter means of communication than mounted messengers. Fire and smoke-signalling were embodied in the general system. The signalling network in Palestine extended to Gaza and thence information was carried across Sinai by mail-horses.

Part IV FORTIFICATIONS

TOWN DEFENCES: WALLS
AND CITADELS

Immediately prior to the Crusader conquest of the Holy Land most of the towns were well fortified. Only Nablus and Hebron were open cities. The defence of the towns was based on their ancient Byzantine fortifications or on Arab defences built on the Byzantine model.

Frankish town defences basically the Byzantine-Arab fortifications

The warlike operations which brought about the capture of such towns did not cause much damage to their fortifications and, having repaired them here and there, the Crusaders continued to use them. Hence, the defensive works of the Crusader towns rested on their ancient fortifications. Apart from changes and improvements in some details, which will be discussed below, no changes took place in the 12th century in the concepts of urban defence or in the plans of the fortifications.

The surviving remains of the walls, or those which can be restored from historical sources, enable us to determine how urban fortification was planned. It was composed of two elements: the walls with their towers and gates, and the citadel. The general plan of the walls of the coastal towns differs from that of the cities of the interior. The enceintes of the inland towns took the form of a square or rhomboid. In the coastal towns the course of the walls formed an elongated trapezoid or ellipse whose longer sides were parallel to the coastline. Some of the coastal towns were fortified by all-round enceintes, while others were undefended on the shore side. Ascalon and Arsuf belonged to the first category; Acre, Caesarea and 'Atlit to the second.

two elements: enceintes and citadels

The length of the perimeter wall varied, depending on the size of the city and the presence or absence of a seaward wall. Ascalon's walls measure 2.7 kilometres, those of Caesarea are 1.2 kilometres long, Acre's are 1.3 kilometres long —here the two sides facing the sea were unfortified—while those of Jerusalem measure 4 kilometres. All had a single wall except Acre, where the line was double, the walls being spaced 30 metres apart. All had rock-cut or excavated moats outside the walls. At Jerusalem, Ascalon and Acre barbicans were built in front of those sections of the ramparts which were particularly vulnerable to attack: the barbican was in front of the north-east wall at Jerusalem, outside the east and west gates at Ascalon and at the north-east corner of Acre.

perimeter walls

The citadel was always built as an independent defensive unit. In some towns it was on the perimeter wall, as at Ascalon, Jerusalem and Banias, in some it was built within the walls, as at Caesarea, Acre and Arsuf; but everywhere it had its own walls, towers and moats. The citadels of the coast towns were built on the shore near the harbour, being so sited in order to ensure protection of the harbour against invasion, to safeguard sea communications even in time of siege, to serve as a refuge for the defenders after the capture of the town, and to

citadels

cover evacuation by sea. In Jerusalem the citadel, the "Tower of David", was built on the west of the city, to defend one of the main city gates and to ensure evacuation in time of siege and capture.

Acre and Ascalon had secondary citadels near those sectors of the walls exposed to greater danger—at Ascalon near the east gate and at Acre not far from the north-east corner.

defence of townships The townships which developed around military and administrative castles were mostly unfortified, and their inhabitants found refuge in times of danger within the walls of the castle. Only at Gaza and 'Atlit were the suburbs defended by their own walls; Montmusard, the suburb of Acre, after remaining open for a prolonged period, was surrounded by a wall in the 1250's. In these few cases the outer wall served as a first line of defence, while the castle acted as the citadel of the townlet.

THE DEFENCE OF OPEN SETTLEMENTS

The undefended Frankish towns and villages were not completely lacking in protection. In each a tower *(turris)* was erected to serve as a fortified stronghold. Towers were also erected on the boundaries of estates, in mining centres, at depots for the collection of agricultural produce and at farmsteads. The defensive function of the towers is well demonstrated in historical sources. William of Tyre related how a Moslem army attacked the Frankish village of Buria (Dabburiya), encircling it at night. "When dawn broke the inhabitants saw that they were surrounded on all sides by the enemy and retreated in haste to a tower which was above the village."[69] The Moslems, surrounding the tower, were able to induce its surrender after four hours. Many of the inhabitants were killed and the remainder, five hundred in number, were taken prisoner. King Baldwin built a tower at Nablus, known as *Turris Neapolitana,* and the inhabitants fled thither during Moslem raids. Similar towers are also mentioned at Jericho and Hebron. William told of the circumstances in which a tower was built in the village of Bethany near Jerusalem, and of its function:

defensive function of towers

"Since the place lay on the edge of the desert and thus might be exposed to the attacks of the enemy, the Queen, at great expense, caused to be built a strongly fortified tower of hewn and polished stone. This was devoted to the necessary purpose of defence, that the maidens dedicated to God might have an impregnable fortress as a protection against the enemy."[70]

These towers were planned in a uniform fashion throughout the country. Each consisted of a two storeyed square structure with walls 12–15 metres long and 10 metres high. They were very solidly built, the walls being as much as 3 metres thick; in some places these were set on a solid base 2 metres high. Such towers were provided with a single entrance; their walls had loopholes for light, air and archery. The structure was surrounded by a low stone wall or timber palisade. The tower's function was one of passive defence and its strength lay in its solid construction; those who took refuge there could not prosecute an active defence, as the single narrow entrance prevented a sortie. The small number of loopholes and the blind areas created by the corners of the structure impeded return of fire.

uniform plan and appearance

The tower's sole value, therefore, lay in the protection which it afforded against predatory forays; if attacked by a regular force it was apt to succumb in a few hours. In the defensive role which it performed the Crusader tower was identical with the keep, as developed by the Normans and built in dozens of places throughout France and England. There are indeed some differences in the details of building: the European tower was often three-storeyed and its entrance, at first-floor level, was by means of steps constructed in the forebuilding. Owing to

difference between Norman keeps and Palestinian towers

shortage of timber for roofing the Franks, unlike the Europeans, were forced to roof their towers with stone vaults, so reducing the interior space and number of storeys from three to two. In Europe the tower walls were reinforced by external buttresses and by small corner turrets. These details were absent in the Holy Land. But despite these differences, there is no doubt that the Norman models, one of the most renowned of which is the Tower of London, were in the minds of the Frankish engineers who constructed the Crusader towers.

However, where the tactical conception inherent in their erection was concerned, the Crusaders were not influenced by the European example. Similar defensive towers were also built by the Byzantines and the Arabs. The need to *similar tactical* defend rural settlements and agricultural estates against predatory raiding pro- *conception* duced identical solutions in the west and in the east; nor were these restricted to *throughout the* the period we are discussing. In 16th-century England "peel towers" were erected *ages* for defence against border forays. Towers with the same purpose were established in Palestine in the Mamluk and Turkish periods. As late as the 1936 disturbances the British administration set up "Pill Boxes" whose functions were identical with those of the Crusader towers. Thanks to their particularly stout structure, remains of more than twenty Crusader defence-towers have been preserved. In some places they survive complete and still serve as dwellings. Elsewhere a huge hall rising to 8 or 10 metres above ground level remains, hanging, as it were, in the air. Such remains are to be found at Burj Misr, Metsad Qorḥa, Metsad Rahav, H. Manoth, Jezreel, Jenin, Qaqun, Qalansuwa, Qula, Nablus, Burj Atot, Beit Tsur, Tel Taninim, al-Bira, Qubeiba, Sinjil, Bethany, Umm-Khalid (Natanya) and Yazur.

no general Students of the military history of Palestine in the Crusader period have *strategic scheme* sought to fit these towers into a comprehensive strategic or tactical scheme. This conception, which implies a general planned initiative, appears to be forced and engenders a distortion of topographical facts and the fabrication of imaginary systems; the *raison d'être* of the towers was simple; namely, to serve as refuges in times of stress for the inhabitants of Frankish villages. Nevertheless, it is indeed true that after they had been erected the towers found their place in the defensive system of the kingdom and fulfilled vital functions there. As most of the villages arose or grew up at important crossroads, or on central highways, the towers could also be used to improve the security of the kingdom's roads.

Elements of fortification were also found in the Frankish manorhouses, monasteries, churches and farmhouses. These buildings were provided with loopholes, corner towers and fortified gates, and their sites were chosen with due consideration for tactical superiority.

276

CASTLES

In the strictly defined sense of the term, a castle is a fortified place built to serve as a permanently defended base for a military force charged with the control of an area. The military force quartered in the castle might operate offensively or defensively, outside the castle walls against an external enemy, or in the capacity of a garrison; it might be used to repress rebellious elements or to impose government upon the population.

Castles were generally erected with a definite purpose in mind. Some were established out of purely military considerations, while others were built to act as centres controlling feudal domains. Changes occurring after their erection led to change of function; thus castles built as frontier fortresses became centres of civilian administration when the frontier moved to a distance as the result of a campaign of conquest (see p. 173), and fortresses built as administrative centres found themselves in the front line during a hostile invasion. Others were built from the beginning to serve several purposes simultaneously. Hence it is generally difficult today to define their *raison d'être* and to classify them precisely. The factor common to all of them was that they were centres of strength and authority. It was thus that the feudal lord maintained his control over his domain and his peasants, and thus that the military commanders safeguarded the security of the realm against the Moslem foe. *changes in function due to changing conditions*

In the conditions of warfare of the period, the overrunning of a region entailed the capture of its castles. A military force could penetrate a country in depth, but so long as it had not gained control of its castles, the invasion was in effect merely a raid and not a conquest. Without a fortified base the invader was forced to evacuate the territory and retire behind his own frontiers. The invader could only secure his control, in an area without castles, by building and garrisoning a new castle from which control could be imposed after the retirement of the main force; thus a noble who received or conquered a domain would set up a castle there, and from this base his knights would sally forth to maintain his rule over it and the serfs who dwelt there. *control of a region required conquest of its castles*

Castles had been built in Palestine in all epochs: Egyptian frontier fortresses of the second millennium B.C., strongholds of David, Solomon and Rehoboam, Hasmonean forts, strongpoints built during the revolt against Rome, the Roman-Byzantine *limes* which defended the frontier and the castles of the Ummayad Caliphs. But at no time were they so important or so numerous as in the Crusader period, the golden age of fortress-building, and the Crusader castles still figure prominently in the Palestinian landscape.

Three main factors led the Franks to invest so much of their energy and resources in the building of fortresses: peril from without, unrest within, and the feudal regime. *three main reasons for castle building*

277

The history of the Crusader kingdom is the history of warfare with the Moslem world which surrounded it. A ceaseless and bloody struggle obliged the Franks to fortify their frontiers in order to prevent the enemy from penetrating the narrow strip of territory, so lacking in strategic depth, which was in their hands. The fact that the Crusader kingdom was the state of an occupying minority, amounting to no more than a quarter of the population, obliged its rulers to watch its Moslem enemies with the utmost vigilance. Although revolts of the Moslem inhabitants did not occur during the period, attempts were made from time to time to throw off the Crusader yoke during invasions of the country by Moslem armies. Likewise, attacks by highway robbers upon travellers, chiefly pilgrims, were frequent, and the king's highways had to be kept secure.

danger from
without

internal unrest

The Crusaders came from a feudal Europe and founded their kingdom in Palestine on a feudal basis. In Europe the castle was the hub from which the lord wielded power over his domain. It was the centre about which the life of the domain revolved, the abode of the military force which imposed the will of the lord, the administrative centre of the domain, the place where taxes were collected, where the court of justice and the council of knights of the fief met. In the conditions of war of the day, the lord of the castle was safe within its walls and independent of his neighbours. When a Frankish noble received a region as a fief, he erected at its centre a fortress which served all these purposes.

feudal regime

The one considerable difference between the castles of the Holy Land and those of Europe lay in the fact that the Frankish lord did not make the castle his residence, preferring to dwell in the city amongst a majority of his own people, and to enjoy its pleasures and excitements. The characteristic way of life of the feudal castles of Europe, with their noble banquets, tournaments and minstrelsy, did not therefore develop in Palestine, where the local castle was no more than a centre for defence, government and administration. The feudal regime was founded on strong bonds between the king and the lords both in terms of rights and duties and, so long as these held, the castles operated as a single system of control through which the entire kingdom was governed. But the castle could also be a divisive factor, making for disruption of the central authority, as proved to be the case with the mediaeval castles of Europe.

The Kingdom of Jerusalem was a state under siege for most of the period of its existence, so that the sense of a common fate and the need for solidarity generally prevailed within it over the forces of disintegration and irresponsibility. The Frankish castles, whether built for frontier-defence and the policing of the roads, or for feudal domination, constituted, together with the fortified towns and the scattered defence-towers of the open settlements, the physical basis on which government and security rested.

unlike European
castles, Frankish
strongholds not
factors of internal
strife

Fortified structures are useless in themselves, without garrisons or field-forces. The numbers manning the fortresses were relatively small and included only a handful of knights. The country's largest castle, that of Safed, held fifty, and the average castle quartered ten to fifteen. In addition each garrison included squires, serjeants, the crews of the siege machines, servants and slaves. The total

garrisons

278

strength of the garrison at Safed was 1,700 in peacetime and 2,200 in time of war.

The garrison strength sufficed to ensure control of the vicinity of the castle against the raids of small forces and irregular units, but could not prevent deliberate invasion by large armies, a task which fell to the field army which gathered in the rear and sallied forth· against the invader. The defensive strategy of the Crusaders will be dealt with more fully when describing the frontier castles.

TYPES OF FORTRESS

Before enumerating the types of Crusader fortress, it is necessary to consider the architectural skill and experience which the Franks brought with them from Europe. Military architecture in Europe had been at its lowest ebb in the centuries before the Crusades began. The only fortifications worthy of the name were those of the Roman period, and these were of two types: city fortifications and fortresses. *architectural skills of the Crusaders*

Most of the Roman towns had been fortified against the barbarians in the final period of the Empire. Urban fortifications were usually constructed to a square plan and included one or two walls with slightly projecting round towers along their length, and gates at the four cardinal points. These Roman defences were retained and repaired by the lords of the towns, generally bishops, and served throughout the Middle Ages to protect and shelter the population from invasion. The remains of Roman fortified camps were also to be found all over Europe, mostly concentrated on the frontiers of the Empire and composing the fortified *limes* (see p. 291). Their plan is standard, in the form of a square, defended by earth ramparts and timber palisades, with four gates. At permanent stations the camp was surrounded by stone ramparts. The new fortifications built in Europe down to the 11th century were of the type known as "motte and bailey," consisting of an enclosure surrounded by a ditch; its spoil earth was piled in the centre of the area which, so raised, created an artificial mound or motte. Along the inner lip of the ditch a palisade was erected, and on the top of the mound a wooden tower was built, surrounded by another palisade. The area between the two palisades was the bailey. The tower had two or three storeys, the ground floor being used as a storeroom. The entrance was in the first storey, a ladder placed outside the building providing access. This storey contained a hall for reception and meals, the living quarters being above. Normally such fortresses were built solely of earth and timber, but where stone was available, masonry walls were added, principally at the gates. In the years before the First Crusade a new period in fortress-building began in Europe. Stone began to take the place of timber and earth and the fortification known as the "Norman keep" became widespread. *urban fortifications in Europe* *"motte and bailey"* *Norman keep*

It was equipped with this primitive knowledge that the Franks encountered oriental military architecture, whose standard was incomparably higher than theirs. Here had been preserved and developed the ancient military techniques which had reached their zenith in the brilliant days of the Roman and Byzantine empires. The Crusading knights, as they made their eastward journey, beheld fortified cities such as Constantinople, Nicaea and Antioch. Hundreds of fortified buildings were scattered throughout Syria, Cilicia and Anatolia—some destroyed, some in continuous use for centuries, some surviving from the Roman period and some built during the long and obstinate conflict waged between the Byzantines and their hostile Moslem neighbours.

oriental castles

The peak period in the history of Byzantine fortification had ended many years before the coming of the Franks, but the Byzantines continued to build their fortifications on the classic models, and the methods which had crystallized in the 6th century, during the reign of the Emperor Justinian, continued to serve as the standard for the construction of fortresses. As we have seen, the Crusaders inherited the urban defences which had not been destroyed, introducing few modifications and repairs. As to the defences of castles, it is not surprising that, much influenced by such numerous examples of well-distilled knowledge, the Franks soon outstripped their teachers. The Crusader fortresses surpassed their predecessors in planning, in the strength of their defences and in the quality of their construction. The reason is without doubt rooted in the need for security, in the demography and in the feudal regime prevailing in the kingdom. These made the building of fortresses essential, regardless of cost. The design of the Crusader fortresses may be divided into three main types, namely the Norman keep, the *castrum* and the "spur-castle." The Norman keep having already been mentioned, the other two types will now be described in greater detail.

THE CASTRUM

The *castrum* (small fort), or in Greek the *tetrapyrgion* (four-towered fort), had four walls surrounding a square, with a square tower at each corner. Dwellings ranged along the inner side of the walls or stood independently in the centre of the court. This was the system on which the fortified camps of the Roman legions, the Roman-Byzantine frontier forts and the castles of the Ummayad Caliphs were planned. The remains of dozens of such structures are to be found throughout the Orient, from Tunisia to the Euphrates Valley, and similar ones are to be seen in Europe.

four-towered fort

The *castrum* was simple in form and easy and quick to erect, ensuring maximum defence with the minimum expenditure of resources. It is no surprise, therefore, that the Franks established most of their forts in the Holy Land on this pattern. The great similarity between the Crusader *castrum* and the Roman-Byzantine *castrum* has led scholars to conclude that the Franks copied the ancient model. While there can be no doubt that they were influenced by it, this influence should not, however, be exaggerated. The plan is so simple, its advantages so obvious and the solutions offered to the problems of defence so elemen-

simple and efficient

tary, that imitation seems superfluous. Rather it is an identical solution arrived at in identical fashion. The builders of the Zionist frontier settlements of the 1930's, or of the Jordanian desert police-stations in the 1950's, used an identical plan, and are not to be suspected of copying ancient models.

The plan of the *castrum* was described by several contemporary chroniclers. Of Castle Darom, William of Tyre related:

the castrum *described by contemporaries*

"... The King had caused to be built on this site a fortress of moderate dimensions, covering scarcely more than a stone's throw of ground. It was square in form and at each corner was a tower, one of which was more massive and better fortified than the rest. There was neither moat nor barbican."[71]

Of the castle of Ibelin:

"They built a fortress of very strong masonry with deep foundations and four towers."[72]

The castle of Blanchegarde he described thus:

"... and a stronghold of hewn stone, resting on solid foundations, was built. It was adorned with four towers of suitable height."[73]

The castle of Chastelet was a "fortification of solid masonry in the form of a square."[74]

Crusader *castra* are widespread throughout Palestine, at Hunin, Mi'ilya, Metsad 'Ateret, Belvoir, al-Fula, Yalu, Latrun, Ma'ale-Adumim, Beit Govrin, Tel Tsafit, Yavne, Deir al-Balaḥ, Ashdod-Yam and Habonim, and constitute the commonsest type among the Crusader fortresses in the country. The *castra* vary in size, and some have modifications on the basic plan. The small forts such as those at Ma'ale-Adumim, Ashdod-Yam, Hunin and Beit Govrin are almost square, their sides being 50–60 metres long. Others, such as Chastelet, are elongated rectangles. The largest is the castle of Belvoir—130 metres long and 100 metres wide. Some are built without projecting corner towers, as at Ma'ale-Adumim and Hunin. In the larger fortresses, where the distance between the corner towers was more than 50–60 metres, and hence too great to ensure effective covering fire from end to end, intermediate towers were built. The usual distance between towers was 40 metres, the towers being square but not solid. They are circular, and solid, only in the Arab fortresses, such as those at Habonim and Ashdod-Yam.

slight differences in plans

The *castra* generally had a single gate, although a few had two. Some (Belvoir, al-Fula, Hunin, Ma'ale-Adumim) were defended by rock-cut excavated moats. Some were also protected by barbicans. The defences of others included a keep —sometimes one of the corner towers specially reinforced (Darom, Metsad 'Ateret). Occasionally a separate tower was built in the middle of the bailey. At Belvoir a keep was built in the form of a rectangle with four corner towers, occupying most of the bailey—in effect a *castrum* within a *castrum*, so that the castle possessed two concentric lines of defence. All the *castra* were erected during the 12th century, chiefly between 1130–1170; their purposes varied as did those who established them, amongst whom were kings, the military orders and feudal lords. We find *castra* which were built to serve as border fortresses (Hunin, Belvoir, Beit Govrin, Tel Tsafit and Yavne), road forts (al-Fula, Ma'ale-Adumim, Yalu, Latrun, Deir al-Balaḥ) and feudal administrative centers (Mi'ilya). The Moslems also continued to build fortresses of the *castrum* type in this period, as for example at Qal'at a-Rabad.

builders

The *castrum*'s strength did not lie in its massive stone walls and complicated defensive installations; nor was it an impregnable stronghold whose defenders awaited siege behind its ramparts. It was designed to serve as a defended base for a military force whose task was to seek out the enemy and engage him in the open field. The tactical conception implicit in its foundation was aggressive defence—the opposite of the concept of passive defence implicit in the Norman keep. It is no coincidence that the *castrum* was selected as the model for all the fortresses of the "Ascalon Strip," and of most of the fortresses of the north-east frontier. William of Tyre described the functions of the *castra* felicitously when he said:

the tactical conception of the castra— aggressive defence

> "Our people resolved to erect fortresses round about. Within these strongholds forces could be easily assembled which from their very proximity could more readily check the enemy forays. Such fortresses would also serve as bases from which to make frequent attacks upon the city [Ascalon] itself."[75]

But if the fortress were besieged, the defenders could not rely upon the strength of the walls and towers, which were too weak to withstand a prolonged siege involving sapping and bombardment. The garrison was bound to adopt active methods of defence in the hope that a relieving force would be rushed to the spot in time to raise the siege. The castle of Darom was breached after a two-day investment, and only saved thanks to the speedy arrival of the relieving force. The castle of Chastelet was taken in five days because the force sent to relieve it lingered at Tiberias. That of Hunin held out in the brief siege of 1179 owing to the active methods of defence adopted by its garrison. The only *castrum* to withstand a prolonged investment was Belvoir, but here the defence was successful because the large garrison carried out frequent sorties and prevented the siege engines and the Moslem sappers from approaching its walls.

disadvantages

Since the function of the *castrum* was an active one, its builders did not select a site which was difficult of access. The *castra* were built on hills with convenient slopes affording a wide field of observation. It is revealing that their building period was restricted to the 12th century, and that after the battle of Hattin no more of this type were erected in Palestine. The aggressive tactical conceptions, based on self-confidence and readiness to meet the enemy everywhere, gave way to a conception of passive defense, which found its expression in another type of fortification.

sites chosen for castra

282

THE SPUR-CASTLE

The spur-castle was a fortress built on a rocky promontory at the junction of two gorges. The ridge or spur selected had very steep slopes on three sides, while the fourth, the saddle of the spur linking it with the high ground, was secured by a rock-cut moat. As such spurs are long and narrow, the plan of such castles was necessarily likewise, and their length along the axis of the spur was several times greater than their breadth.

sites

The exterior walls of the castle were built on the brink of the steep slope, thus enhancing the natural strength of the site and rendering it impregnable. The more gradual slope of the ground at the top of the spur made it possible to erect the castle buildings at various levels, one above the other. An additional line of walls, built within the outer ramparts, created a second line of defence. The weak point of the spur-castle was at its rear, where the promontory joined the plateau. This side, as has been said, was cut off by a moat; behind it was a strong wall, and within it the keep of the castle. The keep was at the highest point of the castle area and dominated all its parts. The spur-castles included some of the largest and finest Crusader fortresses, whose remains, evoking so much admiration and amazement, survive because of their solid construction and their situation in remote and inaccessible spots. For all their brute strength they are decisive evidence of the period of weakness, retreat and pessimism in the history of the Crusader kingdom, when the Franks abandoned the offensive, and ceased to challenge the Moslems in open encounter for the recovery of their lost domains. Seized by fear of open places, they chose instead to shelter in rocky clefts and behind stone walls like tortoises in their shells. In contrast to the *castrum,* whose purpose was to serve as a base for aggressive initiative and action, the spur-castle was founded on the concept of passive defence.

three lines of defence

concept of passive defence

Most of the castles of this type in Palestine were built in the 13th century. Exceptional is the castle of Karak and perhaps of Subeibe, built in the 12th century. Karak, however, is not an independent fortress but a citadel constructed to protect a town, and Subeibe was probably not a Frankish structure. In Western Palestine spur-castles were few, as most of the country's mountainous area was outside the control of the Franks in the 13th century. Their ruins are also relatively rare and slight, the best surviving examples being in northern Syria. The only examples in Palestine of 13th century spur-castles are at 'Atlit, Montfort, Safed and Beaufort. At 'Atlit the castle stands on a promontory projecting into the sea, which is defended by the waves instead of earth slopes. The plan of fortifications at Safed, which lies on a domelike hill, is different, being elliptical and concentric, not elongated or irregular.

most spur-castles built in 13th century

As the main task of the spur-castles was to serve as safe refuges, the emphasis was on the strength of their fortifications, on their ability to withstand prolonged siege, on cunning defensive devices and on relatively comfortable living conditions for their garrisons. The walls, built of huge stones to a thickness of as much as three metres, rise from a rocky base which made undermining extremely difficult. They contain two arrays of firing positions, namely loopholes and machicolations at the top. The projecting towers ensured flanking fire and covered all the dead ground in front of the walls and at the bottom of the moat. There is a second line of defence, whence the defenders could shoot over the heads of their comrades manning the first line. All the gates were built on the plan of the "bent entrance" and were defended by vertical loopholes and portcullises.

Within the spur-castles were immense storerooms for grain, and also cisterns, making it possible to resist prolonged siege; likewise quarters for knights, squires and artisans, the palace of the castellan, a ceremonial hall, prison cells, stables, smithies, armouries, carpentry workshops, flour mills, baths and wine presses. Their garrisons were comparatively large, sometimes numbering as many as several thousand. All those built in the 13th century were erected by the Military Orders.

SIEGE TECHNIQUE

adoption of oriental siege methods

The Crusaders adopted the siege methods and siege machinery in use in the oriental armies, which were vastly superior to the primitive types common in Europe. There were three ways of capturing a fortress: frontal attack, breaching of the fortifications, and prolonged investment aimed at starving out the besieged. An attacking army would generally first try to capture a fortress by a frontal attack without prior preparation; rope ladders with hooks at the end would be thrown onto the ramparts and, when the hooks found hold, the troops would scale them. There was also a mechanical method of scaling known as "the Cat", but the way in which this was operated is not clear. A Frankish source described this machine as follows: "It was intended for scaling the walls and for this reason was called 'the Cat' because after creeping up in the manner of a cat it got a grip of the wall and stuck fast to it." If the frontal attack was repulsed, the besiegers would set about a planned siege with the object of making breaches in the fortifications. The breaching of the walls was carried out in three ways: by bombarding with machines working on ballistic principles, through penetration by means of battering rams and the extraction of stones, and by sapping beneath the wall-foundations.

three ways of capturing a castle

frontal attack planned siege

siege machines

The ballistic weapons were called *petrariae*—in French *periers*—or *mangonels*. These were operated by means of a great weight fastened to the short arm of a lever, which being let fall, raised the end of the long arm with a great velocity. At the end of the long arm a sling with a projectile was attached; when the arm reached the end of its momentum, a special device liberated the projectile and it was flung with great force. These machines could throw stones of a weight of 150 kilograms for a distance of over a hundred yards. Richard Coeur de Lion had a *petraria* that is said to have killed twelve Moslems with one stone. The stone was sent to Saladin, and it was said that "nothing could resist the blows of these stones without being shattered or ground to powder." Another engine was so strong that its stones destroyed half of one of the wall-towers of Acre.

The main breaching implement was the battering ram. This consisted of a *battering ram* long thick beam with a heavy iron head ending in a sharp spike. It was mounted in a timber frame which allowed it to be swung steadily forwards and backwards by a group of men. The blows of the ram struck the joints of the stones and ultimately broke up the mortar between them so that they could be dislodged. The ram was also used to burst open city gates. Fighting men would also advance to the walls under cover of shields to tear down the wall with picks and sledgehammers.

The largest war machine was "the moving tower", known to the Crusaders *moving tower* as the "belfry." This was a huge wooden structure, sometimes as much as 30 metres high, its frame covered with hides soaked in vinegar to prevent its being set alight. The side facing the enemy was protected with iron plates. To its rear ladders were fixed and at the top were a covered platform and a drawbridge with hooks at the end. The whole was set up on timber rollers or a wheeled base; sometimes the lower part was fitted with a battering ram. The tower, high enough to rise above the wall of a fortress, would be brought into position while the archers stationed on its platform drove the defenders from the sector of the wall to be attacked. When the tower reached the rampart, the drawbridge would be lowered so that troops who had climbed the ladders could fling themselves upon the wall.

In addition to these appliances the besiegers mined beneath the foundations of the walls. The following is an account of such an operation: "Meanwhile the . . . *mine* diggers, gradually burrowing by subterranean passages, reached the very foundations of the walls and filled the chasm they had made with logs, to which they set fire. Then, when the fire had consumed the beams upholding the wall, a great part of it gave way. . ."

The besieged, for their part, had various means of defence. "Artillery" was placed on the walls to hurl missiles at the siege-engines, and artillery duels sometimes took place between two opposing machines. Especially effective was *"Greek fire"* "Greek fire," a mixture of raw naphtha, pitch and sulphur in an earthenware container, which was thrown by a mangonel; the material ignited as it struck, stuck to the siege-engines and consumed them. The besieged would lower sacks of straw or faggots to absorb the blows of the battering rams. There were also special implements which were operated from the top of the wall to parry the ram and to lop off its head. Counter-mines were dug against minings, and when sap met sap a subterranean battle would ensue. Sometimes the defence of a fortress was so stout and stubborn that all endeavours at breaching proved in vain. For lack of alternative the besiegers then settled down for a prolonged investment in the hope that starvation would vanquish the besieged. Cases are known in which the siege of a fortress dragged on for several years.

The fate of the besieged after the successful breaching of their defences by force differed from their fate in case of surrender. In the former circumstances

285

they were utterly at the mercy of the victors, who divided the spoil amongst themselves. The prior right to property of the first man who reached it was acknowledged if he raised his banner or shield over it. The history of the Crusader wars is marked by frequent deeds of cruelty wrought during the capture of towns or fortresses. Sieges often ended with the surrender of the besieged when

capitulation their strength had been exhausted or they had been starved out. In such cases there were negotiations on terms of surrender, ending with the signing of an agreement which both sides swore to implement. Usually the besieged were permitted to leave with all the property they could carry and proceed to the nearest town held by their own people. The moment they laid down their arms they could rely only on the decency and honesty of their foes and vanquishers, and many cases are known of the breaking of the terms of capitulation by the victors, ending in frightful butchery, looting, rape and the seizure of captives.

ARCHITECTURAL DETAILS

The tradition of fortress-building is very ancient in Palestine. When the Crusaders came they found not only an advanced knowledge of fortification and splendid examples of the art, but also local builders and architects able to carry

"a ruined fortress out the work. The Frankish chroniclers emphasize the participation of Greek
is one half-built" and Armenian builders in the building of their fortresses. Moslem prisoners were also employed, mostly as masons and builders but also as architects. The continuity of the local art of building finds expression not only in the general plans and details of the fortifications but also in the methods of stone-dressing, wall-building and the form of roofing. Many of the Crusader castles were built on the ruins of ancient structures; the Franks used ancient remains as much as possible and a current saying was that "a ruined fortress is one half-built." The Crusader chroniclers, in describing the circumstances in which many castles were built, stress the presence of ruins or ancient building stones at the places marked for the erection of their fortresses, such as those of Yavne, Gaza, Beit Govrin, Deir al-Balaḥ and 'Atlit.

But notwithstanding the strong traditional influence found in the Crusader structures, many innovations and improvements are discernible in them which led to a different and enhanced style. The use of ribs, which developed into rib-vaulting, is only one example. The Crusader ramparts were also stronger and

unparalleled more massive than those of their predecessors. The improvements in gate-
perfection defences, in the building of wall-towers and their frequency and projection, in loopholes, machicolations and portcullises, in living quarters and storerooms, brought the art of fortification to a level unparalleled before the Crusader period and not attained even by subsequent generations.

286

THE MOAT

Most fortresses were defended by moats, whose function was to prevent the approach of the moving towers and battering rams and the digging of mines beneath the walls. The moat was rock-cut or excavated in soil according to local conditions. In areas without rock the scarps of the moat were reinforced with stone retaining walls. The counterscarp was vertical while the scarp was sometimes sloped like a glacis, although on occasion only at the foot of the wall-towers. True to Byzantine rules, the wall foundations were below the level of the bottom of the moat. The wall of the scarp of the moat covered the lower part of the wall and joined it at a height of 7 or 8 metres. The dimensions of the moat were not the same everywhere; the depth varying from 6 to 12 metres and the width from 8 to 20. The moat was crossed by a drawbridge which, because of the scarcity of long beams, was built in two parts and rested on large masonry piers erected in the middle of the moat. At some castles the approach-road dropped to the bottom of the moat and then rose to the gate (Belvoir, 'Atlit, Safed). Sometimes (at 'Atlit and Safed) special gates were constructed in the counterscarp of the moat, approached by a defended passage built at right-angles to the line of the moat.

dry moats

dimensions

GATES AND POSTERNS

At the beginning of the 12th century the Crusaders continued to build the gates of their fortresses on the Byzantine model with a straight approach protected by a large wall-tower on the axis of the road; the road turned at the foot of the tower at a sharp angle and continued for some distance alongside it, so that the unprotected righthand side of whoever approached would be towards the wall. Opposite the gate the road again turned sharply to enter the first portal of the outer gate, and then the second portal, placed parallel to it. Under the influence of Persian and Arab methods of fortification, however, the Franks began to abandon the Byzantine pattern and to build their gates on the principle of the "bent entrance." A gate-house was built at right-angles to the old straight gateway and at the north end an outer portal was placed at right-angles to the inner portal. Anyone entering now had first to pass through the outer gate and then make a sharp turn towards the inner gate. Most of the gates built from the mid-12th century and in the 13th were built on the plan of the "bent entrance."

Byzantine straight approach

"bent entrance"

As the gate was one of the vulnerable points, the Frankish builders took care to fortify it to a high degree. In addition to the timber doors faced with wrought iron, there were iron gratings or portcullises, which moved in stone slots. The portals were flanked by arrow slits, and archery positions were built in the interior walls of the gate-house, which also had vertical slots in the ceiling through which arrows could be shot and boiling liquids, such as water, oil and molten

defence of gates

lead, could be poured. Concealed posterns or sallyports were built in the wall-towers, leading to the bottom of the moat, and through them the besieged could conduct sudden sorties against the enemy. These also served as exits and entrances for spies and messengers. The way down to them was by means of concealed stairwells constructed in the thickness of the wall. The door of a postern was usually closed by stones which were removed when necessary. Fine examples have been preserved at Caesarea, 'Atlit and Belvoir.

WALL-TOWERS AND FIRING POSITIONS

projecting towers Projecting towers were erected along the ramparts, their function being to cover the areas of "dead ground" created at the foot of the walls and to facilitate flanking fire along them. The towers were square and hollow in all the Crusader castles in Palestine. The castle of Safed, built by the Templars in the 1240's, is the only one in which the Franks used round hollow towers. Round, solid wall-towers are indeed to be found (Ascalon, Ashdod-Yam, Habonim), but these are apparently to be attributed to the early Arab period. Wall-towers were erected *intervals* about 40–50 metres apart, a distance which ensured effective flanking fire covering the sector of the rampart between them. In particularly vulnerable sectors, such as the vicinity of gates, the interval was smaller. The projection of the towers from the curtain walls varies between 4 and 8 or 9 metres and is generally greater in the later fortifications than in the earlier works.

The towers were 2 to 4 metres higher than the surrounding wall, with a single entrance in the lower storey. There was no access from the top of the wall, so that they could be defended independently and, if a break-in were effected and sectors of the rampart seized, the enemy then had to take each tower separately. The roofs of the towers were used as artillery positions.

two ranges of The walls had two ranges of firing positions, one at the top and the other *firing positions* half-way up. The top was crenellated; the archers fired through the embrasures and hid behind the merlons. The defenders of the battlements moved on a *chemin-de-ronde* or wall-walk built over the vaulted roof of the rooms within the wall or in the thickness of the wall. The firing platforms or machicolations were also placed at the top of the wall; these projected in front of the wall and the archers stationed in them fired through slots pierced in their floors and in the outer sides. The vertical shooting made possible by the floor-slots ensured defence of the foundations of the ramparts. No traces of crenellations have sur-*crenellations and* vived in Palestine because of the destruction of the upper parts of the walls, but *machicolations* old drawings show them. Most of the machicolations have also disappeared, but the stone corbels on which they were built survive in some places, such as those at Acre and the Mill of Kurdani. Special vertical slots were built in the gate-houses.

loopholes Halfway up the wall was a second row of firing positions consisting of loop-holes. The Crusader loophole was a wedge-shaped cell built into the thickness of the wall with a narrow slit at the end for the discharge of arrows, but the plan of cells and slits is not standard and in some, the wedge is an extension of a square opening on the inner side of the wall. The ceilings of some are built as pointed arches of gradually decreasing span, and their floors are level or sloping. The early loophole was a simple space between the outer stones of the wall. Later it was cut in the wall-stones, and in the 13th century its lower end was cut to form a funnel directed to the foot of the wall. Not all loopholes were for combat; some were made for light and ventilation, and in several places they were constructed in such a way that the stones at each side could easily be moved, so that in times of peace they were taken out and the arrow-slit became an oblong window.

GARRISON QUARTERS

The castle was planned as an independent logistic unit which when necessary could dispense with the world outside it. Within its fortified areas were erected all the installations and structures which would enable the garrison to live for a prolonged period without bringing in supplies from outside.

stores The first concern was to store foodstuffs. Large storerooms were erected in every castle, some (as at 'Atlit) of astounding size. All these were built with rounded or pointed barrel-vaulting, with thick walls and few loopholes. In their cool darkness dry food could be preserved for a long time. Beside the storerooms were installations for the processing of the food, such as querns for grinding flour ('Atlit, Montfort, Belvoir), wine presses and olive presses. Bread was baked and food cooked in large kitchens, remains of kitchens and baking-ovens being preserved at Belvoir, Montfort and 'Atlit.

water supply A special effort was made to solve the problem of water supply, which was particularly grave in the climatic conditions of the country. All the castles were built in the vicinity of water courses or permanent springs. Large cisterns for rainwater were to be found near the walls of several. The problem of the supply of water in time of siege was solved in a number of ways. The wall of the castle at 'Atlit was built so as to enclose freshwater springs. A wonderful system of water supply by aqueduct was contrived at Safed, but its details have not been clarified. At Belvoir a Roman system of water supply, which carried water into the castle from a small spring rising not far from the fortress, appears to have been utilized. Cisterns for rainwater were cut in all the fortresses, and systems for draining the surfaces of the walls, roofs and courts by means of earthenware and stone channels were constructed. Remains of these systems have survived at Montfort and Belvoir. The capacity of the cisterns at Belvoir was 600 cubic metres, the water being collected from a roof area of 10,000 square metres. In Montreal a secret tunnel with 365 steps led to two reservoirs. If the rainwater was insufficient to fill the cisterns, they were filled with water brought in on the backs of draught animals. The water was drunk by man and beast and even sufficed for the bathhouses, remains of which exist at Belvoir and 'Atlit. Besides foodstuffs the Crusaders stored in their castles building materials, and materials such as iron, wood, fuel and hides, for the making of weapons. Workshops were to be found within the castle area for making and repairing arms.

barracks

The garrison lived in rooms usually built in the walls or in the inner bailey of the fortress. These rooms were small and simple, like those of a monastery, only the castellan's quarters being comparatively sumptuous and roomy. Every large castle had a splendid spacious hall which was used for ceremonies, banquets and councils of war; remains of ceremonial halls at 'Atlit and Montfort are still impressive even in their utter ruin.

chapels

The large castles also had chapels of various forms and sizes. Most consist of a single nave (as at Montfort, Beit Govrin, and perhaps Belvoir). Only at 'Atlit is the church built to a polygonal plan with three apses. The churches were embellished with marble, with wall-paintings and also with stained glass (Montfort).

As already stated elsewhere, the castle was not the abode of feudal lords, but was a military and administrative base. For this reason the mode of life prevailing in the strongholds of Europe did not develop in Palestine. The garrisons occupying the castles belonged chiefly to the Military Orders, which maintained an austerely simple way of life. The rules of the various orders determined the times for guard, sleep, meals, assembly, inspection of storerooms and stables—and created a permanent and inflexible framework for the daily life of the garrison.

FRONTIER FORTRESSES

Crusader frontier defence was assisted by natural factors; the borders of the Kingdom of Jerusalem were the Mediterranean on the west, the desert on the south and south-east, and the Jordan Valley on the north-east. The Crusaders made good use of the defensive advantages furnished by nature, but added man-made courses to the natural barriers along their lengthy frontiers, building and manning fortresses at points where there was risk of penetration. Thus an impressive chain of castles was constructed on the frontier of the kingdom against Moslem military concentrations. But this was not brought about by a concerted effort or by a single individual; rather it was improved, and strengthened as years went by. *natural borders*

The fortified frontier was not a Crusader invention; its plan and execution drew on the rich experience of the Roman and Byzantine Empires. Ever since the 2nd century B.C., the Roman defensive system had been based on chains of forts, known as the *"limes,"* built at regular intervals at strategic points along the frontiers. An example of one such fortified frontier, the *"Limes Palaestina,"* was built in the 4th century along the line connecting Gaza, Beersheba and the Dead Sea. These forts were not designed to stop heavy enemy attacks, but to repel raids and small-scale penetrations. During large-scale offensives the forts acted as observation and signal posts, delaying the enemy for a few days until the populations in the rear had fortified themselves in the principal fortresses and the main force had mobilized to meet the invader. *"limes"*

Although certain differences existed between the structures of the Roman-Byzantine *limes* and the fortified Crusader frontier, the Crusaders used the same strategic and tactical rules as their predecessors. The strength of the Crusader frontier fortresses, and the garrisons stationed in them, was adequate to hold and repel small bands of Moslem raiders, but when large Moslem forces mobilized to invade the country the frontier strongholds could not prevent their penetration. In such cases the second line in the Crusader defensive system, the field force, was at once put into action. When the garrisons of the border castles discerned a movement of large hostile forces, they despatched a report to the neighbouring fortresses, and to the rear, by means which were at their disposal— beacons or carrier pigeons—and then closed the gates of their fortresses. Knowing that they could not halt the enemy, they limited themselves to surprise sorties against groups that had become detached from the main force, or raided the hostile supply-columns. *functions of fortresses*

The main strength of the Crusader field army lay in its armoured cavalry. With their stout swift horses, their long lances, the weight of their weapons, shields and armour, the Crusader knights, physically fit and well-trained, created an offensive arm against which the Moslems were helpless. Their tactical superi- *field army* ority was decisive only when the full weight of their attack was delivered upon a compact enemy formation; otherwise the stroke was wasted on the empty air, and very difficult to repeat. If the enemy was able to elude the assault before it came to close quarters the armoured cavalry lost its tactical advantage and its deficiencies were revealed—the chief of these being poor manoeuvrability.

The Moslems pitted against the Crusader power of assault their main advantage, namely, their high degree of mobility. The Moslem cavalry was lightly

armed, composed of small independent units and trained to carry out swift and unexpected movements. The Moslem cavalryman was trained to shoot accurately while moving rapidly, his main weapon being the bow. High mobility and skilled archery enabled the Moslems to elude the weight of the Crusader force, to outflank it, to check it with a rain of arrows beyond range of personal combat and to harass its flanks.

The wars of the Franks and the Saracens in the east, therefore, involved the trial of power of assault against mobility, and the outcome of the battle was decided by the ability of the combatants to develop their tactical advantages. When the Crusaders were successful in imposing close hand-to-hand combat upon the Moslems, the victory was theirs; when the Moslems were able to evade close combat, outflank the Crusaders and surround them, they were the victors.

An enemy invasion did not always result in a head-on encounter. One of the

basic advantages of the Crusader defensive, as distinct from their offensive strategy, was that, as far as possible, it avoided a decisive battle with the invading enemy. This principle was based on acquaintance with the character and organization of the Moslem army, which comprised mostly independent units mobilized, by order of the sultan, by local emirs throughout the kingdom. Many of the troops were peasants and holders of estates who could be away from home only for a brief period, and who therefore wanted a swift decision which would bring spoils and glory and, above all, release them to go home. Moreover, the supplies of the Moslem army came chiefly from the produce of the land which they invaded; if they tarried long, these sources would be exhausted and difficult logistic problems would arise. The Crusaders' avoidance of a decisive battle therefore compelled the invading general to evacuate the country after a brief period. In many cases the Crusaders followed the course of closely dogging the enemy's movements while refraining from accepting the Moslem challenge. At such times the Crusader general would be under the double pressure of enemy provocation and the ambitions of his own knights, who were eager for battle, spoil and glory. If the general successfully withstood the pressure, the invading enemy general would be forced to evacuate the country. This strategy was followed by the Crusaders on several occasions with great success, and its neglect before the battle of Hattin led to irretrievable defeat. When circumstances rendered the employment of this strategy impossible, the decision turned on an encounter in the open field. Even if the defending army were defeated in the encounter, the invader's victory was not yet complete unless he could seize the country's fortresses.

To serve their purpose in the kingdom's defensive system, the fortresses had to fulfil two fundamental conditions: a) each must be built at a strategic point that was also tactically strong; b) there must be possibility of rapid and effective communication between them. It has been suggested that the Franks neglected to defend certain sectors of the frontiers, but if we scrutinize the chain of border fortresses, we shall see with what perception they built them at every weak spot and facing every point of danger. The second condition was also fulfilled; we find that there existed a system of visual communication whereby beacon-signals could be exchanged between all the border fortresses themselves, and also between them and the rear.

The chief danger of enemy penetration was across the eastern frontier, but the steep mountain scarps which enclose the Valley of the Lebanon, the Jordan Rift Valley and the 'Arava constitute difficult obstacles to traverse from east to west. Only the lateral valleys which crossed the central rift from side to side offered the possibility of easy penetration. These were the weak points selected by the Crusaders for the siting of their castles. The possibility of east-west penetration was not uniform along the whole frontier, and the strength and density of the fortifications varied accordingly. Penetration was almost impossible in the frontier sector traversing the eastern slopes of the Mountains of Lebanon; the steepness of the mountains and their great height prevented actual military movements and hence this sector was not fortified at all. The enemy, in fact, never tried this route. *chief danger— eastern frontier*

Lebanon

Southward, good roads led from Damascus, the natural centre for assembling a Moslem army, through Galilee to the ports, and they were traversed not only by traders and wayfarers but also by the Moslem armies which set out to destroy the Kingdom of Jerusalem. Most of the important campaigns were conducted along these routes over Galilee, and the battles which decided the fate of the Kingdom took place here. It is not surprising, therefore, that this frontier was fortified to the highest degree by the Crusaders. *Galilee*

Seven castles existed along the frontier-line stretching from the Valley of 'Ayun to the Plain of Beit Shean, a distance of 100 kilometres as the crow flies. These were: Qal'at Shaqif (Beaufort), Hunin, Metsad 'Ateret, Safed, Ḥabis Jaldak (on the south bank of the Yarmouk), Belvoir and Beit Shean. To this list must be added the fortified towns of Banias and Tiberias. These castles commanded the central roads and weak points along the border.

Qal'at Shaqif defended the highways leading from Damascus to Sidon and guarded the most convenient crossing of the River Litani, today the Nabatiya-Sidon road. Banias and Hunin were situated on the important route from Damascus through Banias and Tibnin to Tyre. The first protected the descent to the Ḥula Valley from the east; the second, the ascent to the Mountains of Naphtali on the west. Metsad 'Ateret guarded Jacob's Ford and the branch-road from Damascus to Tiberias. The Castle of Safed defended the area between Jacob's Ford and the Sea of Galilee, acting as central lookout over the Mountains of Galilee.

293

The citadel of Tiberias guarded the "Wooden Bridge" south of the Sea of Galilee. The Castle of Ḥabis guarded the roads along the canyon of the Yarmouk and the Crusader domains in the Golan. Belvoir covered the bridge of Naharayim (Jisr al-Majam'a) and the way to Beit Shean, also serving as a lookout post over the Mountains of Gilead. The castle of Beit Shean defended the road to the Plain of Jezreel.

intervisibility The strength of the north-eastern frontier fortresses consisted not only in their siting, but also in their facilities for intercommunication. (On means of communications see p. 269.) The Crusaders could transmit information in a few minutes from the southernmost fortress at Beit Shean to the northernmost on the frontier sector at Qal'at Shaqif, a distance of over 90 kilometres, and in the same way could relay information to the interior of the country. The visual system allowed warning to be given and the far rear to be alerted. Two examples of communication possibilities may suffice. An announcement of the approach of the enemy signalled from the castle of Beit Shean could be transmitted to Qal'at Shaqif by Belvoir, Safed, Marun a-Ras (a village which was the centre of a fief known as *Maron*) and Tibnin. News from Banias, to al-Fula, a distance of approximately 80 kilometres as the crow flies, could be transmitted by Qal'at Shaqif, Tibnin, Maron, Safed and Mt. Tabor.

Pilgrims' Road South of the Plain of Beit Shean Crusader fortifications were less densely distributed. The roads extending from the mountains of Gilead to the Jordan Valley and towards the mountains of Samaria were scarcely used for military purposes in this period and the danger of enemy invasion in this sector was not considered great. South of 'Amman a great chain of fortresses was established. This region, indeed, did not harbour danger of hostile penetration from east to west as in Galilee, but here the Crusaders strove to control the main road from Damascus to Cairo, known as the Pilgrims' Road (Darb al-Ḥaj), which passed along the plateau of Transjordan, Moab, Edom, Eilat and the Sinai Peninsula. Command of this road cut off from each other the main centres of Moslem power, Damascus and Cairo, so impeding a joint onslaught against the Kingdom of Jerusalem. All the fortresses of Transjordan were built along the Pilgrims' Road: they comprised Karak, Tafila, Petra, Shaubak and Eilat (Jazirat Fara'un).

Ascalon So long as the danger of Egyptian invasion threatened through Ascalon, three fortresses protected the frontier sector of the Judaean plain: Beit Govrin, Tel Tsafit and Yavne. When Ascalon was captured in 1153 these castles lost much of their strategic importance.

BELVOIR

"Set amidst the stars like an eagle's nest and abode of the Moon," wrote the historian Abu Shama, of the fortress that looks out from a height of 500 metres over the winding Jordan, the Sea of Galilee and the Mountains of Gilead and Golan beyond.

The prospect from its walls is one of the widest and loveliest in the country; no wonder, then, that its Crusader builders chose to call it "Belvoir," or "Fair View." Because of its elevated situation, the Moslems named it "Star Castle"— Ḥisn Kaukab or Kaukab al-Hawa, "the Star of the Winds."

position

The fortress was of great strategic importance and can be defined as one of the key strongholds in the Crusader system of frontier fortresses. It defended two of the most important Jordan fords, the northerly being at Naharayim (Jisr al-Majam'a), known to the Crusaders as the *Pont de Judair,* on the main road from Damascus through Irbid to Beit Shean, and the southerly Bridge of Sheikh Ḥussein on the highway joining 'Ajlun and Beit Shean. Belvoir also commanded convenient local routes going up from the Jordan Valley westwards.

Thanks to its lofty position, it was possible for Belvoir to communicate by fire signal with a number of other castles, such as Safed, Mt. Tabor and Beit Shean.

Belvoir's history began long before the Crusader period. In the course of archaeological excavations, traces of a Jewish settlement were found nearby, with ruins of houses and an important public building. In the castle itself stones adorned with Jewish motifs such as the seven-branched candelabrum, the incense shovel, the shofar and other decorative designs pertaining to synagogues, were found in secondary use.

history

Belvoir was within the Crusader principality of Galilee, whose capital was Tiberias. When the Crusaders built the castle is unknown, but it is thought that it was erected between the years 1138 and 1140, either by King Fulk or with his aid; this supposition is based on the fact that the same period saw accelerated and intensive fortification work along the frontiers of the kingdom. The first structure was small and modest, and was owned by a French noble named Ivo Velos. He sold it to the Order of Hospitallers in 1168 for 1,400 gold bezants.[76]

The Hospitallers rebuilt the castle completely, so that nothing remained from the former structure. They began to gather neighbouring estates into their possession, adding to the Belvoir lands, by acquisitions or grants, an area of 200 square kilometres containing dozens of villages. In 1182 an indecisive battle was fought between Saladin and the Crusader host on the Plateau of Issachar west of Belvoir, and in 1183 the Moslems captured and burned the nearby castle of Forbelet.

After the battle of Hattin (1187), the Moslem armies laid siege to the fortress of Belvoir, then garrisoned, it would seem, by a full force. The knights, not content with passive defence, made sorties from the castle upon the Moslem units, and defeated one of them on the night of the 31st of December, 1187. They were able subsequently to seize two convoys loaded with supplies and equipment taken by the Moslems from the storerooms of the captured castle of La Fève (al-Fula), and this booty enabled them to replenish the castle's supplies, much reduced in the course of a six months' siege.

long siege

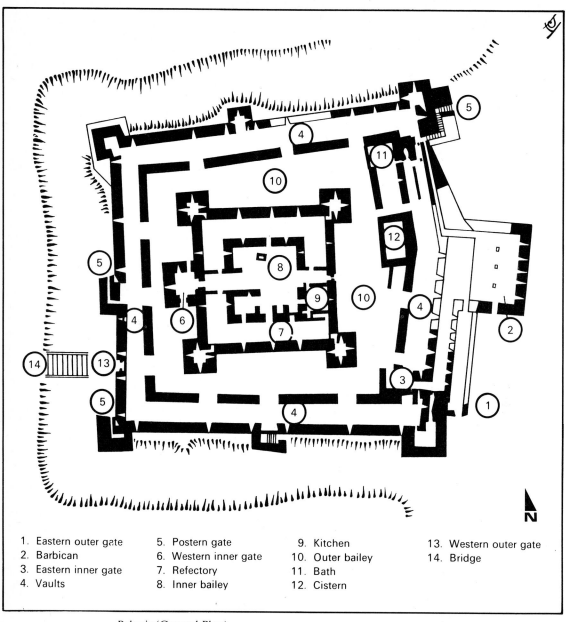

Belvoir (General Plan)

1. Eastern outer gate
2. Barbican
3. Eastern inner gate
4. Vaults
5. Postern gate
6. Western inner gate
7. Refectory
8. Inner bailey
9. Kitchen
10. Outer bailey
11. Bath
12. Cistern
13. Western outer gate
14. Bridge

Saladin takes command

At the beginning of March, 1188 Saladin, seeing that the siege was dragging on indecisively, determined to take over command. According to a Moslem source, he wanted an early capture of the valiantly defended castle "in order to discourage the garrison of Tyre." But he too failed to vanquish Belvoir, and in May abandoned the attempt. He returned at the end of 1188, after taking Safed, the only other castle in Galilee that remained in Crusader hands. The winter of that year had been very severe, accompanied by snow, rain and deep mud, and this made the siege operations difficult. The besieged, whose position commanded the area and camp of the Moslem besiegers, persisted in their stubborn resistance, inflicting numerous losses. The Moslem sappers nevertheless succeeded in undermining the barbican on the east side of the castle and effected a breach in the castle wall. Then they proceeded to the main walls. When the besieged saw that hope had gone, they asked Saladin for terms, and he, admiring their courage, allowed the Hospitallers to leave the fortress with all their belongings and to proceed to Tyre. The castle was occupied on the 5th of January, 1189, eighteen months after the siege had begun, the Moslems leaving a garrison to hold it. The sultan visited Belvoir in 1189 and ordered its walls to be repaired. The Moslem garrison occupied the castle until 1219, when it was dismantled, the work of destruction being completed in 1228. Belvoir was restored to the Franks by the peace treaty signed between Richard of Cornwall and the ruler of Egypt in 1241, and the Hospitallers returned to their estates, which later also included the area between Nazareth and the Sea of Galilee. We have no information concerning the castle's last years or the date of its capture by the Mamluks, but it may be supposed that it was evacuated or taken in 1263, when Baybars wiped out the Hospitaller domains in Lower Galilee.

Belvoir belongs to the *castrum* type of fortress, being the most complete of

sapping

safe-conduct

Belvoir, aerial view

297

its type in the country. Its most interesting feature consists in the fact that it is built as a *"castrum* within a *castrum",* meaning that within the quadrilateral of the outer enceinte, with its corner towers, is an identical square structure with four towers at the angles. We do indeed find a square outer bailey plan with central tower or keep in the middle in other *castrum* fortresses in the Orient, but the central tower is generally of the "Norman keep" type, with two or three storeys. Only at Belvoir do we find a central tower whose plan repeats almost perfectly that of the external fortifications.

moat A moat 10 metres deep and 20 metres wide, cut in the basalt rock, surrounds the fortress on the north, west and south sides. There is no moat on the east side, since the natural slope of the ground here afforded sufficient protection. Instead a barbican was built, the base of which was glacis-shaped, joining the outer curtain at the north-east and south-east corners, thus creating a pentagonal plan. The outer wall had four corner towers and three intermediate towers. The walls

walls are 130 metres long from east to west, 100 metres from north to south, 480 metres in circumference, and 3 metres thick, the area of the fortress being 14

Belvoir, south-west tower

dunams. Around the inside of the outer wall is a barrel vault 6 to 7 metres wide. The area so roofed was divided into halls, and the roof was used as a *chemin-de-ronde* on which the defenders could move. The wall had two lines of firing positions, one on the crenellated top, the other through arrow slits within it.

The towers of the outer wall, like the wall itself, are built of basalt. They are 7 metres high, and erected on a battered plinth resembling a glacis. Their projection from the line of the wall, which is as much as 5 metres, permitted enfilading fire along the wall and the moat. Four of the towers contain hidden posterns leading by steps to the bottom of the moat.

The main approach was on the south, the road descending to the moat at the south-east end and reaching the gate, which was built of white limestone, its jambs surviving *in situ*. A broad road ascends from the gate to an area between the barbican and the castle's main rampart, where it is commanded by a short wall with seven loopholes, of which three remain, then arrives at the barbican tower and turns sharply back upon itself along the main wall to a point situated near the south-east tower at a higher level than that of the lower gate. Here it turns west and enters the second gateway. The lintel of this gateway is built of basalt and its arch is of limestone. It has a portcullis-groove, and two oblique loopholes pierce the jambs, one on each side; the sockets of the gate-hinges and grooves for the bolts are still visible. Within the gate is a barrel-vaulted passage 4 metres in width, flanked by guardrooms. Inside the passage, a northward turn gives access to the castle's outer bailey.

approach and gates

Another gate is situated in the west wall, between the south-western corner tower and the middle tower. The moat was crossed by a drawbridge. This gate was blocked during the siege of 1188. The inner castle is square, each side being 40 metres long with square corner towers. Its height was half a storey higher than the outer ramparts. The main gate to it is on the west side, built in a massive gate-tower. The plan of the gate is of the "bent entrance" type, the outer portal being at right-angles to the inner portal. Long barrel-vaulted halls are built around the inner bailey in two storeys, the southern hall on the first floor is the refectory. Next to it the castle kitchen was found, which contains three large ovens. The chapel of the castle was situated on the second floor of the gate-tower. It was 18 metres long and 7 metres wide. Among the ruins of the chapel statues and reliefs were found, as well as sections of rib vaults. Near the north-eastern corner of the outer bailey, a bathhouse, operated on the "turkish bath" system, was discovered. The water supply, which came from a small spring situated to the south of the castle, was brought inside the walls by an aqueduct. In addition, rainwater was collected from the roofs and walls into two plastered cisterns by a complicated system of earthenware drains and channels.

inner castle

In the course of excavations it was found that the whole castle was built at the same time. The existing structure dates from the Hospitallers' period of occupation, and the original modest castle that was sold to them in 1168 must have been completely dismantled and replaced by the larger structure. After the castle was captured by the Moslems, Saladin ordered its repair, but no traces of the re-

Belvoir, inner bailey

pairs were found. Also there is no sign of a renewed Frankish occupation of Belvoir in the mid-13th century.

The castle has been excavated and restored, and is today the best preserved Crusader castle in Palestine.

HUNIN - CHASTEL NEUF (NEW CASTLE)

position

The castle of Hunin is situated on the vulnerable and dangerous frontier of the Crusader kingdom facing Damascus. Described by an Arab geographer as a "fort which stands on a single rock", it lies on the edge of the steep scarp of the Mountains of Naphtali above the Ḥulah Valley, facing Mount Hermon. It commands the easiest ascent to the northern Mountains of Naphtali along which ran the main road from Damascus, through Banias to Tyre. This highway was one of the chief trade routes of the Middle Ages and control of it gave considerable strategic and economic advantages. Its commercial and military importance led to a constant struggle between the Moslems and the Franks for the control of the main passes—where it climbed the spurs of Mount Hermon east of the Ḥulah Valley and where it ascended the Mountains of Naphtali west of the valley. Castles were established at both these points, on the east at Banias, on the west at Hunin.

300

Belvoir, western inner gate

The Crusaders first penetrated the region in the years 1105–1107, when the Prince of Galilee, Hugh of St. Omer, gained control of it. It was he, apparently, who built the castle of Hunin and so commanded the western pass on the Tyre–Damascus highway. The Prince of Galilee also, in order to maintain control over the continuation of this route westward, erected the castle of Toron (Tibnin) in the northern part of Upper Galilee. In about 1115, for reasons and in circumstances unknown to us, Tibnin was converted into an independent seigneurie which included the whole of northern Upper Galilee with the castle of Hunin. The lord of this seigneurie was a knight named Humphrey (Onfroi). This family *Banias and Hunin* was to become one of the most influential in the kingdom and its head was for many years constable of Jerusalem. The family maintained ties of friendship with the Moslems and its members were well-known as experts in the Arab language and letters. The Crusaders, however, were not content to keep the west side of the Damascus highway firmly in their grip; they sought also to seize control of its eastern defile at the city of Banias. In 1129 they succeeded, but Crusader Banias was a grave threat to Damascus and the Moslems braced themselves for a supreme effort to drive the Crusaders from it. They recaptured Banias in 1132, but the Crusaders persisted and in 1139 retook it. This time it remained in their hands for twenty-five years. But hostilities in the region continued and Humphrey, unable to bear singlehanded the burden of defending the frontier of the kingdom, was forced in 1157 to give half of Hunin and Banias to the Order of the Hospitallers. But the Hospitallers never took possession of the castles (see p. 150) and Humphrey was left to defend alone his domain and the kingdom's frontier. Banias was captured in 1164, this time for good, and subsequently Hunin as well (1167). The Frankish garrison, unable to defend the fortress, set it on fire and retired. The Moslem Sultan Nur a-Din, considering Hunin to be unsuitable as a base since it was so near to the Frankish centres, evacuated the castle and demolished it completely. It was rebuilt at the end of 1178 by Humphrey II, affectionately known as "the old Knight". In the spring of 1179, during a Frankish assault near Banias, he was mortally wounded while protecting with his own person his sovereign, who was also taking part in the expedition.

At the end of May, 1179 Saladin invested Hunin, but raised the siege in the face of the garrison's valiant defence. The family of Toron ceded the castle to King Baldwin IV in 1180. In 1186 Guy de Lusignan, King of Jerusalem, gave the castle and domain of Hunin to Joscelin de Courtenay, who had amassed considerable estates in western Galilee. According to the terms of the cession Joscelin undertook to wed his eldest daughter to the king's brother and to furnish as her dowry the seigneurie of Toron and Hunin. But, a year after the transfer, the battle of Hattin was fought and lost.

After the disaster of Hattin (1187), Hunin was one of the three last Crusader castles remaining in Galilee, together with Qal'at Shaqif and Belvoir. Saladin entrusted his brother al-'Adil with its capture. The garrison held out for five months and surrendered in December 1187. The castle was destroyed by al-

Hunin, castle, north and west sides

Mu'azzam, ruler of Damascus, in 1222 as part of the work of destruction carried out among the castles of Galilee in order to prevent their falling into the hands of the Franks. In 1240 Hunin was returned to the Crusaders by the terms of the peace treaty signed that year, and was included in the Seigneurie of Toron-Tyre. The stronghold was taken by the Mamluks in 1266. The Sultan Baybars rebuilt it a year later, when he also restored the castle of Safed.

The fortress is square, measuring 40 by 40 metres, and without corner towers. *description* A broad rock-cut moat surrounds the walls. The Crusader remains are meagre and stones with 12th century Crusader tooling, with drafted margins, are to be discerned only in the western wall and at the south-east corner. Most of the structures are of the Mamluk period, when the great entrance gate and the vaulted chambers within the fortress were built. The Mamluks also added an elongated fortification south of the Crusader structure and erected a mosque there. This southern portion was completely destroyed in 1837, although remnants of it could still be seen by travellers as late as the middle of the 19th century.

METSAD 'ATERET-CHASTELET

Traces of the castle of Chastelet are visible on a hill on the west bank of the Jordan, about a kilometre south of the Bridge of the Daughters of Jacob. The fortress, which was of the *castrum* type, 140 metres long and 65 metres wide with four square towers at its corners, was defended by a moat and, on the east, by the winding Jordan River. The foundations of an inner structure have been found within the square walled enclosure, apparently the castle keep. The outer walls were built of small basalt blocks partly faced with limestone slabs. Descriptions of the fortress date from the 19th century, when the ruin was still standing. Since that time it has been completely razed to the ground, and its plan is traceable only by aerial photographs.

The castle, whose name meant "the little castle", was erected to defend the ford, which was on the main road from Damascus to Tiberias. According to Christian tradition Jacob crossed the Jordan here on his way to meet his brother Esau (Gen. 32:10), and the Crusaders called the spot "Vadum Jacob," Jacob's Ford. The Arabic name is Maḥdat al-Aḥzan (the Ford of Sorrow) for the Moslem tradition is that it was here that Jacob received the news of the selling of Joseph.

The Crusaders fortified this important crossing in 1178 under growing Moslem pressure. Until then the defence of the frontier in this region had been based on Safed, but the sharpening of the Christian-Moslem struggle induced the Knights Templar, who were the lords of the castle of Safed and responsible for guarding Jacob's Ford, to appeal to the king to build a fortress near the crossing. King Baldwin IV at first refused to comply, since by his agreement with Saladin he had undertaken not to fortify the ford. But at length he responded to the Templars' petition and in October, 1178, arrived there with his entire royal host. The building was carried out under the supervision of the king, who remained on the spot for a prolonged period.

William of Tyre described the castle thus: "The place is ten miles from Banias. Foundations were dug to an appropriate depth on a low hill. In six months a square fort was erected, built of strong stones, with wonderfully high and thick walls." A Moslem chronicler gave further details: "The thickness of the walls exceeded ten cubits, the number of the stones twenty thousand, and each was mortared strongly to the next. The wall was built of dressed stones each seven cubits long."

The fortification of Jacob's Ford caused the Moslems keen concern, since the blocking of the crossing hampered their raids into the Frankish areas, while it made Frankish raids into Syrian territory easier. During the period of building Saladin offered King Baldwin a sum of sixty thousand gold dinars on condition that he cease the work of fortification, but the king refused the offer. After a further offer to pay a hundred thousand dinars for the cessation of the work was rejected, Saladin swore to destroy the castle with his own hands. The castle was completed in April, 1179 and Chastelet was handed over to the Templars, who stationed a strong garrison there. Moslem sources state that there were eighty knights and their squires, fifteen companies of footmen, each fifty strong, as well as craftsmen and servants.

In August, 1179, Saladin marched upon Chastelet with a large force. The Moslems dug a mine beneath the foundations of the castle keep, and when they set a light to the shorings, the tower collapsed. The castellan of the Templars, seeing that there was no further hope, threw himself into the fire. As the Moslem chronicler related: "When the flames reached his side he flung himself into the fiery abyss, fearless of the burning heat, and from this fire he immediately entered another [of hell]." The Moslems stormed the fortress and forced their way into it on the 30th of August, 1179. According to Moslem sources, seven hundred Franks were taken prisoner and some thousand Moslem captives found there were liberated.

The Moslems destroyed Chastelet completely and stopped up its water cisterns. One of their sources says that they filled them with the corpses of a thousand Christians. Baldwin IV, hearing of the enemy's invasion, gathered his entire army and hastened to the aid of the castle's defenders, but while he was still at Tiberias, news came that the fortress had been taken. Chastelet, once destroyed, was never rebuilt.

FORTRESSES OF THE JUDEAN DESERT

TEQOÁ, CARMEL (KH. KURMUL) AND SAMOE (SAMU')

The eastern part of the mountains of Judea, situated east of the main watershed, is a good gauge of the degree of prosperity of the country as a whole in various epochs. Here is a fluctuating boundary line between the cultivated land and the desert, between the permanent agricultural settlements and the realm of the tent-dwellers. The region, called in Hebrew "desert" *(midbar)* (as distinct from "wilderness" *yeshimon*), in Arabic *bariya,* is suitable for permanent settlement based on agriculture, in terms of quality of soil and quantity of rainfall. The existence of such a settlement and its density depend, however, on the security situation prevailing in the populated centres along the line of the watershed and on the ability of the government to prevent incursions by the desert-dwellers.

The eastern part of Mount Hebron has known flourishing periods when many dense settlements thrived there; these are identical with the periods of prosperity in the country as a whole, chief of which was the Roman-Byzantine epoch. When this came to an end with the Arab conquest, a considerable, though very gradual, regression took place in the settlement of the region, the areas nearest to the desert being the first to be evacuated and destroyed. *flourishing periods*

In the Crusader period numerous centres of permanent settlement still existed in the frontier zone. Historical sources describe Teqoá as a town and Carmel as a village. The documents mention numerous permanent villages in regions which, to all intents and purposes, were desert at the beginning of the 20th century. Signs of Bedouin penetration are nevertheless discernible, and the documents record that feudal lords of the area were accepting Bedouin tribes under their suzerainty. Thus the ultimate victory of the desert over the cultivated land in this region should most likely be dated after the time of the Crusaders, to the Mamluk era. This is of great significance in discussing the density of settlement and the relative prosperity of the Holy Land in the period with which we are concerned (see p. 213).

The settlement of the Hebron mountain border was based on three factors: non-irrigated agriculture, pasture, and the trade routes that crossed it. We possess little information on the economy of the Crusader settlements in the area, although it may be assumed that it was largely based on agriculture and pasture. A Moslem historian who lived early in the 13th century reported that the honey of Teqoá was famous.

settlement based on agriculture and trade

The villages benefited from the trade routes crossing the area to reach the Dead Sea and Transjordan; as throughout the territory of the Crusader kingdom, the excellent Roman highways were still in use. There were two main roads, one through Herodium, Teqoá and 'Ein Gedi to a-Safi (Tsoár), and one through Hebron and Carmel to a-Safi. Many boats plied between the western and eastern shores of the Dead Sea and there was a lively traffic in cargo; Lord Maurice of Montreal granted the Hospitallers in 1152 free passage in the Dead Sea ships without payment of transit dues. The inhabitants of Teqoá were engaged in extracting bitumen and salt from the Dead Sea, and the Church of the Holy Sepulchre, which received the town of Teqoá in 1138, was granted the right to continue the enterprise in return for the surrender of Bethany.

strategic importance

The region's strategic importance as a crossroads and defensive belt protecting the centres of settlement was well known to the Crusaders. They themselves used the local roads during their campaigns in Transjordan. In 1100 Baldwin I crossed by the Carmel–a-Safi road on his first campaign to Edom. Fifteen years later he traversed the same route on his way to capture Shaubak and Eilat.

An incident in 1139 in the neighbourhood of Teqoá may serve as an illustration of the perils that beset the settlements of the desert border. That year a large Frankish force set out to campaign in Gilead. A body of Bedouins seized the opportunity provided by their absence, raided Teqoá and sacked it. Its inhabitants fled to the nearby cave of Hareytun, identified by the Crusaders with the Cave of Adullam. A Frankish force which set out from Jerusalem to expel the Bedouins was defeated by them in a battle fought between Teqoá and Hebron.

The Crusaders fortified key points to give protection to the territory and the densely settled area to its rear, and also in order to control the commercial traffic that passed through it. The points selected for fortification were Teqoá, Carmel (Kh. Kurmul) and Samu'. At Teqoá a square tower was constructed; its remains are on the ancient tel, north of the Byzantine ruins.

Teqoá

A fort was erected on the ruins of the large Byzantine church of Carmel in the centre of the ancient settlement. This was a two-storeyed tower, 20 by 15 metres by 10 metres high. Its lower storey was barrel-vaulted and its upper groin-vaulted; the east wall was pierced by three large windows with pointed arches. The tower stood on a battered plinth and was surrounded by a rectangular court

Carmel

Kh. Kurmul, castle,
view from west

60 metres from east to west and 25 metres from north to south. The tower entrance was in its north side. Part of the east wall of the second storey of the structure survives to its full height, with one complete window and parts of two
others. The north section of the vault of the first floor also remains, as well as
the north wall of this storey, which has a loophole. On the north side the battered plinth is visible, but only the foundations remain on the west and south
sides. The eastern wall with its windows, part of the roof and steps going up in
the north wall, could still be seen a generation ago. The fort is built of smooth-
dressed masonry of medium size. Most of the ashlar blocks facing the walls of
the upper storeys have been removed, leaving only the rubble fill.

Carmel was the Frankish military base during one of the invasions of Saladin
into Transjordan. Here King Amalric concentrated his host, calculating that *Frankish military*
from this position he could observe the movements of the enemy's force without *base*
being obliged to leave the populated centres unprotected and so run the danger
that Saladin might "enter from another direction and wreak havoc in the Kingdom."[77] An additional reason was the fact that Carmel possessed abundant water.
"For there was an ancient pool of great extent, which would furnish ample water
for the entire army." This pool still exists at Carmel at the foot of the castle,
north-east of it, fed by two springs which rise from the rocks (see page 266).

The third stronghold of the region was at the village of Samu' (Eshtamoá).
Here, too, as at Carmel, the Crusader tower was built in the area of the Byzantine ruins, this time near the remains of the ancient synagogue.

We do not know when and in what circumstances the fortresses of the Hebron
mountain frontier were captured, but it may be supposed that they were evacuated without fighting after the defeat of Hattin or the fall of Jerusalem. The
fortress of Carmel was used in the Mamluk period too as a posting station on
the royal mail route through Hebron, Carmel, a-Safi to Karak.

Ma'ale Adumim castle and the Red Ascent

ROADS AND THEIR PROTECTION

As in other countries which once formed part of the Roman Empire, the Holy Land was covered by a close-knit system of paved highways. These included main roads linking the provinces, secondary roads and side roads linking towns and military camps. Road-stations existed along the main roads, and distances were indicated by milestones. Throughout the Roman-Byzantine period new roads were built and the existing ones repaired. With the Arab conquest road maintenance was neglected, although the authorities continued to keep the road-stations in good condition and to maintain an organized mail service. *Roman roads*

The Franks continued to use the Roman road system, as they had in other lands. The condition of the roads varied: the metalling of some was preserved, but there were others of which only the track survived. John Phocas tells us that the road from Samaria to Jerusalem was "all paved with stones."[78] On the Jerusalem–Jericho highway, on the other hand, "there was no stone pavement, but nevertheless the outline of it can be faintly traced."[79] *physical conditions*

As in Europe, the Franks did not introduce improvements in the road system of the Holy Land, nor did the central government concern itself with its upkeep and repair. Apparently the little corvée (forced labour) owed by the peasants to their lords also included road repairs. Seigneurial taxes were probably also levied for the repairing of bridges. In striking contrast to the Mamluk period, the Franks built no bridges: at least no bridge erected by them survives, except for a small one on the road to Montfort.

The fine bridges constructed by Baybars along the royal mail route were built with materials taken from Crusader churches and are in a perfect state of preservation (the Jindas bridge near Lydda and the bridge at Yavne). Historical sources do indeed record several bridges in the Crusader period, such as that over the Litani River, the "Wooden Bridge" south of the Sea of Galilee, *Pont de Judair* at the foot of Belvoir, and the "Triple Bridge" on the Yarqon River, but all were built before the coming of the Crusaders. *bridges*

Historical information, and above all the *itineraria,* enable us to determine the principal roads, which correspond in every case to the Roman highways. The most important road was the "Way of the Sea" mentioned in charters as *"Via Maritima",* which ran from Antioch to Egypt. Following the coast as far as Acre, it avoided the dunes of the Bay of Acre, reached Haifa and continued along the coast to 'Atlit, where it crossed the ridge of *Kurkar* (sandstone) hills. Thence it ran east of the hills to Caesarea, and in a straight line to Jaffa. South of Jaffa it followed the edge of the dunes to Yavne and continued southward to Gaza, Rafaḥ and al-'Arish. Many campaigns were conducted along this route. The most detailed account of it is to be found in the writings of the chronicles of the First and Third Crusades. *principal roads: "Via Maritima"*

309

Another international highway was the route from Damascus to Egypt, which crossed the Plateau of Ḥauran and Gilead, reaching the territory of the lordship of Oultrejourdain south of Jerash. Thence it continued southward through 'Amman, Karak and Shaubak to Eilat. Encircling the north-west of the Gulf of Eilat it crossed the Sinai Desert and reached Egypt in the region of Wadi Sidr, south of the Mitla Pass. This road was the most convenient overland line of communication between Egypt and Syria and coincided in part with the "Pilgrim's Road" (Darb al-Ḥaj) to the Moslem holy places in Arabia—hence its geo-political and religious importance. King Baldwin I advanced by this road in 1100, 1115 and 1116, and seized control of the strategic points along it. In the last decades of the first kingdom heavy fighting took place over the various sectors of this highway. In 1170 Saladin seized Eilat and then fortified the road-sector across the Sinai Desert. In 1173 and 1177 the Franks attempted to capture the point at which the road left Egypt, and failed. In the years 1183–4 and 1187 severe fighting took place between Saladin and Reynald of Châtillon lord of Transjordan for the control of the "Road of Edom."

All the international trade routes leading from the Far East and Baghdad towards the coast of Palestine converged on Damascus, whence three principal roads continued to the ports of the Mediterranean: the northerly descended the foot of Mount Hermon to Banias, crossed the northern Ḥula Valley, ascended the Mountains of Naphtali and went on over the plateau of northern Upper Galilee through Tibnin to Tyre. The Crusaders seized control of the western sector of this route when they captured Tibnin (1105–7) and built the stronghold of Toron. In 1129 they also captured Banias. Hard fighting took place throughout the 12th century for the command of this route, chiefly in order to seize its defiles on either side of the Great Rift valley. The central route crossed via Quneitra to Jacob's Ford, and thence via Tiberias, Hattin, the Valley of Beit Netopha and 'Ibillin to Acre. The southern route traversed the Golan Plateau, passed Ḥisfin, descended the steep slope of al-'Al and crossed the Jordan River south of the Sea of Galilee by the bridge of Sinnabris, known as the "Wooden Bridge," or *Jisr a-Sidd.* This route joined the Tiberias–Acre highway at the foot of the Horns of Hattin. Another branch of the southern route passed opposite Beit Shean and continued along the Valley of Ḥarod and the Valley of Jezreel to the coast. The central and southern routes and their two branches were used by the Moslem armies on frequent occasions. Saladin marched along them in 1182, 1183 and 1187. South of the Plain of Beit Shean the roads had no international importance.

As can be seen from a glance at the map, the roads from Damascus to the sea avoided the mountain-massif of Upper Galilee. Nevertheless restricted traffic moved along the secondary road from Tibnin south-westward by Ḥurfeish and Jedin to Acre. This was the route used, for instance, by the caravan of merchants joined by the Spanish-Moslem traveller Ibn Jubayr in 1184. The roads of Upper Galilee were unsuited to the passage of large military forces. When Saladin decided to set out from Qal'at Shaqif for Acre, on learning of the movements of the Crusader forces under command of Guy de Lusignan (1189), he chose the road from Tiberias through Beit Netopha, as the historian Beha a-Din says: "because there was no other in that district practicable for any army."[80] The direct road from Tibnin to Acre was only suitable for small detachments engaged in reconnaissance.

local roads

The local roads, which provided excellent supplementary lines of communication within the country, may be grouped geographically as follows:

a) *The Watershed Route.* This route left the Tiberias–Acre road and continued southwards through al-Fula, Jezreel, Jenin, Sabastiya, Nablus, Jifna and al-Bira to Jerusalem. South of Jerusalem the road followed the watershed through Bethlehem to Hebron. This was the route used by most of the pilgrims who landed at Acre and travelled to Jerusalem.

b) *Roads in Samaria and the Sharon.* An important road was the one from Caesarea through Qaqun to Nablus, where it joined the watershed road. East of the latter a road ran down from Nablus to the Jordan Valley and crossed it by the Damiya bridge. Another road began at Qaqun and followed the Naḥal 'Iron (Wadi-'Ara) to al-Fula. This was traversed by the Templar force (May, 1187) on its way to the battle of Creisson. East of the *Via Maris* an important route ran along the foothills of Samaria via Qaqun, Qalansuwa, Migdal Afeq and Lydda. It was used by Saladin while he was assailing the flank of Richard Coeur de Lion's advance from Acre to Jaffa.

c) *Roads in Judea.* The most important road here was that linking Jerusalem with the *Via Maris*. It had three branches (see p. 313), the principal one making the Beit Ḥoron ascent to Nabi Samwil and joining the watershed route at Beit Ḥanina.

East of Jerusalem the pilgrims' route crossed to the Jordan via Ma'ale Adumim (see p. 324) and Jericho. A branch of an important route in the Shephela went from Beit Govrin by Tel Tsafit to Latrun. Richard Coeur de Lion used this road during his raids in the south of the country (June, 1192). Great commercial and military importance attached to the road from Hebron through Carmel to Tsoár (a-Safi) which was the chief route from Jerusalem to the lordship of Oultrejourdain. Baldwin I marched along it in 1100 on his way to Edom, and Amalric poised his forces at Carmel (Kh. Kurmul) in 1173 in order to prevent the penetration of Saladin along this highway from the same direction.

controlled by seigneurs

The roads were controlled by the seigneurs through whose domains they passed; thus Jean d'Ibelin reserved to himself the "right of the roads" when in 1265 he gave to the Hospitallers broad tracts (already occupied by the Moslems) in the area of Jaffa-Ascalon. Wayfarers were obliged to pay tolls, which were not levied at the frontier-point of the kingdom or seigneurie, but at a castle selected for the purpose. Three such places where tolls were collected are known, namely Tibnin (Toron), Beit Govrin and Deir al Balaḥ (Darom). According to the traveller Ibn Jubayr, the rate of toll was one Tyrian *dinar* and a *qirat* (1/24 of a dinar) per head. This sum was paid to the seigneur, except by merchants carrying transit-goods destined for transmission by sea, or crossing the Crusader

311

kingdom on their way to the Moslem countries. In these cases the right of collection was reserved to the crown and the tax was *ad valorem* at a varying rate. Pilgrims were exempt. The property of a pilgrim who had died *en-route*, however, belonged to the seigneur, and in 1156 the Hospitallers secured the right to inherit all the property of pilgrims who died on the roads in the territory of Nablus.[81]

lack of security

During most of the period travel along the roads was dangerous. Highway robbers, both Moslems and Franks, attacked pilgrims, wayfarers and even regular military units. The chronicles and *itineraria* are full of accounts of such attacks. The Scandinavian Seawolf wrote: "The Saracens set ambushes for Christians . . . How numerous are the corpses by the road-side, torn by beasts of prey", while Daniel the Russian related:

"The Saracen infidels, whose villages are scattered in the hills and the plain, issue from their homes to butcher the wayfarers in these dreadful mountains [between Mt. Tabor and Nazareth]. It is dangerous to traverse this road in a small company and it can be done without fear only with many companions."

Ibn Jubayr reported with enthusiasm a state of affairs on the road from Damascus to Acre, east of Banias. Here there was a large tree, which was the frontier between "security and danger" because of "some Frankish brigands who prowl and rob thereon. He whom they seize on the Moslem side—they capture; but he whom they seize on the Frankish side—they release." He adds that this is "one of the most pleasing and singular conventions of the Franks."[82] William of Tyre related that "bandits emerged from the land of Damascus and so beset the highways that none could go to and from the army without peril, neither could travellers pass along any of the way."[83]

The attacks were made in narrow and winding sectors of the roads convenient for ambush. Places distinguished for such misfortunes earned appropriate names. As already mentioned, the narrow Wadi al-Ḥaramiya, (the Valley of Thieves), between Jifna and Sinjil, was known as the *Vallis de cursu*, "the Valley of Running", owing to the need to pass swiftly through it to escape the ambushes of robbers. The name of Ma'ale Adumim (Tal'at a-Damm) was interpreted by the Franks as deriving from the blood (Hebrew-Arabic—*dam*) spilt there in the attacks of robbers. Other notorious spots for ambushes were a pass through the *kurkar* hills near 'Atlit *(Districtum)*, the hill-passes near Latrun, and the hills between Nazareth and Mt. Tabor.

ambushes

The rulers of the Crusader kingdom ascribed supreme importance to the enforcement of security on the king's highways as vital to the uninterrupted movement of tens of thousands of pilgrims and of the numerous merchant caravans. The kings and seigneurs established fortresses and patrolled the main roads, but the chief burden fell upon the shoulders of the Military Orders. In 1119 Hugh of Payns organized a group of knights whose duty was to convoy pilgrims making their way by the King's Highway. This was the beginning of the Templar Order, which in a few years became one of the principal forces in the kingdom

attempts to secure roads: fortresses and patrols

and even in the entire Christian world. Following the Order of the Knights Templar, the older Order of Hospitallers altered its aims and added to its duty of caring for sick pilgrims, that of protecting them on the roads. Both orders worked to secure the highways, but a division of labour seems to have existed between them. The Hospitallers concentrated their strength in the frontier fortresses and the Templars on the road-forts in the interior. It was characteristic that all the strongholds situated at crossroads and in dangerous localities belonged to the Templars; Latrun, Yalu, Ma'ale Adumim, Qaqun, al-Fula, Ḥ. Qarta *(Destroit),* Safed, Metsad 'Ateret *(Chastelet),* Shefar'am *(Saffran)* and Jezreel *(Petit Gerin),* Yazur *(Casel des Plains).*

Templars' responsibility

AZOR - CASEL DES PLAINS

This is a small fort at the junction of a side road with the road between Jaffa and Lydda. It was taken by the Crusaders on their way to Jerusalem in 1099, being then without garrison. In 1102 it was seized by the Egyptians during the campaign leading to the capture of Lydda and the burning of its church.

The place became famous during the Third Crusade. It was destroyed by Saladin after the battle of Arsuf (September 1191) together with the other fortresses of the Shephela, in order to deny vantage points to the Crusaders on the road to Jerusalem. The fort was rebuilt by the Templars in October 1191 in preparation for Richard Coeur de Lion's movements towards Ramla and Jerusalem, and was seized by the Moslems in 1192 before the battle of Jaffa. By the treaty of that year, which was negotiated in the area between representatives of the belligerents, it remained in the territory of the renewed Crusader kingdom, but was demolished by the Moslems before being handed over to the Franks. Restored at the beginning of the 13th century, it served as a guard post protecting pilgrims on the way to Jerusalem. Remains of the Crusader fort are to be found on the hill in the village; at the summit stands a square tower in a state of complete preservation. Crusader vaults are situated on the south slope; these used to be called "al-Baubariya," the stables, by the Arabs of the village.

THE CASTLES OF AYALON

The Valley of Ayalon is the principal natural communication between the sea coast and the capital, Jerusalem, in the Judaean Hills. The traveller crossing the lower hills of the Shephela reaches an extensive and fertile plain lying at the foot of the steep hill-escarpment and sending narrow fingers deep into it. The supreme strategic importance of the Valley of Ayalon made it the most renowned battlefield in the country. Here Joshua smote the Canaanites, here Saul

strategic importance

and David defeated the Philistines, the Maccabees struggled against the Greeks, the Zealots of the Great Rebellion rose up against the Romans, and Richard Coeur de Lion wrestled with Saladin. Allenby also fought here in the First World War, and heavy fighting occurred at the same spot during the Israel War of Independence.

three main roads Three main roads lead from the coastal plain and the Shephela through the Valley of Ayalon into the heart of the Judaean Hills. The northern road goes via Sha'albim, Beit Sira and Beit Ḥoron (Beit 'Ur); the central road crosses from Beit Nuba via Beit Liqya, Beit Inan, Qubeiba and Nabi Samwil; and the southern route is that traversed today by the main road from Latrun through the hills to Abu Ghosh.

Several routes led from the Valley of Ayalon towards the coast, the most important of which were the Latrun–Gezer–Ramla–Jaffa road and that through Latrun and Yavne to Ascalon. The principal highway from the Shephela to Jerusalem in the Crusader period passed Beit Nuba, Qubeiba and Nabi-Samwil, but this was exposed to the constant raids of brigands and Bedouins at the beginning of the period, and the Egyptians conducted frequent long-range sorties from their base at Ascalon with the aim of severing it. In 1133, in the absence of King Fulk who was at Antioch, the people of Jerusalem, under the leadership of the Patriarch William of Messines, erected a castle to protect the highroad and named it *Castellum Arnaldi*. Of this William of Tyre wrote:

Castellum Arnaldi (Yalu)

"... The Patriarch and the citizens of Jerusalem, putting their trust in the Lord, assembled in full strength at a place near the ancient Nobe which today is generally called Bettenuble. There, on the slope of the hill at the entrance to the plain, on the road leading to Lydda, and from there to the sea, they built a fortress of solid masonry, to ensure the safety of pilgrims passing along that route."[84]

William of Tyre's translator adds that as a result of the building of the fortress, trade was made easier and the price of food fell in Jerusalem.

The question of the identification of *Castellum Arnaldi* has caused disagreement among scholars. Some of them have identified it with a Crusader tower called al-Burj, situated five kilometres north-west of Beit Nuba; others have sought to place it at Yalu, about a kilometre south-west of Beit Nuba.

William of Tyre's description fits Yalu very closely, as the latter is on the slope of a hill at the eastern entrance to the Valley of Ayalon, and looks out over Beit Nuba, lying on the plain not far off. This identification also suits the accounts of *Castellum Arnaldi* at the time of Richard Coeur de Lion's campaigns. The identification of *Castellum Arnaldi* with al-Burj is not appropriate since the tower stands on the other side of the plain and is remote from the Beit Liqya–Qubeiba road. Scholars have been aware of this argument, but some have hesitated to place the *castellum* at Yalu because no Crusader remains of importance have been found there. But during the war of June 1967, as a result of the dismantling of modern structures at Yalu, important Crusader remains were exposed. The building style and plan of these remains resemble those of other fortresses built

wrong identification

during Fulk's reign, thus eliminating any lingering doubt on identification of Yalu with *Castellum Arnaldi*.

The fort is situated on an elongated hill which is the northern continuation of the ridge of Deir Ayyub-Latrun. It commands a wide prospect north-westward and eastward over the northern Valley of Ayalon, the tributaries of Wadi Salman and the slopes of the mountains of Judea. The only sections of the stronghold preserved or uncovered are part of the western wall and a small sector of the southern wall, suggesting that the fortress belongs to the *castrum* type, an oblong plan with square towers in the centre of the long sides. The length of the western and eastern sides was apparently 80 metres. In the centre of the western curtain a square tower is preserved. The length of the northern and southern sides seems to have been 40 metres. The gate was in the south; its arch has not survived, but a hall with pointed barrel-vaulting remains, flanking the gate. Beside this is a spiral staircase, blocked at the end. To its west a gate leads to a corridor. The blocks of the west rampart are roughly cut, their joints filled with gravel. The tower, which projects some 4 metres from the line of the wall, is built of well-cut drafted blocks. There are traces of another vault which probably belonged to the north-west corner tower. The plan of the castle, the style of the arch of the inner gate on the south side and the appearance of the western ramparts indicate that it was built in the 1130's and 1140's, as these details resemble

description of Yalu

Yalu, castle, west wall

315

Latrun, castle, gate area

those of other *castrum* strongholds of the period such as Belvoir and Beit Govrin.

Latrun

In the 1150's the castle was in the hands of the Templars. In 1171 the Templars and Hospitallers, who were neighbours in the area, settled a dispute over lands in the vicinity of Castellum Arnaldi. The erection and garrisoning of the castle ensured the safety of the northern and central roads to Jerusalem but, owing to its position on the northern slope of the Deir Ayyub-Latrun ridge, the castle did not command the southern highway going by Bab al-Wad and Abu Ghosh, or the routes leading south-westward towards Yavne and Ascalon. To gain control of the road system it was necessary to establish another fortress south-west of the Deir Ayyub-Latrun ridge, which projects into the plain like a wedge and cuts it into two. A Templar road-fortress known as *Toronum Militum* or Le Toron des Chevaliers was built here between the years 1150–1170. We have no precise historical information about the date when it was built, and the first source which records it is the book of the Jewish traveller Benjamin of Tudela, who gave the place its Spanish name, *Toron de los Caballeros,* and noted that three Jews lived in the village nearby.

The castle is built on the top of the hill of the modern monastery, where traces of the curtain wall are to be seen, with towers built on a battered glacis-like footing. West of the wall a gate survives, with barrel-vaulting, leading to a corridor; it is flanked by another vaulted structure; on the north side are three rows of halls. The castle was used as a fortified position by the Jordanians, who added concrete emplacements and communication trenches, and partially repaired the series of halls to house their garrison.

316

The name "Le Toron" has undergone interesting transformations. The Arabs converted "Le Toron" to al-Atrun or al-Natrun, which means 'guard' or 'look-out'. After the Crusader period the name Latrun took root and the Christians, not knowing its French origin, saw in it the Latin name *Latro* (robber), hence the tradition that here was the home of "the good thief" *(Boni Latronis)*— Dismos the Egyptian, who recognized Jesus's mission when he was crucified with him (Luke 23:41-43).

The castles of the Valley of Ayalon were captured by Saladin in 1187. Having *Third Crusade* performed valuable service in the defence of the roads to Frankish Jerusalem, they became, after its capture by Saladin, a barrier against the forces of the Third Crusade in their not over-zealous attempts to advance upon the Holy City. The Crusaders, having won the battle of Arsuf in September 1191, captured and fortified Jaffa. Saladin retired to the Yarqon springs and then manoeuvred between Ramla and the Valley of Ayalon with the intention of threatening a Crusader movement eastward, Ramla, Lydda and other castles throughout the Shephela having been demolished in order to deny the Crusaders a base for attack.

The Crusading host, after spending two months at Jaffa, at last set out in November of 1191 on its march to Jerusalem. Saladin evacuated the Shephela *1191* and took up positions in the fortresses of Ayalon. Hard winter conditions hampered Richard's advance; he spent six weeks in the ruins of Ramla, and only at the beginning of December did he set off in the direction of the Valley of Ayalon. In the face of this move Saladin abandoned and destroyed Latrun and, relying on the rainy weather and the deep mud, put his main force into winter quarters in Jerusalem. Richard, having spent Christmas in the desolation of Latrun, set out the next day on his march along the main Jerusalem road. On the 3rd of January, 1192, the greater part of his army gathered at Beit Nuba, an open village *(casale)* below *Castellum Arnaldi*. The situation in the camp was very difficult owing to the stormy weather, heavy rainfall and lack of provisions. The Crusaders from overseas were full of enthusiasm despite the difficult conditions. The longed-for destination appeared to them to be very close, only 22 miles away. But the knights born in the country knew what other armies had learned before them and were to learn again—that the climb through the mountain passes in the winter conditions of Palestine was almost impossible, even if they were not barred by the enemy. The commanders of the Hospitallers and Templars persuaded Richard to retire to winter quarters, and after a week's stay the host retreated to Ramla, arriving there on the 13th of January.

Another attempt to advance to Jerusalem was made by the Crusaders in the summer of the same year (1192). Richard left his base at Ascalon and, turning north by the Beit Govrin road, reached Latrun on the 10th of July. As in the previous winter, his intention was to go up to Jerusalem by the middle route. Crossing the Deir Ayyub ridge and spending the night at *Castellum Arnaldi* *1192* (Yalu), the following day he pitched camp in the plain near Beit Nuba. Here the Crusaders waited for three weeks for supplies and reinforcements. Richard, in the meantime, conducting a number of raids in the direction of Jerusalem as far as Abu Ghosh, Qalunia and Nabi Samwil. The Moslems, for their part, made forays against the supply convoys moving from the coastal towns towards the camp in Ayalon. The threat to Jerusalem was grave and Saladin placed the city in readiness for a siege. Disagreements broke out among the Moslem commanders, some of whom opposed the decision that the army remain shut up behind the walls of Jerusalem and proposed that it go forth and fight a frontal battle to prevent the Franks from reaching the city. While the latter were at Beit Nuba, information was received of the advance of an Egyptian force which had been ordered by Saladin to come to his aid. Richard set out by night southward, attacked the Egyptian army and annihilated it. Loaded with spoils, he returned to camp at Beit Nuba, but the victory did not accelerate the march to Jerusalem. Serious disagreements broke out among the Crusaders as to whether they were strong enough to capture the city, and a commission of experts decided to drop the campaign. Richard's last prospect of reconquering the Holy City faded, and his armies abandoning the Valley of Ayalon, returned to the coastal cities. A short time after this failure a peace treaty was signed between Richard and Saladin (September, 1192), whereby the fortresses of Ayalon remained outside Crusader control. Ayalon returned to Frankish hands in 1229 with the treaty signed by the emperor Frederick II, but the Crusaders were apparently not permitted to refortify Latrun. Nevertheless, in the early 1240's they did so; but in 1244 it was finally captured by the Moslems.

BETHEL - BURJ BEITIN

Bethel, ancient Luz, where Jacob built his altar, was identified by most of the Christian travellers of the Crusader period with Kh. Luza on Mount Gerizim. In this way they followed the Samaritan tradition. Only a few identified it correctly with the village of Beitin, north-east of Ramallah. One of them, an anonymous traveller, wrote: "Machomeria was first called Luza and afterwards Bethel", identifying Bethel with Mahomaria or al-Bira, two kilometres from Beitin. Burchard of Mount Sion, in grand style, locates Bethel in two places: at the beginning of his work he places it near Nablus and further on near Rama— Ramallah. Documentary sources do not mention the place at all.

The Crusader remains are situated half a kilometre from the centre of the village of Beitin. Beside the Ramallah–Jericho road stands a square tower similar in all details to the "Norman keep" structures built for the defence of open settlements. In front of it, foundations of a square curtain wall, probably Byzantine, are visible with an entrance on the south-west side.

The tower is very solidly built and almost entirely preserved. It is 10 metres wide with an aperture on the north. Most of its stones belonged to an older structure and were in secondary use; some are engraved with chased crosses and other ornaments, indicating that they were taken from a Byzantine church.

318

Bethel, tower

EILAT-ILE DE GRAYE

Eilat, the harbour town of the Kings of Judea, an important centre in the Byzantine period and a Jewish settlement after the Arab conquest, was a flourishing townlet just before the Crusader advent. Its inhabitants derived their livelihood from fishing, date-growing and commerce. Eilat is the most important crossroad on the pilgrim routes leading from the Moslem centres of population to the holy cities of the Hedjaz. Pilgrims from Egypt, crossing Sinai, descended to the shores of the Gulf of Eilat by the "Pass of Eilat" ('Aqbat Aila) and met the pilgrims from Syria coming by the ancient "road of the Land of Edom." From there they continued southward by the land of Midian to Medina and Mecca. The importance of this crossroads was both commercial and military, for the Sinai–Edom route was the principal land route linking Egypt and Syria, and when the Crusaders occupied the coastal plain of Palestine, it became the only artery between the two Moslem centres.

strategic crossroad

King Baldwin I reached the region of the Mountains of Edom in the first campaign after his accession, in the winter of 1101, but was not able to gain a hold on this remote area at that time. In the middle of the second decade of the Crusader kingdom, when its north-eastern frontier had become fixed and most of the coastal towns had been captured, he began a war with the strategic aim of estab-

Baldwin I

319

lishing the boundaries of the kingdom at the desert's edge, thus permanently severing the land communication between Syria and Egypt. In the autumn of 1115 the king moved on to Edom and built the "Royal Castle"—*Montreal*—near Shaubak, in the centre of the country and on the main highway. A year later he set out again at the head of a small force to capture and fortify Eilat. His army, numbering not more than forty knights, reached the townlet, which seems to have been unfortified. Its inhabitants escaped by sea, seeking refuge on the island of al-Qureiya or Jazirat Fara'un, 14 kilometres south-west of the town near the western shore of the Gulf. Baldwin and his men seized the town, then crossed the Gulf in boats and captured the island, apparently without opposition. A garrison was left on the island, whose Arabic name al-Qureiye was perverted into a French-sounding one—Ile de Graye—and it was fortified. At one blow and without much effort Baldwin thus achieved his strategic aim, and communication between the Moslem centres was cut. The Franks proceeded to levy tolls on pilgrims and on caravans of traders.

only island fortified

The area between Shaubak and Eilat was organized as an administrative district, governed from Montreal, at first as royal domain. The land of "Oultrejourdain" was given in about 1118 to Roman of Le Puy, with all seigneurial rights. "Oultrejourdain" became one of the principal seigneuries of the kingdom. Roman's heir, Payen le Bouteiller, extended its frontiers northward and built Karak, in Moab, in 1142. On his death the seigneurie embraced the territories of Ammon, Moab and Edom from the River Yaboq (the Zerqa) to Eilat. It reverted to King Baldwin III at the end of the 1150's and he gave it to Philip de Milly, Viscount of Nablus, in 1161. The system of fortifications in Transjordan was both extended and intensified over the years, and by the late 1160's a chain of castles had been raised along the "Pilgrims' Road", consisting of Karak, Tafila, Shaubak, Petra and Eilat.

seigneurie of "Oultrejourdain"

Saladin saw the reopening of the land route from Egypt to Syria as the first phase of his plan to liquidate the Kingdom of Jerusalem. In 1170 he set out for Eilat and the Ile de Graye, leaving his Egyptian base by the Pilgrims' Road, carrying boats in sections on camel-back. The Moslems assembled these upon their arrival on the shore of the Gulf of Eilat and advanced against the Ile de Graye. According to the sources Eilat itself was unfortified, as the account of the attack speaks of "the isle on which Eilat is situated." The Frankish garrison quickly surrendered and was led in triumph through the streets of Cairo. The fall of Eilat opened the way to the Hedjaz, but the castles of Edom and Moab still barred the road to Syria to the Moslems, and many years were to pass before Saladin was able to capture them.

Saladin's conquest

The Franks did not regain control of Eilat. Instead of blocking the Pilgrims' Road on the east side again, they now strove to seize the key position on the western part of the route, on the frontier of Egypt and Sinai. The chief stronghold which commanded the route from the west was Ras Jindi, south-east of the Mitla Pass, where Saladin built a large fortress (Qal'at Jindi). The Frankish forces attacked it in 1173 and 1177, but without success.

Meanwhile the seigneurie of Transjordan remained without a lord. In view of its importance and in the face of the grave Moslem threat to it, the king and his council laid the responsibility for its fate on Reynald de Châtillon, who married its heiress. Late in 1182, Reynald decided to recover Eilat and to make it a base for plundering raids on the maritime trade routes of the Red Sea. He prepared five ships which he brought dismantled to the shores of the Gulf. The Moslem garrison, like its Crusader forerunner, was stationed not in the town but on the island. Reynald laid siege to the latter with two ships, without trying to take it, while the other three, sailing south, began a campaign of robbery and slaughter with the declared purpose of capturing the holy cities of Mecca and Medina. This threat to one of the most important arteries of maritime trade in the Orient, and the grave peril to the safety of the sacred cities, aroused the Moslems to a furious and vigorous reaction. An Egyptian fleet, gathering at Suez, sailed to the Gulf of Eilat and joined battle with the Frankish ships that were blockading the island. One Frankish ship was sunk and its crew was taken prisoner; the second fled to the Egyptian shore, but its sailors were seized by the Moslems and slaughtered. The Moslem fleet then turned southward, chased Reynald's other ships and slaughtered their crews, who had in the meantime left their ships and penetrated deep into the Hedjaz. Thus ended the last attempt of the Franks to seize a posi-

Reynald de Châtillon

Jazirat Fara'un, castle, view from the south

tion in the Gulf of Eilat. Their attempt to gain a hold on the west side of Sinai also failed. The route from Egypt to Syria was forcibly opened, and the encirclement of the kingdom, the first phase of the plan to liquidate it, was complete. The last Franks on the island, prisoners engaged in fishing for the Sultan of Egypt, were seen by the traveller Thetmar in 1217.

The Ile de Graye, known today as "Coral Island", Jazirat Fara'un (Pharaoh's Island) or Al-Qureiye, "the town", lies south of Taba on the west coast of the Gulf of Eilat, some 14 kilometres south-west of 'Aqaba, which is the medieval Eilat (Aila). The distance from the shore of the Gulf to the island is about 250 metres. The island, a solid granite rock, is 300 metres long from north to south and 150 metres broad at its widest point. On the west, facing the shore of the Gulf, lies a shallow lagoon which can be entered by boats at high tide; this was a sheltered harbour in the Middle Ages. The isle has no source of water and its entire supply derives from cisterns. At each end rises a hill with steep sides, the

Jazirat Fara'un   northerly being some 30 metres above sea level and the southerly 24 metres. They are joined by a spur on the east side of the island.

Within the island area are remains of a settlement and defences dating from several ancient periods, but these are beyond the scope of this present work. The mediaeval fortress stands on the northern hill with a flat summit 110 metres long and 30 metres broad. Here a surrounding wall was built which enclosed a lower bailey on the north and dwelling quarters with an upper bailey on the south. The wall is strengthened by square towers of two storeys erected at intervals of 20 to 30 metres. The west part of the wall is preserved to its full height; it had a crenellated top along which is built a *chemin-de-ronde*.

The lower bailey on the north is 60 metres long. Rooms abutting on the west hall appear to have been used as barracks for the garrison. North of the bailey is a large vaulted water cistern.

Inside the court is the quarry from which the building stones appear to have been taken. The gate of the lower bailey is at the northern end of the wall, approached by a steep ascent from the shore.

South of the lower bailey is a complex of living rooms divided into two wings, an eastern and a western. The upper bailey is situated between the wings and north of them, the west wing being composed of a number of two-storey buildings. The west wing contains a lofty keep-like tower which commands the whole castle area; on the jamb of one of the windows of this wing is a reused stone on which a Byzantine or Crusader cross is engraved. South of the east wing is a mosque containing a *mikhrab* or praying-niche.

In the middle of the upper bailey is a water cistern whose ceiling is supported by two pointed arches resting on a single column. The southern complex had an outer gate on the south. Both gates of the lower bailey, the building blocks of the ramparts and the buildings are mostly of roughly dressed granite blocks. Mortar was unnecessary because of their hardness, their crude dressing and their irregularity. The layers range in width down to the very narrow. Limestone blocks are to be found in some of the window lintels and cistern walls.

322

Most of the castle in its present form belongs to later periods (Mamluk and Turkish), but its general plan (upper and lower bailey, wall towers and other building details) should be ascribed, it seems, to the period of Crusader occupation (1116–1170). The Ayyubid style of building is discernible in the cisterns (end of the 12th–beginning of the 13th century).

AL-FULA-LA FÈVE

This castle lay at an important crossroads in the heart of the Valley of Jezreel, where the highway from Jerusalem to Nablus and Tiberias crossed the road from Acre to Beit Shean.

The Crusaders translated the Arabic name of the village of al-Fula to La Fève, The Bean. According to historical sources the castle was in the possession of the Templars, but we do not know when it was built, just as we do not know the dates of other Templar castles. Theodorich (1172) wrote of it as "a castle of no small size in whose ground they [the Templars] have made a large cistern with a wheeled machine."[85] The fortress is also mentioned during the campaigns of 1183 In September and October of that year battles took place in the Valley of Ḥarod between Saladin and the Franks, and the castle of al-Fula was the base for the Frankish army. It is referred to again at the end of April, 1187, when Balian d'Ibelin camped there on his way from Jerusalem to Tiberias. The Templars garrison of al-Fula sallied forth to take part in a punitive expedition which clashed with Moslem forces near Tsipori and was wiped out (Creisson, 1st May, 1187).

Immediately after the battle of Hattin, al-Fula was captured and plundered; it is related that the castle contained livestock and huge storerooms, and may therefore have been a collection depot for produce from the Order's estates in the region. It took the Moslems many months to transfer these stores. As late as the middle of 1188, during the siege of Belvoir, the Knights Hospitaller conducted a sortie against a Moslem convoy loaded with foodstuffs taken from al-Fula.

A village called La Fève is alluded to in 1262 as one of those included in an agreement between the Templars and the Hospitallers.

Very meagre remains of the castle are to be found in the centre of Kibbutz Merḥavya, on an artificial mound isolated from its surroundings by a moat. They include a pointed barrel vault and Crusader building stones scattered over the tel and its vicinity. Travellers who visited the place in the 19th century saw here remains of a square castle of the *castrum* type, evidently with corner towers and surrounded by a moat.

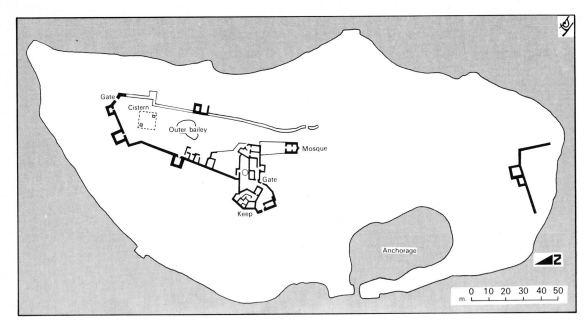

Jazirat Fara'un Castle (Ile de Graye) (General Plan)

MA'ALE ADUMIM - MALDOIM

The Red Ascent

The road from Jerusalem to Jericho and the River Jordan was in the Crusader period one of the principal routes of pilgrim traffic. Having completed their pilgrimage to the holy places of Jerusalem, the Crusaders were accustomed to form large parties in order to go down to Jericho and the site of the baptism of Jesus. On their way down the steep and tortuous descents of the Judean Desert, they were often attacked by highway robbers and Bedouin who lay in wait by the wayside. The hardest and most perilous section was the steep passage winding south of the Canyon of Wadi Qilt, known as "The Red Ascent" or Tal'at a-Damm. This is 11 kilometres long, beginning where Wadi Qilt emerges into the Plain of Jericho and ending among the reddish limestone hills which gave the ascent its name. This sector was already famous in ancient times as a place of ambush by highway robbers, and the Gospels (Luke 10:30) describe an attack by robbers on a wayfarer. In the Roman and Byzantine periods a fort was erected at the top of Ma'ale Adumim and held by a detachment of infantry. The name of the ascent was interpreted as deriving from the ample bloodshed there in encounters with robbers. The Jericho road was still insecure in the Crusader period; in order to ensure the unimpeded movement of pilgrims, the Templars set

324

up a string of forts along the highway, the largest being at the top of the ascent and bearing various names—Adumim, Turris Rubea, Rouge Cisterne and Maldoim. This castle is near the *khan* (caravanserai) where travellers spent the night and which the Crusaders identified as the site of the Inn of the Good Samaritan (Luke 10:33).

Burchard of Mount Sion wrote:

"Four leagues to the west of Jericho, on the road to Jerusalem—is the castle of Adumim, the place where the man who went down from Jerusalem to Jericho fell among thieves. This had befallen many on the same spot in modern times, and the place had received its name from the frequent blood shed there. Of a truth it is horrible to behold and exceedingly dangerous, unless one travels with an escort."[86]

history

The date of the castle's construction is not known but it certainly existed in the 1170's, as Theodorich (1172) mentioned it. In 1187, after Hattin, the castle was captured by a Moslem force which advanced from the Jordan Valley towards Jerusalem. Apparently the castle was empty.

description

The ruins of Adumim are situated north of the Jerusalem–Jericho highway, on a lofty hill from the summit of which Jericho can be seen on the east, and the Mount of Olives on the west. The slopes of the hill are very steep on the south and east side, and more gradual on the west and north sides. The plan of the castle is quadrilateral; the length of each side is 50 metres. A rock-cut moat, 6 metres wide and 4 metres deep, encircles the outer walls. Inside the curtain wall there was a pointed barrel vault. This, once built around the entire inner bailey, has been almost completely destroyed. Its only remnants can be seen in the south-western corner. In the middle of the bailey, nearer to the northern curtain wall, a keep was built, but only part of its vault is still preserved. In its northern wall a loophole can be seen. The castle gate has disappeared but it can be supposed that its position was in the north-eastern corner, where a passage from the moat is still preserved.

In the middle of Ma'ale Adumim, another Templar watch-tower is situated, while still another was found at the beginning of the ascent, not far from Jericho (Beit Jabr Foqani and Taḥtani).

BEIT TSUR - BURJ A-SUR

Near the ruins of the city of Beit Tsur, Kh. Tubeika, one of the fortresses of Rehoboam, son of King Solomon, and close to the spot where a decisive battle took place during the wars of the Maccabees, stands a square tower typical of Crusader "Norman keep" structures. Under the name of Beitsur the locality was given by Hugo of St. Abraham to the Order of Hospitallers in 1136, and it was on the north-east border of the great Hospitaller estate centred on Beit Govrin.

The tower appears to have been built by the Order, probably as an admini-

Beitsur,
tower, west side

strative centre or to mark the eastern boundary of its domain. Another tower, which no longer exists, was built on the northern boundary of the domain of Beit Govrin at a spot called Tamarin. Beitsur is situated not far from the Hebron–Bethlehem road and looks towards 'Ein Dirwa, the Spring of Philip, where Philip baptized the eunuch (Acts 8:38). Burchard of Mount Sion saw its remains in 1283.

The tower at Beit Tsur, like many other square towers, has sides 10 metres long built on a platform of large square stones, apparently re-used. Most of its western wall is preserved to a height of approximately 8 metres and a thickness of 3 metres; it is of dressed ashlar facing, enclosing a rubble fill. A loophole is partly preserved in its centre. Traces of interior stairs remain, leading to the second storey. It is thought that the building was groin-vaulted.

HORBAT ASHDOD YAM - CASTEL BEROART

This is a square castle of the *castrum* type, with corner towers that were circular and solid throughout. It is 60 metres long and 45 metres wide. The only gate, defended on each side by round towers, was in the west wall. The east wall has been covered by shifting sand, but the west flank is preserved to a considerable height together with its towers. In the middle of the 19th century remains of a

326

settlement were still visible but they have since become buried by windblown sand.

The castle is built a few metres from the shore, three kilometres south of the new town of Ashdod and west of the ancient city of the same name. The port was situated here in the Byzantine period and it was still used in the early Arab era. Al-Maqdisi related that there was a castle here, where Byzantine ships sometimes put in bearing Moslem prisoners, and that Palestinian Moslems used to come to ransom them.

The Latin name, *Castellum Beroart,* occurs in marine charts of the 12th century, but nothing is known of the castle or its history in the Crusader period. Its remains appear to be of the early Arab epoch, built on Byzantine foundations. *Omayyad plan* The building's dimensions, its round towers and the arrangement of its gates point, apparently, to an Omayyad structure, and it may be taken as an example of an early Arab copy of a Roman *castrum.* It is even possible that the castle was not used at all in the Crusader period.

Adumim, castle, aerial view

Burj al-Maliḥ and the road to the Jordan

OTHER CASTLES

HABONIM-CAFARLET

This is a small castle built on a sandstone hill rising thirty metres above the Carmel plain, half a mile from the Mediterranean coast. With its perfect walls and circular towers it is one of the finest mediaeval fortresses in the country.

Habonim is situated eight kilometres south of 'Atlit and some 15 kilometres north of Caesarea. It is of the *castrum* type, 58 metres long and 50 metres wide. There are round towers at the corners of the square, walled enclosure, beneath which are vaulted cellars. The only gate, on the south side, is defended by two *position* round towers, one on each flank. The walls are strengthened by external butresses. The castle resembles the one at Ashdod Yam to a surprising degree, in its dimensions, its round towers and the arrangement of its gates. As had been mentioned, the plans of these two castles are identical with those of the fortified palaces of the Omayyad caliphs, such as the one to be found at Ḥ. Minim (Kh. Miniya) on the shore of the Sea of Galilee.

Information which helps to date the fortress of Habonim has been found in

Habonim (Cafarlet), aerial view

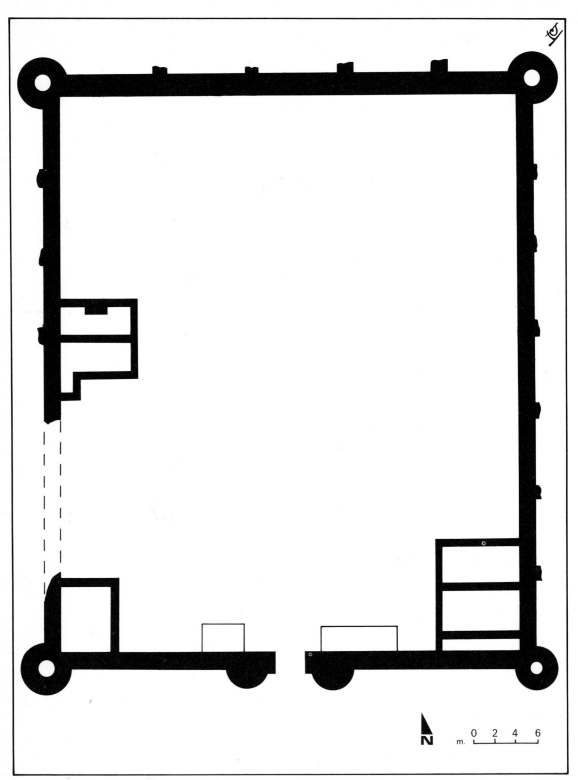

N

m. 0 2 4 6

Habonim (Cafarlet) (Plan)

documents of Moslem historians, who mention that the Omayyad Caliph Hisham, son of 'Abd al-Malik, built a town called Kafar-Lab near Caesarea. Hisham *history* was Caliph from 742 to 743, and in this period the Arab rulers were attempting to increase the population of the coastal plain, which had been ravaged after the Arab conquest, with the object of protecting themselves from invasion by the Byzantine fleet. The historical information on the castle is scant and fragmentary, and exists only in records of sales and grants. The numerous chronicles of the period do not mention it at all, although it is situated on the main coastal highway and the neighbouring forts, such as Dor (Merle), are mentioned.

The charters do not refer to Cafarlet as a castle but as a village *(casale)* belonging to the lordship of Caesarea, which was temporarily handed to the Order of Hospitallers in 1213, mortgaged in exchange for a loan made to the lord of Caesarea. In 1232 Cafarlet was sold for 16,000 bezants to the Templars, who still held it in 1255. It was captured by the Moslems in 1265 after the conquest of Caesarea. Subsequently it appears to have been restored to the Templars, but was taken by the Moslems and destroyed in 1291 at the same time as 'Atlit.

MONTFORT-QAL'AT QURAYN

The castle of Montfort is perhaps the most beautiful and romantic of the mediaeval strongholds of Israel. Its ruins, which spring from a tangled grove of evergreen oaks, commanding as they do a deep gorge through which water flows throughout the year, resemble more than any other fortress in the country the mediaeval castles so common in Europe. It is therefore ironic that this locality in the heart of Galilee should have served as the first centre of the brutal Teutonic Order of St. Mary, which dominated eastern Europe with fire and sword and was the nursery of the notorious "Teutonic spirit."

The castle is built on a steep spur rising 180 metres over the streambed, and extending north-westward between Naḥal Keziv (Wadi Qurayn) on the north *position* and a deep narrow ravine on the south. The slopes of the spur are very steep on the north and south sides, but the gradient is gradual on the west. On the east, a narrow saddle joins the spur to the rest of the hilltop. The Crusaders sundered this link by hewing deep moats into the rock. The gentle drop from west to east enabled them to build the castle at different levels, one above the other, so ensuring defence in depth. The fortress is surrounded by a curtain wall onto which towers were built at regular intervals. Most of the wall has been destroyed, but part survives on the west side of the castle. On its most vulnerable eastern side a high wall was built behind the moat, and behind it the great castle keep was erected, this being its strongest defensive point.

The interior area of the castle is divided into seven parts: these are, from west to east—a) the residence of the commandant; b) the ceremonial hall; c) the chapel; d) the workshops and kitchen; e) the knights' quarters; f) the inner bailey; *internal division*

331

g) the great keep. The only gate is situated on the south slope of the spur. At the foot of the fortress is a large structure whose function will be considered below.

two stages of building

The castle was built in two stages: in the 12th century a small fort was erected here, which was enlarged in the 13th century by the Teutonic knights.

Montfort is a fortress of limited strategic value. It is remote from any important highway, and the two roads which linked it with the inhabited centres, one with Mi'iliya and the other with H. Manot, were local routes of secondary importance. The fortress commands a restricted area and is revealed to the approaching visitor only when he is close to its walls. It looks very much as if its builders deliberately chose an isolated spot which was difficult to reach. In the 12th century it served to protect and administer the domains of the seigneurs of the "royal castle" *(chastiau dou Rei)* at Mi'iliya. The 13th century enlargement was designed by its builders, the knights of the Teutonic Order, to house their headquarters, archives and treasure. For this purpose they chose an unobstrusive locality with good natural defences and remote from highways.

The place was fortified and settled in pre-Crusader periods, for the keep's huge stones appear to be of Roman origin and, during the archaeological excavations of 1926, Roman coins and a decorated Roman urn were found in the castle area.

The fortress, rebuilt by the Crusaders in the middle of the 12th century, was then called *Castellum Novum Regis* ("the new royal castle"), or "the new castle in the mountains of Acre," to distinguish it from the castle of Hunin, which was also known as *Castellum Novum.* It is not clear who owned it in the mid-12th century. It may possibly have belonged to the fief of Mi'iliya (see p. 196) and may have been given in dowry to Joscelin III de Courtenay, together with this fief, in 1179. A document of 1182 indicates that the castle had belonged in the previous period to the king, since he gave it to Joscelin directly, without reference to Mi'iliya, as part of the great exchange transaction effected between the two. Additional evidence of their mutual independence is afforded in the 13th century when these castles were sold by different people (albeit members of the same family) to the Teutonic Order (see below).

history

12th century

Whatever the case, in the 1180's the castle of Montfort was in the possession of Joscelin, who gathered into his ownership broad domains in western and central Galilee. The castle was captured by the Moslems in 1187 and returned to the Crusaders in 1192. Together with the fief it was restored to the Courtenay family and made over after Joscelin's death to his youthful daughter, who had married a French knight, William de Mandelée (Amigdala). In 1228, eight years after the sale of Mi'iliya Castle, Jacques de Mandelée sold the castle of Montfort to the Teutonic Order. This sale appears to have been completed some time after the Teutons, with the aid of pilgrims, had begun to enlarge the fortress. At the beginning of the year 1229 the Christian possession of Montfort was recognized by the peace treaty between the emperor Frederick II and the Sultan al-Kamil. At that time the fortress was already known as "Montfort" (the "strong hill"), while the Teutons translated the name into German and called it *Starkenberg.*

13th century

333

Montfort, aerial view

The Knights of the Teutonic Order transferred their archives and treasure from the capital of the kingdom at Acre to Montfort, although they continued to hold important parts of the city. As the old castle was too small for their needs and its rebuilding required large sums of money, the Master of the Order, Hermann von Salza, appealed to Pope Gregory IX to issue a Bull calling upon the faithful to make contributions to the building of the castle. With the aid of the sums received, the Teutons were able to complete the building of the fortress and make it one of the most magnificent, though not one of the largest, in the realm. An examination of its ruins reveals the limited space allotted to the knights' quarters in contrast to the areas of public use such as the chapel and the ceremonial hall.

As the years went by the Teutons received or acquired wide tracts of land in western and central Galilee, extending from Fasuta in the east to the sea coast in the west and from Tarbiḥa in the north to Kafr Yasif in the south. In all, some fifty villages belonged to their domains in this region. The economic importance of the castle is indicated by the fact that the treasurer of the Order was also the Castellan or commandant of Montfort.

Baybars attacks   In the year 1266 Baybars laid siege to the castle, but was driven off after an obstinate defence. Five years later, in June 1271, the Moslems reappeared before the walls of the fortress and, after a week, their engineers were able to breach the south rampart by mining, and so captured the inner bailey. The Crusaders at first continued to resist, fortifying themselves in the great keep, but the last commandant, John von Sachsen, soon yielded and was permitted to leave in peace for Acre at the head of his knights. Baybars ordered all the timber buildings and a large quantity of arms found within the castle to be destroyed, and the Moslems also emptied the great water cisterns. The Order's treasure and archives were safely transferred to Acre and thence to Europe. This body of records, preserved in its entirety, is an invaluable source on the historical geography of Galilee in the Crusader period. Montfort was never rebuilt.

farm   On the south of the Naḥal Keziv is a large Crusader building of two storeys. This was the central structure of a farmstead which supplied food to the fortress. The ground floor of this building contained stables and barns. A staircase on the west side of the structure, still intact, led to the upper storey, which was roofed with fine Gothic vaulting, also preserved. Other farm buildings were constructed round this block, and the market gardens of the castle extended along the bed of the gorge. The farm was worked by the "Brothers-at-Service" of the Order. The same building protected the steep ascent to the castle and the approach to its water supply. In peacetime the Crusaders drew water from the bed of the Keziv gorge, here a perennial stream, but to ensure a regular water supply during siege, they cut gigantic cisterns into the rock within the castle area and kept them constantly filled with water which they transported on the backs of mules. In the river bed remains of a dam were found which maintained the level of the water and directed it into a channel, leading to watermills situated downstream. These ground sugar cane as well as flour.

334

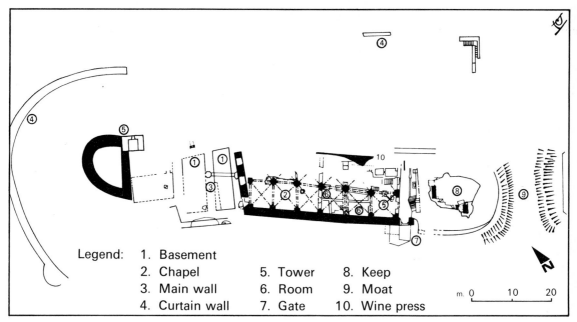

Legend:
1. Basement
2. Chapel
3. Main wall
4. Curtain wall
5. Tower
6. Room
7. Gate
8. Keep
9. Moat
10. Wine press

m. 0   10   20

Montfort (General Plan)

An account from the 13th century refers to Keziv as "a valley most pleasant and celebrated among all the valleys, for its musk-pears, the like of which are found nowhere else for exquisiteness of perfume and excellence of flavor."

A local tradition relates that a secret underground passage connects the lower building with the castle above.

From the lower building, the ascent is by a broad, unpaved road encircling the spur of the hill on the south, above a narrow oak-clad ravine. As we climb, we see *approach* a small Crusader bridge built over the gorge. Here a broad path branches off and, following the gorge upstream, leads to Mi'ilya. The road to the castle continues by a leftward turn, but this is not the original approach, which was further east. To the right of the way, a great wall appears, containing the castle's sewage outfall. A few metres further on, past the castle garth is a great square tower, the only one in the castle surviving to its full height, which reaches 18 metres. It has small windows and loopholes directed towards the streambed of the Keziv. The *castle* tower was originally set in a curving wall, visible from its western corner. Wall and tower acted as a second line of defence to the outer enceinte, which can be seen below on the slope of the spur.

Eastward of the tower are two vaulted rooms which were formerly used as the cellars of the castellan's residence built over them. In one of them lies the base of a large pillar which supported the vault of the ceremonial hall. This has fallen from the upper storey. A steep path ascends from these rooms to the main level of the castle.

The point of entry at the main level was formerly the inner bailey. Its walls and much of its flooring have collapsed over the scarp of the hill. The entrance to the ceremonial hall is to be found in the western (righthand) wall. Most of this area has been destroyed, but its size and splendour can still be discerned. Here the *hall* official receptions and ceremonies of the Teutonic Order were held. The hall was square, 20 metres each way, and the surviving wall is nearly two metres thick. In the centre of the area stands an octagonal column which supported the ribs carrying the vaults of the roof. In the east and only surviving wall, over the entrance, the impressions of the ribs, long since collapsed and fallen, are visible. Huge bases set out against this wall supported the ribs of the eastern vaults of the roof. On the west side of the hall were situated the castellan's residence, the treasury and the records chamber. The castellan's residence was next to the castle garth, which extended to the curving masonry rampart on which stands the square tower near the entrance to the area of the ruins.

All the structures so far mentioned belong to the second period of the castle's history, and were built by the Teutons in the 1230's.

Emerging from the hall gate, we pass a breach in the southern wall on our *chapel* right and reach the chapel of the castle. It is 23 metres long and some 8 metres in width, and divided into three bays by two ranges each of four pillars. Frag-

Montfort, view from south-west

ments of coloured glass were found on the chapel floor during excavation, and it is to be supposed that the windows of the south wall were glazed with stained glass. The chapel contains a circular well.

The east wall of the chapel separated the centre of the castle from the dwelling quarters and workshops. Passing this wall we reach two successive rooms, which were the knights' quarters. The room behind them was the castle kitchen, on one side of which is a small chamber, the castle smithy. Here, during excavation, pieces of armour, broken weapons, a bellows and charcoal were found. Near the smithy was a wine press, with the treading tank to the east and the fermenting tank nearby. Stairs in the vicinity led to the roof of the building, and there was also a well. A short distance from the wine press a capital with carved fleur-de-lys lies upon the ground. *dwelling quarters*

East of the dwelling quarters is a stone-paved court, approached by a paved way from a postern, which was built on the south slope of the spur at the foot of the keep.

The great keep is built of gigantic stones, the remains, apparently, of a Roman fort. It dominates the entire area of the castle and commands a magnificent view of the winding gorge. A large rock-cut, bottle-shaped pit can be seen in the floor of the tower; this was used as a grain silo. East of the tower the rock-cut moat is to be seen, cutting off the castle area from the spur. Beyond the first moat a second, smaller ditch was cut. Between the tower and the moat was a large stone rampart whose remains now lie in the ditch. The main gate of the castle was situated in this wall but its position is not clear. The Crusaders built the keep in a spot which, topographically, is the most vulnerable to penetration. *keep*

The chapel, dwelling chambers and keep were built chiefly in the castle's first period, at the end of the 12th century, but were enlarged in the 13th century.

YEḤI'AM - JUDIN

The remains of this Crusader stronghold form part of the fortified castle built by the Arab sheikh Dahar al-'Omar in the 1160's. The plan of the Crusader structure is not clear, but its remains include the foundations of the eastern central tower and also a series of vaults to the south-west. The castle stood where the road branched off, leading from Tibnin to Acre. The date of its construction is unknown. It seems to have stood in the domain of Mi'iliya and was transferred to the Teutonic Order with the rest of the domain. The traveller Burchard passed the place in 1283 and found the castle in ruins.

KH. AL-BURJ

A square tower on the road from Ramallah to Bir Zeit. Its Crusader name has not been preserved. Remains of the north and east walls of the tower stand to a height of 3 metres.

AL-BURJ NEAR LATRUN

A square tower on the direct highway from Lydda to the Beit Ḥoron ascent. Scholars have identified it as *Castellum Arnaldi* (see p. 314), but this identification does not agree with the historical accounts.

KH. BURJ A-TOT (TURRIS RUBEA, TURRICLEE)

A tower and village in the lordship of Caesarea. It was in possession of the Order of the Templars until 1189, when it passed to the Monastery of St. Mary Latina until 1248, and afterwards to the Hospitallers. The Crusader remains indicate a typical square tower of two storeys, of which the south wall survives, rising to a height of 15 metres, together with the foundations of a fortified courtyard.

Burj a-Tot, tower, interior of south wall

Part V CHURCHES AND
MONASTERIES

"The Holy Land flourished like a garden of delight with many regular clergy, religious persons, hermits, monks, canons, nuns, cloistered virgins dedicated to God, and chaste and holy widows, and breathed sweet perfume, as it were from roses, lilies and violets."—In these words Jacques de Vitry, Bishop of the city of Acre, described the place of religion and its ministrants in the life of the Crusader kingdom. There is no need to dwell at length upon the part played by faith in the creation of the Crusading movement, the depth of religious feeling and intense piety that were the heritage of the Crusaders. Their strong faith inured them to the toils of the journey and to the bloodshed of the battlefield; by virtue of this faith they wrought the most frightful of massacres and for its sake they achieved their aim—the redemption of the Holy Sepulchre.

No sooner had they reached the Holy Land than the Crusaders sought to give tangible expression to their piety by visiting the holy places, collecting the relics of saints, purifying and restoring ancient churches and embarking with all speed upon the erection of churches and monasteries throughout the length and breadth of the country: "Old churches were repaired, new ones were built; by the bounty of Princes and the alms of the faithful, monasteries of regular monks were built in fitting places; Parish priests, and all things appertaining to the service and worship of God, were properly and suitably established everywhere."[87]

building of new shrines

Within a short time of the conquest an attempt was made by the leaders of the Church to translate religious aspirations into political terms and to establish Jerusalem and the entire Holy Land as the domain of Christ's deputy on earth, the Pope, with its government in the hands of the papal representative, the Patriarch of Jerusalem. This attempt was of brief duration and failed, and the kingdom that was founded was a secular one, in which the only secular jurisdiction left to the Patriarch was over the Christian quarter of Jerusalem. The size of the domains of the other princes of the Church was likewise limited, compared with the number and size of the domains of the European prelates. The Crusader kingdom contained only two ecclesiastical seigneuries, the archbishopric of Nazareth and the bishopric of Lydda, small in territorial extent. But the limited political power of the Church did not prevent the concentration into its hands of economic power, principally by the acquisition of tracts of landed property.

secular jurisdiction

ecclesiastical seigneuries

Throughout the entire Crusader period the churches and large monasteries received grants of land and gifts of revenue from the kings and the barons. These grants were not limited to the territory of the kingdom; many of the churches of the Holy Land held extensive landed property in European countries, while the following figures demonstrate the size of their landed property within the realm: the Church of the Holy Sepulchre owned ninety villages in the country;

landed property

the Monastery of the Valley of Jehosaphat owned forty-eight; that of Mount Zion twenty-eight; Mt. Tabor twenty-four.

The establishment of the kingdom brought complicated problems relating to the determination of the boundaries of dioceses and to the location of the Sees. The Holy Land was divided into ecclesiastical dioceses according to a division *dioceses* settled in the Byzantine period (4th–5th centuries). The ruin of the centres of population and the emergence of new ones caused the shifting of Sees and the creation of new ones. Thus the seat of the Archbishop of Galilee was transferred from Beit Shean to Nazareth, and new Sees were placed at Bethlehem and Hebron. Certain Sees were completely abolished, "lest," in the words of Jacques de Vitry, "the dignity of a bishop should be made cheap."

In 1111 Pope Pascal II gave his pledge to King Baldwin I that any area conquered by him would be ecclesiastically subject to the Patriarch of Jerusalem. In the light of this declaration the northern bishoprics of the kingdom, Sidon, Beirut, Acre and Banias, were handed to the Patriarch of Jerusalem, although they belonged, according to the traditional division, to the Archbishopric of Tyre, subject to the Patriarchate of Antioch. When Tyre was captured, these Sees were returned to the Archbishopric of Tyre, which also became subject to Jerusalem. Under the Patriarch of Jerusalem there were four Metropolitans: the Archbishop of Tyre; the Archbishop of Nazareth with one suffragan, the Bishop of Tiberias; the Archbishop of Caesarea with one suffragan, the Bishop of Sebaste; the Archbishop of Petra (Karak) with one suffragan, the Greek bishop of Sinai. The Bishops of Lydda, Bethlehem and Hebron were directly under the Patriarch.

There were no bishops at Jaffa, which was subject to the Prior and Canons of the Church of the Holy Sepulchre, or at Nablus, which was under the Abbot of *monasteries* the Abbey of *Templum Domini* (the Mosque of the Dome of the Rock). The Priors and Abbots of the large monasteries were immediately subordinated to the Patriarch. They were: St. Lazarus at Bethany (Benedictine nuns); St. Mary Latina at Jerusalem (Benedictines); Mount Zion (Augustines); Mount of Olives (Augustines); St. Samuel (Nabi Samwil—Premonstratensians); *Templum Domini* (the Dome of the Rock, Augustines); St. Mary Jehosaphat (Benedictines). The Monastery of Mt. Tabor was theoretically under the discipline of the Archbishopric of Nazareth.

In addition to the large monasteries there were a considerable number of smaller ones, such as that of Palmarea, near Haifa (Cluniac); St. Brocard, St. George de Lebeyne, the monastery of the Three Shades near Lydda; St. Catherine de Montjisart at Tel Gezer; St. Habacuc, near Lydda (Premonstratensians); St. Joseph of Arimathea, at Rantis near Lydda; St. John of the Desert at 'Ein Karem; and Quarantene, at Jebel Quruntul near Jericho. There were also a number of Greek monasteries in the Wilderness of Judea and other places (Tira, Beit Govrin, Sinai, etc.).

number of The number of churches known to us from historical sources is very large. *churches* There were about twenty-seven in Jerusalem, about forty in Acre, and about twelve in Tyre. Even townships possessed two or three each, and every settlement with a Frankish population had a parish church, while numerous churches were scattered in places of pilgrimage. Remains of more than thirty Crusader churches have survived. In terms of status and use these can be classified as follows:

Cathedral Churches: Sebaste, Caesarea, Lydda, Hebron, Bethlehem, Nazareth, Beirut, Sidon, Tyre. These were all on the sites of churches which had survived in whole or in part from the Byzantine period, several of which the Crusaders enlarged or rebuilt, using parts of the remaining structures, or building materials, from the ancient churches. Cloisters were added to all of them, for the use of the Canons of the Cathedral. Remains of such cloisters have been preserved at Sebaste, Bethlehem and Lydda. *cathedrals*

Parish Churches: al-Bira, Qubeiba, Beit Nuba, Ramla, Nablus, Gaza, Jezreel, Qalansuwa. Yavne, 'Atlit, Sinjil and churches at Jerusalem and Acre. As may readily be seen, these are scattered throughout the country. They are to be found wherever there was a Frankish congregation, whether in village, townlet *parish churches* or town. Some were built on the foundations of Byzantine churches, as in Gaza, Ramla, Nablus, and some were newly erected by the Franks when they settled, as in al-Bira, Qubeiba, Qalansuwa, Sinjil, Jezreel.

Abbey-Churches and Chapels: Nabi Samwil, Mt. Tabor, St. Brocard, St. *abbeys* George de Lebeyne and the abbey-churches of the large Jerusalem monasteries. These were among the largest and most splendid of the Crusader churches. Only a small number have survived outside Jerusalem, and in those that remain the other monastery buildings, the monks' quarters, refectories and the like, have disappeared completely.

Castle Chapels: Montfort, Beit Govrin, 'Atlit, Belvoir, Karak, Montreal, had *castle chapels* chapels which served the needs of the garrisons. These are of small dimensions and austere in style.

Churches at places of pilgrimage: Jacob's Well, 'Ein Karem, Abu Ghosh, Emmaus. These were also scattered throughout the country, each connected *places of* with some event in the life of Jesus, the apostles or the saints of the church. Some *pilgrimage* are in centres of settlement and some in remote and isolated localities. Most were built on the foundations of ancient churches. The ministrants were monks or nuns.

Classification of the churches in terms of general architectural plan reveals two principal types:

Buildings with nave and single apse: Marissa (St. Anne), Beit Govrin, Mont- *single nave* fort, St. Borchard, Qalansuwa, 'Atlit (town), 'Imwas, Sinjil.

Buildings with nave, two aisles and three apses (basilicas): Abu Ghosh, al-Bira, Hebron, Yavne, Gaza, 'Atlit (castle), Nabi Samwil, Caesarea, Qubeiba, *basilicas* Tsipori, Ramla, Lydda, Nablus, Nazareth, Mt. Tabor, Beit Nuba, 'Ein Karem and most of the churches in Jerusalem.

Most of the Crusader churches, therefore, were built on the basilical plan, that is with the interior divided by two rows of columns or piers into three parts, the nave and the aisles, terminating at the eastern end with a narrow choir beyond which were three apses. The main entrance was on the west. The ceiling of the nave was higher than that of the aisles and its walls were pierced by clerestory windows. Although the general plan was uniform, there were variations in design and building details. Most of the Crusader churches had an eastern wall or *chevet* with right-angled corners, straight or with square projections. Only a few, at Caesarea, Lydda, Nabi Samwil, Sebaste, 'Atlit (castle) and St. Anne (Jerusalem), possess a rounded or polygonal *chevet*. A transept projecting from the line of the northern and southern walls was rare; the only churches with projecting transepts are at Nabi Samwil and Jacob's Well. All the churches were roofed with groined vaults in the nave and aisles, only Ramla and Nazareth being exceptional in this respect; here the nave has a pointed barrel-vault. This uniform vaulting differs from the churches found in Syria, which frequently have barrel-vaulted naves.

architectural details

The pointed arch is found in all Crusader churches; the arches were flat and wide in the early churches, higher and narrower in the later ones. The columns, colonettes and piers were of various forms—round, square and cruciform. There were also cruciform piers with attached round columns. Some churches have columns, unusual in that, just below the capital, they bend back and never reach the ground. Such columns are characteristic of buildings of the middle of the 12th century, and are common in the Church of the Holy Sepulchre, in St. James' (Armenians), St. Anne's, and St. Mary of the Germans in Jerusalem and also at Abu Ghosh, Ramla, Belvoir and Nabi Samwil.

carvings

Most of the carvings of the Crusader churches consist of bas-relief renderings of foliage or geometrical motifs; a few are of human figures. The commonest motif is acanthus foliage, which had been characteristic of the art of Palestine ever since the Hellenistic period, and it is found adorning the column-capitals and archivolts of portals and windows. Also frequent is the godroon motif, resembling the backs of books in a row, and used to adorn the archivolts of portals and windows. Carvings of human figures are also preponderantly in bas-relief, and few are sculptured in the round. The most beautiful and well-known carvings are to be found on the column capitals of the portal of the Church of the Holy Sepulchre in Jerusalem. Some churches were decorated with mosaic work, as in the Church of the Holy Sepulchre, and the Church of the Nativity. In others there were frescoes, as at Abu Ghosh and Mt. Tabor.

secondary use of Byzantine churches

Many of the Crusader churches were reused Byzantine churches, and in some, such as St. Anne at Marissa, 'Imwas, Nabi Samwil, Nazareth, Nablus, Tayiba, Gaza, the Byzantine buildings were in large part preserved and were merely restored by the Crusaders. In others only traces of the Byzantine churches have survived, and the Crusaders made secondary use of the foundations and building materials, as at St. Anne in Jerusalem, Beit Govrin, Qubeiba, Sebaste, Mt. Tabor, Ramla, and Lydda. The churches built by the Crusaders in the first half of the 12th century belong to the building style termed "Romanesque", which developed in Europe in the 9th–10th centuries and reached its peak in the 11th and early 12th century.

Romanesque style

In the Kingdom of Jerusalem the influence of the architecture of the region of Burgundy and southern France was felt more than that of any other school of Romanesque art. The Crusader structures built in the first two generations of the occupation excel in their massive simplicity and in the sparseness of their decoration. In the first period of their settlement the Crusaders built only what was most essential, and did not have at their disposal the means and time to erect splendid and complex buildings. The architectural result obtained is by no means negligible; they attained perfection and splendour by way of simplicity and austerity. The visitor to the churches of Abu Ghosh and St. Anne in Jerusalem cannot but sense the sanctity which shrouds the dim interiors, and his attention is not diverted by decorations and ornamentation but is drawn at once to the simple altar standing beneath the cupola of the apse.

As the kingdom was consolidated, as its economic and military position improved and as the Franks adapted themselves to the art and architecture of the Byzantine and Moslem east, a change took place in the style of the churches and their decoration; paintings and sculpture became more numerous. The peak *Gothic style* period in the art of church architecture in the Holy Land in the 12th century coincides with the reigns of Baldwin III and Amalric. Between the years 1150 and 1160 the church of Sebaste was built. Here the builders used rib-vaulting and buttresses for the first time, so inaugurating in the country the transition period from the Romanesque to Gothic styles. In the 1160's several of the principal churches were adorned with mosaics and frescoes executed by Byzantine artists. The development of the Gothic building style in the Holy Land was interrupted by the battle of Hattin and the conquest of the greater part of the country. But at the beginning of the 13th century a number of fine Gothic churches were built in the country's maritime towns. Regrettably the overwhelming majority of them were destroyed, but the churches of Cyprus, built in the same period, and the remains of churches at Acre and 'Atlit, may serve as examples of the high artistic standard in the Holy Land just before the end of the Crusader period.

ABU GHOSH-CASTELLUM EMMAUS (FONTENOID)

The village of Abu Ghosh or, to give it its ancient name, Qaryat al-'Anab, was from ancient times a station on the road from the Shephela to Jerusalem. A *site of a Roman* small spring, rising at the lowest part of the plain alongside the route, served *fort* both wayfarers and the village which developed there. A Roman fort was built around the springs in the 1st century A.D. holding a garrison from the Tenth Legion Fretensis. In the 9th century a large caravanserai was erected for wayfarers. The Persian traveller, Nasir Ḥusru, who passed through Abu Ghosh in 1042 on his way to Jerusalem, described it thus: "In the village of Qaryat al-'Anab

347

Abu Ghosh, church and village

caravanserai

is a fine spring with sweet water rising from beneath the rock; about it they have placed troughs and also erected small buildings to lodge wayfarers."[88]

Emmaus of the Gospels

The Catholic tradition, not accepted in Jerusalem prior to the end of the 9th century, identified the village with Emmaus, where Jesus revealed himself to his disciples, as described in Luke 24:13: "And behold, two of them went that same day to a village called Emmaus, which was from Jerusalem about threescore furlongs."

The identification was based on the Latin version of the Bible, the Vulgate, and the tradition was current only amongst the Latins. The eastern churches identified Emmaus with the ancient town of that name which became famous in the wars of the Maccabees, and which was known as Nicopolis in the Roman and Byzantine periods; this is 'Imwas in the Valley of Ayalon. The difference in identification arises from a variation between texts; while the Vulgate states that the village is 60 furlongs from Jerusalem, several Greek texts place it at 160 furlongs from the city.

The first distance suits Abu Ghosh, while the latter corresponds approximately to the distance from Jerusalem to Emmaus-Nicopolis. Differing identifications are revealed in the accounts of two travellers who visited the country at roughly the same period, one being the Latin Theodorich, the other the Greek John Phocas. Theodorich visited Emmaus during a perambulation of the holy places near Jerusalem; first he visited the Monastery of the Cross and then went to 'Ein Karem, Tsova (Belmont) and thence: . . . "near these mountains [of Belmont]

348

is the castle of Emmaus, which the moderns call Fontenoid."[89] John Phocas, on the other hand, described his route from Jerusalem to the coast as going by Nabi Samwil (Armathem) "and at a distance of about seven miles or rather more beyond it, is the large city of Emmaus, built upon a rising ground."[90] From Emmaus, Phocas went on to Ramla (Ramplea).

The identification of Emmaus with Abu Ghosh caused the identification of Modi'in, birthplace of the Maccabees, to be shifted from its correct position north of the Valley of Ayalon near Emmaus-Nicopolis, to Tsova (Belmont) close to Abu Ghosh. Crusader churches existed both at Emmaus-Abu Ghosh and at Emmaus-Nicopolis. In the middle of the 13th century Christian pilgrims were prohibited from moving freely in the area of Jerusalem and were forced to go up to the city by the road through Beit Nuba, Qubeiba and Nabi Samwil. As a result they were unable to visit several holy places near the city. The Frankish tradition of Emmaus was transferred, like other traditions, from the village which could not be visited, to Qubeiba, which was situated on the permitted route, and has survived there to the present day.

transfer of tradition

The village of Abu Ghosh thus went unmentioned for centuries in the accounts of pilgrims, although the Latins returned to Abu Ghosh in the 14th century and set up a church and a hostel there. The latter was destroyed in 1489. In the 16th century the pilgrims reverted to the highway by way of Latrun and Bab al-Wad to Jerusalem, whereupon a new tradition took root at Abu Ghosh, identifying the village with 'Anatoth, where the Prophet Jeremiah was born. In recent times the monks of Abu Ghosh have reverted to the name of the "Fountain of Emmaus", although most Catholics adhere to the tradition connecting Emmaus with Qubeiba.

later history

The Frankish identification of Abu Ghosh with Emmaus, clear in the travel-books, is far from clear in the charters. In those of the Crusader epoch both Abu Ghosh and 'Imwas are known by the name Emmaus, and the fact that both places were in the hands of the Hospitallers further complicates the issue.

Abu Gosh– Emmaus in contemporary charters

Robert of Sinjil *(de Casale Sti Egidii)* made over *"terra Emaus"*[91] to the Hospitallers in 1141 and, by an agreement between the Order and the Church of the Holy Sepulchre, the latter was to receive a half-tithe from this area. The agreement mentions lands and other Casalia in the hills adjacent to Emmaus. One of the Casalia is Huldre, Ḥulda in the Shephela south-west of 'Imwas. The document leaves no doubt that the land of Emmaus was the land in the northern Valley of Ayalon. The fact that the Order of Hospitallers entertained certain claims upon *Castellum Arnaldi,* which is Yalu close to 'Imwas, provides supplementary evidence that this area was in their hands.

In 1168 *Castellum Emmaus* was mentioned in another Hospitaller domain extending west of Jerusalem and including Aqua Bella, near Abu Ghosh. The names of the other points referred to in this document[92] permit no doubt that Abu Ghosh is here intended. A Commander of Emmaus is alluded to among the functionaries of the Order of Hospitallers in a third document, dated 1186. Most scholars do not distinguish between the two places called Emmaus, stating that

site of the Hospitaller Commandery was at 'Imwas

349

the same place is meant. Hence they note that the Commandery of the Hospitallers was at Abu Ghosh. This location of the Order's centre at the mountain village cannot be reconciled with the information that Tsova (Belmont) was another administrative centre under a castellan. As the close proximity of two such centres is unacceptable, the Hospitaller Commandery should be placed at 'Imwas rather than Abu Ghosh, and it is to be supposed that *Castellum Emmaus* was subordinate to the Hospitaller centre at Tsova (Belmont).

Emmaus-Abu Ghosh was the last halting-place of the armies of the First Crusade before they proceeded to their destination—Jerusalem. The pilgrims, weary from their long journey, "passed the night peacefully in the enjoyment of abundant water and a goodly supply of the necessary food."[93]

last halting-place of First Crusade before Jerusalem

While the Crusaders were at Abu Ghosh, envoys reached them from the Christian inhabitants of Bethlehem, asking for a Frankish force to protect them and the Church of the Nativity. Tancred set out at midnight at the head of a hundred horsemen, reaching Bethlehem, "six miles from Emmaus," at dawn.

Abu Ghosh, church (Plan)

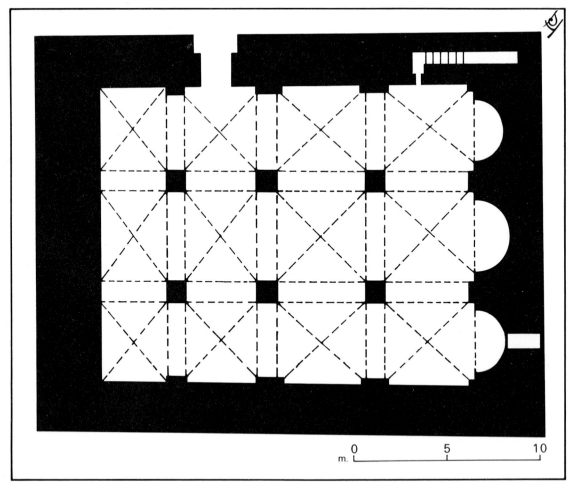

0   5   10
m.

Emmaus is not mentioned in the chronicles of the period, except during the *Third Crusade* "Third Crusade." In the one of the razzias conducted from Richard's camp at Beit Nuba (1192), the king reached Emmaus.

The Crusading age has left here one of the most beautiful Romanesque churches in the Holy Land; its structure, which was not destroyed by the Moslems, was used first as a mosque and then as a stable. The French consul at Constantinople, the Marquis de Vogüe, who investigated the churches of the country, obtained it from the Turks in 1873; it was restored and reconsecrated in 1907. The church appears to have been partly built on the foundations of a Roman fort, some of the stones of its walls being taken from the ruins of the fort.

The plan of the building is that of a "simple basilica", a nave and two aisles, *description of* terminating in three apses built with a flat eastern wall or *chevet*. Three rows of *church* square pillars divide the interior into four bays. The hall is 20 metres long and 15 metres wide. The northern wall is 2.80 metres thick, the western 3.70 metres, and the entire church is roofed by a groined vault. The arcades dividing the nave from the aisles have pointed arches. The vault of the nave is higher than that of the aisles, and rests on pointed arches supported by short, bent columns with capitals having a double-leafed design. The church is lit by a narrow window in the central apse, a large one with four rounded arches in the west wall of the nave, and by rows of windows in the north and south walls. The entrance is from the north. On the north wall are obliterated frescoes, although at the beginning of the century paintings could still be made out over the apses. They are Byzantine in style, but the inscriptions beneath them are in Latin. There is a crypt beneath the eastern part of the church, also ending in three apses. A spring, the Spring of Emmaus, rises in the middle of the crypt, its water being collected in a marble basin. Red painted stars can still be seen on the walls and ceiling of the crypt.

The exterior walls of the church are constructed of stones of various sizes, roughly dressed and partly bossed, mainly at the corners. They carry numerous mason's marks. The joints are not parallel. The courtyard of the building is strewn with relics of Roman times, including the engraved badges and inscriptions of the Tenth Legion. To the east of the church are remains of an Arab caravanserai, and in the close vicinity buildings of the Crusader period have been found, among them a hall and a watch tower.

DEIR AL-ASAD-ABBEY OF ST. GEORGE DE LEBEYNE

A Benedictine abbey was built in the first third of the 12th century, near the village of al-B'ina (Frankish St. George de Lebeyne), in central Galilee. The *12th century* origin of the tradition upon which the abbey and the village were named is unknown. However, late Frankish sources place there the birthplace of St.

George. Two abbots of St. George are mentioned in the documents, one in the year 1140 and the other in the year 1160[94]. The area around the village was called *"Terra Sancti Georgii"* and belonged to a small fief in the royal domain of Acre. The abbey also owned large tracts of land. In 1179, part of the fief of St. George was given by the king to Joscelin III and thereafter was included in the fief of Mi'ilya (Chastiau dou Rei). It was captured by Saladin in 1187, but

13th century

was again in the hands of the Franks at the beginning of the 13th century: in the 1220's the abbey was inhabited by monks. "From Saphet to St. George five leagues. There is a church of Black Monks."[95] In 1220, the Teutonic Order acquired one third of the fief of St. George, as part of the transaction that gave them Mi'ilya. The abbey was captured by Baybars in the 1260's and destroyed. In 1271, Prince Edward of England, later King Edward I, attacked the village of St. George and returned laden with much booty.

Burchard (1283) mentioned the "village called Sangeor where this saint is born. This stands in an exceedingly fat, fertile and beauteous valley, among hills."[96] The tradition of St. George was kept by the Moslems who called the

16th century

ruined abbey "Al Khadr" (the "evergreen", the Arabic name for both Elijah and St. George). In the middle of the 16th century the ruin was given by the Sultan Suleiman the Magnificent to a Moslem holy man from Baghdad called al-Asad (the lion), who settled in it with his family. Asad died in 1569 and was buried near the abbey. Afterwards the name of the village which sprang up around the abbey was changed to Deir al-Asad (the monastery of the lion). The Arabs still call a cave near the village al-Khadr. The ruin of the abbey is one of the most impressive of its kind in Palestine. The structure consists of a church,

Deir al-Asad
(St. George
de Lebeyne),
abbey, south side

a cloister and a tower. The church is of the basilical type with a nave 5 metres wide and two aisles 2.5 metres wide. It was divided into three bays and terminated with three apses, now destroyed. The aisles and the nave had groin-vaulting, supported on square piers. The capitals of the piers are simple, without relief. There are three portals on the western side. The central, leading to the nave, is larger and the two side portals are smaller. Three lancet windows in the southern and northern walls illuminated the interior. There were three more windows in the western wall, above the portals.

description

The cloister is situated north and west of the church. The entrance was from the south, where a broad pointed-arch portal still exists. It leads to a small courtyard on the north of which a barrel-vaulted hall, 20 metres long, lies intact. East of the courtyard is a series of vaults, abutting onto the western wall of the church. North-west of the main building stands a square tower. The walls were built with small, regular ashlar with bossed blocks at the corners. The piers, columns, arches and cornices were very elegantly carved. Most of the area is still inhabited by Arab families, who have partitioned the buildings.

MOUNT CARMEL
THE MONASTERY OF ST. BROCHARD

Mount Carmel has been regarded as a holy mountain from early times and many traditions are associated with it. Its name, "God's Vineyard", is synonymous

353

with fertility. Its tangled woods rising above the coastal plain and the Bay of Acre, its numerous caverns and almost impenetrable reaches—all these have made it a dwelling-place and centre of activity for men of God, monks and *earlier history* recluses, whether of the monotheistic faiths or of the pagan religions. The mountain's chief claim to sanctity had been by virtue of its ties with Elijah the Prophet, and several localities (Muḥraqa, the Altar of Elijah, Elijah's Cave, Elijah's Spring) are held sacred because of their associations with him and his deeds.

Christian monks settled on the mountain at the dawn of Christianity. In the year 412 John, Patriarch of Jerusalem, gave a Rule to the Hermits of Carmel. Numerous Christian saints, such as St. Spiridion and St. Euthymius, dwelt here and Benedictine monks established a monastery on the mountain, called St. Margaret.

Most of the monks who lived there dwelt in solitude in caves, neither organized in orders nor under any fixed Rule. The Carmelite Order was founded in the middle of the 12th century. Tradition holds that the Prophet Elijah appeared in a dream to a priest of Calabria called Berthold (later canonized), and bade him *beginning of
Carmelite
settlement* go to the sacred mountain and set up a monastery there. The priest sought the aid of Aimery of Limoges, Patriarch of Antioch, then in Jerusalem because he had fled from Reynald of Châtillon, Prince of Antioch. Aimery approached King Baldwin III and the Patriarch of Jerusalem, who assisted Berthold in estab-

St. Brochard, chapel and hermit's cave

lishing his monastery. The spot chosen was above Elijah's Cave, on Cape Carmel, where remains of an ancient church had been found. The monastery was named after the Blessed Virgin, and a defensive wall and cells were built for the ten monks who assembled here.

The monastery was visited in 1185 by John Phocas, who related that Berthold had "built a small defensive wall, a tower and a small church, had gathered some ten monks and now dwelt in this holy place."[97] In 1187 the monastery was destroyed by Saladin after the battle of Hattin. After the Third Crusade (1192), the Carmelite monastery was rebuilt, but was moved from Elijah's Cave to Naḥal Siaḥ (Wadi Saiaḥ), south of the village of Kababir. The builder of the new monastery was St. Brochard, who succeeded St. Berthold as head of the establishment. St. Berthold himself may have been privileged to witness the restoration as he was reputed to have died only in 1200 at the age of 115. *building of a new monastery*

The site selected for the monastery had a number of advantages: two springs rise from the streambed, the soil is fertile, it is remote from the highway and hidden from wayfarers. After its restoration Brochard asked that the Order be granted a fixed Rule, and in 1207 Albert, Patriarch of Jerusalem, granted this "to our dear son Brochard and to the very dear brothers, the other hermits, who live under his authority near the Spring of Elijah on Mount Carmel."[98] The Rule was ratified and then modified several times during the 13th century. St. Brochard died in 1231, but the monastery continued to exist and its monks grew in number. It was described in the late 1220's as follows: *Rule of Carmelites ratified*

"On the slope of the same mountain is a very fair place and delicious, where dwell the Latin hermits, who are called Brethren of Carmel; where is a little church of Our Lady, and throughout this part there are plenty of good waters which issue from the very rock of the mountain."[99]

Two other sacred sites are noted at this period: one is the Church of St. Margaret at the top of Cape Carmel, where the Carmelite monastery is today, over the Latin monastery of St. Elie; the other is the birthplace of St. Denys, Francheville, whose whereabouts have not been verified.

In 1243 Simon Stock, an Englishman from Kent, was appointed head of the monastery; he instituted the Order's cloak (scapulaire). King Louis IX of France visited him in 1252. It was at this time that the monks rebuilt the Monastery of St. Elie near Elijah's Cave. The Monasteries of *Saiadj,* that is St. Brochard, and of *"Mar Elias"* (St. Elie) are among the lands referred to in the agreement between the Sultan Qalaun and the Franks. Burchard of Mount Sion visited the Monastery of St. Elie at this period and stayed there. The end of the Carmelites in Palestine came in 1291 when the Mamluks attacked the monastery and butchered the monks, who went to their death singing the "Salve Regina". The gorge is known among Christians as "the Valley of the Martyrs" in their memory. *end of Crusader period*

The monastery is built on the southern slope of Naḥal Siaḥ, 2 kilometres from where the wadi opens into the Carmel Plain. The gorge is rich in water and its soil is fertile. West of the monastery rises the spring of 'Ein Siaḥ which provides irrigation for a large orchard. Within the confines of the monastery the spring of *description*

355

al-Faraj rises from a rocky cranny; its water is collected in a small rock-cut reservoir. Opposite the monastery is the Hermits' Cave, which has two levels; the lower "hall" is circular with a great rock pillar at its centre supporting the ceiling. Seats are hewn around the walls, and rock-cut steps lead to the upper level which resembles a verandah.

The central structure of the monastery is large and majestic; its western wall climbs the wadi slope, while the northerly is constructed along the stream bed. The entrance gate, with a rounded arch in the west wall, leads into a small court behind which is another gate, today blocked. South of the gate a stairway leads to a large entrance hall, 18 metres long with a barrel-vaulted roof, whose walls have been preserved to their full height. The hall is lit by small apertures in the walls. At its southern end a staircase ascends by a broad vaulted corridor to the upper level of the monastery, where there are remains of various structures. The most important of these is a chapel, whose walls have been restored. It consists of a nave without aisles, divided into three bays, and an apse. The chapel, built of soft limestone, is 18 metres long and six metres wide. In the middle of the south wall is the opening of a circular stairwell whose steps, leading to the roof, have been restored.

In the centre of the upper level of the monastery is a small chapel, built in the mid-19th century by the Carmelites.

MOUNT QUARANTENE
(MOUNT OF TEMPTATION)

According to Christian tradition, the mountain overlooking the oasis of Jericho and the Jordan Rift is the place where Satan tempted Jesus during the forty days in the wilderness (Luke 4:1–3). As early as the first centuries A.D. hermits dwelt on the mountain and a chapel was erected on the spot. In the Crusader period a monastery was set up at Jebel Quruntul, subordinated to the canons of the Church of the Holy Sepulchre. The Patriarch of Jerusalem, William, gave the monastery the tithes of the city of Jericho in 1136. It also possessed rights to the use of the mills at the foot of the mountain.

Mount of Temptation

Many pilgrims visited the place and it is described in several *Itineraria*. The fullest account was given by Theodorich, who visited it in 1172: "At the top is a gate . . . and when you have passed through it and proceed a little farther, you will find a chapel built on to a grotto, made by human labour and dedicated to our Lady."[100]

Further up the mountain were two more gates and past them a small chapel where a saint called Pilgrimus was buried. Anchorites dwelt in the numerous caves scattered on the slope of the mountain, at the top of which was a Templar castle.

Templar castle

Theodorich wrote:

357

St. Brochard, monastery, staircase

"The crest of Mount Quarantana and its subterranean caves are full of victuals and arms belonging to the Templars who can have no stronger fortress or one better suited for the annoyance of the infidels."[100]

MOUNT TABOR

site of worship and war

The dome-shaped mountain, which rises so unexpectedly to a height of 588 metres above sea level and 400 metres over its surroundings, was a cult place and military position from ancient times. Its summit commands broad views from the mountains of Upper Galilee to the mountains of Gilboa and from the mountains of Golan and Gilead to the Carmel range. The wide prospect not only brought men nearer to God, but also ensured military control over most of the routes in the north of the country. It is not surprising, therefore, that the summit of Mount Tabor should be rich in the remains of various religions and that, from the days of Barak ben Avinoam down to those of Napoleon, the fate of the area should have been decided in battles fought on its slopes or in its vicinity. In the Crusader epoch, too, the mountain served as the setting both for worship and for war.

From the 3rd century, Mount Tabor was believed to have been the place of the Transfiguration of Jesus (Mark, 9).

Tancred builder of monasteries

When Tancred the Norman reached the mountain in the summer of 1099 he found a Greek monastery on its summit dedicated to the prophet Elijah (St. Elye). Tancred, who had just set up his capital at Tiberias, established another monastery on the summit called St. Salvator, and gave it to the Benedictines. A short time afterwards yet another monastery was built, dedicated to Moses (St. Moise).

The Russian traveller Daniel, who visited the mountain in 1106–7, left the following description:

"A rocky platform is to be found on the summit of Tabor, on the east side, and here took place the Transfiguration of our Lord Jesus. Today a great church is to be seen there, dedicated to the Transfiguration. Near it in the same place is another church dedicated to the holy prophet Moses and a third to the holy prophet Elijah. The entire place of the Transfiguration is surrounded by thick walls built of dressed stone blocks, with doors of iron. Water is found in plenty on this mountain. Fields of wheat are to be seen there, as well as vines and all sorts of vegetables."[101]

destroyed in 1113

In 1113 the monasteries on the mountain were destroyed by a Moslem force commanded by Maudud, who had invaded Galilee. A year or two later, the monks returned and restored the ruins. The Benedictines, who meanwhile had accepted the discipline of Cluny, began an extensive agricultural development in the villages of their large domain. This affected more especially the growth of Dabburiya (Buria) which lies at the foot of the mountain.

358

The Moslems again invaded the district of Mt. Tabor in 1182. The village of Dabburiya was attacked and most of its inhabitants were killed or taken prisoner. The monasteries themselves were attacked in July. The Moslems ascended to the summit of the mountain, "a feat hitherto unknown", to use William of Tyre's own words, plundered the Greek monastery of St. Elye and also tried to break into the Latin monastery, "but", wrote William, "the monks with all their household and the people from the village nearby retired within the monastery, which was defended by a wall with towers",[102] and after a valiant defence they successfully repulsed the Moslems.

invasion of 1182

Some three years after these events Mount Tabor was visited by the Greek traveller John Phocas. He described two monasteries, that of the Transfiguration belonging to the Latins and the other belonging to the Greeks. In the former was an altar "surrounded with a brazen railing; --- there is to be seen a boss of exceeding whiteness, whereon is carved the figure of the Holy Cross, and from which an unspeakable perfume is breathed forth, and delights the senses of those who visit it."[103]

After the battle of Hattin (1187), Mount Tabor was taken without resistance and its monks banished. The second phase in its history in the Crusader period began in 1211. The Franks having conducted repeated campaigns into the heart of Galilee, Sultan al-'Adil, the brother of Saladin, realized the need to secure control of the area. In that year he established a huge fortress on Tabor, the walls of which surrounded the entire summit. The Moslems were thus able to control the roads used by the Franks from Acre eastwards, which passed the foot of the mountain, and to present a direct threat to their capital. The Moslems devoted much effort to the work of fortification and the sultan supervised the builders in person.

building of a Saracen castle (1211)

The Franks made no attempt to interfere with the work, though the danger it represented was clear to them. Only six years after the fortress had been completed and manned did they try to capture it. In 1217 the Fifth Crusade reached the country. After a long-range foray to Ḥauran and the Jordan Valley, the leaders of the Crusade decided to direct their efforts to the capture of Tabor, whose seizure would open the way to the reconquest of the whole of Galilee.

At the end of November 1217, the Frankish troops set out from Acre under the command of Jean de Brienne, King of Jerusalem. They climbed the mountain from the west, clashing with bodies of Moslem troops which had sallied out from the fortress to prevent their ascent of the steep path. After an initial Frankish victory the Moslems retired behind its mighty walls, against which the Franks were helpless as they had brought no siege machinery. They attempted to scale the walls with ladders, but were driven back. After a few days they abandoned their attack and retreated to Acre. The campaign had not attained its objective, but al-Mu'azzam, al-'Adil's son, decided to evacuate Mount Tabor and to demolish its fortifications, since its maintenance and garrisoning tied down forces beyond his capacity; had it fallen complete into Frankish hands they would have gained a vantage point which would have enabled them to control the whole of

Frankish attempt to capture Tabor failed (1217)

Moslems demolish their castle

359

Lower Galilee. For long months al-Mu'azzam's troops were engaged in demolishing the towers and breaching the walls of the giant stronghold, retiring eastwards as soon as they had done so. The destruction of the fortress heralded a new Moslem strategy, the main feature of which was the demolition of every fortification in the north of the country which might become a strongpoint for the Crusaders. A year after the demolition of the fortress, al-Mu'azzam began the dismantling of the rest of the Galilean strongpoints, including Belvoir, Safed, Hunin and Qal'at Shaqif. The fortress remained in ruins until 1229, when it was *settlement by* settled by Hungarian monks who built themselves a small chapel. In 1241 the *Hungarian monks* place reverted to the Franks by the peace treaty of Richard of Cornwall. Six years later, in 1247, it was again captured by the Moslems and in 1255 restored to the Franks. The monks recovered their property, but could not defend it against the constant attacks of the Moslems.

The Hospitallers, viewing with envy the control of their rivals, the Templars, over the surroundings of Safed, cast their eyes upon Mount Tabor; not only did its military value attract them, but also, and perhaps principally, the monastery's rich possessions. The Grand Master of the Hospitallers petitioned Pope *ceded to the* Alexander IV for the cession of the mount and the monastery's properties to the *Hospitallers* Order. After the monks had confirmed that they were unable to hold it, the Pope gave the place to the Hospitallers in exchange for a specific undertaking on the part of the Order to fortify and garrison it with a force of forty knights. The strength represented by this number will become clear to us if we compare it with the number of knights quartered in the huge castle of Safed, where a force of fifty knights represented less than ten percent of the entire garrison.

We do not know how far the Hospitallers fulfilled their obligations, but it does appear that many repairs were made to the walls of the Ayyubid fortress. *evacuation* When the last test came in the year 1263, the defenders did not put up much *without fighting* resistance, and evacuated it without fighting. Baybars' troops completed the demolition of the walls and also destroyed the Latin and Greek monasteries.

From the accounts of the Russian Daniel, and William of Tyre, it is clear that in the 12th century the fortress on the mount was confined to the Latin monastery, while the Greek monastery was unfortified. Remains of the Crusader fortress, which according to the sources included walls, towers and an iron gate, are preserved around the Church of the Transfiguration at the southern side of the summit.

Burchard of Mount Sion visited the mount in 1283: "And there to this day are shown the ruins of three tabernacles or cloisters ... Moreover, there are exceeding great ruins of palaces, towers and regular buildings now lurking places for lions and other beasts. There is royal hunting to be had here."[104]

The Ayyubid fortress built by al-'Adil in 1211–1212 is one of the largest and strongest fortifications built in the Holy Land in the 13th century. It surrounds *description of* the entire summit of the mountain and the length of its ramparts is as much as *Saracen castle* 1 750 metres. We may note for comparison that the circumference of the walls of the castle of Safed, the most extensive of the castles in the Holy Land,

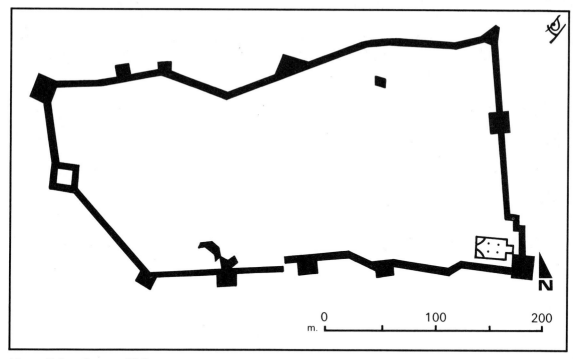

Mount Tabor, Saracen Wall

amounted to 850 metres. The fortifications of Mount Tabor are almost comparable in their circumference to those of the town of Caesarea, which encompassed 1,850 metres. The fortress consists of a high stout wall with ten square towers. The length of the north side is 580 metres, of the southerly 450 metres and of the easterly and westerly 250 metres. On the south, west and east a moat is cut in front of the wall, whose sides and base are battered, glacis-fashion. No moat was cut in the north sector of the enceinte, as the slope is here so steep as to make scaling impossible. For this reason only one tower was built on this side as against five on the south. The fortress had one gate on the west, the "Damascus Gate," over whose ruins the modern entry gate to the monastery area is built, known as the "Nazareth Gate"—in Arabic Bab al-Hawa or the "Gate of the Wind."

huge dimensions

The walls and towers are built of bossed stones in the Ayyubid style of the day, which resembles that of the Crusaders, but is a little rougher, as the boss was smoothed down with a pointed chisel. In the precincts of the mountain there are traces of numerous inscriptions indicating the date of construction of the fortress and the name of al-Mu'azzam, Sultan of Damascus. No signs of Crusader repairs have been found in the walls, which were destroyed by the Moslems in 1218; hence we may doubt the historical testimony that the fortress was rebuilt by the Hospitallers after 1255. The Order did indeed concentrate considerable military force here and made Tabor an administrative centre, but apparently

361

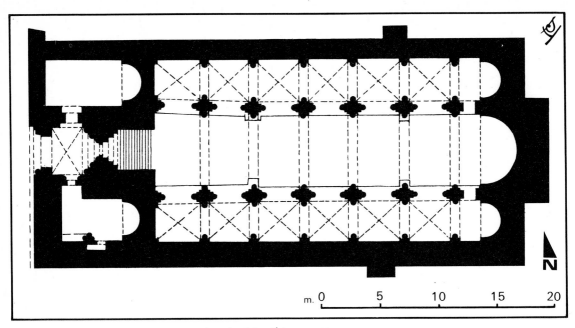

Mount Tabor, Church of St. Salvator (Plan)

church saw no point in reconstructing the huge circuit of the Ayyubid walls, and fortified itself within the area of the defended monastery in the south-eastern corner.

The Church of St. Salvator, or of the Transfiguration, built at the beginning of the 12th century and completely destroyed by Baybars, was rebuilt by the Franciscans in the present century. Remains of the original edifice comprise the crypt and the lower part of the outer walls. The Crusader church took the form of a nave and two aisles. $27\frac{1}{2}$ metres long, which ended in three apses. The central apse created a square projection *(chevet)* in the east wall, and the interior was divided into six bays. Below the main level is a crypt 28 metres long, at whose west end are two chapels, one dedicated to Moses and the other to the Prophet Elijah.

The Greek Orthodox monastery of Elijah is also built on the foundations of a Crusader church, which likewise had a hall with a nave and two aisles.

NABI SAMWIL
ST. SAMUEL DE MONTJOIE

The hill on which by tradition the Prophet Samuel was buried was known to the Franks as Montjoie, or the Hill of Joy. Situated on the main road from Beit Nuba through Qubeiba to Jerusalem, it was so called because the pilgrims caught their first glimpse of the Holy City from its summit. The tradition of the burial here of the Prophet Samuel took root as early as the Byzantine period and

Hill of Joy

362

a church was built on the hill top. Greek travellers identified it as Ramah (I Sam. 25:1) and the Latins as Silo (Shilo).

A monastery and church of the Order of Premonstratensians stood on the summit in the Crusader period. The place was given to the Order by Baldwin II (1118–1131) together with a broad domain including the entire tract at the foot of the hill, which stretched eastward to the Jerusalem–al-Bira (Mahomeria) road and southward to a point beyond Beit Iksa. The monks appear to have established a storehouse for the collection of produce, similar in plan to that of the Hospitallers at Qula. Its remains survive at a ruin known as al-Burj, on a hill south of Nabi Samwil. The church was erected in 1157 over the tomb of the Prophet Samuel, and a small Frankish settlement developed around it.

Premonstratensian monastery

Nabi Samwil was captured by Saladin in 1187 and during the campaigns of 1191 it was used as a rear base by the Moslems. In 1241 it seems to have returned to the Crusaders under Richard of Cornwall's peace treaty. The church remained in ruins until the beginning of the present century, when a mosque was set up in

Nabi Samwil, north aisle

its place. Considerable parts of the Crusader church remain in the present structure.

The original building, on the plan of a Latin cross, consisted of a nave 36 metres long and 8 metres wide. To the east of it is a transept 23 metres long. A circular apse was built, projecting from the east wall *(chevet)*. North of the nave was an annexe the same length as the nave, divided into three bays and roofed with groined-vaulting. Below the nave is a rock-cut crypt, with the cenotaph of the Prophet Samuel at its centre. The entrance to the crypt is from the northern annexe. The plan of the church of Nabi Samwil, with its projecting transept, is unusual among the Frankish churches of the Holy Land.

THE MONASTERIES OF THE WILDERNESS OF JUDEA

The desolate slopes of the Mountains of Judea, falling towards the Jordan Rift and the Dead Sea, have always been an abode of hermits, "those who have despised the world and its luxuries for the Kingdom of Heaven's sake, who endure its unendurable heat, and by means of quenchable fire quench that which is unquenchable."[105] In the 5th century A.D. a special type of ascetic organization developed in the Wilderness of Judea, the *Lavra*. Solitary anchorites settled in caves and cells near one another, in the proximity of the dwelling-place of some famous holy hermits. They retained their independence and their solitude, but met for prayer and common meals. The first teacher of the hermits of the *Lavrae* in the Wilderness of Judea was St. Euthymius of Melitene, who in 403 set up what was later to become the Monastery of St. Sabas (Deir Mar Saba). During the 5th century monasteries living under the Rule of St. Basil were also established in the desert. Most of the *Lavrae* were destroyed in 614, during the Persian invasion, but were restored after the brief reconquest of the country by the Byzantines. The Arab conquerors left the hermits of the Wilderness of Judea to themselves and their communities continued to exist. In the Crusader period a considerable number of hermits of European origin joined the hermitages, but most continued to belong to the oriental Greek Church. We shall sketch briefly the monasteries which existed in the Crusader period. The main writer to leave descriptions of them was the Greek monk, John Phocas of Crete, who showed a particular interest in the localities belonging to men of his own church.

KHAN AL-AḤMAR—ST. EUTHYMIUS

This monastery contains the tomb of St. Euthymius of Melitene, the teacher of the hermits who dwelt in the caves of the Wilderness of Judea. In the 12th century a number of Greek monks lived in the monastery which, according to John Phocas' account, was fortified by towers and walls. The monastery was destroyed in 1187 and at a later period was converted into a *khan* or caravanserai for the use of Moslem pilgrims on their way to the nearby Nabi Musa.

DEIR MAR SABA—ST. SABAS

The largest and most renowned monastery in the Judaean Wilderness was founded in 405 by St. Euthymius. His disciple, St. Sabas, set up on the spot the monastery buildings which were named after him. In 614 the monks were murdered by Chosroes the Persian and the monastery was destroyed. Restored in the Arab period, the monastery had forty monks in the Crusader period, including six who, according to John Phocas, "conversed directly with God". Besides these many dwelt in caves in the side of the Kidron gorge. The monastery enjoyed the special favour of the kings of Jerusalem and Queen Melisende granted to it villages and lands in the royal domain. The life of the monastery was not disturbed by Saladin, but in 1269 Baybars ordered it to be destroyed. It was called Deir a-Siq by the Moslems, after the reach of the Kidron gorge close by, and known by that name. According to a Moslem source three hundred monks dwelt there at the time of Baybars. The place was enlarged in the 1840's, with the help of the Russian government.

DEIR AL-QILT—ST. GEORGE DE CHOZIBA

This place was an abode of hermits as early as the 4th century A.D. John Phocas described it: "On the opposite side of the ravine is the monastery of Choziba, a thing not to be believed when described, and inspiring wonder when beheld; for the cells of the monks are the mouths of caves and the church itself and the cemetery are excavated out of solid rock---in this monastery I saw many holy men :.."[106]

The monastery was abandoned in 1187 and remained in ruins for seven hundred years. In 1880 Greek Orthodox monks returned thither and rebuilt it.

ST. THEODOSIUS

Deir ibn-'Ubaid, or Deir Dosi, lies beside the road from Jerusalem to Beit Saḥur. In the 12th century it was a monastery surrounded by walls and towers. John Phocas related that a church stood in the middle of the monastery, with a circular roof, and below it a grotto containing the tomb of Theodosius. Its Frankish name was *St. Theodosius Coenobiarcha de Laberria* ("of the desert"). In the year 1218, the Pope Honorius III confirmed to the abbot of that monastery the possession of properties which included a church, hospital, shops and oven in Jerusalem, hospitals in Ascalon, Jaffa and Cyprus, lands and two ships with free passage on all seas.

MONASTERIES OF THE JORDAN RIVER

The place in the Jordan River where Jesus was baptized (Matthew, 3) was one of the most important points of pilgrimage in the Holy Land. Theodorich related that sixty thousand pilgrims sojourned with him on the banks of the river. The pilgrims camped in "the Garden of Abraham," planted around the Spring of Elisha, where "they are protected on three sides by the garden itself from the ambuscades of the infidels; on the fourth side they are guarded by patrols of the Hospitallers and Templars."[107] They would go out from Elisha's Spring to the Jordan after sunset, each carrying a lamp.

place of baptism
The place of baptism was marked by a large stone on which Jesus was said to have stood when he was baptized. Nearby were four monasteries, of St. John the Baptist, St. Chrysostom, St. Gerasimus and the Archangel Michael. That of St. John the Baptist (Qasr al-Yahud), situated close to the place of baptism, is one of the oldest in the Holy Land and already existed in the 4th century A.D. It was twice destroyed in the Crusader epoch, once by the Moslems in the 1140's, and a second time in an earthquake, but was restored by the Byzantine emperor Manuel Comnenus, apparently in the 1160's. The emperor restored and adorned a number of sacred sites in the Crusader kingdom at that time, including the Church of the Nativity in Bethlehem. The monastery was fortified and occupied by a Templar garrison.

SABASTIYA-ST. JEAN DE SEBASTE

Shomron, the ancient capital of the Kingdom of Israel, magnificently adorned by Herod the Great, was no more than a small village known as *Sabastiya* when it was captured by Tancred the Norman in 1099. The remains of the splendid
remains of Herodian structures aroused the curiosity of the Crusaders and they were de-
Herodian scribed with enthusiasm by the chroniclers and travellers. Sebaste had been the
structures seat of a bishop from the beginning of the 4th century, and was renowned as a place of pilgrimage by virtue of an ancient tradition that the body of St. John the Baptist, who was beheaded at Machaerus, east of the Dead Sea, had been brought by his disciples and buried there. His body was burnt by Julian the Apostate and its ashes scattered, but the head was saved because it had already been taken to Alexandria, from there to Constantinople, and subsequently to
tomb of St. John Poitou in France. His finger was also saved from burning and likewise, accord-
the Baptist ing to some accounts, his arm. The tomb was located in the cave in which the

Sebaste, church, aerial view

prophets Elisha and Obadiah were also buried and, some said, Elizabeth and Zachariah, the parents of St. John the Baptist.

A Greek monastery stood at this spot before the arrival of the Crusaders, who restored the episcopal See to Samaria. The borders of the diocese coincided with the boundaries of the territory of the Byzantine Sebaste. The Crusaders built a church on the ruins of the ancient Byzantine church between 1150 and 1160. *Greek monastery* The Crusader church was one of the most magnificent in the Holy Land and was surpassed only the the Church of the Holy Sepulchre in Jerusalem. Near it were *bishop's palace* the bishop's palace and a large monastery.

Sebaste and its vicinity were noted for their fertility; Benjamin of Tudela wrote that Samaria was "a land of streams, gardens, orchards, vineyards and olives". Pilgrims visited Sebaste in large numbers and their contributions enriched the Church and the bishop, whose revenues from this source were so large that he *area noted for* bound himself to give a tithe of them to the Church of Mount Zion in Jerusalem. *fertility* The church was encrusted with gold and silver and hung with precious cloths. In 1187 Sebaste was captured by Saladin and the church became a mosque, never reverting to the Crusaders. However, the small Greek monastery, which had been there before the Crusader conquest, remained and Burchard of Mount Sion visited it as late as 1283, enjoying the hospitality of the monks.

description Remains of the Crusader church are to be found within the Arab village of Sebastiya, to the east of the ruins of the Israelite and Herodian city. It is built over the foundations of an ancient Byzantine church; the walls of the Crusader structure remain to a considerable height, and also remnants of its piers and columns. Steps lead from the south to a sunken court and thence to the main entrance in the west wall. The church is 50 metres long and 25 metres wide, its area being divided into a nave and two aisles terminating in a narrow transept with three apses to the east. The central apse, polygonal in form, projected from the line of the east wall *(chevet)*.

The church was built by European builders in the early Gothic style. In its centre is a chamber containing steps, leading to the sepulchral cavern where tradition had it that St. John the Baptist, his parents Elizabeth and Zachariah, and also the prophets Elisha and Obadiah were interred.

A mosque was built in the area of the transept in 1893. The nave and aisles were divided into six bays. Buttresses were built against the thin south wall to carry the weight of the vault, but such reinforcement was not required for the massive northern wall. The blocks of the walls are cut to uniform size and dressed; the joints are parallel and little mortar was used.

West and south of the church are remains of large vaults, thought to be part of the Latin cloister.

Part VI   THE FRANKISH WAY OF LIFE

THE DAILY LIFE OF THE FRANKS

The chroniclers of Crusader times did not concern themselves with describing the day-to-day life of the Frankish inhabitants of the Holy Land. The little that is known to us on the subject is culled from fragmentary information and from passing observations scattered broadly over contemporary literature. Consequently any attempt to reconstruct the way of life of the Franks, and to give an account of their diet, dress and leisure-time occupations, must encounter numerous difficulties. We can only describe some aspects of their daily human activity, and to do so we must avail ourselves to some extent of the accounts of the mode of living of their contemporaries in Europe and the East. An additional difficulty lies in the fact that the Crusader period extends over nearly two centuries; a long time, in the course of which pronounced changes took place in the ways of life and in material culture. The paucity of available information does not enable us to follow these changes in detail. Nevertheless one important phenomenon can be traced with great clarity, namely the process of "orientalization" which overtook the Franks the longer they lived in the country. The phenomenon is not peculiar to the first Frankish immigrants, but continued with each fresh wave of new arrivals.

After a relatively brief stay in the land, the Franks began to change their habits and their European behaviour, and progressively to adopt many of the customs of the indigenous population. This was first and foremost a natural process of adaptation to climate, physical conditions, to diet and general ways of living, which were so different from those they were used to in their lands of origin, and which necessitated considerable changes of habit in daily life. It was in the nature of things that this adaptation took the form of an imitation of the life of the local inhabitants, which was better suited to the conditions of the country. The imitation was the more pronounced because in many spheres the natives enjoyed a higher standard of material culture than that prevailing in contemporary Europe. The Franks, who had become the rulers and masters of the country, inherited all the tastes of eastern culture and very swiftly grew accustomed to its external attributes. This orientalization found its expression in most spheres of life and examples will be given as we proceed. But it would be a mistake to think that this imitation of eastern customs was accompanied by a loss of identity; nor is it to be concluded that the process of self-adaptation went deeper than the superficialities of daily existence. The Franks did not cast off many of their European habits, and even while they became accustomed to eastern dress and diet, they remained fundamentally Europeans. Even the children of mixed marriages, and the second and third generation of Franks born in the country—upon whom Jacques de Vitry poured oceans of contempt and whom he compared to Saracens —remained, despite the similarity in their mode of living, westerners rather than

fragmentary information

"orientalization"

superficial self-adaptation

Franks remained fundamentally Europeans

371

easterners at heart. The gulf between the Franks and the natives, whether Christians or Moslems, remained unbridged until the departure of the last Frank from the shores of the Holy Land.

The following descriptions do not embrace the entire Frankish population of the Holy Land. Owing to the lack of information on the other social classes, our treatment will be restricted to the nobles and wealthy burgesses who lived in the principal cities.

THE APPEARANCE AND DRESS
OF THE FRANKS

the majority French

The Franks who lived in the Holy Land came from all parts of Europe, and included Scandinavians and Spaniards, Scots and Hungarians, Bohemians and Navarrese, English, Italians and Germans, though the majority were from the various regions of France, chiefly Flanders, Lorraine, Normandy, the Auvergne, Burgundy and Provence. According to Usamah the ideal knight was tall and slender—"if the knight is thin and tall, the Franks admire him more." Most Franks cannot have corresponded to this ideal.

beardless

The Frankish male was beardless and clean-shaven like the European of his period. An anonymous traveller wrote: "[The Franks] are the only one of all these races who shave the beard."[108] The natives grew beards: the Greeks grew long unkempt ones, and the Syrians beards that were cut and carefully tended. It is interesting that all the Crusader kings had large beards, and the beard of Baldwin II flowed down upon his chest. Some at least of the Franks born in the country seem to have begun to grow beards as the years went by, considering the beard to be "an honour to the face and the dignity and glory of man."[109]

hair worn long

Shaving was with a large, not very sharp, knife. In contrast to Europe, soap was used and the custom was to be shaved once or twice a week, usually by a barber. In Jerusalem the barbers concentrated near the Church of the Holy Sepulchre, but the attendants at the public baths also shaved their customers. Hair was worn fairly long, to the shoulders. According to one testimony, the Franks went bare-headed, but this must be assumed to mean that they went uncovered at home or in the shade. There is no doubt that when they were in the sun they covered their heads, wearing either the European cap with narrow brim, the Arab *kafiya* or turbans.

head gear

clothes

In peaceful times the Frank wore European clothes—undergarments, long stockings, a shirt with long, tight sleeves and over it a short jacket with short sleeves. On his feet he wore shoes, or high boots made of soft leather. In winter, under the influence of the oriental style, he began to wear a fur-trimmed mantle, and King Baldwin I "always wore a mantle hanging from his shoulders."[110] Ibn Jubayr saw Frankish men dressed in cloaks with "their trains falling behind." The Franks also imitated the eastern shoes with upturned toes. Their

372

clothes were of cotton, wool, linen and silk, embroidered with gold and very splendid, the colours being gay and vivid, generally red, green, yellow, black and gold.

In battle the Frankish knight wore a hauberk—a coat of chain mail weighing some 30 kilograms, reaching to the knees and with long sleeves. Underneath he donned the gambison, a tunic made of quilted cotton. The arms and legs were protected by metal-coated guantlets and metal shoes: the head was covered by the *mail* the hood of the hauberk, over which was the helmet. The latter was conical or pot-shaped at the beginning of the period, with a piece of metal which descended from the forehead and protected the nose. Another triangular piece of metal protected the mouth and neck. At the end of the period the helmet had become a metal box supported on the shoulders, with a grating to protect the face. A surcoat of coloured silk was worn over the armour.

The hair of Frankish women was worn in long plaits falling each side of the face. Their costume was magnificent. Ibn Jubayr described the dress of a bride *long plaits* whom he saw on her wedding-day at Tyre:

> "She was most elegantly garbed in a beautiful dress from which trailed according to their traditional style a long trail (train) of silk. On her head she wore a gold diadem covered by a net of woven gold, and on her breast was a like arrangement."[111] *magnificent costumes*

The dress of the Frankish women covered the whole body, much more so than the dress of European women. Jacques de Vitry says that the Franks "wrap up both themselves and their daughters with clothes, that they may not be seen." The Frankish women learned the use of cosmetics from their eastern sisters, and adorned themselves with splendid and costly jewellery.

HOUSING AND DOMESTIC EQUIPMENT

The Crusader dwellings were sometimes single-storeyed, but more often had two floors, a room on the second being known as the *solarium*. In the towns a house would often consist of one or two shops at street level, with a dwelling above for *single-storeyed* the merchant and his family. The *haute bourgeoisie* and the nobility lived in *houses or* "palaces" planned in typical oriental style, composed of a square of rooms sur- *"solarium"* rounding a paved central court. Such buildings had one main entrance, and all other doors and windows, together with a row of verandahs, looked onto the court. In the wealthier houses the windows were glazed and in others they were closed by wooden shutters. Roofs were without exception flat. There were cel- *flat roofs* lars below ground-level.

We do not know how the various rooms were used, but it may be supposed that the ground floor contained the kitchen and dining-hall, while the bedrooms were in the second storey. The kitchen contained an oven and a large water tank, *rooms* the former being made of baked clay bricks and possessing a large opening in its

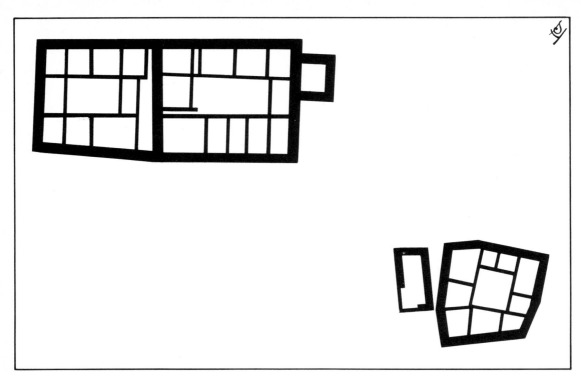

Acre, Frankish house

side and a chimney at the top. The pots were inserted through the opening, and outside it revolved the spits on which meat was roasted. We do not know exactly what the cooking utensils were, but they certainly included pots, a cauldron, pans, bowls, flour-sieves, a hatchet, a stirring stick, large spoons and knives.

kitchen The kitchen possessed a cupboard for condiments and a vessel for pickles, a hook for hanging meat and hand-mills for grinding pepper and small quantities of grain. The cook worked on a table. Rubbish was thrown into the cellar through a hole in the kitchen floor.

The table at which meals were taken stood in the hall with benches placed around it, and it was covered with a cloth at mealtimes. Among the eating utensils were knives, spoons, deep earthenware bowls and bowls of wood, glass decanters and splendid glass goblets. The food was brought from the kitchen on large trays, the meat being carved at table. The hall was also used for social pur-

table customs poses after meals, and when the remnants had been cleared away the family and visitors would sit, perhaps listening to minstrels while they sipped wine and sampled confections and sweetmeats. For lighting the Franks used tallow candles and torches, tapers and oil lamps.

We do not know how the bedrooms were furnished, but the Crusaders brought with them the European bed-frame and did not sleep on the floor as did the orientals. The beds had deep soft mattresses and pillows.

The washing habits of the Franks changed after their arrival in the Holy Land.

374

Whereas in Europe they had been in the habit of washing only rarely, the local climate obliged them to wash their bodies frequently and they went to the bathhouse for this purpose. The women are known to have gone there three times a week[112] and it is to be supposed that the men washed even more frequently. The Military Orders insisted very strictly that their members wash, and before entering an Order the novice was obliged to bathe in a communal bathhouse.

The baths were of a type of sweat-bath exactly like the modern Turkish bath. Several contemporary accounts exist, and make it clear that the method of washing was identical with that still customary in bathhouses in eastern countries. The bather entered an anteroom containing niches with couches and benches. Here he undressed, wrapped himself in a large towel and put on sandals. Usamah complained that the Franks did not wrap themselves in towels but bathed naked. From the anteroom they entered a narrow corridor and then the sweating room, which was heated by a furnace outside the building, its heat being inducted through earthenware pipes. The room had stone benches, and stone bowls full of water round the walls. When he had perspired sufficiently the bather called an attendant, who rubbed his body with a cloth and soap. The wealthy and the

baths

Belvoir, kitchen

Belvoir, bath

prominent bathed in private cells attached to the sweating room, and the attendant would shave those who wished it. Having finished washing, the bather returned to the anteroom, where he donned his clothes and rested a little. The bathes were seigneurial monopolies *(ban)*. Archaeological remains of Frankish bathhouses have been found at Belvoir and 'Atlit.

FOOD AND DRINK

varied and rich

meat

The food of the Franks was rich and varied. Their tables were graced by numerous meat dishes, amongst which were chicken, quail, crane, pigeon, partridge, mutton, beef, wild boar, ibex, roebuck and hare. Some of the meat was obtained by hunting, but some was bought from butchers; Jerusalem had special markets for poultry, cattle and pork. Cranes and wild boars, whose meat is tough and ill-tasting, were eaten after prolonged cooking, and were included in the menu because the Franks liked hunting them and liked eating what they had killed. There were marine and freshwater fish in plenty; the Franks were also fond of eels.

376

Cooked vegetables included beans, broad beans, peas, artichokes, asparagus, *vegetables* rice and lentils. Those eaten raw included lettuce and cucumbers. Amongst the fruits were bananas, oranges, lemons, ethrogs, the sycamore fruits known as *fruits* "Pharaoh's figs," dates, carobs, grapes, peaches, plums, figs and quinces, and with them almonds and other nuts. One source emphasized that "in this land one hardly finds pears, or apples or cherries."[113]

Fresh fruit and confections of fruit cooked with extra sugar were served for dessert. Burchard noted the excellent peach conserves made in the city of Acre. There were numerous kinds of sweets, including varieties of candy (Arabic *dibs*), made of solidified fruit and honey-sugars, filled with almonds and other nuts, and also cakes of all sorts. Currants, dried figs and dates were also eaten.

The Franks ate hen and turkey eggs and used the milk of goats, cows and buf- *dairy* faloes, making butter and cheese from it. For cooking they used olive and ses- ame oil, and also animal fats and vinegar. While honey was still used in Europe, the Franks sweetened their food with sugar. Its sweetening capacity was three times as great, enabling them to prepare sweetmeats and cakes such as could not be made overseas. They were accustomed to flavouring their foods with much *sweet meats* garlic, mustard and pepper, and used many other seasonings in cooking, attach- ing great importance to the preparation of various kinds of sharp sauces. The condiments were purchased at special shops known as *apothecae,* where aro- matic herbs were sold both for cooking and medicinal purposes. One of the large *spices* markets in Jerusalem was known as the Street of Herbs. Pickles were eaten, and prepared with lemons and bitter oranges. Burchard wrote that "the natives make pickles to eat with fowls, fish and other food, and thus make food very palat- able."[114]

The bread was made of wheat flour; both raised and unleavened bread were *bread* used, the latter resembling oriental *"pitta."* Bread was not baked at home but in public bakeries, which were the monopoly of the seigneur.

The profession of cook was regarded as honourable, and among the respected burgesses of Jerusalem we find "Guillelmus coquus" acting as witness in grants. Jean d'Ibelin's cook received an annual rent of eighty bezants, the highest rate *cooks* payed to a serjeant. The cities had public kitchens where cooked food could be purchased, and the main market street in Jerusalem was known as the "Rue Malquisinat" (Street of Bad Cooking), where food for pilgrims was cooked.

Meals were accompanied by wine, but winegrapes had not been grown by the *wines* Moslems, whose religion did not permit them to drink wine. Hence the Franks grew grapes for wine in various localities, and according to Burchard "the wine of the Holy Land is very good and noble."[115] The most renowned vineyards were in the neighbourhood of Bethlehem, 'Ein Gedi, in the valleys near Jerusalem, at al-Bira and Qubeiba, at Akhziv, near Sidon and at other places along the coast. In summer wine was drunk chilled with snow from Lebanon. Jacques de Vitry wrote: "All through the summer cold snow is brought down to Jerusalem in two or more days' journey from Lebanon,—which, when mixed with wine, makes it as cold as ice. This snow is preserved by being covered with straw."[116]

Wine was sold in taverns, where it was kept in casks and sold retail in bottles. The wine merchants advertised their wares in a way known also in Europe. Usamah related that in Nablus someone would be sent out to draw attention to the merchant's wines: "He would take some wine in a bottle and go around announcing it by shouting; 'So and so the merchant has just opened a cask full of this wine. He who wants to buy some of it will find it in such and such a place.' "

beer Another alcoholic beverage was beer. It was called *vinum cerevisii* or by its Arabic name of *focay,* and was made from barley. Cooled fruit-juices *(sorbet),* the chief Moslem drink, were also served on Frankish tables.

As can be seen from the above account, the Frankish diet was rich and varied. In its variety and mode of cookery it surpassed European food. The Frankish cooks learned much from the local wizards of the kitchen, though the Moslem cuisine remained superior to the Frankish, as can be seen from the following anecdote told by Usamah. A Moslem was invited to dinner by a Frankish knight: "The knight presented an excellent table with food extraordinarily clean and delicious. Seeing me abstaining from food, he said: 'Eat: be of good cheer! I never eat Frankish dishes but I have Egyptian women cooks and never eat except of their cooking.' "[118]

AMUSEMENTS: FESTIVALS AND BANQUETS

It would be unrealistic to differentiate between the Franks' work and leisure-hours, at least when we speak of the Frankish nobles and knights. When not engaged in their profession, which was war, they were free to amuse themselves indoors or out, since affairs of state and their domains took little time.

The nobles spent most of their time hunting on horseback using spears. They

hunting hunted beasts of prey such as lions, bears, leopards, wolves and wild boars, and also deer, ibex and hares. King Fulk was mortally injured chasing a hare in a hunt near Acre. A special favourite with the Franks was falconry, or the hunting of birds with the aid of molten falcon and hounds. Usamah related an episode during a hunt in which he participated at Acre. A Genoese had brought a molten falcon and hounds. "Whenever the falcon was flown at the cranes, the bitch would run right below the falcon, so that the moment the falcon clutched a crane and brought it down, the hound would grab the crane in its teeth, and the bird could not escape."[119] Foxes were also hunted with hounds. There was famous hunting on Mt. Tabor, in the Ḥula Valley, in the forest of Banias and on the Plain of Acre.

Racecourses were to be found near the large towns, where races were held and

races regular tourneys took place. Ibn Jubayr wrote that the plain before the walls of Acre at the mouth of the River Na'aman was a wonderful place; "as a course for horses there is none to compare with it. Every morning and evening the Lord of the town rides over it, and there the soldiers parade."[120]

Usamah described a racecourse near the town of Tiberias. Tourneys were central events in the life of the nobility, and nobles came from far and near on the invitation of the host, to the appointed place. The rival groups formed up on the open field and each knight chose his opponent. When the sign was given the knights went into combat with their lances. Slowly the ranks thinned and the knight who vanquished the largest number of "enemies" was declared the hero of the day. The audience, among whom were the ladies of the contestants and the inhabitants of the city, stood at the edge of the field. The event was accompanied by various entertainments and competitions. "The cavaliers went out to exercise with lances. With them went out two decrepit aged women whom they stationed at one end of the racecourse. At the other end of the field they left a pig which they had scalded and laid on a rock. Then they made the two aged women run a race while each one of them was accompanied by a detachment of horsemen urging her on. At every step they took, the women would fall down and rise again, while the spectators would laugh. Finally one of them got ahead of the other and won the pig for a prize."[121] *tourneys*

When not engaged in some outdoor activity, the Franks spent their time in their homes, in the palaces of their friends, in the markets. Their chief game was dicing, which they played everywhere. They also played chess and other more "civilized" games. They spent a considerable part of their time drinking in taverns; drunkenness was very widespread among the Franks. Prostitutes were numerous. Minstrels, mimes and actors played before the public in the city squares; these professionals were considered to be of inferior class and were referred to by Jacques de Vitry along with drunkards and pimps. *dicing*

drinking

The chief livelihood of these various entertainers was derived from appearances on festive occasions. Festivals and banquets were held to mark family or state events, which were celebrated with great pomp and splendour, eating and drinking being accompanied by singing, music, miming, plays and Arab dancing women. The musical instruments were numerous. A chronicler mentioned a few of them: "The trumpets clanged, horns sounded and the shrill intonations of pipe, and the deeper notes of the tambourine and harp, struck upon the ear; soothing symphonies were heard like various voices blended in one." As typical of the many accounts of such festive occasions we may cite the description of the coronation banquet of Henry II, the last in the Holy Land which was held at Acre: *entertainers*

muscial instruments

"They celebrated for fifteen days at a place in Acre called the Auberge of the Hospital of St. John, a very large palace. This was the finest banquet known for a hundred years, and included tourneys and rejoicing. They mimed the Round Table and the queen of Femenia, that is, knights dressed like women jousted together. They also mimed nuns jousting with monks and Lancelot, Tristan and Palamides and other pleasant comely sports."

Acre, defended gate to Genoese Square

MEDICAL CARE

The Franks enjoyed a standard of medical care much more advanced than that which had been their lot at the same period in Europe. There were numerous hospitals, as many as four being mentioned in Jerusalem, with others in Acre, Nablus, Ascalon, Jaffa, Tiberias and Tyre. The most renowned and advanced medical institution was of course that of the Order of Hospitallers, in whose hospitals at Jerusalem, Acre and Nablus the sick, chiefly pilgrims, received skilled and devoted treatment. Each hospital had four physicians and four surgeons and the regulations of the Order laid down all details for the diet of the sick, the arrangement and covering of their beds, their times of treatment, medicines and other needs. The highly progressive methods in the Frankish hos- *progressive methods* pitals resulted mainly from the influence of the Arab medical institutions already existing in the principal cities of the East. The Frankish hospitals in the Holy Land served as prototypes for the hospitals which began to develop in Europe in the 13th century. Throughout the Crusader period local physicians were looked upon as superior to the Frankish doctors. William of Tyre says that the Franks "scorn the medicines and practice of our Latin physicians and believe *Frankish medicine inferior to local* only in the Jews, Samaritans, Syrians and Saracens." Usamah also gave a wry description of Frankish medicine.

Medicine was the sole profession in which it was permissible to engage only *examinations* after passing an examination before a board of physicians headed by the local bishop. Treatment included blood-letting (also as a preventive prophylactic measure), bandaging and stitching, and cauterization with red-hot iron or white-hot lead, amputations, ointments, diets and various medicines. The medicines and the diets were designed to restore the balance of the humours in the body, whose impairment was regarded as the cause of the illnesses, including insanity. As the humours, phlegm, blood, bile and black bile, were combinations of different values—cold and wet, warm and wet, warm and dry and cold and dry respectively—the medicines were classified according to the degree of warmth, coldness, dryness and wetness which they caused. On this basis the physicians determined the diet or medicine which would restore the balance.

Anyone could buy any drug at an *apotheca*. The apothecaries prepared syrups from sugar and spices and various mixtures of powders and herbs. The *apothecae* were strictly supervised and a special board of inspection composed of specialist apothecae apothecaries, acting on behalf of the viscount, examined the quality of the syrups and drugs, offenders being liable to fines.

381

INDUSTRIES AND CRAFTS

BUILDING AND BUILDING MATERIALS

The principal building material in the Holy Land was stone. Owing to the short- *stones*
age in the country of timber suitable for building, nearly all the Crusader constructions were of masonry. Only such components as doors, shutters, galleries
and external facings were of wood. Crusader building-stones are generally very
handsome, of equal size, cut with precision in uniform style, and laid with level
horizontal joints in even layers of mortar. As a result the walls of Crusader structures are distinguished by the perfection of their frontages and the cleanness of
their lines, and convey a feeling of strength. The exterior walls were built of
dressed blocks on both faces, called ashlar, a filling of rubble mixed with gravel
and thick, tough mortar being inserted between the two faces. The filling itself
was so strong that in many places it has been preserved despite the fact that the
dressed blocks have fallen away or been dismantled. Where, as in a number of
places, the Crusaders exploited parts of ancient structures or scattered building
blocks for secondary use, regularity of the stone and straightness of jointing
could not be strictly observed, but they still took great care to build the corners
of their structures with well-cut masonry.

The size of the building blocks varies. In some places they are of gigantic dimensions, as in 'Atlit castle, where the length attains to 170 cm., and the depth
to 90 cm. Crusader masonry blocks cut in the 12th and early 13th century are *size and type*
generally larger than those from the 1230's onwards. The masons normally used
stone quarried in the vicinity of the building under construction; thus Belvoir
castle was built of the very hard basalt quarried locally. In the region of the
coastal plain the walls were built of blocks of *kurkar,* a rock composed of rough
sand and sea pebbles solidified by the permeation of rain and seawater, which
have dissolved the calcareous material and the residual organic matter. In the
northern coastal region the *kurkar* is hard, but in the region south of Caesarea
it is less so. In western Galilee, the Jerusalem mountains and Beit Govrin, marble in various colours, from pink to yellowish, was cut and used to face important buildings. Remains of Crusader quarries survive to this day, chiefly in the
vicinity of 'Atlit and Jerusalem. The blocks were given a rough primary dressing in the quarry and transferred by ox-cart to the building site, where the stone
received its final dressing under the direction of the master mason.

The Crusader builders understood the characteristic degrees of hardness of
the different stones and adjusted the amount of cement and its strength to that of *cement*
the masonry. At Belvoir, where the stone is hard, a thin layer of cement was laid,
while in the buildings of the coastal plain, at Caesarea, Arsuf and Ascalon, where
it was soft and crumbling, a thick layer of cement was applied. Here the cement

became so hard that it survives in massive lumps today, although the stone which it was meant to bind has almost crumbled away. The Crusader cement is made of a mixture of earth, lime and sand, mixed with whole or ground sea-shells or, where there were ruins, also with potsherds.

Crusader stone-dressing is divisible into two principal class:

a) Boss-blocked. The surface was roughly tooled with a sharp chisel which left round marks at irregular intervals. A narrow frame was cut back round the edges of the face with a broad-headed chisel, thus creating a projecting boss in the centre of the block, framed by a smooth drafted margin.

boss-blocked

b) "Pitted" masonry. The surface of the stone was tooled with a toothed mason's axe which left evenly spaced oblique lines of marks and no projecting boss. In several localities a smooth drafted margin was cut along the edges of the stone to surround the pitted centre. Bossed tooling was learnt from the local masons, for it had been common in the East for centuries and is frequently found in Hellenistic building. Its resemblance to Hellenistic masons' work is so great that archaeologists studying architectural remains in the area in the 19th century attributed Hasmonean structures to the Crusaders. The style is characteristic of Crusader building up to the first decades of the 13th century.

"pitted" masonry

From approximately 1220 onwards, most building blocks fall into the second category. It should be observed that embossed tooling could be done in half the time required for the pitted style, and that speed of dressing was of great importance in the building of the exterior walls of fortresses and cities in the period of initial settlement and fortification in the 12th century. It is apparently for this reason that most of the exterior walls of the fortresses were rebuilt of embossed masonry, whereas the walls of the interior structures, and of churches and other non-military buildings, are of pitted masonry.

In nearly all Crusader buildings, masons' marks are incised on the stones. These take various forms; letters of the Latin alphabet, crosses of various types, such as the Maltese cross, the arrow-cross and the Greek cross, various geometric figures, and symbols such as the *fleur-de-lys*. These marks are found chiefly on stones cut for special purposes, such as quoins, voussoirs and the like, but also on simple wall blocks. Their purpose is not clear; they may have been cut by the masons to mark their output, or perhaps they were used to help the builders set the blocks correctly.

masons' marks

To strengthen the walls the Franks, like the Moslems before them, used solid stone columns which they laid to pass through the thickness of the wall and the fill, between the outer and the inner stone courses. The columns gave cohesion to the wall, converting its three parts into one consolidated mass, and increasing its resistance to the blows of the battering ram and to earthquakes, which were frequent. Examples of this technique of building with columns (see also p. 97) are to be found at Ascalon, in the seawall and the eastern wall, and at Caesarea, in the wall of the citadel.

stone columns

Moslem sources reported that in some castles such as the Tower of David in Jerusalem, Montfort and Chastelet both mortar and lead were used to tie the

lead bars

blocks. Such lead bars, weighing 2.5 kilograms, were found in Belvoir. The lime used in mortar, for lime-washing or to line cisterns, was made in lime-kilns; the *calcis furnax* appears on several occasions in documents, standing in the open field and serving as a landmark on the boundaries of villages or estates.

lime-kilns

Timber parts were nailed together with large iron nails. Gates were faced with a layer of tin, iron or lead attached with nails. They turned on large iron hinges and were secured by thick iron bolts. Drains, water pipes, and air vents were made of fired earthenware.

timber part

POTTERY AND GLASS-MAKING

Crusader pottery was influenced mainly by the Arab and imitated it both in forms and technique to such an extent that it is hard to distinguish between Frankish vessels and those of the Arabs and Mamluks. It is to be supposed that most of the craftsmen were non-Frankish natives. The ribbing is flat, the bands being very broad and the furrows narrow but not deep. A considerable proportion of the pottery is black and many of the vessels are decorated with geometric motifs. Especially frequent are glazed bowls and pots painted in light bold colours with designs cut into the clay before firing. Cruciform motifs and other Christian symbols sometimes appear on the pots. Strips of glazed tiles were used to face the walls of private houses and public buildings. There was a considerable importation of Chinese porcelain, which was subject to a high excise; part remained in the country, but most of it was exported to European countries.

Frankish pottery identical with Arab

Glass-making is one of the oldest industries in the Holy Land and its invention has been attributed to the Phoenicians. Its centres in the Crusader period were Tyre and Acre. William of Tyre related:

"A very fine quality of glass is also marvelously manufactured out of sand which is found in this same plain [Tyre]. This is carried to far distant places and easily surpasses all products of the kind. It offers a material suitable for making most beautiful vases which are famous for their transparency."[122]

Tyrian glass

The Moslem traveller Idrisi added (1154): "They make here long-necked vases of glass and pottery." And Jacques de Vitry reported: "In the territory of Tyre and Acre they make the purest glass by cunning workmanship out of the sand of the sea, that is out of sand and sea-gravel."[123]

The glass was manufactured in sheet-form, for the making of coloured windows and mirrors, and also blown for the making of bottles, vases and goblets. The mixture of ash and sand was placed in crucibles, which were inserted into the furnace. After the mixture had been smelted the blower blew air into it through a long pipe and turned the blown vessels with the help of a potter's wheel. To prepare sheet glass the mixture was first blown, a bubble was created, and its ends cut; it was then flattened out and again heated. Window panes

method of manufacture

were manufactured also in the form of circular panes of blown glass 20 cm. in diameter resembling very short shallow dishes. While the vessel, or sheet of glass, was still hot, it was drawn and painted upon and then put into a special kiln for firing. A complete Crusader glass-smelting furnace was found in excavations conducted at Samariya, the Frankish Somelaria, near Acre.

The Venetians, who held considerable parts of the city of Tyre and its regions, seem to have taken local skills back to their home city, and from this the renowned Venetian glass-industry developed.

TEXTILES, SILK AND PRINTED FABRICS

Cotton and flax were grown in the Holy Land on a large scale. According to Burchard:

> "Cotton grows on certain shrubs which are about as tall as a man's knee, and are annuals. Their leaves are like vine leaves, but smaller. Upon them grow pods wherein is the cotton. They are gathered at Michaelmas."[124]

textiles Thread spun from the cotton was used for making textiles. In Frankish sources the fabrics were termed boueran and bordat, and a cloth made of a mixture of flax and cotton was called fustian. The spinning and weaving seem to have been carried on in small workshops and, as had been the practice of the country since ancient times, by the wives of the *fellaḥin* who grew the cotton. By royal regulation, the cloth sold had to be of standard length and breadth. Wool textiles (camelots) were woven from camel's hair, and the wool spun from sheep and goats' hair.

silk The finest and most expensive of the fabrics was that made of silk. This had been made and spun in the country since the Byzantine epoch. It was woven locally or exported in skeins to be woven in Europe. The silk fabrics manufactured in the Orient were both splendid and costly, and much in demand. Idrisi related that the white "tafeth" of Tyre was especially beautiful. "Also a sort of white cloth stuff which is exported thence to all parts, being extremely fine, and well woven beyond compare. The price is also very high and in but few of the neighbouring countries do they make as good a stuff."[125]

Silk textiles were of many kinds, some of them interwoven with silver and gold thread. Taffeta and cendal cloth are mentioned, the latter being unrivalled in its smoothness, and obliged to pass royal inspection before it was sold. Brocade, satin, velvet and other fabrics are also referred to. The fabrics were magnificently embroidered. Various kinds of fur were also worked locally.

dyeing The dyeing of textiles was a royal monopoly. Benjamin of Tudela reported that "there was in Jerusalem a dyeing plant which the Jews purchased annually from the King so that no man should carry out dyeing in Jerusalem except the Jews only." The Jews engaged in the dyeing of cloth throughout the realm. The cloth was first soaked in water to shrink it, and then in special clay (fuller's earth) which prepared the fabric to absorb the dye in which it was afterwards steeped. The Franks favoured bright bold colours. The dyes were produced locally. Woad grows wild in Palestine. Indigo was grown in the Jordan Valley and Tyrian purple was manufactured in the coastal plain. Alum as a mordant was brought from the Dead Sea.

OTHER LOCAL PRODUCTS

Salt was obtained by quarrying in the salt mountain of Sodom or produced from the seawater of the Mediterranean by evaporating in salt-pans. The pans *salt* near 'Atlit are mentioned, and also the *Turris Salinarum,* "Tower of Salt," salt-pans at the mouth of the Crocodile River.

The Dead Sea yielded bitumen, which was used for medical purposes. Fetullus reported: "From the lake bitumen is extracted which is useful for doctors."[126] *bitumen* Bitumen and salt from the Dead Sea were collected chiefly by the inhabitants of the township of Teqo'a near Bethlehem.

The centre of soap manufacture in the Crusader period, as today, was at Nablus. Soap-making factories are also referred to at Tyre, Jerusalem and Acre. *soap* It was made of a mixture of olive oil and alkali, the manufacture being a royal monopoly which was granted or leased out.

The region has no deposits of iron ore or non-ferrous metals, except in the mountains in the vicinity of Beirut. Metal work was confined to that of the metal-smith and included, beside weapons, the making of iron tools for domes- *metals* tic use. Sources mention the metal-smiths of Nablus, Acre and Jerusalem and traces of a copper industry have been found at Caesarea. Iron and copper were the chief metals used. There is evidence of the very high quality of the work of the Frankish smiths, in the magnificent grill that surrounded the rock in the Mosque of the Dome of the Rock, part of which is today preserved in the Moslem Museum on the Temple Mount.

One of the important and well-established crafts of the country was the mak- *souvenirs and* ing of sacred vessels and souvenirs and the working of fine gold and silver ob- *religious objects* jects. Throughout the Crusader period there was a lively export of sacred relics; they were also made and sold to pilgrims, and various objects of religious significance were sent to Europe, including crucifixes, medallions, candelabrae, vases and holy books bound in ivory inlaid with gold or carved wood. The quality of the precious metals was subject to royal inspection and the goldsmiths and silversmiths were concentrated in special streets.

THE LAND THROUGH THE
EYES OF THE CRUSADERS

"Now you must know that, as a matter of fact, the whole of the Holy Land was, and is to this day, the best of all lands, albeit some who have not carefully regarded say the contrary."[127] In this fashion Burchard of Mount Sion described the country in which he sojourned in the kingdom's last days, when most of it had been ravaged and laid waste by the Mamluks. The accounts of the earlier and later travellers, indeed, are full of the country's praises, and speak of its fertility and abundant crops. Some of them also knew that its fertility was no more than a shadow of its great prosperity in more ancient times. Theodorich wrote: " ... all works and constructions of that people [the Jews] and of the entire province, have been destroyed."[128] The remains of the large cities, the ruins of the palaces and temples of Sebaste, Beit Shean and Caesarea, roused the enthusiasm and wonder of the travellers. They described with special interest the plants and fruits which had been unknown to them in Europe. The banana they termed "the apple of paradise," and the sycamore tree, "Pharaoh's fig." They describe at length the orange, the lemon, the sugar cane, cotton, balsam and the date.

unknown plants

Various natural phenomena were explained by means of legend. Not only could no fish live in the Dead Sea nor creature drink from it, wrote Fetellus, but "if any bird has flown above the sea, falling there, it dies."[129] According to Fetellus the water of the Sea of Galilee was drinkable because " ... it is of such character in itself that without receiving the filth of the city and of the neighbouring castles, it would be rendered undrinkable, and smelling."[130]

natural phenomena

Jacques de Vitry explained the frequent earthquakes which afflicted the country in his time by saying that the severest occurred on the coast, "because of the violence of the winds, which being borne by the breath and impulse of the waves in underground places and caves in the earth, as the enclosed and rushing air had no free vent, shake the earth with strong trembling and blows."[131]

There are also many strange accounts of the animals of the country. In addition to those known today, lions, leopards, baboons and buffaloes were mentioned. An anonymous traveller told the following story:

animals

"At Joppa, on the sea beach, there is a rock 'Adam', whereunto an exceeding great, nay, an infinite multitude of the fishes called salmon resort in summertime, bearing long yellow lines upon their backs, and after kissing the stone, as though it were a holy place, depart swiftly."[132]

Ernoul gave the following account of the snakes of Jericho:

"Near this city is a field which is full of serpents. There they catch the serpents of which the ointment is made, and I will tell you how they catch them. The man who catches them makes a ring round the field, and goes saying his charms, singing round the ring. All the serpents who have heard him come to him, and he catches them as easily as he would a lamb---Now there are some wise ones amongst these serpents, who, when they hear him begin his song, stop one of their ears against the ground, and stop the other with the tail, so that they may not hear, and thus they escape."[133]

miracles The wondrous tales and miraculous traditions concerning holy places were legion. These legends recurred repeatedly; one anonymous traveller told of a field at Hebron from whose earth the first man was made.

"In Ebron is that field whose earth is red, which earth is dug up by the inhabitants, and is exported to Egypt for sale and brought as an exceeding precious dung, because it is said to be true that of this earth Adam, the first man, was made. The aforesaid field, however widely and deeply it be dug into, yet by God's ordinance will be found at the end of the year to be filled up as before."[134]

Abraham's terebinth among the Oaks of Mamre was said to possess medicinal virtue---"Whosoever carries a piece thereof with him when riding his horse doth not stumble."[135]

John Phocas recounted a miracle which occurred to a Spanish monk who dwelt in a cave on the banks of the Jordan. Two lions were wont to come to him every Sabbath and to look at him as if begging for food. He gave them vegetables and bread made of wheat or barley flour. Once, when they came to the old monk, he had nothing to share with them, because he had eaten nothing for twenty days, so he said to them: "Since I have no means of getting food for myself and you, you must go along the channel of the Jordan and bring me a small piece of wood to make little crosses. These I will give to pilgrims and they will give me alms with which I can buy victuals for you and myself."[136] The lions listened and appeared to understand him. They went away and after a time returned with two branches of wood.

Many of the tales were merely quoted or repeated from ancient literature, but a considerable number were stories composed during the Crusader epoch. In contrast to this collection of miraculous tales and imaginary accounts it would be well to cite extracts from the account of Fulcher of Chartres, who visited the Dead Sea region at the end of 1100 with Baldwin's army. The description is exemplary for its clear limpid style, lacking all imaginary additions. It stands in striking contrast to the writings of the majority of the Frankish chroniclers and travellers:

"The waters [of the Dead Sea] are so salty that neither four-legged creatures nor birds can drink from them. I, Fulcher of Chartres, made an effort to do so and dismounting from my mule on the shore of the lake, tasted the water and found it bitterer than hellebore. The sea is called the Salt Sea because nothing can live in it and no fish can remain there. The River Jordan flows into it from its north end but no river or lake flows out from its south side. Near it is a mountain in an equal measure salty, certain parts, but not all, of which are as hard as the hardest stone and as white as snow. The salt of which it is composed is known as rock salt and splinters of it are often seen falling from the top of the

390

mountain to its bottom. We went round its north side [*sic*—the correct side is the southern] and found a small town called Segor (as-Safi), pleasantly situated and very rich in the fruit of the palm known as dates, whose taste is very sweet: we lived on them because we could get nothing else. On the first rumour of our coming, the Arabs dwelling in this country fled except for a few wretched ones blacker than pitch whom we left there like the most worthless weeds. On some trees here I saw a sort of fruit inside which I found nothing but black powder when I broke its outer shell."[137]

NOTES

LIST OF ABBREVIATIONS

Ibn Jubayr	The Travels of Ibn Jubayr, tr. R. J. C. Broadhurst. London, 1952.
Ibn al Qalanisi	The Damascus Chronicles of the Crusades, ed. H. A. R. Gibb, London, 1932.
Lane Poole	Lane Poole S. 'Saladin'. Beirut, 1964 (Reprint).
Le Strange	Le Strange, G. 'Palestine Under the Moslems'. London, 1890.
PPTS	Palestine Pilgrim's Text Society, in 12 Vols. (Vols. IV, V, VI, XII). London, 1892–6.
RH	Regesta Regni Hierosolymitani,Comp. R. Rohricht. Innsbruck, 1893. Additamentum, 1904.
Usamah	Memoirs of an Arab-Syrian Gentleman (Usamah Ibn Munqidh). Tr. P. K. Hitti. New York, 1927.
WT	William of Tyre, 'A History of Deeds Done Beyond The Sea.' Tr. E. A. Babcock and A. C. Krey. New York, 1943.

[1] Ibn Jubayr, p. 317
[2] Ibn al Qalanisi, p. 139
[3] PPTS Burchard, p. 51
[4] Raymond d'Aguilers RHC, occ III, p. 354
[5] Le Strange, p. 88
[6] ibid, pp. 85–86
[7] WT, 8; 20
[8] ibid, 11; 27
[9] PPTS John of Wurzburg, p. 69
[10] Ibn al Athir. Lane Poole, p. 229
[11] ibid, p. 236
[12] PPTS Theodorich, p. 5
[13] ibid, ibid, p. 6
[14] ibid, ibid, p. 5
[15] ibid, ibid
[16] RH, 278
[17] ibid, ibid p. 22
[18] John of Wurzburg, ibid, p. 46
[19] RH, 214

[20] John of Wurzburg, ibid, p. 46
[21] Theodorich, ibid, p. 31
[22] Le Strange, p. 329
[23] PPTS Phocas, p. 11
[24] Le Strange, p. 330
[25] Ibn Jubayr, p. 318
[26] Le Strange, p. 328
[27] ibid, p. 401
[28] WT, 17; 22
[29] ibid, 17; 29
[30] ibid, 17; 22
[31] PPTS Fetellus, p. 47
[32] ibid, City of Jerusalem, p. 32
[33] WT, 19; 10
[34] Ibn al Qalanisi, p. 217
[35] ibid, p. 335
[36] WT, 18, 12
[36a] RH. 325
[37] ibid, 15; 9
[38] Ibn Jubayr, p. 315
[39] WT, 7; 24
[40] Albert of Aix, RHC Occ., VII; 43

[41] Phocas, ibid, p. 34
[42] WT, 11; 5
[43] ibid, 20; 19
[44] ibid, 15; 25
[45] Oliverus, Historia Damiatina etc. pp. 169–171
[46] WT, 14; 22
[47] WT, 17; 12
[48] ibid; ibid
[49] Burchard, ibid, p. 26
[50] WT, 15; 25
[51] ibid, 15; 24
[52] RH, 1114
[53] RH, 346
[54] RH, 229, 656
[55] RH, 457
[56] RH, 302
[57] WT, 20; 20
[58] Theodorich, ibid, p. 60
[59] RH, 469
[59a] RH, 656
[60] Ibn Jubayr, p. 317
[61] RH, 458
[62] PPTS Jacques de Vitry, p. 28

63 Burchard, ibid, p. 99

64 Theodorich, ibid, p. 31

65 RH, 425

66 RH, 104

67 Theodorich, ibid, p. 64

68 Le Strange, p. 24

69 WT, 22; 14

70 ibid, 15; 26

71 WT, 20; 19

72 ibid, 15; 24

73 ibid, ibid

74 ibid, 21; 26

75 ibid, 14; 22

76 RH, 448

77 WT, 20; 28

78 Phocas, ibid, p. 17

79 ibid, p. 26

80 Beha a-din, PPTS, p. 154

81 RH, p. 321

82 Ibn Jubayr, p. 315

83 WT, 21, 926

84 ibid, 14; 8

85 Theodorich, ibid, p. 64

86 Burchard, ibid, p. 63

87 de Vitry, ibid, p. 26–7

88 Le Strange, p. 481

89 Theodorich, ibid, p. 57

90 Phocas, ibid, p. 34

91 RH, 205

92 RH, 458

93 WT, 7; 24

94 RH, 354, add. 199

95 City of Jerusalem, ibid, p. 47

96 Burchard, ibid, p. 32

97 Phocas, ibid, p. 35

98 RH, 489

99 City of Jerusalem, ibid, p. 31

100 Theodorich, ibid, p. 47

101 Daniel, PPTS, p. 101

102 WT, 22; 26

103 Phocas, ibid, p. 14

104 Burchard, ibid, p. 43

105 Phocas, ibid, p. 23

106 ibid, ibid, p. 25

107 Theodorich, ibid, p. 48

108 PPTS Anon. Pilgrims, p. 28

109 de Vitry, ibid, p. 68

110 WT, 10; 2

111 Ibn Jubayr, p. 320

112 de Vitry, ibid, p. 65

113 Burchard, ibid, p. 100

114 ibid, ibid, p. 100

115 ibid, ibid, p. 101

116 de Vitry, ibid, p. 92

117 Usamah, p. 165

118 ibid, p. 169

119 ibid, p. 226

120 Ibn Jubayr, p. 325

121 Usamah, p. 167

122 WT, 13, 3

123 de Vitry, ibid, p. 93

124 Burchard, ibid, p. 99

125 Le Strange, p. 344

126 Fetellus, ibid, p. 13

127 Burchard, ibid, p. 99

128 Theodorich, ibid, p. 2

129 Fetellus, ibid, p. 7

130 ibid, ibid, p. 29

131 de Vitry, ibid, p. 91

132 Anon. Pilgrims, ibid, p. 36

133 PPTS, Ernoul, p. 59

134 Anon. Pilgrims, ibid, 37–8

135 ibid, ibid, p. 38

136 Phocas, ibid, p. 28

137 Fulcher, III 379–80.

INDEXES

Names of frequently recurring items, such as Jerusalem, Kingdom of Jerusalem, Franks, Moslems, etc., are not listed.

A. INDEX OF PLACE NAMES

The names of places in this book are generally those used by the Survey of Israel in its maps. As some Arabic place names are referred to in the existing literature, cross-references will refer the reader to the names used in this book.

B. NAME INDEX